BEST LOVED RECIPES
OF THE AMERICAN PEOPLE

Books by Ida Bailey Allen

COOKBOOK FOR TWO

GASTRONOMIQUE

SOLVING THE HIGH COST OF EATING

SUCCESSFUL ENTERTAINING

BEST LOVED RECIPES OF THE AMERICAN
PEOPLE

IDA BAILEY ALLEN

Best Loved
Recipes of the
American People

ILLUSTRATIONS BY
REISIE LONETTE

DOUBLEDAY & COMPANY, INC.
GARDEN CITY, NEW YORK

ISBN: 0-385-08189-8
Library of Congress Catalog Card Number 72–89290
Copyright © 1973 by Doubleday & Company, Inc.
All Rights Reserved
Printed in the United States of America

Contents

Introduction

The preparation of *Best Loved Recipes of the American People* has been uniquely exciting and rewarding to me. It is a distillation of a lifetime career devoted to communication with the American homemaker, primarily in the vital fields of nutrition and food preparation.

The emphasis in this volume, as you will have guessed from the title, is upon foods that have become American favorites over the centuries, since the Pilgrims first set foot upon land in this wild and bewildering New World an ocean away from what had been home. The American continent offered all kinds of challenges to the early settlers, not the least of them the preparation of various strange foods, such as corn, for which there were no English equivalents at all!

Some of the fine, venerable old recipes they brought over with them—Yorkshire pudding, for instance, which housewives in the 1600s prepared as an accompaniment to venison in the absence of domestic cattle. And gradually the list grew over the centuries until it now includes all manner of modern-day specialties you will find in this book, like sloppy Joes, oven-fried chicken, barbecued franks with beans and lemon meringue pie.

Perhaps you are wondering about my sources for the many hundreds of recipes in this book. During my career as a home economist I have served as food editor of numerous magazines and newspapers, conducted several radio series, appeared on television and lectured from coast to coast. I have talked directly with homemakers in cities, towns and villages across the country and learned from them what they liked most to cook and to eat; and my mail through the years has brought clear proof of the foods that are most welcomed on American tables. And yet, as I pondered this collection, I found it challenging to decide just which recipes could be considered *best loved* by the American people. There are of course the splendid old standbys, such as

Parker House rolls, pot roast, apple pandowdy, hopping John, chicken fricassee, Virginia roast ham, election cake and Welsh rabbit, to name but a few. Then there are the new dishes that in turn win enough popularity to join the ranks and eventually become favorites. Beef Wellington has been popular now for over a decade. The little relatively new, delicious game hens are appearing more and more often on American tables. So are such succulent stews as beef Bourguignonne, cassoulet and coq au vin. Swiss fondue, once considered quite exotic, is now available packaged in supermarkets. In fact, as the world shrinks, so expands the American cuisine, already one of the most cosmopolitan in the world.

America, as a nation formed by groups of people from many lands, has a great diversity of foods to offer. Any number of delicious, homey foods from "the old country" are much treasured as American favorites today. There's sauerbraten from Germany, pizza from Italy, lamb stew from Ireland, chili from Mexico, goulash from Hungary, quiche from France, egg foo yung from China—the list is long, and still growing. Add these and numerous others to the grand old recipes that reflect our own regional cookery, such as Indian pudding, hangtown fry or jambalaya, and you have a rich field indeed to choose from!

Some recipes have changed considerably with the passage of time. You will find two recipes for a much-favored early seventeenth-century beverage called syllabubs in these pages, but neither bears much resemblance to one that was given to me by a very old lady from Massachusetts, who admonished me to follow the instructions *exactly*. "Place in a large bowl two pints of white wine or port, some nutmeg rasped and a plenty of sugar. Milk into this rapidly near four pints of milk, to raise a good froth. Let it stand. The drinker may be pleased to put clouted cream, pounded cinnamon and sugar on the top."

Now, it would be difficult to follow these instructions to the letter. Much of the cookery done in the early days was done by guesswork. Today, however, any recipe worthy of the name is reliable and can be followed exactly, for consistently mouth-watering results.

There are certain guidelines to good cookery, and one of the first is simply this: read the recipe through to the end. Be sure you have the necessary utensils or workable substitutes on hand before you start. Then consider the ingredients. While listing any you may have to buy, check to be sure that you have a sufficient amount of such provisions as flour, baking powder, sugar, salt, shortening, etc. on your pantry shelves. It's often the staples we're sure of that run out, right in the middle of things. Once you have your ingredients and utensils assembled, *follow the recipe.* Don't deviate if you want to be sure of success. Remember that all measurements are level unless otherwise specified, and oven temperatures are carefully selected to produce the best results.

I am sure you will find your own favorites in *Best Loved Recipes of the American People.* May you enjoy these with a hearty appetite—and add many others over the years!

IDA BAILEY ALLEN

BEST LOVED RECIPES
OF THE AMERICAN PEOPLE

Menus

Remember that there's more to a meal than just the cooking. Careful planning and preparation are your secrets to successful and nourishing menus.

The wise menu planner will consider budget, the size and type of group to be served, the nutritional balance of foods and the over-all appearance of the finished dishes.

Don't be afraid to vary these menus or to try new recipes. A new dish is always a pleasure for your family and your guests. Be imaginative, consider color, texture and temperature, and create your own exciting menus. Here are ideas to help you get started with menus for various occasions. Check the Index for location of the starred (*) recipes.

Breakfast

NUMBER ONE

> Baked or Fried Sausage Links
> Fluffy Egg Flapjacks* and Maple or Maple-Blended
>   Syrup
> Bowl of Assorted Seasonable Fruits
> Coffee, Tea or Milk

NUMBER TWO

    Cranberry Juice Cocktail
    Fried Breakfast Oatmeal Slices*
    Poached Whole Apples*
    Coffee, Tea or Milk

NUMBER THREE

    Baked Apples* or Stewed Fruit
    Heated Shredded Wheat Biscuits with Whole Milk
    Scrambled eggs*
    Toasted Split Rolls Spread with Butter or Margarine
    Coffee, Tea or Milk

NUMBER FOUR

    Cantaloupe Wedges
    Cinnamon Orange French Toast*
    Sausage Links
    Coffee or Milk

NUMBER FIVE

    Pineapple Juice
    Cooked Dark Farina Served with Whole Milk and
        Brown Sugar
    Bacon, Cheese and Tomato Sandwiches on Enriched
        Bread Toast
    Coffee, Tea or Milk

NUMBER SIX

    Orange Juice
    Cooked Oatmeal with Whole Milk and Sugar
    Enriched Bread Toast Spread with Butter, Margarine
        or Peanut Butter
    Coffee, Tea or Milk

CONTINENTAL BREAKFAST

Fresh Orange Juice or Half Grapefruit
Oven-Fresh Rolls, Croissants or Toast with Jams or
Honey
Pot of Coffee or Tea

PENNSYLVANIA DUTCH BREAKFAST

Bowls of Dutch Pretzels* in Heated Milk
Scrapple*
Red Ripe Tomato
Apple Turnovers*
Coffee

SOUTHERN BREAKFAST

Orange Juice
Poached Eggs on Quick Regular Hominy Grits
Fried Ham and Buttered Toast
Coffee, Tea or Milk

Brunch

NUMBER ONE

Chilled Grapefruit Juice
Scrambled Eggs Gala* with Pan-Fried Ham
Baked Bananas Caribbean*
Cinnamon Cake*
Coffee, Tea or Milk

NUMBER TWO

Mixed Fruit Compote or French Onion Soup*
Eggs Fried with Virginia Ham
Fried Potatoes with Green Peppers*
Hot Asparagus Tips on Tomato Slices
Orange-Honey Rolls*
Coffee, Tea or Milk

NUMBER THREE

Melon of Choice
Canadian Bacon
Baked Eggs in Sour Cream*
Home-Fried Potatoes
Blueberry Crumb Cake*
Hot or Iced Coffee or Tea
Milk

NUMBER FOUR

Chilled Assorted Fruit Juices
French Toasted Sandwiches*
Slices of Peeled Fresh Oranges and Halved Seedless
     Green Grapes
Hot or Iced Coffee
Milk

NUMBER FIVE

Tomato Juice Piquant*
Broiled Halved Rounds Smoked Ham
Oven French Fries*
Hard-Cooked Eggs with Curried Vegetables*
Toast Rounds
Assorted Fresh Fruits
Coffee, Tea or Milk

Lunch

NUMBER ONE

Split Pea or Lentil Soup*
Southern Corn Bread*
Eggs à la Swiss* on Green Beans
Orange Gelatin
Coconut Macaroons*
Coffee, Tea or Milk

NUMBER TWO

Cream of Green Pea Soup*
Croutons
Superb Turkey Salad* with Shredded Lettuce
Strawberry Tallcake*
Hot or Iced Coffee or Tea
Milk

NUMBER THREE

Chilled Apple-Cranberry Juice
Ham-Swiss Cheese Salad*
Toast
Pineapple, Bananas and Dark Sweet Cherries
Old-Fashioned Brownie Cookies*
Coffee, Tea or Milk

NUMBER FOUR

> Mixed Vegetable Salad with Yogurt Thousand Island
>   Dressing*
> Poached Eggs on Deviled Corned Beef Burgers*
> Tomato Catsup
> Crisp Rolls
> Strawberry Shortcake*
> Coffee, Tea or Milk

NUMBER FIVE

> New England Oyster Stew*
> Oyster Crackers
> Hot Potato-Bacon-Egg Salad*
> Crisped French Bread
> Coddled Apples*
> Coffee, Tea or Milk

NUMBER SIX

> Cream of Tomato Soup
> Fillets of Sole Florentine*
> Baking Powder Biscuits*
> Lime Sherbet Topped with Sugared Sliced Strawberries
> Coffee, Tea or Milk

NUMBER SEVEN

> Waldorf Saladettes*
> Baked Eggs with Rice and Cheese, Mushroom Sauce*
> Old-Fashioned Succotash*
> Ice Cream Slices with Fresh Raspberry Melba Sauce*
>   (see Fresh Peach Melba Compote)
> Hot or Iced Coffee or Tea

NUMBER EIGHT

> Chilled Tomato Soup
> Sliced Smoked Pork with Mustard
> Potato Salad*
> Slices of Cheddar Cheese
> Ice Cream with Drained Crushed Pineapple
> Coffee, Tea or Milk

NUMBER NINE

> Hot Gazpacho*
> Bread Sticks
> Chicken à la King Bake with Ham Deviled Eggs*
> Fresh Spinach Salad*
> Strawberry Shortcake*
> Coffee, Tea or Milk

NUMBER TEN

> Chicken Paella*
> Amontillado Sherry
> Tossed Salad of Lettuce and Avocados
> Crème Brûlée*
> Coffee

NUMBER ELEVEN

> Tomato Juice Piquant*
> Beef Stroganoff*
> Green Peas with Small White Onions
> Crusty French Bread
> Lady Baltimore Cake*
> Coffee, Tea or Milk

Dinner

NUMBER ONE

Grated Cabbage, Carrot and Raisin Saladettes
Marinated Spiced Beef* with Gravy
Quick Hominy Grits
Rutabagas with Basil Lemon Butter*
Baked Pears Oregon*
Coffee, Tea or Milk

NUMBER TWO

Holland Red Bean Soup*
Croutons
Cheese Soufflé*
Baked Tomato Halves*
Chopped Spinach
Applesauce
Jelly Roll*
Coffee, Tea or Milk

NUMBER THREE

Big Tossed Mixed Vegetable and Greens Salad
Crusty Italian Bread
Cheese Polenta with Tomato-Meat Sauce*
Rhubarb-Mince Tarts*
Coffee, Tea or Milk

NUMBER FOUR

Tomato Bouillon*
Fish Fillets Baked in Foil*
Tomatoes and Hominy*
Hot Chopped Spinach
Peach-Prune Compote
Coffee, Tea or Milk

NUMBER FIVE

Cream of Spinach Soup*
Croutons
Baked Fillets of Red Snapper à la Santa Rosa Island*
Baked Celery
Florida Lime Pie*
Coffee, Tea or Milk

NUMBER SIX

Avocado Slices on Lettuce with Tomato French Dressing
Bread Sticks
Beef and Mushroom Stew, French Style*
Spicy Apple Crisp*
Coffee, Tea or Milk

NUMBER SEVEN

Chilled Pineapple Juice
Roast Prime Ribs of Beef au Jus*
Jill's Roast Potatoes*
Celery and Radish Slaw
Marinated Orange Slices*
Coffee, Tea or Milk

NUMBER EIGHT

Grapefruit Halves Broiled with Honey
Pepper Steak*
Baked Potatoes Duchesse*
Fresh Spinach Loaf*
Raspberry Charlotte*
Coffee, Tea or Milk

NUMBER NINE

Chilled Grapefruit Sections
Leek Soup*
Tournedos* with Sauce Béarnaise*
Whipped Potatoes
Cucumber-Lettuce Salad
Cherries Jubilee*
Coffee, Tea or Milk

NUMBER TEN

Hot Vegetable Juice (Canned) with Lemon Wedges
Skillet Sweet-Sour Pork Chops*
Browned Sweet Potatoes
Country Cranberry Sherbet*
Coffee, Tea or Milk

NUMBER ELEVEN

Vichyssoise*
Croutons
Roast Beef Salad*
Buttered Corn on the Cob
Half-Frozen Pineapple and Watermelon*
Coffee, Tea or Milk

NUMBER TWELVE

> Sardine Saladettes on Lettuce
> Roast Cornish Game Hens*
> Wild Rice*
> Zucchini with Sliced Carrots
> Baked Valencia Oranges*
> Coffee, Tea or Milk

NUMBER THIRTEEN

> Halves of Grapefruit
> Rolled Roast Shoulder of Lamb with Cranberry Relish*
> Pan-Roasted Potatoes
> Brussels Sprouts
> Sacher Torte*
> Coffee, Tea or Milk

NUMBER FOURTEEN

> Melon Wedges
> Liver, Bacon and Tomato Slice Platter*
> Whipped Potato
> Zucchini Vinaigrette
> Pineapple Sherbet* with Fresh Strawberry Garnish
> Coffee, Tea or Milk

NUMBER FIFTEEN

> Tomato-Onion Soup
> Croutons
> Blanquette of Veal*
> Flaky Boiled Potatoes with Parsley*
> Zucchini Sauté
> Plum Betty* with Hard Sauce*
> Coffee, Tea or Milk

NUMBER SIXTEEN

New England Corn and Oyster Chowder*
Hot Buttered Rolls*
Vegetable Platter of Cauliflower Sections with Cheese
    and Bacon*
Baked Acorn Squash*
Pan-Fried Zucchini
Coconut Custard Pie*
Coffee, Tea or Milk

POULTRY DINNER

Tossed Mixed Greens Salad with French Dressing
Corn Pudding*
Fried Chicken with Gravy*
Baking Powder Biscuits*
Blueberry Cream-Cheese Fluff*
Coffee, Tea or Milk

COLONIAL DINNER

Oxtail Soup*
Small Baking Powder Biscuits*
Roast Ham Virginia*
Raisin Sauce from Old New England*
Pan-Roasted Sweet Potatoes
Broccoli Parmesan
Red and White Cabbage Patch Salad*
Marble Spice Cake New England*
Coffee, Tea or Milk

NEW ENGLAND DINNER

Lobster Bisque*
Crisp Crackers
New England Boiled Scrod*
Vegetable Platter Consisting of Buttered Cauliflower,
    Carrots, Green Peas
Fresh Apple Pie*
Sharp Cheese
Coffee, Tea or Milk

SOUTHWESTERN DINNER

Halved Grapefruit
Rolled Stuffed Flank Steak* with Tacos*
Black-eyed Peas*
Broiled Tomato Halves*
Caramel Cup Custards*
Coffee, Tea or Milk

NEW YEAR'S DINNER

Homemade Pâté de Foie Gras* with Crackers
Crisp Celery and Olives
Roast Leg of Lamb Gratiné*
Diane's Mashed Potatoes*
Poached Brussels Sprouts*
Heated Raisin Tudor Fruit Cake* with Hard Sauce*
Coffee, Tea or Milk

ST. PATRICK'S DAY DINNER

Citrus Fruit Sections in Cups
Irish Lamb Stew*
Irish Cream Scones*
Brown Betty
Cheddar Cheese
Coffee, Tea or Milk

THANKSGIVING DINNER

Citrus Fruit Cocktail
Avocados in the Half Shell
Roast Turkey with Moist Crumb Stuffing*
Giblet Gravy*
Parsley and black olives
Whipped Sweet Potato
Creamed Brussels Sprouts
Bacon-Chive Corn Meal Muffins*
Cranberry Jelly
Salad of Tomato Slices with Pickled Beet Strips
Fresh Apple Pie*
Pumpkin Pie*
Coffee, Tea or Milk

CHRISTMAS DINNER

Grapefruit Halves Topped with Cherries
Celery hearts, Radishes, Olives
Roast Beef with Yorkshire Pudding*
Pan Gravy*
Creamed Onions
Buttered Brussels Sprouts
Tossed Salad Bowl
Cheese Sticks
Steamed English Plum Pudding*
Hard Sauce*
Coffee, Tea or Milk

CHINESE-AMERICAN DINNERS

Crunchy Salmon-Cheese Ball*
Spareribs Oriental Style* on Mushroom Chow Mein
Piquant Fried Rice*
Assorted Fresh Fruits
Fortune Cookies (purchased)
Tea

Cream of Green Pea Soup*
Chinese Fried Rice with Ham*
Coleslaw*
Glazed Nut-Orange Cupcakes*
Coffee, Tea or Milk

ITALIAN DINNER

Big Tossed Mixed Green Salad with Herbed Italian
    Dressing*
Lasagne with Meat, Cheese and Cream Sauce*
Compote of Fresh Fruits
Caffè Espresso, or Coffee, Tea or Milk

NEAR-EASTERN DINNER

Tomato Bouillon*
Broiled Veal Chops
Fried Eggplant*
Whipped Potato
Sharp Pepper Relish*
Kadayif*
Turkish Coffee*

TERRACE DINNER

Coleslaw-Filled Tomatoes
Tongue Molded in Aspic*
Brown Mustard Sauce
Apricot Corn Bread*
Deep Dish Blueberry Pie*
Hot or Iced Coffee or Tea

SIX-COURSE PROGRESSIVE DINNER MENU

First Course: Tomato Juice Piquant*
                    Assorted Canapés, Olives
Second Course: Mushroom Soup Madeira*
                    Small Croissants
Third Course: Quick Lobster Casserole*
                    Parslied Rice Pilaff
Fourth Course: Roast Duck à l'Orange*
                    Sweet Potato Rhumba*
                    Assorted Pickles
Fifth Course: Tossed Green Salad
                    Sesame Seed Sticks*
Sixth Course: Strawberry Cream Pie*
                    Coffee

Supper

SUNDAY NIGHT SUPPER

Melon Wedges or Grapefruit Sections
Beef Sukiyaki with Vegetables and Rice*
Lemon Meringue Pie*
Coffee or Tea

TERRACE SUPPER

Jellied Tomato Soup
Olives
Mixed Pickles
Cucumber Sticks
Salad Niçoise*
Thin-Sliced Buttered Pumpernickel
Corn on the Cob
Thin-Sliced Fresh Pineapple Sweetened with Sugar
Hot or Iced Coffee or Tea or Milk

PICNIC

Cheese-Pecan Balls*
Hawaiian Cube Steak Sandwiches*
Tomato Slices
Potato Chips
Corn on the Cob
Orange Marmalade Sunshine Cake*
Assorted Soft Drinks
Hot or Iced Coffee or Tea

Appetizers

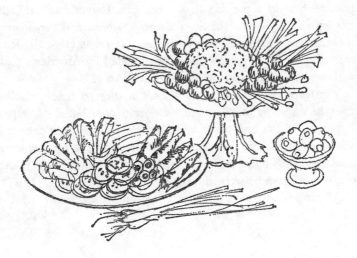

An appetizer is "something that stimulates the desire for food" and that's just what the forerunner to a meal should be—provocative, satisfying but not filling. Most countries have their own devices for whetting the appetite—either as a cocktail accompaniment or as a prelude to a meal: the Italian *antipasto*, the French *hors d'oeuvre*, the Swedish *smörgåsbord* and the Spanish *tapas*. Many of the favorites gathered here came originally from countries far away, others have been created by American cooks without any reference at all to customs abroad!

Whatever the appetizer, it doesn't matter so much whether you choose to serve a hot one or a cold one, but don't repeat the same flavors and tastes you plan to serve in your entree. A crab meat bouchée, for instance, should not be a forerunner to a main course featuring crab; in fact, it's often wise to plan a contrast in tastes between the appetizer and the entree.

All recipes are for six servings unless otherwise stated.

HOMEMADE PATÉ de FOIE GRAS

¼ cup finely chopped
  mushrooms
1 tablespoon butter
½ pound liver sausage
1 (3-ounce) package cream
  cheese
¼ cup heavy cream

1 teaspoon Worcestershire
  sauce
½ teaspoon paprika
Water cress (optional)
Canapé crackers or toast
  rounds

Brown mushrooms slightly in sweet butter. Beat together all ingredients except water cress and crackers until they make a smooth paste. A sprig of water cress is optional. Chill in refrigerator. Serve on crackers or toast rounds with cocktails. May be used for thin tea sandwiches also.

ARTICHOKE CUPS

Remove the centers from canned artichoke hearts, leaving ⅛ inch shell. Chop the centers with an equal quantity of chopped pimiento and half the quantity chopped browned almonds. Fill the centers.

BLUE CANAPÉS

½ cup crumbled blue cheese
½ cup toasted chopped Brazil nuts
16 ripe olives, chopped
Canapé crackers or toast triangles
Brazil nut slices

Mash cheese and mix with toasted Brazil nuts and olives. Spread on crackers or toast and garnish each with a slice of Brazil nut. Slide under the broiler for a few seconds or serve cold. Makes 20 canapés.

CANAPÉS DE PESCADITO

3 tablespoons butter or margarine
3 tablespoons flour
½ teaspoon salt
Few grains pepper
1 cup milk
½ cup fine-chopped Brazil nuts
2 tablespoons minced green pepper
2 teaspoons minced onion
¼ teaspoon Worcestershire sauce
1 (7-ounce) can tuna fish, flaked with a fork
Toast diamonds
Pimiento strips
Brazil nut slices

Melt butter in a saucepan; blend in flour, salt and pepper; gradually add milk; cook over low heat until thickened and smooth, stirring constantly. Add Brazil nuts, green pepper, onion, Worcestershire sauce and tuna. Spread on toast and slow-broil, about 5 minutes. Garnish each canapé with a strip of pimiento and a Brazil nut. Serve hot. Makes 20 canapés.

CHEESE AND BACON APPETIZERS

1 cup milk	1 egg yolk
1 cup grated sharp Cheddar cheese	1 teaspoon water
	4 to 6 strips partially cooked
1 teaspoon dry mustard	bacon, cut into small pieces
1 tablespoon flour	Parsley sprigs

Mix milk and cheese in top of double boiler and cook until cheese melts. Mix mustard and flour and moisten to paste with water. Add this to milk-cheese mixture. Add egg yolk mixed with 1 teaspoon water. Cook in double boiler until it thickens. Spread crackers with this paste and top with piece of partially cooked bacon. Place under broiler and complete cooking of bacon. Top with a tiny sprig of parsley. (This is another recipe that can be made ahead—paste can be kept in jar in refrigerator for 2 to 3 weeks.)

CHEESE-PECAN BALLS

½ pound Roquefort cheese	2 teaspoons onion juice
1 (8-ounce) package cream cheese at room temperature	½ teaspoon salt
	1 cup fine-chopped pecans

Combine the first four ingredients. Refrigerate until firm. Shape into balls about three-fourths inch in diameter; roll in the chopped pecans. Refrigerate until serving time. Makes 50 balls.

CHEESE WAFERS

1 pound sharp cheese, grated	⅓ teaspoon red pepper
¼ pound butter	1 cup flour
1 teaspoon salt	
3 teaspoons Worcestershire sauce	

Knead all ingredients together with fingers until well blended. Form into a roll about 2 inches in diameter. Wrap in waxed paper or foil and put in refrigerator for at least 24 hours. Slice very thin, arrange on baking sheet and bake in a 450° oven for about 7 minutes.

CHILI-PECAN ROLL

½ pound processed American cheese
1 (3-ounce) package cream cheese
½ teaspoon salt
¼ teaspoon instant minced onion
½ teaspoon instant minced garlic
Pinch ground red pepper
2 teaspoons fresh lemon juice
¾ cup fine-chopped pecans
3 tablespoons chili powder
Round crackers

Have cheeses at room temperature; mix thoroughly. Add remaining ingredients except chili powder and crackers. Mix well. Shape into rolls, 4 inches long and 1½ inches in diameter. Chill 30 minutes or more. Dust evenly with chili powder. Refrigerate until firm and ready to serve. Cut into slices ⅛ inch thick. Serve on round crackers. Makes approximately 3 dozen canapés.

CRUNCHY SALMON-CHEESE BALL

In the oriental tradition, fish is considered to be a symbol of wealth and good luck. This salmon-cheese ball hors d'oeuvre—rolled in crisp chow mein noodles—is delicious when spread on colorful fresh vegetables such as cucumber slices, halved cherry tomatoes, small celery sticks, raw mushroom caps, etc. It is equally good on Melba toast or crackers.

2 cups canned salmon, skin and bones removed
1 (8-ounce) package cream cheese at room temperature
1 tablespoon lemon juice
1 teaspoon horseradish
1 teaspoon onion juice or grated onion
¼ teaspoon salt
⅛ teaspoon liquid smoke (purchased)
1 (3-ounce) can chow mein noodles
3 tablespoons minced parsley
Crackers or vegetables

Flake salmon and combine with cream cheese, lemon juice, horseradish, onion juice, salt and liquid smoke. Mix well and chill until firm. Crush chow mein noodles lightly and combine with parsley. Shape salmon cheese mixture into a ball and roll in the noodles. Chill and serve as appetizer, providing a spreader and thin slices of Melba toast, crackers or small pieces of sliced fresh vegetables.

CUCUMBER CANAPÉS

1 (8-ounce) package cream cheese at room temperature	Salt
1 tablespoon butter	Toast rounds
½ cup finely chopped and drained cucumber	Paprika
Few drops onion juice or little grated onion	Stuffed olives (optional)
	Green pepper (optional)

Cream the cheese and butter and mix thoroughly with cucumber, onion juice and salt. Serve on toast rounds. Sprinkle with paprika. Garnish with finely sliced stuffed olives and thin shreds of green pepper if desired.

STUFFED HARD-COOKED EGGS

For appetizer or hors d'oeuvre service and great in the picnic basket! Shell and quarter hard-cooked eggs. If to be an appetizer, the stuffing should be firm and the eggs quartered for finger eating. For an hors d'oeuvre at a buffet supper the filling may be soft.

Stuffed Eggs: Cool the eggs, shell, rinse and dry. Halve lengthwise. Scoop out the yolks; blend with ¼ the quantity of any of the savory pastes that follow, plus ¼ the quantity of whipped unsalted butter. Pack level into the empty egg-white halves and refrigerate. Cut in quarters. Dust the yolks with paprika, minced fresh dill or parsley; or decorate with bits of truffle, green or ripe olives, capers, black or red caviar.

Savory Pastes for Fillings: These include sardine spread; lobster, anchovy or shrimp paste; Maine lobster spread; crab meat spread; cheese spreads of all kinds; tuna sherry spread; Smithfield ham spread; liver pâté and many others.

Filled Eggs: Shell and halve hard-cooked eggs lengthwise. Scoop out the yolks. For 4 yolks blend in ½ tablespoon each mustard and mayonnaise. Half fill the empty egg whites with red or black caviar, plain or with minced chives; or use chopped smoked oysters, mussels or shrimp. Heap with the egg-yolk mixture, decorate with designs made by the tines of a fork. Top with a bit of truffle, a small sautéed mushroom, a slice of red radish, a dot of canned pimiento or clusters of capers. Chill. Serve in single small lettuce leaves.

STUFFED EGGS À LA RUSSE

Remove the shells from 6 hard-cooked eggs, cut them crosswise into halves; remove the yolks and fill the spaces from which these were taken with caviar, minced sardines, salmon or tuna fish. Press the yolks of the eggs through a sieve, moisten thoroughly with mayonnaise and put a spoonful on each half egg. Have ready rounds of well-buttered bread and slices of small ripe tomatoes. Put a slice of tomato on each round of bread, then a half egg on the tomato. Garnish with parsley.

GUACAMOLE

1 soft large ripe avocado	4 drops Tabasco
1 juicy tomato, skinned	½ teaspoon salt
2 tablespoons olive oil	Crackers
½ tablespoon lemon juice	
4 slices crisp cooked bacon, crumbled	

Mash soft and mix all ingredients together except crackers. Heap in bowl. Chill; serve on crackers.

HORS D'OEUVRE TARTS

1 recipe Rich American Pie
Pastry (see Index) or a mix
2½ tablespoons sesame seeds
2 (3-ounce) packages cream
cheese
2 tablespoons minced fresh
chives or 1 tablespoon
freeze-dried chives

1 (4¾-ounce) can liver
spread or 1 (4½-ounce)
can deviled ham
Almonds, pitted black olives,
radishes or apple slices

Prepare pie pastry as usual, mixing sesame seeds into flour or dry mix. Chill; roll pastry into large rectangle; with cookie cutter shape into small 2-inch scalloped rounds. Press each lightly into small muffin pan. Bake about 15 minutes in hot (400°) oven, or until golden brown. Cool and fill as follows: First a layer of 1 package cream cheese smooth-mixed with chives; a second layer of either liver spread or deviled ham; then a top layer of remaining package of plain cream cheese stirred until smooth. Garnish with almonds, pitted black olives, radishes and/or thin-sliced red-skinned apple. Refrigerate. Serve within 4 hours. Makes about 3 dozen tarts.

MOUSSE DE FOIE GRAS EN ASPIC

½ pound chicken livers
Water
¾ cup consommé or clear
chicken broth
½ cup mixed coarse-chopped
celery with chopped onion
and parsley
1 envelope unflavored gelatin

¾ cup cold water
2 tablespoons dry sherry
1 teaspoon Worcestershire
sauce
2 tablespoons chopped parsley
4 ounces cream cheese
Salt to taste

Simmer chicken livers in water to barely cover until pink color disappears. Put in blender; buzz until smooth. Meantime, simmer vegetables in the consommé about 15 minutes. Soften gelatin 5 minutes in cold water; add to boiling consommé. Stir until dissolved. Strain. Add sherry, Worcestershire sauce and chopped parsley. Pour ¼ the consommé mixture into 6 or 8 individual 4-ounce molds or custard cups; tilt to coat. Refrigerate until firm. Break up cream cheese; add to liver in blender and buzz while adding remaining consommé mixture. Fill molds. Refrigerate 3 to 4 hours, or until firm.

CHOPPED CHICKEN LIVERS

¼ cup chicken fat or butter
½ pound chicken livers, quartered
1 medium-sized onion, peeled and diced
2 eggs, hard-cooked and chopped

½ teaspoon salt
¼ teaspoon pepper
Pinch of thyme
Lettuce leaves or crackers

Melt fat in skillet; sauté livers and onion for about 8 minutes, or until livers are cooked and onion is golden. Cool. Chop livers; mix with onion and fat. Combine liver mixture with eggs; stir in salt, pepper and thyme. Chill. Serve in lettuce-lined cups or as a spread for bread or crackers.

HOT MACKEREL CANAPÉS

Fry 3 tablespoons each minced onion and green pepper in 2 tablespoons butter. Add ¼ cup solid-pack tomatoes. Stir in the contents of 1 can mackerel, well drained. Season with freshly ground black pepper. Simmer until thick. Serve hot on small squares of toast. Makes 36 canapés.

MUSHROOM NUT CANAPÉ SPREAD

Put 3 ounces shelled Brazil nuts through the food chopper, using the finest blade. Drain 1 (3-ounce) can chopped mushrooms, saving the liquid for other uses. Chop mushrooms very fine. Combine nuts and mushrooms with 1 (3-ounce) package cream cheese and ¼ teaspoon each salt and celery salt. Spread on bread or toast rounds. Makes 36 canapés.

STUFFED MUSHROOMS

20 medium-sized fresh mushroom caps
⅓ cup chopped mushroom stems
2 tablespoons fine-chopped onions
1 tablespoon butter or margarine
½ cup fine dry bread crumbs
½ cup chopped Brazil nuts
⅓ cup cooked or canned tomatoes
½ teaspoon salt
¼ cup grated American cheese
⅛ teaspoon pepper
2 teaspoons lemon juice

Wash and dry mushroom caps. Cook mushroom stems and onions in butter slowly for 5 minutes (do not brown). Combine all ingredients except mushroom caps; mix well and stuff mixture into the mushroom caps. Arrange on a baking sheet; broil 10 to 15 minutes until browned on top. Serve hot. Makes 20.

MUSHROOM TOAST

From 1½ pounds mushrooms reserve 6 good-sized caps. Wipe with damp cloth, set aside. Wipe remaining caps and stems, chop. Melt 2 tablespoons of butter in a frying pan, add a few drops of lemon juice, a hint of mace and salt and pepper to taste. Gently cook the mushrooms until they are done, about 10 minutes. In the meantime, fry the caps separately, keeping them whole; put the chopped mushrooms on fried or toasted rounds of bread, which have been spread with lemon butter, top with the 6 mushroom caps, sprinkling them lightly with minced parsley.

OYSTERS ON THE HALF SHELL LUCULLAN

Fill large scooped metal plates with crushed ice. Top with 6 large oysters on the half shell, delicately laced with pink caviar. Center with shredded horseradish. Garnish with lemon sections.

LYNNHAVEN OYSTERS

For each person allow 6 oysters on the half shell. Place the oysters in a baking pan; on each oyster put a bit of horseradish and a few drops of lemon juice; then lay on each a very small strip of thinly sliced bacon. Place in a 375° oven and bake until the oysters ruffle and the bacon is brown. Serve very hot on a good-sized plate with sprigs of parsley between the oysters and a lemon basket filled with Tartar Sauce (see Index) in the center of each plate.

OPEN OYSTER CANAPÉS

Dry 1 pint oysters on absorbent paper. Dip in slightly beaten egg; dust with salt and pepper; dip in fine dry bread crumbs. Sauté in butter; serve on half slices of toast spread with Tartar Sauce (see Index). Garnish with water cress.

OYSTERS ROCKEFELLER

¼ cup butter
½ cup fine bread crumbs
½ cup defrosted frozen
    chopped spinach
2 tablespoons minced onion
1 tablespoon fine-chopped
    parsley

1 tablespoon dry sherry
Salt and pepper to taste
1 dozen large oysters on the
    shell
Grated Parmesan cheese

Cream the butter and mix in the bread crumbs. Add spinach, minced onion, parsley and sherry. Mix thoroughly. Season to taste with salt and pepper. Spread generously over the top of each oyster in the half shell. Dust with grated Parmesan cheese. Place in a large baking or broiling pan. Bake in a moderately hot (400°) for 10 minutes, or until browned. Serve immediately. Serves 4 as an appetizer.

SMOKED BABY OYSTER CANAPÉS

2 tablespoons catsup
½ teaspoon Worcestershire
 sauce
2 slices white bread, decrusted,
 cut in squares and toasted

2 (3½-ounce) cans smoked
 baby oysters
1 tablespoon minced parsley

Mix together catsup and Worcestershire. Toast bread squares and spread with catsup mixture. Meantime, either broil smoked oysters, or sauté in a little of their oil. Place 2 oysters (more if very small) on each toast square. Dust with minced parsley. Serve hot.

PIZZA CRACKERS

Spread round buttery crackers or square white crackers with thin-sliced mozzarella cheese or cottage cheese. Spread over a thin layer of tomato sauce; sprinkle with oregano (or thyme) and grated Parmesan cheese. Bake in a hot (400°) oven 10 minutes, or until the cheese melts. Serve at once.

PRUNE AND BACON APPETIZERS

Steam 18 prunes and remove the pits. Insert in each prune a small piece of chutney and a pecan. Wrap a narrow piece of bacon around each prune, insert toothpick to hold together. Broil until bacon is crisp.

ROQUEFORT COTTAGE CHEESE DIP

Crumble 1¼ ounces Roquefort cheese and add to 1 cup creamed cottage cheese; mix well. Stir in ½ teaspoon onion juice. Add enough sour cream to give good dipping consistency, about ½ cup. Serve with potato chips, crackers, crisp raw vegetables or ripe pears.

SARDINE AND ANCHOVY CANAPÉS

Remove the bones and tails from anchovies or sardines and pound or rub the flesh until very smooth; or substitute for either kind of fish sardine or anchovy paste, which may be purchased in tubes. Spread toasted or fried bread with the paste, garnish the edges with pimiento butter or stiff mayonnaise put through the pastry tube or bag, and in the center of each lay a small, thin slice of lemon, on which 2 crosswise strips of pimiento are placed.

SAVORY BRAZIL NUT SPREAD

½ pound liverwurst
2 tablespoons mayonnaise
1 teaspoon table mustard
½ cup fine-chopped toasted
 Brazil nuts

Toast rounds
⅓ cup crushed Brazil nuts

Mash liverwurst and blend with mayonnaise and mustard. Mix with chopped toasted Brazil nuts. Spread the mixture on toast rounds and garnish the edges with crushed Brazil nuts. Place the canapés under a broiler until heated through, about 3 minutes, and serve hot. Makes 20 canapés.

Toasted Brazil Nuts: Spread the shelled nuts on baking sheets and bake in a moderate (350°) oven 15 to 18 minutes, turning occasionally to brown evenly. Allow nuts to cool—then chop them.

SESAME SEED STICKS

1½ cups sifted flour
½ cup enriched corn meal
1 teaspoon salt
1 teaspoon paprika
½ cup shortening at room
 temperature

1 cup grated sharp cheese
1 egg, beaten
¼ cup milk
½ cup dairy sour cream
2 tablespoons sesame seeds

Sift together first four ingredients. Chop in shortening until like coarse crumbs. Stir-mix in cheese, egg and milk. Knead gently 5 times on lightly floured surface; roll into two 4×18-inch rectangles; spread with sour cream; strew with sesame seeds. Cut across into strips 4×½ inches. Bake on pastry sheets in hot (400°) oven for 10 minutes, or until light brown.

HOT LOBSTER CANAPÉS

Slowly fry ½ cup fine-minced celery and 1 tablespoon minced onion in 1 tablespoon butter. Drain 1 3½- or 4-ounce can lobster meat, pick over and mince. Add to the fried vegetables. Season with ⅛ teaspoon powdered dill, salt and pepper to taste. When hot, serve on small squares of toast. Makes 36 canapés.

TINY COVERED SANDWICHES

White bread, toast rounds, rye bread, pumpernickel rounds can be used. Take your choice of fillings:
Chive cream cheese and minced clams with clam juice to blend.
Cream cheese and anchovy paste.
Chopped pimiento, crushed pineapple and cream cheese.
Deviled ham and chopped dill.
Cream cheese and chopped black olives.
Minced cucumber, onion and water cress.

SARDINE PATÉ SPREAD

Press excess oil from 12 sardine fillets; put fish through sieve. Stir ¼ cup unsalted butter until creamy. Mix or blend with the sardines and 1 tablespoon lemon juice. Yields 1¼ cups.

SWEDISH LEAF

On a good-sized lettuce leaf arrange 1 heaping teaspoonful each of shredded herring and celery blended with mayonnaise, 2 heaping teaspoonfuls of chopped hard-cooked egg blended with chili sauce or catsup, and caviar to garnish. Makes 1 serving.

TINY SWEDISH MEAT BALLS

Grind together three times ½ pound each ground raw beef and fresh pork. Fry 1 teaspoon finely chopped onion in 1 tablespoon butter or margarine. Add to the meat. Stir in 2 tablespoons fine, soft bread crumbs, 1 teaspoon salt, ⅛ teaspoon pepper, ¼ teaspoon ginger or nutmeg and ⅓ cup water. Mix and blend until smooth. Shape into very small round balls and fry in butter. Shake the pan occasionally so they will brown evenly. Serve hot or cold. If served hot, pour over any remaining butter.

VIRGINIA WHET

6 half slices white bread, cut ½ inch thick	1½ cups grated Cheshire cheese
3 tablespoons butter	1 tablespoon minced parsley
6 anchovy fillets	2 tablespoons melted butter

Sauté bread in butter. Place anchovy fillet lengthwise on each piece. Cover thickly with cheese and parsley mixed; brown under broiler, basting occasionally with additional melted butter. Serve very hot.

WATER-CRESS CANAPÉS

General directions: For 2 dozen canapés use ½ bunch water cress; discard the stems; cut the leaves medium-fine. Combine all the other ingredients except the water cress. Add water cress, stirring lightly. Cover rounds of white or whole wheat bread with the chosen spread:

Anchovy Spread: Cream 1 (3-ounce) package cream cheese with 1 tablespoon anchovy paste and 1 teaspoon lemon juice. Add ½ bunch prepared water cress.

Smithfield Ham Spread: Combine ½ cup deviled Smithfield ham or spread and 1 tablespoon mayonnaise, and add ½ bunch prepared water cress.

Roquefort Spread: Mash 3 ounces Roquefort or blue cheese, and add 2 tablespoons catsup and ½ teaspoon paprika. Stir in ½ bunch prepared water cress.

Soups and Chowders

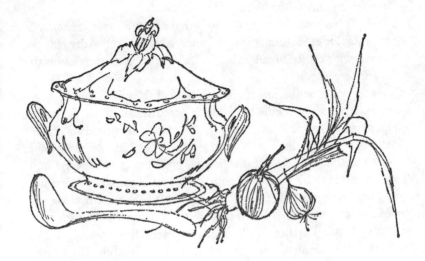

"Soup's on!" is an old cry that used to summon the pioneers to the table in our country's earlier days. Soups at that time may have taken hours to make or the stock pot may have simmered on the stove for days. Excellent homemade soup can be made in a trice today with the help of a blender.

If you've gotten out of the soup habit, try a clear consommé as a prelude to dinner or consider a hearty chowder to be served with crusty bread, salad and cheese for a marvelous lunch or supper.

Any soup containing meat, chicken, fish, milk, cheese, eggs or beans, peas or lentils has enough protein to make it the main event in a meal. When eighteenth-century homemakers made chowder, it was thick with seafood and vegetables, a hearty kind of soup that made a meal satisfying even for growing boys and hungry men. In Rhode Island and New York, clam chowder was often made with tomatoes, while a bit to the north along the Massachusetts coast, no "self-respecting" cook would dream of using them. Further south, many types of fish and vegetables varied the formula into seafood stews and gumbos. Back from the coasts in the prairie regions, vegetables became the chief ingredients of chowders. Today it's each to his own, and tastes include minestrone, borscht and boula boula! Make your own favorites and then from time to time try someone else's favorite soup.

All recipes are for six servings unless otherwise stated.

CHILLED SOUPS

It was years ago in Europe that chilled soups—usually made with fruits—were invented and one wonders why they are not served more often in our own country. In the warm weather cold soups made either with a fruit basis such as the famous European cherry soup, or with a savory base such as Jellied Madrilène (see Index), are most refreshing. Creamed soups like Vichyssoise (see Index) are winning ever-widening favor.

A FEW QUICK HOT SOUP COMBINATIONS

There are many soup combinations that go well together and will transform a can of ordinary soup into a quickly prepared, superb taste experience. Let your palate and your imagination be your guide. For example try mixing tomato and oyster soups together and garnish with oyster crackers. Or a can of oyster soup with some milk and celery soup added, plus a pinch of onion salt, makes another different, distinctive easy-to-make soup. A few more ideas: corn chowder and tomato soup garnished with bacon; oxtail and celery soups garnished with a lemon slice; mock turtle and pea soup with a dash of sherry.

QUICK COLD SOUPS

You can "cook" delicious, nutritious and refreshing soups right in your refrigerator. Simply keep cans of condensed soup chilled, and to serve just mix or blend the soup with ice water or cold milk. Several soups preferred for chilling include: tomato, green pea, black bean, beef broth and consommé. Cream soups, such as asparagus, chicken, mushroom, potato or vegetable also are favorites.

Garnish with whipped or sour cream, water cress, chopped parsley or chives, fine-shredded carrot, diced pimiento or green pepper, lemon slices or grated rind, or sliced stuffed olives.

MONEY-SAVING SOUPS FROM FOOD ODDMENTS

Cooked Vegetables: Combine bits of leftover cooked vegetables to make a cream soup.

Bones from Meat or Poultry: Brown the bones from roast or poultry. Fry 1 sliced onion in margarine with ½ teaspoon sugar; add the bones, celery tops, 1 diced carrot, some canned tomato, and a little thyme; pour in 2 quarts cold water; simmer 2 hours. Strain, thicken and serve with croutons or small toast rounds.

Bread Crumbs: Sprinkle fine dry bread crumbs into any fish or meat soup as thickening.

Leftover Cereal: Use leftover rice, oatmeal or farina to thicken any soup.

Outer Lettuce Leaves: Fine-chop enough outer leaves of lettuce to make 2 cups. Add some chopped celery tops and 1 chopped onion, peeling and all. Simmer in 1 quart of water for 20 minutes and rub through a sieve. Add 1 cup undiluted evaporated milk; when boiling, thicken with 2 tablespoons each of margarine and flour, blended. Season with salt, pepper and nutmeg.

Dried Cheese: Grate the cheese from dried rinds and pass with any plain vegetable soup.

A Meal from a Soup: Transform any thin meat or vegetable soup into a meal by putting a slice of bread fried in butter or margarine in each soup plate, topping with a poached egg, then pouring in the soup.

CHEDDAR CHEESE SOUP

2 medium carrots	⅛ teaspoon pepper
1 medium onion	1 quart heated chicken broth
3 tablespoons butter or margarine	½ pound sharp Cheddar cheese, grated
½ cup minced celery	2 cups heated milk
¼ cup flour	2 tablespoons minced parsley
½ teaspoon salt	

Peel and finely chop carrots and onion. Melt butter in a 2-quart saucepan. Add carrots, onion and celery; sauté until softened. Add flour, salt and pepper and stir to make smooth paste. Gradually stir in chicken broth making smooth sauce. Stir in cheese; cook-stir until it melts. Add milk. Serve topped with parsley.

QUICK CHICKEN MINESTRONE

1 package chicken noodle soup	1 cup cooked or canned red
1 cup mixed cooked vegetables	kidney beans
(canned or frozen)	1 tablespoon minced parsley

Make up chicken noodle soup following package directions. Simmer 5 minutes. Add remaining ingredients, except parsley. Simmer 5 minutes more. Serve in bowls and dust over parsley.

QUICK CURRIED CHICKEN SOUP

Reconstitute 2 (10½-ounce) cans of chicken soup as directed on the can. Add ½ tart apple, grated, and ⅓ teaspoon curry powder blended with water. Garnish with diced avocado and pimiento.

WON TON SOUP

These Chinese dumplings, served in a canned meat, chicken or vegetable soup, make a satisfying and unusual substantial opening or luncheon main dish.

First, prepare the canned soup; 2 minutes before it will be done, add the won tons; cover and steam 15 minutes.

Won Ton Chinese Dumplings

1½ cups presifted flour	Salt and pepper to taste
½ teaspoon salt	½ tablespoon minced
1 egg	onions (optional)
2 tablespoons cold water	2 tablespoons minced fresh or
1 cup minced cooked pork,	canned mushrooms
shrimp, beef, veal or poultry	(optional)

Won tons are really made in two parts:

The Dough: Sift together flour and salt. Beat and add egg; mix in water. Turn onto floured surface; work until smooth as in making noodle dough. Let stand 15 minutes. Roll as thin as paper; cut in 3-inch squares, ready for the filling.

The Filling: Mix pork, shrimp, beef, veal or poultry, salt and pepper to taste, onions and mushrooms if used. Put 1 teaspoon of filling in center of each square of dough. Fold over diagonally to form triangles and press edges together with fork. Boil 15 minutes in salted water or thin meat, chicken or vegetable soup.

BOUILLABAISSE

¼ cup olive oil
1 section garlic, minced
1 onion, sliced
1 carrot, diced
1 tablespoon minced parsley
¼ teaspoon crushed fennel seeds or 1 teaspoon minced fennel tips
1 teaspoon saffron
2 teaspoons salt
¼ teaspoon rosemary
1 pound halibut steak, diced
1 pound striped-bass fillets

4 cups Court Bouillon (see Index)
¼ cup tomato paste
2 pounds squid, sectioned (optional)
12 clams in the shell
1 pound lobster meat or rock lobster tails (cooked or canned)
1 (10½-ounce) can mussels
¼ cup dry white wine or sherry

Heat the oil in a 4-quart kettle. Add the garlic, onion, carrot, parsley and fennel. Slow-fry until golden. Add the saffron, salt and rosemary. Layer in the diced halibut and bass. Heat the Court Bouillon and tomato paste together; pour over the fish. Cover; simmer 15 minutes. Scrub the clams in the shell (or use 1 jar canned clams and liquid); add with the squid if used. Simmer 10 minutes. Add the lobster meat and the canned mussels with their liquid; heat 5 minutes. Stir in the sherry.

Ladle over toasted French bread in deep soup plates. The French bread may be spread with unsalted butter or discreetly flavored garlic butter before toasting.

CHOPPED CLAM AND TOMATO SOUP

3 cups seasoned tomato juice
1 cup hot water
½ teaspoon Worcestershire
 sauce

3 drops Tabasco
2 (7½-ounce) cans chopped
 clams and juice
1 tablespoon minced parsley

Combine first four ingredients and simmer 5 minutes. Stir in chopped clams. Simmer 5 minutes more. Serve garnished with minced parsley.

MANHATTAN CLAM CHOWDER

3 tablespoons diced salt pork
2 medium-sized onions,
 chopped
1 quart boiling water
1 quart shucked clams
1 pint sliced potatoes
1 carrot, diced
1 teaspoon salt

1 teaspoon pepper
1 clove of garlic, crushed
¼ teaspoon thyme
1 tablespoon flour
1 tablespoon butter or a
 substitute
1 pint canned tomatoes

Put the pork in the soup kettle and slowly fry out the fat. Then add the onions, cook gently for 3 minutes, add the water and, when boiling, the clams, potatoes, carrot and seasonings. Simmer for 1 hour and thicken with the flour and butter rubbed together. Then add the tomatoes, let cook a few moments and serve.

NEW ENGLAND CLAM CHOWDER

3 tablespoons diced fat salt pork
2 medium-sized onions, peeled and chopped
1 quart boiling water, fish stock or bottled clam juice
1 quart shucked clams

1 pint thin-sliced potatoes
1 teaspoon salt
¼ teaspoon pepper
1 tablespoon butter
1 tablespoon flour
1 pint milk

Fry out fat from salt pork in a 2-quart kettle. Add onions; sauté gently 3 minutes. Add water, clams, potatoes and seasonings. Cover; simmer 1 hour. Rub together butter and flour. Add a little of hot clam chowder and stir smooth. Return to cooking clam chowder and slowly bring to boil. Stir in milk. Simmer-cook 5 minutes. Serve in soup plates or bowls.

ONE-DISH COCONUT FISH-MEAT SOUP

1 fresh or 1 package grated coconut (unsweetened)
½ pound salt beef (corned beef)
1 (3- to 4-pound) king fish or red snapper
2 quarts water
2 peeled onions
3 shallots
2 stalks celery
1 green pepper, seeded

Pinch basil (preferably fresh)
4 cloves
2 bay leaves
¼ teaspoon cumin seed, crushed
½ teaspoon salt
2 to 3 tablespoons corn meal
2 beef bouillon cubes
Corn meal mush wedges or pilot crackers

Note: If using fresh coconut, take it out of shell, cut in pieces and grate it in blender.

Put grated coconut in bowl, cover with 1 quart boiling water and put aside. Wash salt beef, cover with boiling water and put aside. Remove head from fish; set aside.

Next, prepare fish bouillon. Boil water and add 1 onion, 2 shallots, 1 stalk celery, 1 green pepper, all cut in large pieces, together with basil, cloves, bay leaves, cumin, salt, and the head of the fish; let boil 20 minutes. Then turn heat very low; add fish cut up in slices and let simmer another 20 minutes. Then strain; remove fish head, and put clear bouillon back to boil with salt beef, cut in small pieces. Cut fine remaining onion, shallot and celery stalk and put with salt meat to cook until meat is tender. Meanwhile, remove flesh from bones of fish and flake medium fine; put aside.

Put coconut with water through cheese cloth and press out every drop of coconut milk. Discard coconut. When salt meat is tender, sprinkle corn meal over it and stir until absorbed. In large kettle, combine with reserved coconut milk, flaked fish and two bouillon cubes. Heat, but do not boil. If necessary, correct seasoning. Serve with corn meal mush wedges or pilot crackers.

COURT BOUILLON

This is the liquid used in poaching or so-called "boiling" fish. If fish head and bones are available, they are added, and the drained court bouillon may be presented in cups as bouillon with a garnish of canned baby shrimp and/or seasoned un-sweetened whipped cream.

2 cups dry white wine	1 bouquet garni*
5 cups water	1½ teaspoons salt
⅓ cup minced onion	6 peppercorns

Combine all ingredients except the peppercorns in a 2-quart saucepan. Simmer 20 minutes. Add the peppercorns. Simmer 10 minutes; put through a fine strainer and use.

* One or two sprays of parsley, a little thyme, and a bay leaf tied together so that they may readily be removed from the stock after cooking.

CRAB GUMBO FILÉ

Filé powder, used in making all types of gumbos, was originated by American Indians. It is a powder made from the tender leaves of young sassafras trees. The early Creole settlers of

Louisiana adopted it and used it in many savory dishes. Filé powder is available at fine food stores and in the spice sections of some supermarkets.

1 whole green pepper, seeded and diced
1 cup diced celery
1½ cups drained solid-pack, canned tomato, mashed
1 quart clam broth, canned or bottled
1 onion, peeled and sliced
1 cup okra, fresh, canned or frozen, sliced, stems removed

¼ teaspoon powdered bay leaf
⅓ teaspoon thyme
3 cups water
3 (6-ounce) packages frozen Alaska king crab meat
6 drops Tabasco
1 teaspoon Worcestershire sauce
½ teaspoon filé powder
4 cups cooked long grain rice

In a 2½-quart saucepan, combine green pepper, celery, tomato, clam broth, onion, prepared okra, bay leaf, thyme and water. Bring to boiling point. Simmer 25 minutes. Remove all shell from crab meat; cut crab meat into small pieces; add to soup in saucepan and bring slowly to boil. Season with Tabasco, Worcestershire and filé powder. Simmer 5 minutes. Spoon rice into soup plates. Ladle over the gumbo filé.

MANHATTAN FISH CHOWDER

3 pounds cleaned fish (any light-fleshed kind, salt water or fresh water fish)
2 quarts cold water
¼ pound sliced salt pork
2 cups cooked fresh, canned or frozen mixed vegetables (carrots, peas, green beans and celery)
1 (1-pound 12-ounce) can tomatoes

⅓ cup flour
2 teaspoons salt
⅓ teaspoon pepper
¼ teaspoon each ground thyme, marjoram and dill
1 tablespoon freeze-dried chives or 2 tablespoons minced fresh chives

Rinse fish thoroughly. Cut off heads, add to cold water with fish. Bring to slow boil. Simmer 30 minutes or until fish barely flakes when tested with fork. Remove fish (discard heads). Save fish liquid. Carefully separate skin and bones from fish;

flake fish coarse. Fry salt pork until fat runs freely and pork is light brown in color. Dice with scissors. (Save fat.) Add pork to fish liquid with mixed vegetables and tomatoes. Bring to boil. Add fish. Add flour to salt pork fat; stir until smooth. Add ¼ cup of hot chowder, stirring until all lumps disappear, then return to cooking chowder. Add seasonings. Simmer 5 minutes. Garnish with chives. Serve in bowls.

NEW ENGLAND FISH CHOWDER

2 cups peeled diced raw potato
3 cups boiling water or fish stock
2 tablespoons minced onion
1 teaspoon salt
½ teaspoon pepper
1 bay leaf
1½ cups flaked cooked fish or 1 pound fish fillets, cooked and flaked
3 cups milk
1½ tablespoons flour
1 tablespoon butter or margarine
Minced parsley

Combine potato, boiling water, onion and seasonings. Cook 15 minutes, or until potato is tender. Add fish. Bring to boil; then stir in milk. Mix flour with butter; stir in ½ cup liquid from cooking chowder; return to chowder and stir-cook until boiling. Dust with parsley; pass pilot crackers or old-fashioned oyster crackers.

PORTUGUESE FISH SOUP

1 cup minced onion
2 tablespoons olive or salad oil
6 cups hot water
⅓ cup minced parsley
1 pound haddock fillets or other white-meat fish
1 (6-ounce) can shrimp, diced
2¼ teaspoons salt
⅛ teaspoon ground black pepper
¼ teaspoon basil seasoning powder
3 hard-cooked egg yolks, mashed
6 slices toasted French bread
½ cup toasted slivered almonds (optional)

Sauté onion in olive or salad oil in 2½-quart saucepan. Add hot water, parsley, fish, shrimp and seasonings. Cover. Cook over medium heat for 10 minutes, or until fish is flaky. Stir in egg yolks. Serve over toasted French bread in soup bowls. Garnish with slivered toasted almonds if desired.

LOBSTER BISQUE

1 tablespoon butter or margarine	½ cup fine-crushed saltine cracker crumbs
1 tablespoon flour	½ teaspoon Worcestershire sauce
½ teaspoon salt	
⅛ teaspoon pepper	⅓ cup heavy cream
1 cup milk	3 tablespoons fine-minced parsley
4 cups Lobster Stock	
2 cups fine-minced lobster meat†	

Melt butter. Stir in flour, salt and pepper; slowly stir in milk until mixture bubbles. Add Lobster Stock, lobster meat, cracker crumbs and Worcestershire sauce. Bring to slow boil. Add cream. Serve in soup plates. Dust with parsley.

† Two good-sized boiled Maine lobsters will be needed.

Lobster Stock: Boil lobster shells after meat has been removed with ½ teaspoon pickling spice, 1 teaspoon salt, ⅛ teaspoon pepper and 5 cups cold water. Cover; simmer-boil 1 hour, then strain.

LOBSTER OR CRAB BISQUE

1 tablespoon butter	2 cups minced lobster or crab meat
1 tablespoon flour	
1 pint hot milk	½ cup cracker crumbs
½ teaspoon salt	Worcestershire sauce or lemon juice (optional)
¾ teaspoon minced parsley	
1 quart fish stock	Minced parsley

Melt the butter, add flour, milk and seasonings, as in making white sauce, then stock, fish and crumbs. Season further if desired with a little Worcestershire sauce or a hint of lemon juice, and just before serving sprinkle with parsley.

FRENCH OYSTER SOUP

1 pint shucked oysters	2½ tablespoons flour
1 pint cold water or 1 cup each water and bottled clam juice	2½ tablespoons butter or margarine at room temperature
1 tablespoon minced peeled onion	3 cups milk, scalded
¼ cup fine-chopped celery	Salt and pepper to taste
Generous dash ground mace or nutmeg	1 tablespoon cold water
	2 egg yolks, beaten

Wash oysters and fine-chop. Place in a 3-pint saucepan. Add water, onion and celery; simmer 20 minutes. Stir together mace or nutmeg, flour and butter; when smooth add ¼ cup of the milk; stir into oysters; add remaining milk. Cook-stir until boiling. Add salt and pepper to taste. Add 1 tablespoon cold water to beaten egg yolks. Stir into cooking soup, but do not boil. Serve at once.

NEW ENGLAND CORN AND OYSTER CHOWDER

2 slices fat salt pork or 2 tablespoons bacon drippings	¼ teaspoon paprika
	2½ cups scalded milk
2 tablespoons minced onion	2 tablespoons flour
2 cups diced potatoes	1½ tablespoons cold milk
3 cups boiling water	1½ cups raw or canned oysters and liquid
2 cups canned cream-style corn	1 cup boiling water
1 teaspoon celery salt	Dash of paprika

If pork is used, cut it into dice and try out the fat; if drippings, melt and heat. Add the onion; sauté until it begins to turn color; add the potatoes and the water. Simmer 15 minutes, or until the potatoes are tender. Add the corn, seasonings and scalded milk. Blend the flour with the cold milk and bring to a boil. Meantime, simmer-boil the oysters five minutes in the additional boiling water (or heat canned oysters and liquid). Stir into the corn mixture. Heat but do not boil. Finish off with additional dash of paprika.

NEW ENGLAND OYSTER STEW

½ cup minced celery
2 tablespoons butter
1 pint medium-sized oysters, washed
3 cups water

½ teaspoon salt
Few grains white pepper
1 quart milk
Paprika to taste
Crisp oyster crackers

Sauté the celery in the butter slowly 3 minutes. Add the oysters, water and seasonings. Simmer till the edges of the oysters ruffle or curl. Meanwhile, scald the milk and add to the oysters. Add paprika. Serve with crackers without reheating.
Note: In many places in New England 1 cup clam broth (canned or bottled) replaces 1 cup of the milk.

MANHATTAN TUNA CHOWDER

2 slices bacon, diced
1 large onion, peeled and sliced
2 cups pared cubed potatoes
1 cup pared diced carrots
½ cup diced celery
2 (1-pound) cans tomatoes

2 cups water
1½ teaspoons salt
1 teaspoon thyme
¼ teaspoon pepper
2 (6½- or 7-ounce) cans tuna in vegetable oil
3 tablespoons chopped parsley

Sauté the bacon until crisp in a 3-quart saucepan. Add onion; sauté until tender but not brown. Add potatoes, carrots, celery, tomatoes, water, salt, thyme and pepper. Simmer uncovered 30 minutes. Coarse-flake tuna and add with its oil. Simmer 5 minutes longer. To serve, dust with chopped parsley.

MOCK TURTLE SUPERB

1 cup green peas	Few grains salt
1 can mock turtle soup	Grated Parmesan cheese
1 cup hot water	
½ cup heavy cream, beaten stiff	

Rub green peas through sieve and mix with turtle soup and hot water in ovenproof casserole. Top with whipped cream to which salt has been added. Sprinkle with generous amount of grated cheese and place in oven until very hot and cheese is melted. Serve in soup cups. Serves 4.

JELLIED BEET SOUP

6 large beets	4 tablespoons sherry or 1
2 cans consommé	tablespoon lemon juice
2½ cups water	2 teaspoons gelatin dissolved in
1½ teaspoons salt	2 tablespoons cold water
1 teaspoon Worcestershire sauce	Slice of lemon
	Minced parsley

Grate raw beets and cook slowly in the consommé and water for 30 minutes. Keep pot covered except to check to see if too much water is cooking away, in which case add a little more. Strain, add salt and other seasonings. Stir dissolved gelatin into soup liquid, stirring until well blended. Chill for about 10 hours before serving. Garnish with a slice of lemon sprinkled with minced parsley.

JELLIED MADRILÈNE

2 envelopes unflavored
  gelatin
½ cup cold water
2 cups tomato juice
½ teaspoon grated onion
1 cup canned chicken broth
1 cup sauerkraut juice

1 piece lemon rind
½ teaspoon salt
⅛ teaspoon pepper
Worcestershire sauce to taste
6 lemon slices
6 sprigs parsley

Add gelatin to cold water; let stand 5 minutes. Combine tomato juice, onion, broth, kraut juice, lemon rind, salt and pepper. Heat to boiling point and strain, making a stock. Dissolve gelatin in it. Cool. Season with Worcestershire to taste. Refrigerate until firm, about 4 hours. Serve in bouillon cups or small bowls. Garnish with lemon slices and parsley.

BEEF GUMBO WITH RICE

2 pounds best-quality stewing
  beef, tenderized
½ pound cooked ham
3 tablespoons margarine or
  cooking oil
1 pint canned or 1 quart
  fresh okra, sliced
1 medium onion, peeled and
  minced
3 medium-sized green peppers,
  seeded and chopped

1 cup solid-pack canned
  tomatoes, mashed
2 quarts cold water
2 teaspoons beef bouillon
  powder
1 dried pod red pepper
6 cups cooked flaky converted
  rice

Cut beef and ham in 1-inch cubes. Fry meat in large heavy deep kettle until well browned in margarine or oil. Stir in okra, onion, peppers, tomatoes, water and bouillon powder; add red pepper pod. If fresh okra is used, add okra last when gumbo is practically done. Cover; simmer 45 minutes, or until meat is fork-tender. Remove pepper pod. Add extra water if liquid boils down too much, or gumbo will be too thick. Serve in warmed deep soup plates or large shallow bowls; top with cupful of cooked flaky rice.

QUICK BEEF SOUP

½ pound ground raw beef	1 teaspoon salt
1 tablespoon butter or beef fat	⅓ cup pearl barley
1 medium-sized onion,	2 quarts cold water
chopped	1½ teaspoons salt
1½ cups diced raw potato	⅛ teaspoon pepper
1 cup diced raw carrot	

Break up the meat with a fork and fry it until brown in the butter or beef fat. Brown the onion slightly with the meat. Add the potato, carrot, salt, barley and water. Season with the salt and pepper. Cover and simmer for 1 hour. Serve in bowls.

MULLIGATAWNY SOUP

1 onion	1 apple, peeled, cored and cut
1 carrot	into pieces
1 small white turnip	1 bay leaf
4 tablespoons butter	Pinch of thyme
1 pound lamb	1 teaspoon lemon juice
1 teaspoon curry powder	1 cup rice, cooked
6 cups chicken bouillon	

(Consult your butcher when you buy the lamb—ask him for a lean cut with the fat and skin removed and the meat cut in small pieces.) Begin making this soup by slicing the onion thinly; cut the carrot and turnip, and sauté vegetables in butter. When golden brown add the lamb to the pot and sear, then add the curry powder. Stir well, cook for about 5 minutes more before adding hot chicken bouillon. Bring to a boil, skim, then add apple, bay leaf and thyme. Turn heat to simmer, cover and let cook for 2 hours. Add water if liquid cooks down. Strain. Put lamb pieces back in strained soup and bring to a boil again. Then add the lemon juice. Simmer about 5 minutes more. Add rice, heat thoroughly.

OXTAIL SOUP

2 oxtails, disjointed
3 tablespoons butter or
   margarine
½ cup sliced carrot
¼ cup sliced onion
½ cup diced celery
2 quarts soup stock or 2 quarts
   water and 4 teaspoons
   bouillon powder

¼ teaspoon ground clove
1 tablespoon minced parsley
3 tablespoons flour
¼ cup cold water
Salt and pepper to taste
Croutons

Rinse oxtail pieces well and drain. Melt butter or margarine in soup kettle; add oxtails and vegetables; fry until slightly browned. Add soup stock, clove and parsley. Cover closely; simmer 2 hours, or until oxtails are fork-tender. Add more soup stock from time to time so there will be 2 quarts soup left when it is done. When cooked, thicken with flour stirred smooth in ¼ cup cold water. Bring to boiling point; season to taste. Garnish with croutons.

PHILADELPHIA HOT POT

1 pint mixed vegetables,
   prepared for cooking
1 pound fresh honeycomb
   tripe, washed, drained and
   cut up
3 tablespoons butter or
   drippings
1 pound stewing lamb or
   mutton, freed from fat and
   cut up in small pieces
¼ pound lean salt pork, diced

1 small bay leaf
1 clove
1 sprig each parsley, thyme
   and marjoram
3 quarts cold water
½ pint diced potatoes
Salt and pepper to taste
⅓ cup flour
⅓ cup butter
2 eggs yolks, beaten (optional)

Vegetables in season may be used in making this soup—the pint being made up of equal parts of beans, carrots and celery; peas, onions and beans; tomatoes, eggplant and onions, etc. Fry the tripe in the soup kettle in butter or drippings until light yellow. Add the mutton, salt pork and the seasonings, tied together in a bit of cheesecloth, with the cold water. Closely cover the mixture, bring to boiling point and simmer for 2 hours; then add the vegetables and potatoes. Simmer 20 minutes or until tender. After cooling, remove the fat, season hot pot to taste with pepper and salt, then thicken with flour and butter creamed together. When boiling, stir the soup into egg yolks if a very rich effect is desired.

CHILLED AVOCADO SOUP

2 fully ripe avocados	¼ teaspoon onion salt
1 cup chicken broth	Pinch white pepper
1 cup light cream	1 teaspoon lemon juice
1 teaspoon salt	2 lemon slices

Halve avocados lengthwise, twisting gently to separate sections. Insert sharp knife directly into seed and twist to lift out. Peel avocado halves; then blend with chicken broth in electric blender until smooth, about 2 minutes. Combine and mix with cream and seasonings, and pour into large glass jar. Cover and refrigerate at least 3 hours or overnight. Stir in lemon juice. Garnish with lemon slices.

BEAN AND SPINACH SOUP

1 cup white or kidney beans	2 tablespoons savory fat
2 quarts boiling water or liquid from cooked smoked ham	2 cups water
	1 teaspoon beef extract
1 bay leaf	3 cups chopped cooked or canned spinach
1 medium-sized onion, peeled and chopped	2 tablespoons flour
	2 tablespoons cold water
1 section garlic, chopped	Salt and pepper to taste

Wash the beans and cover with the boiling water or ham liquid. Soak 50 minutes. Add the bay leaf, onion, and garlic sautéed in the fat. Cover and simmer till the beans are soft, about 2 hours.

Then add the water, beef extract and spinach. Bring to boiling point. Add the flour blended with 2 tablespoons cold water. Cook and stir till boiling. Season to taste with salt and pepper.

BLACK BEAN SOUP

1 pint black beans	¼ teaspoon pepper
2½ quarts boiling water	1 teaspoon celery salt
1 tablespoon flour, browned	1 tablespoon lemon juice
1 tablespoon butter	1 hard-cooked egg, diced
1 teaspoon salt	½ lemon, sliced thin

Soak the beans overnight in cold water to cover. In the morning, drain, add the boiling water and simmer until the beans are soft, adding more water during the cooking, if necessary—there should be no less than 2 quarts of soup when completed. Work through a sieve to purée, or buzz in blender. Return to the heat, and thicken with the flour and butter rubbed together. Add the seasonings and lemon juice and, just before serving, the egg and the lemon.

BORSCHT

2 cups shredded fresh beets	1 cup shredded cabbage
1 cup chopped fresh carrots	1 tablespoon lemon juice
1 cup peeled chopped onions	6 tablespoons sour cream
2⅔ cups salted water	
1 (10½-ounce) can beef broth plus ⅔ cup water	

Cook beets, carrots and onions uncovered in 2⅔ cups of boiling salted water 20 minutes. Add beef broth plus ⅔ cup water and shredded cabbage and cook uncovered 15 minutes longer. Add lemon juice and serve in bowls, topping each with 1 tablespoon of sour cream.

BOULA BOULA

2 cups fresh green peas, shelled	2 cups canned green turtle
Boiling salted water	soup
1 tablespoon sweet butter	1 cup sherry
Salt and pepper to taste	½ cup heavy cream, whipped

Cook the peas in water until tender. Make a purée by straining them through a fine sieve or whip in a blender. Reheat the purée with butter. Add salt and pepper to taste. Add turtle soup and sherry to purée and heat to just under the boiling point. To serve, place soup in serving cups, top with whipped cream and put the cups under the broiler to brown whipped cream topping. Serves 4.

CARROT AND BEEF SOUP

1½ pounds beef bones	1½ teaspoons salt
2 quarts cold water	⅓ teaspoon pepper
6 medium-sized carrots	2 tablespoons minced parsley
1 medium-sized onion, minced	

The beef bones should be cracked. Put them in the cold water. Scrape the carrots and add with the onion, salt and pepper. Bring slowly to boiling point, then simmer until liquid is half reduced. Strain; remove any bits of meat from the bones and add to the soup with the carrots cut in thin slices. Add the parsley and boil up again.

CELERY CREAM SOUP

Outer stalks and tips of a good-sized bunch of celery	1½ teaspoons salt
2 tablespoons butter or margarine	⅛ teaspoon pepper
1 onion, peeled and minced	1 pint milk
1 quart cold water	2 tablespoons flour
1 bay leaf	1 egg (optional)
	1 tablespoon minced parsley

Remove any strings from celery stalks and dice stalks. Melt butter in kettle; add celery stalks and onion, and cook gently together 5 minutes. Add water, bay leaf, and celery tips tied loosely in a piece of cheesecloth. Cover and simmer 1 hour; then remove celery tips. There should be 3 cups of liquid left. Add salt, pepper and milk; thicken with flour rubbed smooth with a little extra milk. If using the egg, beat until light; pour in some of the hot soup, then stir back into the main mixture and cook 1 or 2 minutes. Do not boil. Add parsley and serve.

CHICK-PEA SOUP

1 pound chick-peas	3 bouillon cubes
2 quarts boiling water	1 teaspoon salt
2 onions, sliced	1 bay leaf
½ cup diced celery	1 cup 1-inch-length noodles
1 tablespoon butter or margarine	2 tablespoons minced parsley or chives

Wash the peas. Put in a 3-quart saucepan; pour over the boiling water and let stand 50 minutes. Next fry the onions and celery in the butter. Add to the peas and water; add bouillon cubes, salt and bay leaf. Bring slowly to boiling point. Cover and simmer till the peas are tender, about 2 hours. Then add the noodles and cook 12 minutes longer. Add the parsley or chives.

CHINESE VEGETABLE SOUP

2 tablespoons butter	½ teaspoon sugar
1 cup shredded celery	1 teaspoon salt
1 cup shredded carrot	⅛ teaspoon pepper
1 shredded green pepper	¼ teaspoon soy sauce or Kitchen Bouquet
½ cup shredded mushrooms	Cooked fine noodles
4 cups chicken stock	

Melt the butter in a kettle; add the vegetables and cook together 3 minutes. Add the chicken stock and seasonings and simmer until the vegetables are tender, about 25 minutes. Just before serving add the soy sauce and noodles.

CORN CHOWDER

2 slices fat salt pork or bacon drippings	1 teaspoon celery salt
	¼ teaspoon paprika
2 tablespoons minced onion	4 cups milk, scalded
2 cups diced potatoes	2 tablespoons flour
3 cups boiling water	1 tablespoon cold milk
2 cups fresh or canned corn pulp	

If pork is used, cut it into dice and try out the fat; if drippings, melt and heat. Cook the onion until it begins to turn color, add the potatoes and the water, and simmer until the potatoes are tender. Add the corn, seasonings and scalded milk, thicken with the flour blended with the cold milk, and bring to a boil. Simmer 2 to 3 minutes before serving.

CREAM OF GREEN PEA SOUP

1 (1-pound) can green peas	2 tablespoons flour
2½ cups cold water	1 teaspoon salt
2 tablespoons butter or margarine at room temperature	⅛ teaspoon pepper
	2 cups heated milk
	½ teaspoon onion juice

Combine peas with their liquid and cold water in 2-quart saucepan. Bring to rapid boil; simmer 20 minutes. Rub through sieve or food mill. Reheat. Mix butter, flour, salt and pepper together until smooth. Add ¼ cup of hot liquid; stir until smooth and return to boiling soup. Stir in milk and onion juice. Simmer 3 minutes to blend flavors. Crisp whole wheat crackers are a recommended accompaniment.

CUCUMBER SOUP

2 medium cucumbers
1 quart buttermilk
1 tablespoon chopped green
  onion
1 teaspoon salt

¼ cup fine-chopped parsley
Dash pepper
Cucumber slices
Parsley sprigs

Pare cucumbers. Scoop out and discard seeds. Grate or put through food chopper. Combine with buttermilk, onion, salt, parsley and pepper. Mix well. Cover and chill about 4 hours. Just before serving in chilled cups, mix again. Garnish with cucumber slices, parsley sprigs.

GAZPACHO

8 fresh tomatoes
2 medium cucumbers
1 large onion
2 garlic sections
2 medium green peppers
2 cups soft bread crumbs
2 cups water or light stock
1 teaspoon hot red crushed
  pepper

1 teaspoon salt
⅓ cup Spanish olive oil
¼ cup cider or wine vinegar,
  or more to taste
Stuffed green olives
Minced parsley
Chopped celery

Skin the tomatoes, peel and seed. Peel and halve the cucumbers, discard the seeds. Peel and chop the onion and garlic; seed and chop the green peppers. Put all the vegetables through the medium knife of the food chopper or a fine sieve. Combine the bread crumbs and water or stock. Let stand 10 minutes. Add the vegetables. Stir in the seasonings, olive oil and vinegar to taste. Chill at least 2 hours, or overnight. Serve in soup bowls. Garnish with sliced stuffed green olives, minced parsley and chopped celery.

GARBANZO BEAN-SAUSAGE CHOWDER

1 pound garbanzo beans (chick-peas)
¼ teaspoon baking soda
2½ quarts boiling water
2 tablespoons butter or margarine
1 large onion, peeled and sliced
1½ cups sliced peeled potatoes
1 cup peeled carrot rounds

1 pint solid-pack canned tomatoes
½ cup elbow macaroni
1 cup cubed eggplant
1 cup diced ham, bologna or coarse-chopped cooked smoked pork
1 teaspoon sugar
Salt and pepper to taste
Garlic or sesame bread

Place the beans in a 3-quart saucepan with the baking soda and boiling water. Cover. Let stand 50 minutes. Boil until tender, about 1½ hours. Two quarts of liquid should be left. If not, add water to make up the quantity. Melt the butter or margarine; add the onions; sauté until limp. Mix in the remaining ingredients. Stir into the beans and liquid. Cover. Simmer-cook 30 minutes, or until the vegetables are bite-tender. Season to taste with salt and pepper. Serve in soup plates or shallow bowls; pass warm garlic or sesame bread.

HOLLAND RED BEAN SOUP

2 (No. 2) cans red kidney beans
1 (No. 2) can solid pack tomatoes, mashed
2 tablespoons instant onion or 4 tablespoons minced fresh onion
2 envelopes beef broth powder

3 cups water
½ teaspoon salt
⅛ teaspoon pepper
2½ tablespoons dry sherry or 1½ tablespoons water and 1 tablespoon sherry flavoring
2 tablespoons minced fresh parsley or dill

In 2-quart saucepan combine all ingredients except wine and parsley. Cover and simmer 30 minutes. Rub through sieve or food mill. Reheat. Add wine or wine flavoring. Garnish with parsley or dill.

SCOTCH KALE SOUP

5 cups strong hot beef stock	3 tablespoons rolled oats
1½ cups chopped kale	Salt and pepper (optional)

Combine and simmer until the rolled oats are soft, about 30 minutes. Season, if necessary, with salt and pepper.

LEEK SOUP

6 thin-sliced leeks with ⅔ of tops removed, the very tender portions saved for garnishing	1 cup milk
	2 tablespoons butter or margarine at room temperature
1 cup peeled thin-sliced potato	2 tablespoons flour
	1 cup half and half
4 cups boiling water	½ cup minced fresh parsley or the tender portions from leek tops
3 tablespoons chicken bouillon powder	
½ teaspoon celery seed	Fine-grated Cheddar or
1 teaspoon seasoned salt	Swiss cheese (optional)

Combine first six ingredients in double-boiler top. Cover; boil 20 minutes, or until vegetables are fork-tender; add milk. Place over boiling water. Stir-mix butter and flour. Add ¼ cup of the cooking soup; stir until smooth; return to the cooking soup. Add half and half; cook-stir 3 minutes, or until thick. Serve in bowls. Garnish with minced parsley or minced tender leek tops. Pass grated Cheddar or Swiss cheese if you like.

LENTIL SOUP

1 pound lentils	1 tablespoon vinegar
8 cups water	¼ teaspoon mustard
1 teaspoon salt	6 to 8 frankfurters, sliced
4 carrots, diced	1 tablespoon flour
4 onions, sliced	½ cup water
1 bunch celery, cut fine	

Soak lentils in salted water overnight. Simmer for 1 hour until soft. Add vegetables, vinegar and mustard and simmer another 30 minutes. Add frankfurter slices and simmer 30 more minutes. Mix the flour with the ½ cup of water and blend into soup. Cook about 5 minutes.

MINESTRONE

1½ cups cooked chick-peas
1 cup peeled sliced carrot
1 large onion, peeled and chopped
1½ cups diced celery
1 cup peeled thin-sliced zucchini
½ teaspoon rosemary

¾ cup high-protein spaghetti cut in 1-inch lengths
1 quart water
2 tablespoons olive oil or butter
Beef stock or bouillon
Salt and pepper to taste
Grated Parmesan cheese
1 cup cooked green peas

Combine first six ingredients. Add spaghetti, water and olive oil or butter. Cook 30 minutes, or until vegetables are tender. Add stock or bouillon to make 2 quarts. Boil 5 minutes. Season to taste. Garnish with Parmesan cheese and green peas.

MUSHROOM SOUP MADEIRA

½ pound fresh mushrooms
3 tablespoons butter
1 tablespoon chopped onion
1 green pepper, seeded and minced
2 (14½-ounce) cans beef consommé

1⅓ cups water
Generous dash nutmeg
2 tablespoons Madeira wine
½ cup wild rice, canned
6 thin lemon slices

Wash and trim the mushrooms. Shred both crowns and stems. Melt the butter in a 2-quart saucepan. Add the onion and green pepper. Simmer until limp. Stir occasionally; add the mushrooms. Cook-stir occasionally for 5 minutes. Add the beef consommé and water. Bring to rapid boil. Add the nutmeg and the wine. Into each soup plate spoon a tablespoon of wild rice. Pour in the soup. Float on a thin slice of lemon.

FRENCH ONION SOUP

3 tablespoons butter or
margarine
3 cups thin-sliced onions
1½ quarts beef stock

Salt and pepper to taste
Rounds of toast
Grated Parmesan or sharp
American cheese

Melt the butter or margarine; add the onions and slow-fry until yellowed. Heat the soup stock; add the onions, simmer 3 minutes, and season to taste with salt and pepper. Transfer to large individual earthenware soup bowls. Top each with a round of buttered toast covered with grated cheese. Place under the broiler or in a very hot oven until the cheese melts.

POTATO CHOWDER

¼ pound ham or lean salt
pork, diced small
1 medium-sized onion,
chopped
6 white potatoes, peeled and
thin-sliced
1 teaspoon salt
⅛ teaspoon pepper

1 tablespoon minced parsley
2 cups boiling water or beef
stock
1 tablespoon butter
1 tablespoon flour
3 cups milk
Toast, dark bread or cheese
crackers

Combine the ham or salt pork and onion in a small heavy kettle and cook together until the onion begins to turn yellow. Add the potatoes, salt, pepper, parsley and boiling water or stock; simmer about 12 minutes, or until the potatoes are nearly tender. Cream together the butter and flour and add to the cooking chowder. Add the milk; cook-stir until boiling and serve with toast, bread or crackers.

SPINACH SOUP ITALIAN

5 cups clear soup stock (any
    kind) or 5 cups water and
    5 teaspoons instant bouillon
¾ cup cooked rice (any kind)
1½ cups fine-chopped cooked
    spinach

⅛ teaspoon grated nutmeg
Grated Romano or Parmesan
    cheese

Heat the soup stock to boiling. Add the rice, spinach and nutmeg. Heat until boiling again. Serve bubbling hot in soup
bowls. Pass the cheese.

SPRING SOUP JULIENNE

1 cup peeled carrots cut in
    narrow strips
½ cup fresh mushrooms cut
    in narrow strips
¼ cup shredded green beans
½ cup celery cut in narrow
    strips

1 tablespoon narrow strips
    mild onion
1½ cups boiling salted water
1 (10½-ounce) can beef broth
2½ cups hot water
6 teaspoons chopped chives

Combine carrots, mushrooms, green beans, celery and onion;
cook 15 minutes in boiling salted water until liquid practically
evaporates and vegetables are bite-tender. Combine broth and
water; bring to boil. Add vegetables and juice. Do not cook
further. Serve in small bowls. Garnish with 1 teaspoon chopped
chives atop each serving. Seeded rolls are a good accompaniment!

SPRING VEGETABLE SOUP

6 leeks
1 carrot
2 cups raw asparagus tips
1 cup string beans

3 tablespoons butter
2 cups raw shelled peas
1 quart water
Salt and pepper

Cut white part of leek into small pieces, dice carrot, and cut asparagus tips and string beans into small pieces. Heat butter in soup pot and add these vegetables and the peas. Simmer covered for 5 minutes, then add water and seasoning. Cook for 20 minutes.

TOMATO BOUILLON

1 (8-ounce) can tomato sauce, seasoned
1 (10½-ounce) can beef bouillon, condensed
2½ cups water
1½ cups tomato juice
½ teaspoon horseradish
4 dashes Tabasco
¼ cup dry red wine

In a 2-quart saucepan combine the ingredients, except the wine, in the order given. Simmer 10 minutes. Add the wine.

CREAM OF ONION SOUP

2 cups fine-chopped raw onions
1½ cups water
⅓ teaspoon sugar
1 teaspoon salt
⅛ teaspoon pepper
1 quart milk
2 tablespoons flour
2 tablespoons butter or margarine
1 egg (optional)

Combine onions, water, sugar and seasonings; simmer 20 minutes. Add the milk and bring to a boil. Cream together the flour and butter, add to the soup, and cook-stir until it thickens. If the egg is used, beat until light, pour a little hot soup into it, return to the soup in the kettle, and stir for ½ minute over a low heat. If desired, each serving may be sprinkled with minced parsley.

Cream of Corn Soup: Follow the recipe for Cream of Onion Soup, using, instead of onion, 2 cups green corn kernels put through the chopper.

Cream of Carrot Soup: Follow the recipe for Cream of Onion Soup, substituting for onion 1½ cups peeled carrots, put through the food chopper with 1 slice onion. Cook the carrots in chicken or veal stock instead of water. When done, add a dash of nutmeg.

Cream of Cabbage Soup: Follow the recipe for Cream of Onion Soup, substituting for onion 2 cups fine-minced white cabbage. Pour the hot soup into the beaten egg; and just before serving add 3 tablespoons sour cream; sprinkle with a little paprika.

Cream of Spinach Soup: Follow the recipe for Cream of Onion Soup, substituting chopped cooked spinach for onion. Season with a little nutmeg.

Canned Vegetable Cream Soups: Follow the recipe for Cream of Onion Soup, substituting for the onion fine-chopped canned vegetables. The vegetable liquid should be used to replace part of the water. Any vegetable may be used.

VICHYSSOISE

4 leeks, well-cleaned
1 medium-sized onion, peeled
  and sliced thin
4 tablespoons butter
6 medium-sized potatoes,
  peeled, sliced thin
1 quart water or white
  consommé

2 cups milk, heated
2 cups light cream, heated
¾ teaspoon salt
1 cup heavy cream
¾ cup fine-chopped chives

Slice white part of leeks; lightly brown with onion in butter; then add potatoes. Add water or consommé. Boil 35 minutes. Mash and rub through very fine sieve; or put in blender and buzz 2 minutes. Add milk, light cream and salt; bring to boil. Cool, rub through sieve or blend again and add heavy cream. Serve very cold, sprinkled with chives. Serves 8.

Note: If using a blender in making vichyssoise, put in ⅓ to ½ the mixture at each blending. Cup of heavy cream may be omitted, and light cream or whole milk substituted to reduce calories.

WATER-CRESS LETTUCE SOUP

Small head lettuce, shredded	Dash of pepper
Small bunch water cress	1 teaspoon chervil
3 tablespoons butter	½ cup cream
6 cups chicken broth	1 egg yolk, well beaten
Salt	

Cook lettuce and water cress in butter for 5 minutes but do not let brown. Add broth, salt, pepper and chervil. Simmer gently, covered, for 30 minutes. Add cream and egg yolk, mixed, and continue cooking until soup is hot. (Do not overcook, however, as it may curdle.)

Fish and Shellfish

Fish

Visit a moderate-priced or plush restaurant at noon and see what so many men are ordering: Fish! Seafood chowders when available, shellfish, including shrimp, scallops, clams, mussels and Maine lobster; fillets of fish sautéed or baked, fish steaks from the grill, old-fashioned codfish cakes, bouillabaisse—the famous French multi-fish stew. Ask some of the men why they often choose fish as their luncheon entree and they will probably say, "We don't get it cooked like this at home."

Fish is one of the finest protein foods, equivalent to meat in nutrition, low in cholesterol and even easier and often quicker to cook. Good cooks should recognize fish as the great food it is— and learn how to prepare it for real appetite appeal.

Keep in mind that fish should not be cooked at a high temperature or for an overlong period of time; overcooking makes fish dry and flavorless.

All recipes are for six servings unless otherwise stated.

WALNUT-FRIED BOSTON SOLE

6 fillets fresh Boston sole or flounder
1½ teaspoons salt
¼ teaspoon pepper
10 tablespoons flour
4 large egg whites, beaten stiff but not dry

2 tablespoons unseasoned fine cracker crumbs
2 cups sliced walnut meats
½ cup hot melted butter— more if needed
6 lemon wedges
12 sprigs water cress

Season fillets with salt and pepper; dust with flour. Dip fillets, one at a time, into egg whites, then into a mixture of cracker crumbs and sliced walnut meats, coating each fillet thoroughly. Slide them at once into a 12-inch heavy skillet containing hot melted butter. Sauté over low flame 5 to 8 minutes on each side, or until tender and golden brown. Tested with fork, fillets should flake when done. Garnish with lemon wedges and water cress.

BAKE-FRIED FISH

The simplest possible way to prepare fish fillets, fresh, or frozen and thawed. Allow ½ pound a person.

Coat the fish generously with mayonnaise. Dust with salt and pepper, coat with fine dry crumbs. Place in a well-buttered pan; bake in a hot (400 to 425°) oven for 15 minutes, or until brown. Place briefly under broiler for additional browning if desired, but watch for burning. Serve with lemon slices and Tartar Sauce (see Index).

CARIBBEAN PICKLED FISH

2 pounds boned halibut, swordfish or haddock
1 tablespoon salt
½ teaspoon ground black pepper
⅓ cup flour
1 cup olive or salad oil
¾ cup cider vinegar
¼ cup water
3 tablespoons instant onion
3 tablespoons minced green pepper

6 large bay leaves
½ teaspoon whole allspice
¾ teaspoon whole black pepper
¼ teaspoon instant garlic
⅔ cup pitted small whole green olives
2 dried hot-red peppers, broken in half
4 cups shredded crisp chicory
Pimiento-stuffed olives

Slice fish into serving pieces ½ inch thick. Mix salt, black pepper and flour; rub half into the fish; roll fish in remainder. Heat ¼ cup of oil in large skillet. Add fish; sauté on both sides about 10 minutes. Transfer fish to large bowl. Combine remaining ingredients except oil, chicory and pimiento-stuffed olives in saucepan. Heat to boiling point; boil 1 minute. Pour over fish; add remaining oil. Cover. Refrigerate. Marinate up to 24 hours or more. Serve cold on platter covered with shredded crisp chicory. Garnish with pimiento-stuffed olives.

CIOPPINO

1 cup chopped onion
1 medium-sized green pepper, halved, seeded and chopped
½ cup sliced celery
1 carrot, pared and shredded
3 cloves of garlic, minced
3 tablespoons olive oil
2 (1-pound) cans tomatoes
1 (8-ounce) can tomato sauce
1 teaspoon crumbled basil leaf
1 bay leaf
1 teaspoon salt
¼ teaspoon pepper
1 pound swordfish or halibut steak, fresh, or frozen and thawed

1 dozen mussels or 1 dozen clams in shell; 1 (10-ounce) can clams in shell may be substituted for fresh clams
1½ cups dry white wine
1 (8-ounce) package frozen, shelled, deveined shrimp, thawed
½ pound fresh or frozen scallops, thawed
2 tablespoons minced parsley

Sauté onion, green pepper, celery, carrot and garlic in olive oil until soft in a kettle or Dutch oven. Stir in tomatoes, tomato sauce, basil, bay leaf, salt and pepper. Heat to boiling; reduce heat; cover; simmer 2 hours. Discard bay leaf.

While sauce simmers, remove the skin from swordfish or halibut; cut into serving pieces. Using a stiff brush, thoroughly scrub the mussels, cutting off the "beards," or the clams, under running water to remove any residue of mud and sand. Stir wine into sauce in kettle. Add swordfish or halibut, shrimp and scallops. Simmer covered 10 minutes longer. Place mussels or clams in a layer on top of fish in kettle; cover; steam 5 to 10 minutes, or until the shells are fully opened and fish flakes easily. Discard any unopened mussels or clams. Ladle into soup plates or bowls. Sprinkle with parsley. Delicious served with sourdough bread or crusty French or Italian bread.

ESCALLOPED COD OR HADDOCK

A favorite fish dish of old New England.

1½ pounds flaked boiled fillets cod or haddock	1½ teaspoons seasoned salt
	1 teaspoon onion juice
2 cups medium-thick White Sauce (see Index)	½ cup seasoned bread crumbs
	1 tablespoon butter, melted

Combine fish, White Sauce, salt and onion juice in buttered low 3-pint baking dish. Top with crumbs mixed with butter. Bake 20 minutes, or until golden brown, in moderate (350 to 375°) oven.

OVEN-FRIED CODFISH CAKES

2 cups canned codfish flakes	1 tablespoon catsup
2 tablespoons chopped onion	1 tablespoon salt
2 tablespoons melted fat or oil	1½ cups dry bread crumbs
2 eggs, beaten	½ cup melted fat or oil
3 cups mashed potatoes	

Separate fish into small flakes. Cook onion in fat or oil until limp. Combine eggs, mashed potatoes, catsup and salt with fish and onion. Portion fish mixture into cakes of ¼ cup each. Roll in crumbs. Space in single layer on well-oiled shallow pan. Pour additional fat over cakes. Bake 8 to 10 minutes in extremely hot (500°) oven, or until browned on the bottom. Turn carefully and bake 3 to 5 minutes longer, or until brown all over. This may be prepared in advance.

FISH FILLETS BAKED IN FOIL

3 pounds fish fillets (any kind)	1 teaspoon salt
	¼ teaspoon pepper
6 white onions	1 tablespoon minced parsley
6 small carrots	1½ tablespoons lemon juice
⅓ cup butter or margarine	6 thin slices Swiss cheese

If fish is frozen, thaw until a knife goes through easily before cooking. Cut each fillet into 3 portions. Place each in center of 8-inch square of buttered double-duty aluminum foil. Peel and thin-slice onions and carrots. Place over fillets. Melt butter. Pour 1 scant tablespoon over each serving. Dust with salt, pepper and parsley. Sprinkle with lemon juice. Top with cheese. Fold foil over fish and close all edges with tight double fold. Place on cookie sheet. Bake 30 minutes in hot (425°) oven. Serve in foil.

BAKED FILLETS OF FLOUNDER SOUBISE

Just a suggestion—try serving this with parslied boiled potatoes and fried tomatoes or eggplant!

½ cup chopped onions	1 teaspoon seasoned salt
1½ cups White Sauce (see Index)	Butter or margarine
Butter or margarine	½ cup grated cheese (optional)
6 fillets of flounder	

Combine onions and White Sauce. Thoroughly butter a deep earthen or glass baking platter. Lay the fillets on this; dust with seasoned salt, cover with sauce, dot with additional butter; dust with cheese; bake 30 minutes in moderate (350 to 375°) oven.

FISH 'N' CHIPS

1 pound fish fillets, fresh, or frozen and thawed	Oil for frying
Salt and pepper to taste	1 (1-pound) package frozen French fried potatoes
1 egg, beaten with 1 tablespoon water	Tartar Sauce (see Index)
Fine dry bread crumbs	Lemon slices (optional)

Cut fish into serving pieces. Add salt and pepper to egg mix. Dip fish in this mixture, then coat carefully with bread crumbs. Heat oil to 375°; fry fish 4 to 5 minutes on each side until nicely browned. Remove, drain on paper toweling. Add French fries to

fry pan, cook until browned. Drain. Serve with fish and plenty
of Tartar Sauce. Garnish with thin slices of lemon if desired.

FISH CURRY INDIA

3 tablespoons chopped onion
1 section garlic, peeled and
    crushed
3 tablespoons cooking oil
2 teaspoons curry powder
1 whole clove
1 small apple, cored and
    chopped

3 whole canned tomatoes,
    drained
1 teaspoon salt
1 cup hot water
Juice of ½ lemon
2 pounds fish fillets, halved
    (any kind)
2 tablespoons chopped parsley

In skillet that can go-to-table, sauté onion and garlic in oil until
color turns. Stir in curry; cook ½ minute to develop flavor; add
clove, apple and tomatoes. Slowly stir-cook 7 to 8 minutes. Stir
in salt, water, lemon juice. Add fish. Cover. Slow-cook 12 minutes, or until fish begins to flake. Lift fillets occasionally with
pancake turner so they will not stick. Dust with parsley.

BAKED STUFFED FISH FILLETS

2 pounds thin-sliced whiting,
    flounder or red perch fillets,
    thawed, if frozen
1 recipe homemade or
    packaged herb bread
    stuffing

¼ cup butter or margarine
Salt and pepper to taste
3 teaspoons water
1 recipe Herb Sauce (see
    Index)
Lemon wedges

Arrange 1 layer of fish fillets in buttered baking pan. Spread
with stuffing. Top with second layer of fish. Brush generously
with butter or margarine; dust with salt and pepper. Add water
to pan. Bake in moderate (350°) oven for 35 minutes, basting
occasionally with liquid from pan, or until, when tested with
fork, fish flakes easily. Meantime, prepare Herb Sauce while
fish is baking. Remove fillets to heated platter, pour over sauce.
Garnish with lemon wedges.

ROLLED FILLETS OF FLOUNDER

2½ pounds fillets of flounder,
  fresh, or frozen and thawed
Juice of ½ lemon
1 teaspoon salt
⅛ teaspoon pepper
½ teaspoon minced green
  onion or peeled shallots
⅓ cup butter (preferably
  unsalted)

6 tablespoons dry vermouth or
  vegetable juice
6 rounds toast
1½ cups plain or wine-
  seasoned White Sauce (see
  Index)
6 small pitted black olives

Brush fillets with lemon juice; dust with seasonings; spread with onion; roll up and secure with wooden picks. Rub 6 deep muffin pans (or 5 ounce custard cups) thickly with butter. In each place a rolled fillet. Add 1 tablespoon vermouth or vegetable juice to each. Cover with buttered foil; bake 20 minutes in moderate (375°) oven. Unmold on round of toast. Top with plain or wine-seasoned White Sauce. Garnish with a black olive.

FILLETS RED SNAPPER A LA SANTA ROSA ISLAND

Pensacola (Fla.) red snapper is the Gulf Coast's blue ribbon contribution to the nation's cuisine. Fried, or stuffed with cashews or dropped into the broth of southern gumbo, the red snapper provides a subtle yet distinct flavor all its own.

3 pounds red snapper fillets
1½ teaspoons salt
¼ teaspoon pepper
2 tablespoons lemon juice

1 teaspoon ground oregano
2 sections garlic, peeled and
  minced
3 tablespoons olive oil

Sprinkle fillets with salt, pepper, lemon juice and oregano. Place in well-oiled low baking pan. Bake 40 minutes or until fork-tender in 350° oven. Meanwhile, mince garlic and fry it in olive oil. Spoon over fish before serving.

LANDLUBBER FISH FILLETS SPECIAL

2 pounds yellow perch fillets or
    other fish fillets, fresh, or
    frozen and thawed
1 teaspoon salt
⅛ teaspoon pepper

2 cups herb-seasoned bread
    stuffing
¼ cup oil or melted fat
3 slices bacon

Skin fillets if necessary. Sprinkle both sides with salt and pepper. Line a 12-compartment well-oiled muffin pan with fillets in rounds, overlapping ends. Fill center of each with bread stuffing. Brush tops with fat; place ¼ slice bacon on each. Bake in moderate (350°) oven for 25 to 30 minutes, or until fish flakes easily when tested with fork.

FILLETS OF SOLE FLORENTINE

2 packages frozen chopped
    spinach, thawed
2 pounds fillets of sole, fresh, or
    frozen and thawed
Sprinkling of salt
Pepper
2 tablespoons dry sherry mixed
    with 1 tablespoon flour

2 cans frozen cream of shrimp
    soup, thawed
3 tablespoons grated Parmesan
    cheese
2 to 3 tablespoons butter

Cook spinach half the time indicated on the package. Drain thoroughly. Place in large buttered baking dish. Lay fillets cut in serving pieces in single layer on top. Sprinkle with salt and pepper to taste. Add sherry and flour mixture to soup and pour over fish. Sprinkle with Parmesan cheese, dot with butter. Bake uncovered 20 to 25 minutes in 375° oven. If desired, run quickly under broiler for browning.

FILLETS OF TROUT MARGUÉRY

2 trout, filleted
½ cup butter
½ teaspoon freeze-dried shallots or ½ tablespoon minced onion
1 cup dry white wine or 1 cup white grape juice and 1 teaspoon lemon juice
1 pint shucked fresh or thawed frozen oysters and their liquid

2 bay leaves
⅓ cup flour
3 tablespoons butter
1 teaspoon salt
⅛ teaspoon pepper
1 cup cooked shrimp
1 cup cream
1 tablespoon minced fresh mushrooms
4 butter-sautéed mushroom tops

Place fillets in pan with butter and shallots. Add wine or grape juice, liquid drained from oysters and bay leaves. Bring to boiling point. Simmer 6 minutes, or until fish flakes. Remove from pan. Save liquid. Place fish on heated platter. Blend flour and additional butter in saucepan. Slow-stir in fish liquid. Add salt, pepper. Meantime heat shrimp and simmer oysters in their own juice until edges "curl." Arrange on fillets of trout. Add cream to fish sauce. Stir in minced mushrooms. Heat and pour over fish. Garnish each serving with whole mushroom cap. Serves 4.

FISHBURGERS

1 pound fish fillets, fresh, or frozen and thawed
2 tablespoons butter or margarine
¾ cup hot milk
1 cup fine soft white bread crumbs
½ teaspoon salt
¼ teaspoon paprika
1 tablespoon lemon juice

Grated rind of ¼ lemon
1 egg, slightly beaten
Flour
Margarine or oil for sautéing
6 toasted split buns
½ cup Tartar Sauce (see Index) (homemade or purchased)
Corn relish (purchased)
Lettuce

Pass fish through food chopper, using medium blade. Add butter to milk and pour over bread crumbs. Cook-stir over low heat to form thick paste. Add seasonings, lemon and egg. Mix into fish and cool. Shape into round flat cakes containing 1 rounded tablespoonful each. Roll in flour. Sauté in margarine or oil until lightly browned on both sides, about 12 minutes altogether. Serve in toasted buns spread with Tartar Sauce. Garnish with corn relish on lettuce cups.

FISH CHILI

1½ quarts boiling water
1 pound red kidney beans
1½ teaspoons salt
1 cup converted rice
2 onions, peeled and sliced
2 sweet green peppers, cored, seeded and sliced
1 section garlic, peeled and minced

2 tablespoons butter or margarine
1 tablespoon chili powder
¼ teaspoon pepper
1 (6-ounce) can tomato paste mixed with 1¼ cups water
1 pound frozen or fresh fish fillets (any kind)

Pour boiling water over beans. Add salt. Cover and let stand 50 minutes. Boil 1¼ hours. Add rice; cook together until both are almost tender, about 20 minutes. Meantime, sauté onions, green peppers and garlic in butter or margarine until limp. Stir into beans and rice. Add chili powder and pepper and tomato paste mixed with water. Simmer 10 minutes. Cut fish in ½-inch dice and add. Simmer 20 minutes. Serve very hot in shallow bowls.

FISH PUFFS

1½ cups stiff, well-seasoned hot mashed potato
1 tablespoon butter
¾ cup minced tuna, salmon or other fish

¼ teaspoon Tabasco
¼ teaspoon powdered onion
1 egg, well beaten
1 egg yolk, beaten
Parsley

Into mashed potato beat butter, fish, Tabasco and powdered onion, egg and egg yolk. Drop by teaspoonfuls (or use a pastry tube) onto oiled cookie sheet. Bake 15 minutes in hot (400°) oven, or until puffy and brown. Garnish with parsley.

BAKED FLOUNDER

6 fresh or 2 (1-pound) packages frozen fillets of flounder
1 teaspoon salt
¼ teaspoon pepper
½ teaspoon oregano
1 pound shrimp, cooked and chopped
1 cup coarse white bread crumbs
1 tablespoon minced onion
1 tablespoon chopped parsley
½ teaspoon salt
⅛ teaspoon cayenne
Caper Sauce (see Index)

If fillets are frozen, thaw on refrigerator shelf or at room temperature. Sprinkle fillets with salt, pepper and oregano. Arrange half the fillets in oiled broiler pan or in shallow pan lined with oiled foil. Mix shrimp, crumbs, onion, parsley, salt and cayenne. Spread portion of this stuffing on each fish fillet in pan. Top each with second fillet, sandwich fashion. Bake 25 to 30 minutes in moderate (375°) oven, or until fish flakes easily when tested with fork. Baste 3 times with half the Caper Sauce; pass sauce that is left.

CASSEROLE OF HADDOCK FILLETS

2 pounds fillets of haddock, fresh or frozen and thawed (halved)
6 small onions, peeled and sliced
3 tablespoons cooking oil
3 tablespoons butter
¼ cup flour
1 teaspoon salt
⅛ teaspoon pepper
1 spice bag*
1 tablespoon lemon juice
½ cup mild vinegar
1 teaspoon sugar
1¼ cups chicken or fish bouillon
3 tablespoons minced parsley
6 slices decrusted toast, cut into triangle points

Fry fillets and onion in oil and butter in wide heavy stew pan until lightly browned. Dust in flour and seasonings; add spice bag. Spoon over lemon juice, vinegar, sugar and bouillon. Simmer 30 minutes. Transfer to heated deep platter. Dust over parsley. Garnish with toast points.

* In a 6-inch square of cheesecloth or heavy gauze, tie 1 whole clove, ¼ bay leaf and 8 shredded fresh celery leaves.

FRIED FISH WITH GINGER SAUCE

2 pounds swordfish or haddock
   steaks
1¼ cups sifted flour
1 teaspoon salt
1½ tablespoons olive oil
1 egg, lightly beaten

½ cup cold water, plus
   2 additional tablespoons
Vegetable oil for deep frying
Parsley and radishes
Ginger Sauce

Cut fish in 6 serving sections. With sharp knife, make incisions ⅛ inch deep on top and bottom of each section forming ½ inch squares. Thoroughly mix flour, salt, olive oil, egg and water, making a smooth batter. Heat vegetable oil for frying to 375°, or until a cubelet of bread browns in it in 1½ minutes. Dip sections of fish in batter. Slide each piece gently into deep fat. Fry until golden brown. Turn once. Drain on crumpled paper towels. Serve hot on warm platter, garnish with parsley and radishes. Pass Ginger Sauce.

Ginger Sauce: Drain contents of 1 (2½-ounce) can mushrooms (reserve liquid); chop mushrooms fine. Put in a quart saucepan with 3 tablespoons vinegar, 2 tablespoons chopped scallions, 2 tablespoons sugar, 1 tablespoon soy sauce, ¼ cup chopped crystallized preserved ginger, and reserved mushroom liquid mixed with enough water to make ½ cup. Slow-boil 5 minutes. Stir ½ tablespoon cornstarch smooth with 2 tablespoons cold water. Stir into the boiling sauce. Continue to cool. Stir 3 minutes, or until thickened.

MACKEREL BAKED-IN-MILK

Everyone enjoys "plain fare" once in a while—this may have been a favorite of your grandmother's—or perhaps even your great-grandmother's!

1 (3-pound) fresh mackerel	⅓ cup butter or margarine
½ cup flour	1½ cups heated milk
1½ teaspoons salt	1 cup boiling water
¼ teaspoon pepper	

Dress and split mackerel. Lay mackerel skin side down on heat-proof baking platter. Dust mackerel all over top with flour, salt and pepper mixed.

Dot fish with bits of butter. Add milk and water, nearly covering fish. Bake about 25 minutes in moderate (350°) oven, or until flaky and slightly browned.

BAKED SALMON

This is an interesting way to cook salmon, because the flesh remains an orangey pink (salmon pink) and tastes subtly different from that of poached salmon, which has a more delicate flavor. It has the added advantage that you can cook the whole fish without all the nonsense of a special fish kettle.

Have your fish man prepare salmon, or do it yourself as follows: Slit the salmon along the belly and remove the gut. Scrape away the congealed blood that lies beside the backbone. Remove the gills, but keep the head on. Rub the whole salmon over with soft butter. Wrap it well in waxed paper or aluminum foil, as if it were a parcel. Put this "parcel" in a large roasting pan. Bake in a moderate (350°) oven, allowing 10 minutes to the pound. Let the salmon cool slightly before removing it from the paper. This will give the flesh a chance to set. Carefully skin the fish. Put it on a long plate and garnish it with thin-sliced cucumber, lemon wedges and parsley.

If you want to eat the fish cold, do not unwrap it for a couple of hours.

A 5-pound salmon should serve 8 to 10 people.

NEW ENGLAND BOILED SCROD

Scrod | 2 slices lemon
½ teaspoon mixed pickle | ½ teaspoon salt
  spice

Wrap fish in cheese cloth. Place it in boiling water or broth made from the fish head and trimmings, to which spice, lemon and salt have been added. Simmer covered 10 minutes if 1 inch thick; if in a large piece, 15 minutes to a pound. Serve with sauce of your choice.

SHAKER FISH BALLS

2 cups chopped leftover cooked fish (any kind) or 2 (7-ounce) cans tuna | 1 tablespoon minced-fine onion (optional)
4 cups peeled, chopped, cooked white potatoes | 1 teaspoon salt
2 egg yolks, beaten | ¼ teaspoon pepper
1 tablespoon minced-fine parsley | 3 tablespoons flour
 | Vegetable oil for deep frying
 | 6 slices crisp fried salt pork
 | Salt Pork and Milk Gravy

Combine fish and potatoes, egg yolks, parsley, onion, salt and pepper. Mix lightly with fork. Taste and add more salt and pepper if desired. Form into balls the size of an egg. Dust over with flour and let stand 15 minutes to firm. Heat vegetable oil (2 inches deep) in heavy deep kettle until frying thermometer registers 375°, or cubelet of bread when dropped into fat browns in 1 minute. Carefully slide in the fish balls. Fry until golden brown. Drain on crumpled paper towels. Serve garnished with the fried salt pork slices and accompanied by Salt Pork and Milk Gravy.

Salt Pork and Milk Gravy: Fry ¼ pound thin-sliced salt pork until well browned. Reserve 6 slices for garnish. Chop remainder into bits. Next make 2 cups White Sauce (see Index); add chopped fried salt pork and 1 tablespoon minced chives. Serve hot.

SOLE- OR FLOUNDER-STUFFED ARTICHOKES

To prepare artichokes, wash and cut off stems at base and remove small bottom leaves. Trim tips of leaves and cut off about 1 inch from top. Stand artichokes upright in deep saucepan; add ¼ teaspoon salt for each artichoke and add 2 to 3 inches boiling water to pan. Cover and boil gently 35 to 45 minutes or until base of artichokes can be pierced easily with fork. Remove artichokes to platter turning them upside down to drain. If they are to be stuffed, gently spread leaves and remove "choke" (thistle portion) from center of artichokes with metal spoon.

6 teaspoons butter or margarine	¾ cup chicken broth or bouillon
6 small fillets of sole or flounder	¾ cup dry white wine
1 teaspoon salt	4 lemon slices, halved
⅛ teaspoon pepper	1 recipe Mock Hollandaise Sauce
1 teaspoon dill weed	
6 artichokes, prepared as directed above	1 teaspoon lemon juice
	½ cup heavy cream, whipped

Place 1 tablespoon butter on each fish fillet; dust with salt, pepper and dill weed. Roll up jelly-roll fashion; stuff rolls into center of prepared artichokes. Place in low ovenproof dish. Pour broth and wine over artichokes. Add lemon slices; cover and bake 30 minutes in moderate (350°) oven. Keep artichokes warm. Pour ½ cup of wine-broth liquid into saucepan and boil fast until reduced to 2 tablespoons. Meanwhile, in top of double boiler, have Hollandaise Sauce ready over hot, but not boiling, water. Stir in lemon juice and reduced liquid. Just before serving sauce, fold in whipped cream.

Mock Hollandaise Sauce: Mix ¼ cup instant nonfat dry milk crystals with ¼ cup ice water. Whip until soft peaks form, about 3 to 4 minutes. Add 1½ tablespoons lemon juice; continue beating until stiff peaks form, about 3 to 4 minutes longer. Lightly fold into ¾ cup mayonnaise (purchased). Stir-heat to serving temperature over hot water.

SOLE VERONIQUE

4 egg yolks
1 whole egg
½ pound sole or other white fish, cut in strips
1 teaspoon salt
1 teaspoon dried tarragon

4 tablespoons heavy cream
½ cup soft bread crumbs
8 fillets of sole
Court Bouillon for Sole Veronique
Sauce Veronique

First, prepare fish forcemeat: Place egg yolks, whole egg, sole strips, salt, tarragon and heavy cream in electric blender. Blend 1 minute, or until fish and other ingredients are combined into a heavy paste. Add bread crumbs and blend until smooth. Taste and correct seasoning. Spread fillets of sole with fish forcemeat. Roll and fasten with picks. Place rolled fillets in Court Bouillon and poach until fish flakes easily when tested with a pick or fork. Remove fillets, reserving broth, and arrange in a baking or au gratin dish. Pour Sauce Veronique over fish. Glaze under a broiler. Serves 8.

Court Bouillon for Sole Veronique:

½ cup white wine (or fish stock)
½ cup water
Salt and pepper to taste

2 sprigs parsley
1 small onion
Few whole cloves

Combine wine, water, salt and pepper to taste, parsley and onion stuck with cloves. Simmer 4 minutes.

Sauce Veronique:

4 tablespoons butter	1 cup milk
3 tablespoons flour	Salt, pepper, nutmeg
½ cup fish broth (reserved from poaching fish in Court Bouillon)	½ cup cream
	2 egg yolks

Melt butter in saucepan. Add flour and cook until slightly colored. Add fish broth and stir until smooth. Gradually add milk and continue stirring until thickened. Cook 5 minutes. Season to taste with salt, pepper and nutmeg. Stir in cream and egg yolks. Heat through, stirring constantly. Do not let sauce boil.

SPANISH FISH PIE

Pastry:

4 cups sifted all-purpose flour	¾ cup firm shortening
1½ teaspoons salt	6 tablespoons cold water
2 teaspoons baking powder	2 teaspoons fine dry bread crumbs
1 egg	

Sift together first three ingredients. Heap and make hollow in center. Break in egg; add shortening. Chop and mix with pastry blender until soft and crumbly, gradually adding cold water (if too dry, add 1 tablespoon more). Shape into ball. Roll scant ¼ inch thick on slightly floured surface. With pastry, line 2 8-inch piepans or 1 8×12-inch shallow pan. Dust bottom of pastry with fine dry bread crumbs; press in.

Filling:

2 pounds thin fresh fish fillets—
flounder, whiting or sole
⅓ cup olive oil
⅓ cup sliced peeled onion
½ teaspoon oregano
½ teaspoon rosemary
3 medium tomatoes, thinly
sliced

2 green peppers, seeded and
thinly sliced
1½ teaspoons salt
¼ teaspoon pepper
¾ cup grated Parmesan and
Romano cheese
Hard-cooked eggs
Cooked peas

Brush fish fillets generously with olive oil and layer evenly in crust-lined pan. Sauté onion in remaining olive oil. Spread over fish. Dust with oregano and rosemary. Alternately layer on tomatoes and green peppers; dust with salt and pepper. Cover with grated cheese. Bake 35 to 40 minutes in moderate (375 to 400°) oven, or until crust browns and fish is fork tender. Garnish with sliced hard-cooked eggs and cooked green peas.

CHILLED STRIPED BASS

1 (3- to 4-pound) cleaned
striped bass
Juice of 2 lemons
2 teaspoons salt
¼ teaspoon Tabasco

Boiling water
Asparagus tips, chilled
2 hard-cooked eggs
Fish Aspic
1 cup Tartar Sauce (see Index)

Place fish in long deep pan or roaster. Add lemon juice, salt, Tabasco and boiling water to cover. Bake-boil, covered, in hot (425°) oven for 20 to 30 minutes, or until fish begins to look flaky. Drain and reserve liquid. Cool. Transfer to large platter. Garnish with asparagus and sliced hard-cooked eggs. Surround with coarse-chopped Fish Aspic. Pass Tartar Sauce.

Fish Aspic: Strain and measure hot fish liquid. (There should be 3 cups.) Add 2½ teaspoons unflavored gelatin softened in ¼ cup cold water. Add more seasoning if necessary. Pour into

7×11-inch pan; refrigerate 3 to 4 hours, or until firm enough to cut.

ROAST STUFFED STRIPED BASS

1 (3- to 4-pound) whole striped bass	¼ cup melted butter
1 teaspoon salt	Soft-Shelled Crabs Sauté
¼ teaspoon pepper	Shrimp Sauté
Fish Stuffing Mousse	Lemon basket filled with parsley spriglets
1 tablespoon cooking oil	Brown Butter-Lemon Sauce

Order a 3- to 4-pound whole striped bass or other large fish, cleaned, scaled and boned, but with head, tail and fins left intact. Wash in cold water; rinse, drain, and blot on absorbent paper towels. Rub interior with salt and black pepper. Fill with Fish Stuffing Mousse. Fasten together with wooden picks. For ease in moving cooked fish, cut a long strip of heavy-duty aluminum foil (about 28×12 inches). Place in oiled roasting pan, with ends standing up. Oil the foil. On it carefully place prepared fish. Brush it with cooking oil. Place in moderate (350°) oven and roast 1 hour uncovered, or until flesh flakes when tested with fork. Baste 3 times with melted butter. Using foil, lift fish out and slide it onto long heated platter. Arrange Soft-Shelled Crabs Sauté on top near center down length of fish. Place Shrimp Sauté on top of crabs. Cover side opening of fish with parsley spriglets. Perch lemon basket filled with parsley near head of fish. Pass Brown Butter-Lemon Sauce.

Fish Stuffing Mousse:

1 pound fish (any white-fleshed fish, especially cod)	Dash of pepper
	2 egg whites
½ teaspoon salt	2½ cups heavy cream

Pound and mix fish with seasonings, gradually mixing in egg whites. Rub through fine sieve, and place it in saucepan on crushed ice. Then work it up with wooden spoon and gradually fold in cream. Use for stuffing large fish.

Soft-Shelled Crabs Sauté: Dust 6 cleaned soft-shelled crabs with 1 tablespoon salt, and ⅛ teaspoon pepper mixed with 1 tablespoon flour. Sauté about 6 minutes in equal parts cooking oil and butter.

Shrimp Sauté: Clean and devein 6 good-sized shrimp. Sauté as described above for soft-shelled crabs, until shrimp are curled and pink in color.

Browned Butter-Lemon Sauce: Melt ⅓ cup unsalted butter and slowly heat it until light brown. Beat in 1 tablespoon lemon juice or to taste.

KABOBS OF SWORDFISH

2 pounds swordfish, steaks, fresh, or frozen and thawed
12 small onions, peeled and parboiled
12 cherry tomatoes
12 fresh medium mushroom caps

Marinade:

1 onion, peeled and sliced
1 carrot, peeled and sliced
3 sprigs parsley
½ teaspoon crushed thyme leaves
1 bay leaf
½ cup dry white wine or white grape juice
⅓ cup cooking oil
4 peppercorns, crushed
1 large section garlic, peeled, or ¼ teaspoon instant garlic

Cut swordfish into 24 (1½-inch) cubes. Combine and mix marinade ingredients. Add swordfish. Refrigerate 1 hour or more. Drain; reserve marinade for basting. On 4-inch skewers impale first a cube of fish, then onion, tomato and mushroom cap. Continue this sequence until 4 cubes of fish are on each skewer. Brush kabobs with drained marinade. Place on grill 4 inches from source of heat. Cook 5 to 6 minutes, turning frequently with tongs.

Venison Kabobs: Instead of swordfish use venison steak cut in cubes, first treated with instant tenderizer according to package directions, then marinated and completed as described in recipe.

BLUE TROUT SPECIAL FOR FISHERMEN

The trout should be live and weigh about ⅓ pound each. Stun trout one at a time by a blow on the head; clean at once (leave on head and tie loosely to tail). Plunge into 2½ quarts boiling fish broth containing ½ cup cider vinegar. Poach 10 to 12 minutes. Trout will turn blue. Serve 1 to a person. Garnish with parslied potato balls and lemon slices.

SESAME SEED TROUT

Brush the cleaned fish with oil and dust with salt, pepper and enough sesame seeds to make a coating. Grill the fish over hot coals, or on an indoor grill, until browned on one side; turn carefully with a broad spatula and brown the reverse side.

Complement this mild-flavored fish with a piquant green olive sauce, a whipped butter sauce, or a sour cream sauce. Or serve additional sauces, if your fisherman returns with enough to feed a crowd. Or omit the sauce and serve the trout accompanied with a piquant kraut relish. The crisp, crunchy texture and tart flavor of kraut is a tasty foil for trout.

TUNA LOAF

2 (7-ounce) cans tuna	1 tablespoon parsley flakes
2 tablespoons farina	1 teaspoon salt
½ cup milk	⅛ teaspoon powdered dill
1 large egg, beaten	2½ cups cooked fresh or
1 teaspoon scraped onion or	frozen vegetables
½ teaspoon instant onion	Danish Sauce

Chop tuna fine. (If flaked canned tuna is purchased, no need to chop.) Stir farina into milk; cook-stir until boiling and thick. Add to tuna. Beat in remaining ingredients except vegetables and sauce. Transfer to oiled 5×9-inch loaf pan; set in a pan; pour in 1 inch water. Bake 35 minutes, or until brown and firm to the touch, in a moderate (350 to 375°) oven. Let stand 5 minutes. Loosen edges; unmold on a heated platter. Serve surrounded by mixed vegetables in Danish Sauce.

Danish Sauce: Into 1½ cups medium-thick White Sauce (see Index), stir 1 teaspoon lemon juice and 2 tablespoons mayonnaise. Reheat; do not boil.

TUNA PATTIES

⅔ cup mayonnaise
1 tablespoon lemon juice
¼ cup chili sauce
1 clove garlic, mashed
2 tablespoons minced parsley
2 (7-ounce) cans tuna, drained
  and flaked

2 cups fresh bread crumbs
¼ cup fine-chopped onion
1 cup fine-chopped celery
½ teaspoon salt
Freshly ground pepper

In large bowl, stir mayonnaise, lemon juice, chili sauce, garlic, parsley until smooth. Add remaining ingredients including generous sprinkling of pepper and blend thoroughly. Form into 6 patties. Sauté in lightly oiled frying pan over medium heat till browned, about 5 minutes each side.

BAKED WHITEFISH

1 (3-pound) whitefish, scaled,
  cleaned and boned
1 teaspoon salt
⅛ teaspoon pepper

Corn Bread Stuffing
Melted butter
Parsley
Lemon sections

Heat oven to moderate (375°). Sprinkle interior of fish lightly with salt and pepper. Spoon Corn Bread Stuffing into fish. Fasten sides of fish together with wooden picks or small skewers. Place fish on a large seasoned and oiled hardwood plank. Brush fish with melted butter. Bake about 40 minutes, or until fish flakes easily when tried with fork. Garnish with parsley and lemon sections.

Note: If whitefish is unavailable, use haddock, cod or red snapper, all delicious with Corn Bread Stuffing.

Corn Bread Stuffing:

3 cups crumbled corn bread	½ teaspoon salt
¼ cup fine-chopped peeled onion	Dash of pepper
2 tablespoons chopped parsley	1 egg, slightly beaten
1½ teaspoons crushed thyme	¼ cup butter or margarine, melted

Combine all ingredients in order given, tossing lightly.

FROGS' LEGS SAUTÉ

Allow 2 pairs of frozen frogs' legs to a serving. Do not thaw. Rinse with cold water.

For 8 pairs of frogs' legs, combine 1 teaspoon salt, ⅛ teaspoon dill or tarragon, 1 tablespoon lemon juice and 1½ cups Court Bouillon (see Index) or water; bring to boiling point. Add the frogs' legs; simmer 5 minutes, or until nearly tender. Drain.

Frogs' Legs Meunière: Dip the prepared frogs' legs in milk, then in seasoned pancake mix. Sauté in butter until golden brown. To the saucepan add 3 tablespoons whipped butter and ½ tablespoon lemon juice. Stir until melted and the frogs' legs are coated.

Shellfish

Webster calls oysters, clams, mussels, scallops, shrimp, crayfish, crabs, lobster and rock lobster "aquatic animals" and you may think of them as ornery beasts when you carefully select fresh crabs and lobsters that are alive and kicking, or choose clams and oysters whose shells must be very tightly closed. The shellfish that come straight from their underwater homes are superior, of course, but those that have been quick-frozen are good too, and some interesting and tasty dishes can be made with the canned product if necessary.

All recipes are for six servings unless otherwise stated.

BAKED DEVILED CLAMS

18 clams in shells (opened by fish dealer)
2½ medium-sized onions, peeled and fine-chopped
2 cups fine-chopped celery (strings removed)
½ section garlic, peeled and crushed, or ⅛ teaspoon garlic powder
1½ teaspoons curry powder
½ teaspoon ground ginger
½ teaspoon salt
¼ teaspoon pepper
1 tablespoon cornstarch
½ cup dry sherry or 2½ tablespoons sherry flavoring and 5½ tablespoons water
2 tablespoons fresh lemon juice
½ cup mayonnaise
½ cup heavy cream, whipped (not sweetened)

Drain clams; reserve juice and shells, scrubbed to remove sand. Coarse-chop clams and set aside. In a 1-quart saucepan, combine clam juice, onions, celery, garlic and chopped clams. Bring to boiling point. Simmer 10 minutes, or until bite-tender—do not overcook. Stir in curry, ginger, salt and pepper. Simmer 2 minutes. Stir cornstarch into sherry and lemon juice, then into clam juice mixture. Cook-stir until the latter thickens and clings to pan. Cover. Set aside until cold. Spoon into clam shells; fill completely. Combine mayonnaise and whipped cream. Spread over filled clams. Bake 12 minutes in moderate (350°) oven, or until heated and slightly browned.

NEW ENGLAND CLAM FRITTERS

1 (8-ounce) can chopped clams	½ teaspoon lemon juice
1 cup and 2 tablespoons sifted flour	½ cup clam juice
½ teaspoon baking powder	1 teaspoon melted butter or salad oil
¼ teaspoon salt	Vegetable oil
2 egg yolks	Catsup (optional)

Drain juice from clams and measure it; there should be ½ cup. If not, add water as necessary. Sift together flour, baking powder and salt into bowl. Hollow center; drop in egg yolks; add lemon juice and half clam juice. Mix well. Add remaining clam juice gradually, pressing batter to remove any lumps, then melted butter. Fold in chopped clams, well drained. Heat vegetable oil 2 inches deep to 370° in a heavy 2½-quart saucepan. Drop in batter by tablespoonfuls (dip spoon in boiling water each time so it will not stick to spoon). Fry 5 minutes or until golden brown all over. Drain on crumpled towels. Serve as is, or with catsup. Serves 4.

FRIED CLAMS

1 egg, separated	½ cup sifted flour
1 tablespoon butter, melted	2 tablespoons cold water
2 tablespoons cold water	6 clams
⅛ teaspoon salt	Fat for frying

Beat the egg white stiff, yolk until creamy. Add butter, 2 tablespoons water, salt to yolk. Stir in flour. Gradually beat in 2 tablespoons additional water. Fold in beaten egg white. With tongs dip clams one by one into batter, using as little as possible.

Slip clams into hot (360 to 375°) fat. Fry until golden brown. Drain on absorbent paper. Serves 1.

MAINE CRISSCROSS CLAM PIE (Modernized)

1 (10½-ounce) can chopped clams
½ cup milk (about)
1 cup small cubes cooked or canned potatoes
1 cup cooked or canned diced carrots
1 teaspoon minced onion or ¼ teaspoon instant onion

2 tablespoons flour
Salt to taste
1 recipe Rich American Pie Pastry (see Index)
1 teaspoon fine dry bread crumbs

Drain off clam liquid; add enough milk to make ⅔ cup. Add to potatoes, carrots, onion and flour. Stir in clams. Add salt to taste. Line a 9-inch pie plate with ½ the pastry, rolled a scant ¼ inch thick. Dust lightly with bread crumbs; press in. Spoon in clam and vegetable filling. Cover with crisscross strips of pastry. Bake 10 minutes in hot (400°) oven. Reduce heat to 375° and bake 25 minutes more.

MARYLAND CRAB CAKES

1 pound crab meat
1 cup fine soft bread crumbs (no crusts)
1 large egg

1 tablespoon table mustard
¼ teaspoon pepper
½ teaspoon salt
Butter or margarine

Fine-flake the crab meat and combine with other ingredients except butter. Mix well. Shape into flat cakes containing 1 tablespoon each of mixture. Fry in butter or margarine until lightly browned. Mushroom sauce, or a rich cream sauce seasoned with dry sherry, makes an excellent accompaniment.

CRAB RAVIGOTE IN AVOCADO HALVES

1 (7-ounce) can crab meat
⅓ cup sliced celery
2 tablespoons toasted shredded
    almonds
½ cup Ravigote Dressing
3 medium-sized avocados
    peeled, halved, pits removed

1 tablespoon lemon juice
6 parsley spriglets
1½ cups chicory leaves
    (about)

Lightly mix together crab meat, celery, toasted almonds and Ravigote Dressing. Chill at least 30 minutes. Brush avocado centers and edges with lemon juice. Fill avocado centers with crab meat mixture. Chill again. Top each serving with parsley spriglet. Place on salad plates. Wreathe each avocado half with a few curly chicory leaves.

Ravigote Dressing: Combine 2 tablespoons mild vinegar, 3 tablespoons olive oil, 1 tablespoon minced onion, ½ teaspoon Dijon mustard, 1 drop liquid garlic, 1 chopped hard-cooked egg, 1 teaspoon chopped parsley, ⅛ teaspoon crumbled dry tarragon leaves, ½ teaspoon salt, ⅛ teaspoon black pepper. Stir thoroughly.

CRAB MEAT IMPERIAL

2 pounds lump crab meat
½ cup mayonnaise
3 pimientos, chopped
1 teaspoon salt

⅛ teaspoon pepper
½ teaspoon dry mustard
2 tablespoons mayonnaise
Paprika

Remove any remaining shell particles from crab meat. Combine mayonnaise, pimiento, salt, pepper and mustard. Mix lightly with crab meat. Place in 6 well-oiled ramekins. Top each with a dot of additional mayonnaise. Dust with paprika. Bake 20 to 25 minutes in moderate (350°) oven, or until bubbly and brown.

CRAB MEAT ON SHELLS
(Deviled Hard Crabs)

¼ pound butter, melted	1 teaspoon fresh minced parsley
12 salted crackers, crushed to crumbs	1 teaspoon Worcestershire sauce
1 tablespoon mayonnaise, beaten with 1 egg	3 tablespoons dry sherry
Salt and pepper to taste	1 pound crab meat, well picked
¼ teaspoon dry mustard	Sprigs of parsley
	Lemon wedges

Clean and butter 6 to 8 large crab backs, or shallow shells or ramekins. Over the cracker crumbs pour melted butter, reserving some crumbs for sprinkling over top of crabs. Add mayonnaise, beaten with egg, seasonings, sherry. Mix in crab meat lightly with fork, to prevent breaking the pieces. Fill shells generously with the mixture, but do not pack down. Sprinkle with remaining crumbs and bake in medium (350°) oven about 30 minutes. Serve at once with sprigs of parsley. Lemon wedges may be served separately.

Note: The preceding recipe provides 6 to 8 servings, depending on size of the containers used. May be prepared in advance and refrigerated, ready to heat and serve.

BOILED LOBSTER

Lobster should be bought alive (green), then either boiled by the dealer or boiled at home. The claws are usually plugged with a wooden peg, which prevents the lobster nipping. It may either be plunged alive into boiling salted water or first killed by cutting with a sharp knife just where head and body meet. Plunge the lobster head first into boiling water salted in the proportion of ½ cup of salt to 2 quarts of water. Cook 20 to 30 minutes, according to the size, then drain and cool quickly. When cold it is ready for such further preparation.

Cold Boiled Lobster: Cook the lobster as directed; when cold, remove the large claws, then lay it on its back and with a very sharp knife split lengthwise from head to tail. Lay the halves cut side uppermost on a platter, add the large claws, which should be slightly cracked for the easier removal of the meat, and garnish with lettuce. Serve with mayonnaise to which a few capers have been added.

To Remove Cooked Lobster from the Shell: Cook and split the lobster as directed. Remove the tail meat from the shell (this will come out of each half easily without breaking), take out the intestinal cord which runs the length of the lobster and which will be found near the back. Pick the meat carefully from the head, the sand pouch which is in the middle of the head, and the gills which lie at each side of the head close to the shell. The greenish fat and the bright red coral are choice portions and should be carefully saved. There is very little that is edible in the small claws and these are generally used for garnishing. The large claws, however, contain a good proportion of solid meat, and they should be cracked and the meat removed.

The shell and trimmings may be cooked with celery, a tiny bit of onion, and a bouquet of herbs to make a fish stock for lobster bisque.

QUICK LOBSTER CASSEROLE

1½ cups fresh white bread crumbs	1½ cups diced cooked celery
¼ cup melted butter or margarine	3 hard-cooked eggs, sliced
1 (7-ounce) can lobster meat, small-diced	2 cups well-seasoned White Sauce (see Index)
	¼ teaspoon Tabasco

Grease with butter or margarine a 3-pint low casserole that can go-to-table. Stir together crumbs and melted butter. Spread half in casserole. Combine lobster meat, celery, hard-cooked eggs, White Sauce and Tabasco. Layer with remaining crumb mixture.

Bake 15 to 20 minutes in a moderate (375°) oven, or until lightly browned. (If prepared ahead, refrigerate and heat 30 minutes before serving.)

LOBSTER, FISHERMAN'S STYLE

6 small (4-ounce) South
   African rock lobster tails
⅓ cup olive oil
3 sections garlic, peeled
1 medium-sized onion, peeled
   and chopped
1 tablespoon minced parsley

1 bay leaf, crumbled fine, or
   ½ teaspoon dried thyme
¾ cup dry white wine or use
   white grape juice
1 cup water
Salt and pepper to taste
Rice

Cut lobster away from soft under shell, then pull flesh partly away from outer shell (if frozen, hold lobster tails under running hot water so that it will be easier to loosen the flesh). Pour olive oil into skillet or top-of-range casserole; sauté garlic sections until yellow and soft, then mash, with tines of fork, into oil. Add onion, parsley, bay leaf or thyme, cook over low heat until onion is soft. Add lobster tails, cook covered until shell is bright red and white flesh is translucent. Add wine, water, and salt and pepper to taste; simmer 5 minutes more. Serve in a casserole with rice.

LOBSTER NEWBURG

¼ cup butter
3 cups cooked or canned
   lobster meat
1 tablespoon cornstarch
1½ cups light cream
Yolks of 3 eggs
1 teaspoon salt

⅛ teaspoon cayenne
1 teaspoon lemon juice
2 teaspoons California dry
   sherry
½ tablespoon brandy
Toast or rice

Melt butter; cut lobster into large dice and cook it with butter 5 minutes, stirring continuously. Add cornstarch and cook a moment longer. Add 1 cup of the cream. Bring to boiling point. Place over hot water (double boiler or chafing dish); add yolks of eggs slightly beaten with the remaining cream, and stir constantly until thickened. Add seasonings, lemon juice, sherry and brandy. Serve in small heated casseroles with toast points, on toast, or over flaky cooked rice.

LITTLE LOBSTER PIES

6 tablespoons butter
¾ cup dry sherry
3 cups lobster meat, fresh or
   2 (10½-ounce) cans
½ cup butter

3 tablespoons flour
2½ cups light cream
5 egg yolks
Lobster Pie Topping

Melt the butter; add the sherry; boil 1 minute. Add the lobster meat; let rest at least 10 minutes. Melt the remaining butter. Stir in the flour and cook-stir 1 minute, or until bubbling. Remove from the heat. Slow-stir in the cream and the liquid drained from the lobster. Return to the heat; cook-stir until thick and smooth. Beat the egg yolks. Stir in ¼ of the sauce, a little at a time. Return to the saucepan. Heat over hot water. Cook-stir until thickened, about 3 minutes. Remove from the heat; add the lobster. Transfer to buttered individual small casseroles or large ramekins. Strew with Lobster Pie Topping. Slip under the broiler to brown.

Lobster Pie Topping: Combine 1½ cups cracker meal, 1 tablespoon crushed potato chips, ½ cup paprika, ½ tablespoon grated Parmesan cheese and ½ cup butter; spread over the pies.

MAINE LOBSTER STEW

1 (1½- to 2-pound) Maine
   lobster
3 tablespoons butter
1 cup bottled clam broth
1 quart milk or 1 pint each
   milk and half and half,
   heated

Salt, pepper and celery or
   onion salt to taste

Cook lobster as usual—plunge it in plenty of boiling water, head bown. Boil 15 minutes, or until it turns red. Cool. Remove and dice lobster meat. Slightly sauté meat in butter. Add clam broth. Simmer 5 minutes. Stir in milk and half and half. Bring to slow boil. Simmer 10 minutes. Season to taste with salt, pepper and celery or onion salt. Cool fast; refrigerate 5 hours or more to blend flavors. Reheat in double boiler. Serve at once.

MUSSELS IN WHITE WINE

A delightful way of preparing this delicate and plentiful shell-fish. Serve as soup or appetizer.

1 cup dry white wine	1 clove garlic, mashed
¼ pound butter	4 dozen mussels, thoroughly
1 cup chopped onion	scrubbed, "beards" removed
2 tablespoons chopped parsley	

In a large kettle, combine all ingredients and cook covered over high heat for about 5 minutes until shells open, shaking pan a few times. Lower heat, simmer 8 to 10 minutes longer. Serve in shallow soup plates.

OYSTERS BAKED WITH CANADIAN BACON

1 tablespoon butter	½ pound thin slices Canadian
1½ pints shucked small	bacon, cut in half
oysters	Buttered toast
Pepper	

Rub a 7×11-inch baking dish with butter. Into it turn oysters in their liquid. Dust sparingly with pepper—no other seasoning or the delicate flavor will be clouded. Edge with half-slices of Canadian bacon. Bake 25 to 30 minutes in moderate (350 to 375°) oven, or until edges of oysters "curl" and bacon lightly browns. Pass buttered toast.

OYSTER BAR STEW

¼ cup butter or margarine
2 dozen medium-sized oysters
   with oyster liquid
1 cup bottled clam broth
1 quart milk
1 cup light cream or half and
   half

1½ teaspoons Worcestershire
   sauce
½ teaspoon paprika
½ teaspoon salt
⅛ teaspoon pepper
Few grains cayenne

Melt butter in top part of 2½-quart double boiler. Add oysters; cook over boiling water 10 minutes, or until edges curl. Add remaining ingredients. Heat thoroughly over boiling water.

HANGTOWN FRY

This dish, according to some Californians, originated during the Gold Rush in 1849. A lucky miner demanded the finest and most expensive meal available at the Cary House in Hangtown. He slapped his fortune in nuggets on the counter, and upon being informed that oysters and eggs were the most expensive foods on the menu, told the cook to put them together and serve up the results.

1 dozen oysters, shucked
All-purpose flour seasoned
   with salt and pepper
9 eggs

Fine cracker crumbs
3 tablespoons butter
1 teaspoon salt
Dash pepper

Drain oysters; dry between paper towels. Dip each one in all-purpose flour seasoned with salt and pepper, then into 1 well-beaten egg and finally into cracker crumbs. Melt butter in a large skillet and brown oysters on both sides. Beat remaining 8 eggs with 1 teaspoon salt and a dash of pepper. Pour egg mixture over oysters and cook until firm on the bottom. Turn with a large spatula and cook the second side 1 to 2 minutes longer. Serves 4.

PIGS IN BLANKETS, PROVINCETOWN

16 oysters, shucked
Cracker crumbs

Salt and black pepper
16 slices bacon

Roll each oyster in cracker crumbs to coat thoroughly, sprinkle lightly with salt and black pepper and fasten strip of bacon around each with a toothpick. Fry slowly until bacon is crisp, or if preferred, broil 4 to 5 inches from heat about 5 minutes, or until bacon is crisp. Remove toothpicks before serving.

BROILED DEEP SEA SCALLOPS

2 pounds frozen sea scallops
3 eggs
1½ teaspoons salt
¼ teaspoon pepper

2 cups fine dry bread crumbs
⅓ cup butter or margarine
Tartar Sauce (see Index)

Thaw and wash scallops; drain on absorbent paper; cut in halves. Beat eggs; add seasonings; stir scallops into this. Cover sparingly with crumbs. Rub baking pan thoroughly with butter. Layer scallops (not touching each other) in pan. Dot with butter or margarine. Broil at moderate heat, allowing 7 minutes if small, 10 minutes if large. Turn once. Pass Tartar Sauce.

COQUILLES ST. JACQUES

1 pound sea scallops
1 cup white wine
¼ cup water
1 onion, peeled and chopped
Salt and pepper to taste
Bouquet garni (parsley, bay
   leaf, celery stalk, thyme)
¼ pound mushrooms

Juice of 1 lemon
3 tablespoons butter
3 tablespoons flour
1 cup milk
1 egg yolk
Buttered bread crumbs
Grated Parmesan cheese

Wash scallops and poach in white wine and water together with the onion, salt and pepper to taste and the bouquet garni for 5 to 6 minutes. Drain the scallops, saving the broth for the sauce, and cut into small pieces. Put scallop broth back on the stove, bring to a boil, and cook down until you have about ½ cup. Fine-chop the mushrooms and combine with the lemon juice; cook together about 4 minutes.

Melt butter, stir in flour until smooth, then cook-stir until mixture bubbles. Add milk and continue to cook-stir slowly until mixture resembles thick mayonnaise. Add the scallop broth and blend it in thoroughly. Beat up egg yolk. Add sauce to beaten egg yolk very gradually, stirring constantly.

Combine scallops, mushrooms and sauce. Fill 6 scallop shells or a greased baking dish and sprinkle with the buttered bread crumbs and Parmesan. Place under the broiler to brown. Serve immediately.

SCALLOPS AU DIABLE

¼ cup butter or margarine	⅛ teaspoon salt
4 cups diced sea scallops	⅛ teaspoon cayenne
(approximately 1½ pounds)	½ cup chili sauce
½ cup flour	1 teaspoon lemon juice
½ teaspoon table mustard	1 tablespoon minced parsley

Melt butter and heat without browning. Roll scallops in flour, shaking off any which does not cling; then cook 5 minutes in hot butter. Mix and add all remaining ingredients. Cook 5 minutes more. Accompany with flaky rice.

DEVILED SCALLOPS

Wash and drain 2 (10½-ounce) packages frozen and thawed scallops. Cut in halves. Roll in 3 tablespoons vegetable oil, then in 3 tablespoons flour. Add 1 tablespoon each minced onion, lemon juice and grated Parmesan cheese, ½ teaspoon Worcestershire sauce, 1 teaspoon salt and ½ teaspoon minced parsley. Turn into well-oiled low quart baking dish. Bake 20 minutes, in moderate (375°) oven. Top with 1 fresh or firm canned tomato, diced, and 2 tablespoons frozen chives. Continue to bake 10 minutes more.

FRIED SCALLOPS

1 quart scallops (approximately 1½ pounds)	Fat or oil for frying
Egg	Bacon, parsley and lemon wedges
Salt and pepper to taste	Tartar Sauce (see Index)
Bread crumbs	

See that the scallops are thoroughly dry, roll them in slightly beaten egg, then in seasoned bread crumbs. Repeat the egging and bread crumbing a second time because in cooking the scallops shrink somewhat and give off part of their juices. Fry in deep hot fat or oil hot enough to brown a piece of bread in 1 minute. Drain on paper toweling. If desired, garnish with crisply cooked bacon, parsley and lemon wedges. Serve with Tartar Sauce.

SHRIMP CREOLE IN A RICE RING

1 large onion	2 tablespoons chopped onion tops
2 sections garlic, peeled and diced	2 tablespoons chopped green pepper
½ cup cooking oil	2 tablespoons fine-chopped celery
1 (1-pound) can whole tomatoes	1½ cups rice for a ring, cooked by package directions
1 (8-ounce) can tomato sauce	Parsley sprigs
2 pounds shrimp, shelled	
3 cups hot water	
Salt and pepper to taste	
4 tablespoons fine-chopped parsley	

Cut onion fine and fry with garlic in oil until soft. Add canned tomatoes and tomato sauce, being sure to crush any whole tomatoes, and cook until oil comes over top. Add shrimp and simmer-cook 10 minutes. Stir in hot water. Slow-simmer until mixture is consistency of a medium-thick sauce. Add salt and pepper to taste. Stir in parsley, onion tops, green pepper and celery. Continue to cook 15 minutes. Serve in ring made from rice; edge with parsley.

SHELLFISH PAELLA

1½ pounds shrimp, fresh or frozen
1 (5-ounce) can lobster meat
9 clams, fresh or canned
½ teaspoon saffron
¼ cup hot water
2 tablespoons salad oil
½ cup medium-chopped onion
¼ cup medium-chopped celery
1 section garlic, peeled and minced

1½ cups uncooked rice
3 cups chicken broth or 1½ cups bottled clam broth and 1½ cups water
1½ teaspoons salt
¼ teaspoon pepper
½ teaspoon oregano
2 pimientos, medium-chopped
2 cups cooked frozen or canned green peas

Cook and clean shrimp. Drain can of lobster; separate pieces; remove any small bones. Set aside three colorful lobster pieces for garnishing. If clams are fresh, scrub well and place in covered kettle with 1 inch water. Add saffron to hot water to soften.

Heat salad oil in 2½-quart saucepan. Add onion, celery and garlic; slow-sauté over low heat 5 minutes or until wilted. Add rice; cook-stir 2 minutes to brown lightly. Stir in broth and salt; strain into the saffron-hot water, bring to a boil. Cover; slow-cook 15 minutes, or until rice absorbs the liquid. While this cooks, steam clams if fresh in water 10 minutes, or until opened. Stir pepper, oregano, pimiento and peas into rice.

To assemble, layer rice, half the shrimp, the lobster and 4 clams shelled or all the canned clams in buttered casserole. Cover; heat 10 minutes in moderate (350°) oven. Remove and arrange remaining shrimp at edge in a semicircle; top with any remaining clams in their shell. Garnish with colorful reserved lobster.

INDIO SHRIMP CURRY

This recipe calls for fresh dates. If they are not available, pasteurized dates may be used but they make a sweeter curry.

1½ pounds raw shrimp
¼ cup butter or margarine
1½ tablespoons curry powder
1 teaspoon salt
1 cup fine-chopped celery
4 tablespoons instant minced onion
3 tablespoons flour
1½ cups water

1 (14½-ounce) can evaporated milk
1¼ cups fresh California dates, sliced
4 cups hot flaky rice
1½ cups chopped green onions
½ cup chutney
½ cup toasted slivered almonds

Cook, shell and devein the shrimp; rinse under cold water; reserve four for garnishing. Melt the butter in a large skillet. Blend in the curry and salt. Add the celery and sauté until translucent. Add the instant minced onion and the flour; stir until thoroughly mixed. Gradually add the water and milk. Cook-stir over medium heat until thick. Slice the dates; add with the shrimp; heat thoroughly. Serve over the rice. Garnish with the reserved shrimp and a few halved dates. Pass the green onions, chutney and slivered almonds in separate bowls.

LOUISIANA SHRIMP GUMBO YA-YA

½ cup shortening
½ cup flour
1½ teaspoon salt
¼ teaspoon pepper
1½ cups fine-chopped onion
1 section garlic, peeled and minced
1 large green pepper, cored, seeded and minced
2 (8-ounce) cans tomato sauce
1½ quarts (6 cups) hot water

1 pound fresh okra, washed, stemmed and chopped, or 2 (10½-ounce) packages frozen okra
4 (4½-ounce) cans shrimp, rinsed, or 1 pound fresh or frozen shrimp
2 teaspoons filé powder
1 tablespoon cold water
6 cups boiled rice

Melt shortening in heavy 4-quart pot or saucepan. Stir in flour, salt and pepper. Cook-stir until golden brown. Add onion, garlic, green pepper. Simmer-cook-stir until vegetables are limp. Stir in tomato sauce. Then stir in hot water and okra. Simmer 1 hour. Add shrimp, simmer 15 minutes. Remove from heat. Mix filé powder with cold water and stir in. Spoon 1 cup rice into each soup plate or shallow bowl. Ladle over the gumbo.

SHRIMP COCKTAIL

1 quart water	1 teaspoon salt
1 onion, sliced	3 dozen medium-large fresh
1 whole clove garlic	shrimp with shells, washed
1 bay leaf	in cold water
1 stalk celery with leaves, sliced	Cocktail Sauce

Simmer first six ingredients 5 minutes. Strain liquid into a large kettle, bring to a boil, add shrimp and simmer 5 to 8 minutes or until pink. Drain and cover with cold water to chill. Drain, remove tiny legs from shrimp, peel. Slit shrimp along back to expose vein; remove with sharp knife point. Rinse quickly in running water. Drain and chill again. Serve with Cocktail Sauce.

Cocktail Sauce: Combine ¾ cup catsup with ¼ cup prepared horseradish, the juice of 1 lemon, and 1 to 2 dashes of hot pepper sauce, according to taste. Makes about 1 cup.

SHRIMP FOO YUNG

1 (6-ounce) can small shrimp, washed and drained	¾ cup small-diced celery
¾ teaspoon fine-grated lemon peel	¾ cup peeled diced onions
	8 eggs, slightly beaten
2½ tablespoons fresh lemon juice	¾ teaspoon salt
	4 tablespoons cooking oil
1½ cups drained, canned bean sprouts	Soy sauce

Cut shrimp in halves crosswise. Combine with the next five ingredients. Add to beaten eggs and salt. Fry on hot oiled griddle as for pancakes, using ½ cup of the mixture for each one. Turn once. Pass soy sauce.

SHRIMP-SCAMPI

"Shrimp-Scampi" is the name of a scampi entree dressed up with the word "shrimp." Scampi is a shellfish native to the Adriatic and parts of the Mediterranean, but it is seldom that it can be found in the United States, and then it is frozen. As scampi resembles shrimp, medium-large or jumbo shrimp can be used instead.

2 pounds medium-large or jumbo shrimp, fresh or frozen (uncooked)
1¼ cups butter
1 cup olive oil
3 tablespoons chopped green onion
3 tablespoons chopped parsley

3 cloves garlic, finely minced
1½ tablespoons fresh lemon juice
1¼ teaspoons crushed basil
1¼ teaspoons crushed oregano
1½ teaspoons salt
Fresh-ground black pepper

Peel and devein shrimp, leaving tails attached. Split down the inside lengthwise. Do not cut through shrimp. Spread open butterfly style and place in large shallow baking pan. Do not put shrimp in layers. Heat butter and olive oil. Add all remaining ingredients except pepper and pour over shrimp. Grind pepper lightly over shrimp. Bake 5 minutes in a preheated, hot (450°) oven. Remove from oven. Place under broiler for 5 minutes, or until shrimp are flecked with brown. Serves 8.

Note: Shrimp-Scampi ready to bake may be refrigerated until baking time.

SWEET-SOUR SHRIMP

2 tablespoons butter or
   margarine
1 onion, peeled and thin-sliced
½ cup thin-sliced celery
1 (13-ounce) can pineapple
   tidbits, not drained
1 green pepper, seeded and
   cut into bite-sized chunks
2 tablespoons brown sugar

2 tablespoons soy sauce
½ teaspoon grated lemon peel
3 tablespoons cornstarch
4 tablespoons fresh lemon juice
1 cup chicken or vegetable
   bouillon
2 cups or 2 (4½-ounce) cans
   medium-sized shrimp
1 can Chinese noodles

Melt butter in large skillet. Add onion and celery; slow-sauté 3 minutes, or until semi-soft. Add pineapple, green pepper, brown sugar, soy sauce and lemon peel. Mix cornstarch and lemon juice. Stir into skillet. Then stir in bouillon. Stir-simmer until thick and boiling. Stir in shrimp. Heat 4 minutes at low temperature, do not boil. Serve over Chinese noodles.

Beef

"Let's face the fact that being a good cook means, first of all, being able to cook meat well," writes James Beard, a fellow author and food authority. I agree that meat is the main attraction of most major meals! Of course, as important as cooking meat is buying it. If you're uncertain about selecting the right cut and best quality meat be sure to consult your butcher. (Even supermarkets have a buzzer that will call forth a butcher to give advice and to get you the kind and cut of meat you want.)

Americans are more enthusiastic about beef than any other meat. Young children usually elect hamburgers as their favorite, and we all know how many people consider roast beef or steak to be "tops" in eating pleasure. There are uncounted ways to prepare beef including the best-loved recipes included here. (When buying beef look for meat that is red and firm with a marbled texture. The exterior fat should be creamy-white and crumbly.)

All recipes are for six servings unless otherwise stated.

CORNED BEEF HASH CREOLE

2 tablespoons vegetable oil
1 cup chopped onion
½ cup sliced Pascal celery
½ green pepper, chopped
1 small section garlic, peeled and chopped
1 whole canned tomato, drained

1 (1-pound) can corned beef hash
Salt and pepper
Scrambled eggs
Parsley

Heat vegetable oil in 9-inch fry pan. Add chopped vegetables; slow-sauté 5 minutes or until translucent; stir often. Add tomato; crush into vegetables; sauté 1 minute; do not burn. Stir in corned beef hash using fork, so chopped ingredients will not be mashed. Season to taste with salt and pepper. Pat down; slow-brown; light brown crust should form. Fold over; turn onto heated good-sized platter; spoon scrambled eggs at each end. Garnish with parsley.

CORNED BEEF PLATTER

4 to 5 pounds corned beef, brisket or plate
Water as needed
1 tablespoon vinegar
1 bay leaf
12 medium potatoes, peeled
12 whole peeled baby carrots

6 medium-sized onions, peeled
1 green cabbage (about 2 pounds)
Minced parsley
Paprika
Radishes or bread-and-butter pickles

Wash corned beef. Place in a 3-quart kettle. Cover with cold water; add vinegar. Slowly bring to boiling point. Drain off water. Pour in fresh boiling water to cover. Add bay leaf. Cover. Simmer until tender from 3½ to 4 hours for brisket, 2½ hours for plate corned beef. Add potatoes, carrots and onions during the last 40 minutes, but cut cabbage in wedges and cook separately in boiling salted water until bite-tender, from 25 to 30 minutes. When corned beef is done trim off excess fat. Slice meat across grain. This recipe makes enough for two meals.

Arrange overlapping down the center of heated large platter, cooked potatoes at one end, dusted with minced parsley. Arrange sections of cabbage at other end, carrots dusted with paprika down each side. Garnish with radishes or bread-and-butter pickles. Some people like horseradish with corned beef; others prefer Dijon-type mustard.

DEVILED CORNED BEEF BURGERS

1 (12-ounce) can corned beef, not chilled, and flaked
1 egg, beaten
1 slice bread, crumbled fine
¼ teaspoon instant onion

¼ cup chili sauce
1 tablespoon table mustard
⅛ teaspoon Tabasco
Vegetable or toast

Combine all ingredients except vegetable or toast in a quart-sized bowl and mix thoroughly. Shape into 6 flattened patties. Place in oiled shallow pan. Bake 20 minutes in moderate (375°) oven, or pan-fry if you like. Serve as is with vegetable or on toast.

FRIZZLED CREAMED DRIED BEEF

1 (4-ounce) package
wafer-thin dried beef
3 tablespoons butter or
margarine
3 tablespoons flour
2½ to 3 cups milk

⅛ teaspoon pepper or to taste
Boiled potatoes or buttered
toast
1 tablespoon minced parsley
(optional)

With fingers, pull dried beef into easy-to-eat pieces. Place in sieve; scald with boiling water; drain. In 3-pint saucepan melt butter or margarine. Add dried beef; slow-cook until it begins to sauté or "frizzle"; do not brown it. With fork, stir in flour, browning it slightly. Gradually stir in milk, using 2½ cups for medium-thick sauce or 3 cups for thinner sauce. Cook-stir until boiling. Add pepper. Spoon over boiled potatoes or toast. Dust with parsley for color.

BOILED BRISKET OF BEEF

1 medium onion, peeled
6 whole cloves
3 quarts boiling water
1 bay leaf
2 cloves garlic, peeled
2 stalks celery

2 tablespoons vinegar
2 tablespoons sugar
2 teaspoons salt
4 pounds lean brisket of beef
Horseradish (optional)

Stud onion with cloves. Combine water, bay leaf, garlic, onion, celery, vinegar, sugar and salt in a large kettle. Cover and boil for 30 minutes. Add beef. Cover and simmer-cook 4 hours, or until meat is fork-tender, adding additional boiling water if necessary. When meat is done, remove, slice and arrange on a hot platter. Good with horseradish.

BEEF À LA MODE

2 cups water
⅓ cup plain or herb vinegar
1 teaspoon salt
1 teaspoon poultry seasoning
¼ teaspoon mace
3 whole cloves
1 carrot, peeled and sliced

2 sprigs parsley
2 lemons, sliced with the peel
4 to 5 pounds round, chuck
    or brisket of beef
2 tablespoons cooking oil
¼ cup dry wine (optional)
Lemon wedges

Make marinade by combining water, vinegar, seasonings, vegetables and ⅔ of the lemons. Bring to boiling point and simmer 15 minutes. Place meat in deep bowl. Strain over vinegar mixture. Cool quickly; cover and refrigerate 24 hours; turn occasionally. Remove meat and drain, but save the marinade. Put meat in 4-quart heavy saucepan; brown in oil and add remaining lemon. Add marinade, wine if used, and bring to boil. Cover; simmer 3 hours. Slice meat and garnish with wedges of lemon.

BEEF POT ROAST CREOLE

3 to 4 pounds any cut beef,
    suitable for pot roasting
3 sections garlic, peeled and
    slivered
1¼ teaspoons salt
¼ teaspoon pepper
¼ cup meat fat or shortening
1 cup fine-chopped celery
2 medium-sized onions, peeled
    and chopped

2 medium-sized sweet green
    peppers, seeded and chopped
½ cup chopped parsley
1 cup drained and mashed
    canned tomatoes
1½ cups boiling water
3 beef bouillon cubes
Gravy

Pound meat thoroughly with meat mallet to tenderize it. Make 12 incisions with a sharp knife; press into each a sliver of garlic. Dust with salt and pepper. Slow-brown all over in meat fat in large heavy 4-quart saucepan; then remove. To saucepan add celery, onions, green peppers, parsley and tomatoes. Cook until they change color. Add water and bouillon cubes. Return pot roast to saucepan; bring to a brisk boil. Then cover and simmer 3 hours or until fork-tender. Remove meat and keep warm. Serve with Gravy.

Gravy: To vegetables and juice in saucepan, add 3 tablespoons enriched flour stirred smooth with 3 tablespoons cold water; slowly stir in 1½ cups boiling water; bring to a rapid boil. Add 4 drops Tabasco.

HUNGARIAN POT ROAST

3 tablespoons fat (any kind)
4 or 5 pounds beef tied for pot roasting
2 teaspoons seasoned salt
2 teaspoons paprika
3 tablespoons fresh or frozen minced onion

2 rye crackers, fine-crumbled
2½ cups any soup stock or beef bouillon
12 medium-sized potatoes, peeled and halved
Paprika

Heat fat in deep heavy 4-quart kettle. Rub beef all over with seasoned salt and paprika. Slow-brown all over. Add minced onion and fry 1 minute. Stir fine-crumbled rye crackers into 1 cup of the soup stock and add. Cover and simmer-cook 2¼ hours or until nearly fork-tender. Then add 1½ cups boiling stock or enough to make a gravy. At same time, put potatoes around pot roast. Dust them with paprika. Cover and simmer-cook 30 minutes, or until fork-tender. Nice served with pickled beets. Serves 8.

POT ROAST SPANISH

¼ teaspoon powdered
   marjoram
2 bay leaves, crushed
1 section garlic, crushed
1 green pepper, cored and
   minced
1 small onion, fine-chopped
3 to 4 pounds boned rump of
   beef or chuck, rolled

¼ cup olive oil
1 (1-pound) can tomatoes,
   mashed
1 tablespoon sugar
¼ teaspoon ground cinnamon
⅛ teaspoon ground cloves
1 cup red wine
1 tablespoon red wine vinegar
2½ teaspoons salt

Mix marjoram, bay leaves and garlic. Add green pepper and
onion and rub over meat. Cover; let stand 1 hour at room
temperature. Measure olive oil in deep heavy kettle; place meat
in it, and brown in oil over high heat. Add tomatoes, sugar,
cinnamon, cloves, wine, vinegar and salt; cover. Simmer-cook
3 to 4 hours, or until meat is fork-tender.

POT ROAST WITH WINE

3 cups water
⅔ cup cider vinegar
2 tablespoons salt
1 teaspoon whole peppercorns
1½ teaspoons poultry
   seasoning
¼ teaspoon mace
1 onion, peeled and sliced

1 carrot, peeled and sliced
6 cloves
3 to 4 pounds top round of beef
¼ cup beef drippings
5 slices lemon
1 cup dry red wine
3½ tablespoons flour
¼ cup cold water

Combine first nine ingredients; bring to boiling point; simmer
30 minutes. Strain over beef. Cover; let stand 24 hours; turn
occasionally. Remove and drain beef (save the liquid). Melt
beef drippings in large heavy kettle; add lemon and then the
beef; slow-brown all over. Pour in liquid drained from meat;
close-cover; simmer 3 hours or until beef is almost tender; turn
twice. Add wine and simmer 1 hour more. Remove meat; keep

it hot. About 2½ cups liquid should be left. To make gravy, add flour stirred smooth in additional cold water. Cook-stir until boiling; season to taste; simmer 3 minutes. Pass in gravy boat.

SAUERBRATEN WITH GINGERED GRAVY

5 pounds rolled pot roast of beef

2 teaspoons salt

½ teaspoon pepper

1 medium-sized onion, peeled and sliced

½ cup chopped celery stalks and leaves

½ cup thin-sliced peeled carrot

6 whole cloves

4 peppercorns

2 bay leaves

2 cups wine vinegar

1 quart boiling water or enough to cover the beef

2 tablespoons beef fat or vegetable oil

1 tablespoon butter

Puffy dumplings (recipe on biscuit mix package)

Minced parsley

Gingered Gravy

In a deep 4-quart bowl, place meat. Mix and add next eight ingredients. Pour in wine vinegar and water. Cover. Refrigerate and marinate at least 24 hours. Remove meat from refrigerator. Drain off and save liquid. Brush off any spices that may have adhered to meat. In large deep, heavy fry pan, brown meat all over in beef fat and butter. Strain in reserved liquid. Cover; bring to boil. Simmer 3 hours. Remove meat and keep warm.

Place the meat on heated large platter; surround with puffy dumplings made by following recipe printed on a box of biscuit mix, and dust them with minced parsley. Pass Gingered Gravy separately. Serves 10 to 12.

Gingered Gravy: Melt 2 tablespoons butter in a 3-cup saucepan. Stir in 5 tablespoons flour and 1 tablespoon sugar. Slow-brown, stirring often. Then stir in reserved liquid. When boiling, cover and simmer 10 minutes, or until thickened. Stir 10 old-fashioned, crushed ginger snaps into this and continue to stir until smooth.

MARINATED SPICED BEEF

4 pounds rump or round roast
  of beef
1 teaspoon salt
½ teaspoon ground thyme
2 teaspoons powdered mustard
2 tablespoons parsley flakes
6 whole cloves
½ teaspoon whole black
  pepper
¼ teaspoon ground sage
2 tablespoons grated lemon
  peel
2 bouillon cubes
2 cups boiling water
1 onion, peeled and sliced
½ cup cider vinegar
3 tablespoons shortening

Place beef in close-fitting pan. Combine remaining ingredients except shortening, and pour over beef. Marinate in refrigerator 24 hours or more; turn several times. Remove beef from pan; save marinade. In skillet, brown beef on all sides in shortening. Place meat in roasting pan. Add marinade. Cover with foil, roast 2½ to 3 hours in slow (325°) oven, or until fork-tender. Remove meat. Enough for 2 meals.

ROAST PRIME RIBS OF BEEF AU JUS

Use a meat thermometer to determine accurately the required doneness of all roasted meats. The thermometer should be inserted in the meat before starting it to roast. Plunge the thermometer into the thickest portion but do not let it rest on the bone.

Place the roast, fat side up, in an uncovered pan. Dust with 1 teaspoon seasoned salt and ⅛ teaspoon pepper mixed for each 2 pounds of meat. Roast 15 minutes in a hot (450°) oven. Reduce the heat to 350°, and roast to the desired doneness. Do not baste the meat. The fat on the top of the roast does this automatically.

When done, add 3 tablespoons rich beef stock or bouillon or dry sherry to the juices in the pan. Turn off the oven heat. Leave the oven door open and let the roast stand 15 minutes to set. This treatment makes carving easier and generates sufficient juice in the pan to serve as gravy. This slightly thickens itself as the low oven heat coagulates and cooks the proteins in the meat juices.

Timetable for Standing Rib Roast of Beef: Rare: Allow 20 minutes to the pound or 140 to 145° on a meat thermometer. Medium rare: Allow 25 minutes to the pound or 160° on a meat thermometer. Well done: Allow 40 minutes to the pound or 170° on a meat thermometer.

Yorkshire pudding is the traditional accompaniment for roast beef. Recipe follows.

YORKSHIRE PUDDING

1¼ cups sifted flour
¼ teaspoon salt
1¼ cups milk at room temperature

2 eggs at room temperature
6 tablespoons hot beef drippings

Sift together flour and salt. Beat in milk with rotary beater. Beat eggs very light and add. Measure 4 tablespoons drippings from roast beef into an 8×8-inch loaf pan and heat till smoking hot. Pour in pudding mixture. Bake 15 minutes in hot (400°) oven. Then baste with 2 tablespoons beef drippings; lower heat to 350° and bake 15 minutes more, or until puffy and golden brown. Serve hot. Break into squares with a fork, as cutting makes it heavy.

For special savor, add ½ teaspoon powdered mixed herbs to the pudding mixture. Or add 1 teaspoon sage, ¼ cup minced onion, generous sprinkling pepper.

ROAST BEEF HASH

3 cups chopped (not dry) roast beef
1½ cups fine-chopped boiled potatoes

1 tablespoon fine-chopped onion
Salt and pepper to taste
3 to 4 tablespoons butter

Combine beef and potatoes. Add and mix onion, salt and pepper to taste. Melt butter in a 10- to 12-inch skillet. Spread in hash mixture and fry until well-browned, then roll up as you would an omelet. (Try serving this with a garnish of ¾ cup sour cream, mixed with 3 tablespoons well-seasoned tomato sauce.)

OVEN-BRAISED SHORT RIBS OF BEEF

3 short ribs of beef, cut in
   2-inch lengths
1 teaspoon dry mustard
1 tablespoon flour
1 teaspoon salt
½ teaspoon pepper
2 tablespoons vinegar

1 onion, sliced and peeled
2 cups beef broth or 2 cups
   water and 2 teaspoons beef
   broth powder
6 medium-sized potatoes,
   peeled and halved

Rub beef all over with mustard, flour, salt, pepper and vinegar mixed together. Place in 3-quart casserole; let stand to marinate 1 hour before cooking. Place onion on meat; pour around beef broth; cover. Bake 2 hours in moderate (350°) oven. After beef has cooked 1 hour, uncover, drain and arrange potatoes around it (save the liquid). During last ½ hour, beef and potatoes will brown. Skim fat from broth and make gravy from reserved liquid.

SWEET-SOUR SHORT RIBS

3 pounds short ribs of beef
2 teaspoons salt
⅓ cup flour
2 tablespoons fat
1 cup sliced peeled onion
1 section garlic, peeled and
   minced

1½ cups hot water
1 bay leaf
¼ cup vinegar
½ teaspoon Tabasco
1 tablespoon brown sugar
¼ cup water

Order short ribs cut into individual servings; remove excess fat. Combine 1 teaspoon salt and flour; roll meat in this mixture; reserve leftover flour. Heat fat in large skillet; add meat and brown well all over. Remove meat to heavy pan. Add onion and garlic to skillet; sauté until onion is limp. Add to short ribs. Combine hot water, bay leaf, vinegar, Tabasco, brown sugar and left-over salt; pour over short ribs. Cover and simmer or slow-bake 2 to 2½ hours, or until fork-tender. Remove ribs to serving platter and keep warm. To thicken gravy, make paste of 2 tablespoons reserved flour and ¼ cup water. Stir rapidly into meat juices. Boil 3 minutes. Accompany with hot buttered noodles.

BROWNED SPARERIBS OF BEEF

3 pounds spareribs of beef (cracked for easy serving)	2 tablespoons seasoned salt
1 teaspoon pickling spice	2 quarts boiling water
1 large onion, peeled and sliced	1 teaspoon seasoned salt
1 cup celery leaves, pressed down	6 white potatoes, peeled and halved lengthwise

Combine ingredients, except last two, in 6-quart kettle; cover. Simmer 2 hours, or until meat is fork-tender. Strain and save broth. Arrange meat in one layer in large roasting pan. Dust with additional seasoned salt. Tuck in halved potatoes. Pour around 1½ cups broth. Bake 35 minutes at 350°, or until browned and potatoes are fork-tender. Make a gravy from pan drippings and 1½ cups reserved broth.

BROILED BEEF STEAK

Slash fat in several places at edge of a 1½-inch sirloin, porterhouse, or rump steak so meat will not buckle while cooking. Spread lightly with butter; dust with salt and pepper. Place on oiled, preheated broiler, 3 inches from source of heat. Broil 3 minutes, or until well browned. Dust with salt and pepper. Turn with cooking tongs.

Broil until browned on second side; dust with salt and pepper. Reduce heat; broil a total of 16 minutes for steak cut 1½ inches thick; a total of 20 minutes if cut 2 inches thick. This will give you a steak medium-well done. You may vary the cooking time by 2 to 3 minutes more or less, according to whether you want it well done or rare.

When done, spread over 1 tablespoon softened unsalted butter to each pound of steak. Pass bottled meat sauces of choice in the original containers, their hallmark of excellence.

STEAK DIANE

Sauce:

2 tablespoons butter	¾ cup sour cream
1 tablespoon minced shallots or red onion	1 tablespoon fine-chopped parsley
18 medium mushrooms, sliced profile style	¼ teaspoon fresh-ground black pepper
6 tablespoons demi-glacé (beef jelly)	

Melt butter; add shallots and mushrooms. Sauté 5 minutes. Add demi-glacé and cream; stir-cook over low heat 3 minutes; add parsley and pepper.

Meat:

6 ½-inch filets mignons	6 tablespoons brandy or 2 tablespoons brandy flavoring and 2 tablespoons water
1 teaspoon salt	
⅛ teaspoon pepper	
3 tablespoons butter	

Season meat; in second skillet sauté both sides in butter until golden brown but still rare. Pour brandy and flame. (If brandy flavoring is used, do not flame.) Cover with sauce. Accompany with wild rice.

LONDON BROIL MAÎTRE D'

2 pounds flank steak	Maître D'hôtel Butter (see Index)
1 tablespoon French dressing (not sweet)	6 strips each green pepper and pimiento (optional)
¾ teaspoon salt	
⅛ teaspoon pepper	

Brush steak with French dressing; cut slits at each end to prevent curling. Dust with salt and pepper. Broil under high heat until well browned on both sides, about 8 minutes altogether. Cut in diagonal (slanting) slices no more than ¼ inch thick. Top with thin slices Maître D'hôtel Butter. Garnish with green pepper and pimiento strips if desired.

PANNED CUBED BEEF STEAKS

6 individual cubed beef steaks	¼ teaspoon pepper
1 tablespoon lemon juice	¼ cup butter or margarine
½ teaspoon garlic powder	Lemon butter
1½ teaspoons salt	

Brush cubed steaks all over with lemon juice. Mix and rub in garlic powder, salt and pepper. Melt butter in large skillet. Sauté cubed steaks until browned, about 7 minutes on each side. Present sizzling, each steak garnished with thin slice of lemon butter.

PEPPER STEAK

2 teaspoons coarse ground black pepper	2 tablespoons butter
3½ pounds Porterhouse steak cut 1½ inches thick	2 tablespoons olive or salad oil
½ teaspoon garlic salt	¼ cup dry red wine or ½ cup beef bouillon
	¼ cup cognac

Rub black pepper into both sides of steak. Sprinkle lightly with garlic salt. Heat butter and oil in large heavy skillet over high heat. Add steak and sear on both sides. Cook 7 to 10 minutes on each side. Remove steak to serving platter. Add wine or boiling bouillon and cognac to pan and heat for 1 minute. Pour over steak.

BUTTER-ROASTED SIRLOIN STEAK

3 pounds sirloin steak, 1½   1½ teaspoons salt
  inches thick   ¼ teaspoon pepper
½ cup butter

Thoroughly rub low baking pan just large enough to hold the
steak with half the butter. Heat in oven until butter sizzles.
Place steak in pan. Spread thin layer of remaining butter over
top. Dust with seasonings. Bake 30 minutes in moderate (375°)
oven for medium rare. Baste occasionally with 2 tablespoons extra butter, melted.

ROLLED STUFFED FLANK STEAK

2 pounds flank steak, 2 inches   4 green onions, fine-chopped
  thick   ¼ cup coarse-chopped parsley
1 section garlic, peeled, or ½   ½ cup coarse-chopped celery
  teaspoon garlic powder   1 egg, beaten
5 chorizos (Mexican or   ¼ cup cooking oil
  Spanish sausage)   1 cup beef broth

Split flank steak almost through. Spread open, and lay it out
flat. Rub with garlic or dust with garlic powder. Remove skins
from sausages. Crumble sausage meat fine. Add onions, parsley,
celery and egg. Mix well to make stuffing. Spread this over flank
steak to within ½ inch of edge. Roll up steak loosely, holding
in stuffing; keep in shape with a few picks, if needed. Brush
rolled flank steak all over with oil. Place in roasting pan. Bake
30 minutes in hot (425°) oven. Add broth and continue to bake
1½ hours or until flank steak is fork-tender. Baste every 20
minutes with broth. If necessary use ¼ cup extra broth.

Serve stuffed flank steak sliced, accompanied with a sauce of
your choice.

SWISS STEAK IN FOIL

2½ pounds boneless chuck ½ inch thick, cut into 6 serving portions
1 envelope onion soup mix
1 (3-ounce) can sliced mushrooms
1 (1-pound) can tomatoes, drained, reserve juice
1 clove garlic, crushed

Pinch of salt
Generous sprinkling fresh-ground pepper
½ cup reserved tomato juice
1 tablespoon cornstarch
2 tablespoons whiskey, brandy or sherry (optional)
2 tablespoonfuls chopped parsley

Arrange steak on slightly overlapping, large piece heavy duty foil, about 20 inches in length. Sprinkle with soup mix, drained mushrooms, drained tomatoes, which have been chopped up, and garlic. Mix salt, pepper, and the ½ cup reserved tomato juice with the cornstarch and the whiskey, brandy or sherry if used. Pour over all and sprinkle with parsley. Fold foil, double-edge, seal tightly. Place in baking dish and bake at 350° for 2½ hours.

SWISS STEAK IN SKILLET

1½ pounds bottom round steak, cut ½ inch thick
¼ cup flour
1 teaspoon salt
¼ teaspoon pepper
4 tablespoons butter or margarine
4 small onions, peeled and thin-sliced

½ teaspoon salt
1 bay leaf
1 teaspoon Worcestershire sauce
1 cup canned tomatoes, mashed
1½ cups hot broth or water

Pound steak, working in flour mixed with salt and pepper. Cut steak in 6 portions for serving.

Melt butter or margarine in large ovenproof skillet. Add steak and onions and sauté until both are browned. Dust with additional salt; add bay leaf and Worcestershire. Spoon in tomato. Add broth or water; close cover. Bake 1 hour in slow (325°) oven, or until fork-tender. Serve from skillet.

TOURNEDOS

These smallest of steaks cut from the narrow part of the beef tenderloin should be sliced 1 inch thick and trimmed to be neat and round. If necessary, fasten them into shape with wooden picks, but be sure to remove them before serving.

Two or three tournedos or miniatures are served to a person at a dinner. But two or even one is sufficient for a light luncheon entree.

After cooking, the tournedos are completed with a glamorous garnish which gives each type a special name. Interesting vegetables without much sauce, except butter, accompany tournedos, but they must be compatible with the garnish.

To Cook Tournedos: Season with salt and pepper, using 1 teaspoon salt and ⅛ teaspoon pepper to the pound. Fry in plenty of unsalted butter, allowing about 6 minutes on each side for medium well done. Then garnish. Here are a few suggestions. Imagination will supply many more.

Tournedos Béarnaise: Sauté tournedos as directed. To serve, place each tournedo on a broiled thick slice of tomato. Top with Sauce Béarnaise (see Index). Garnish of cress, small parslied potato balls and buttered baby green beans.

Tournedos Rossini: Sauté the tournedos as directed. Place each upon a butter-sautéed round slice of bread. Top each tournedo with a round slice of pâté de foie gras, a slice of truffle the climax.

Tournedos Henri IV: Sauté the tournedos as directed; set each on a round slice of butter-sautéed bread. Edge with a pastry-tubed ribbon of Sauce Béarnaise (see Index). Top each tournedo with a drained canned artichoke bottom heated in butter and centered with a cutout of canned red pimiento.

Tournedos Hollandaise: Sauté tournedos as directed. Place each on a small round of broiled ham steak. Spread the tournedos with Hollandaise Sauce (see Index). Slip under the broiler 1 minute to brown. Top each with a sautéed mushroom crown dusted with minced parsley. Accompaniment, braised, whole red-plum tomatoes, or tomato slices oregano and water cress.

Tournedos Roman: Sauté tournedos as directed. Place each on a very large sautéed mushroom crown, turned upside down and stuffed with smoked ham pâté. Garnish with sautéed chicken livers and small mushroom crowns in sherry-flavored White Sauce (see Index); trim with water cress.

BEEF WELLINGTON

Traditionally made with the expensive and elegant fillet of beef, Beef Wellington can be equally delicious made with the more accessible eye-of-the-round. Here is the first of two recipes for Beef Wellington.

1 beef eye round (about 3
    pounds)
2 tablespoons brandy or cognac
1 cup sherry
½ cup beef consommé,
    undiluted
1 onion, sliced
1 carrot, sliced
1 stalk celery, sliced
1 section garlic, halved

Butter at room temperature
2 (10-ounce) packages frozen
    puff pastry shells, thawed
1 (4¾-ounce) can liver pâté
½ cup finely chopped
    mushrooms, fresh, or canned
    or ½ cup finely chopped
    pitted black olives
1 egg, slightly beaten

In bowl, combine beef with next seven ingredients. Marinate meat 24 hours, turning occasionally. Remove, pat dry. Reserve marinade. Rub entire surface with soft butter. Roast on rack in

425° oven 1 hour, or until meat thermometer registers 130°. Remove. Reserve drippings. Cool meat.

Roll out pastry shells to form rectangle about 14×16 inches. Spread meat all over with pâté and mushrooms, or olives, combined. Place beef top side down on pastry. Draw up edges. Wrap securely. Trim, and brush all over with egg to seal and glaze. Place on baking sheet seam side down. Bake in preheated 425° oven, 25 to 30 minutes, or until pastry is puffed and golden brown.

If desired, make gravy with reserved marinade and drippings.

QUICK BEEF WELLINGTON

A new way to make the classic elegant Beef Wellington by using modern methods and budget ideas.

1 family steak, 2 inches thick, cut from round, chuck or rump	Beef Liver Pâté
	1 egg, beaten with ¼ cup milk
2 tablespoons water	Sauce Béarnaise or
Instant seasoned meat tenderizer	Cumberland Sauce (see Index)
4 sticks package pie pastry mix or 2 standard recipes flaky pie pastry	

Prick meat at ½ inch intervals with kitchen fork; pat over water; dust all over with meat tenderizer. Use no salt. Roll up meat; tie in four places to give beef tenderloin shape. Immediately broil all over 20 minutes. Cool; cover with pastry as follows: Roll pastry ¼ inch thick on 18-inch square of waxed paper. Spread over Beef Liver Pâté almost to edges. Place steak in center. Bring dough at each end up over meat; cut out corners for easy folding; bring up and fold in sides; gently press together all seams. Place the Wellington seam side down on baking sheet. Gently remove waxed paper. Cut fragments of pastry into decorative motifs; brush with egg beaten with ¼ cup milk, and arrange motifs on Wellington; brush loaf all over with egg-milk mixture. Bake 15 minutes in hot (450°) oven, or until golden brown. To serve, cut across the grain in thin diagonal slices. Serve with Sauce Béarnaise or with Cumberland Sauce.

Beef Liver Pâté:

1 pound beef liver (or chicken livers)
1 teaspoon instant seasoned meat tenderizer
2 large onions, peeled and thin-sliced
4 tablespoons chicken fat
1 (4-ounce) can mushroom stems and pieces, drained (reserve liquid)

2 tablespoons grated raw onion
Mushroom liquid or dry white wine
Salt and pepper to taste

Cut out veins and slice skin from beef liver. Dust meat tenderizer evenly over entire surface. To insure penetration and retain natural juices, pierce liver deeply with kitchen fork at ½-inch intervals. Use no salt. Sauté onions in 2 tablespoons of chicken fat in skillet until translucent. Add liver; sauté 6 to 10 minutes, or until well done. Cool. Slice liver; add sautéed onions and mushrooms; put through fine blade of food grinder, or use a blender. Combine with remaining chicken fat and grated onion. If necessary, add enough mushroom liquid or dry white wine to make pâté spreadable. Add salt and pepper to taste. Chill.

BEEF BOURGUIGNONNE

½ cup beef fat
12 small white onions, peeled
2 pounds steak, bottom or top round, or chuck
2 tablespoons flour
1½ teaspoons salt
½ teaspoon pepper

¼ teaspoon powdered thyme
½ pound mushrooms, sliced
1 cup beef bouillon or 1 cup water and 1 teaspoon beef bouillon powder
1 cup dry red wine

In a 2-quart kettle, heat beef fat until it melts freely; remove any brown pieces; add onions. Stir-sauté until lightly browned; remove onions and set aside. Meantime, cut steak into bite-sized pieces; brown in fat in kettle. Stir in flour and seasonings. Add reserved onions, mushrooms, bouillon and wine. Cover. Simmer 3½ hours, or until fork-tender. Or transfer to casserole, and bake 3 hours or more in slow (325°) oven. Add more bouillon if it becomes too dry. Accompany with garlic French bread and a tossed green salad.

Note: All alcohol in the wine evaporates during cooking.

BEEF CASSEROLE CREOLE

2½ tablespoons beef drippings	½ teaspoon sugar
1 stalk celery, minced	1 (1-pound) can tomatoes
2 green peppers, shredded	1 (4-ounce) can mushrooms
1 section garlic, minced	½ cup dry red wine (optional)
3 medium onions, peeled	½ cup pimiento-stuffed olives,
2 pounds round steak	sliced
2½ tablespoons flour	12 whole pimiento-stuffed
1½ teaspoons salt	olives
¼ teaspoon pepper	Buttered noodles

Melt beef drippings in skillet. Add celery, green peppers, garlic, and onions; sauté until softened and slightly browned. Cut meat into bite-sized cubes. Mix together flour, salt and pepper; then stir in meat. Add to skillet; sauté until browned. Stir in sugar, tomatoes, canned mushrooms and liquid, and wine. Transfer to buttered 3-quart casserole; cover. Bake 2 hours in a moderate (350°) oven. Stir in sliced olives 5 minutes before completion. Garnish with pimiento-stuffed olives. Serve with buttered noodles.

BEEF GUMBO WITH RICE

2 pounds best-quality stewing
beef, tenderized
½ pound cooked ham
3 tablespoons margarine or
cooking oil
1 quart fresh or 1 pint canned
okra, sliced
1 medium-sized onion, peeled
and minced
3 medium-sized green peppers,
seeded and chopped

1 cup drained and mashed
canned tomatoes
2 quarts cold water
2 teaspoons beef bouillon
powder
1 dried red pepper
6 cups cooked flaky converted
rice

Cut beef and ham in 1-inch cubes. Fry meat in large, heavy, deep kettle until well browned in margarine or oil. If fresh okra is used, add and brown slightly; stir occasionally. If it is canned, add okra last when gumbo is practically done. Stir in onion, peppers, tomatoes, water and bouillon powder; add red pepper pod. Cover; simmer ¾ hour, or until meat is fork-tender. Remove pepper pod. Add extra water if liquid boils down too much, or gumbo will be too thick. Serve in warmed deep soup plates or large shallow bowls; top with cupful of cooked flaky rice.

MARINATED BEEF KABOBS

1½ pounds chuck or round
steak
½ cup cooking oil
¼ cup fresh lime juice
1 teaspoon dry mustard
¼ teaspoon powdered thyme
1 bay leaf
⅛ teaspoon powdered basil
⅛ teaspoon powdered
rosemary
½ teaspoon salt

⅛ teaspoon pepper
1 medium onion, peeled and
chopped
2 medium onions, peeled and
sliced
1 green pepper, seeded and
sliced
1 (6-ounce) can mushroom
caps
1½ tablespoons melted butter
or margarine

Cut steak into 1½-inch cubes. In 2-quart bowl, blend and mix cooking oil, lime juice, seasonings and chopped onion. Add meat and stir to coat with this marinade. Let stand 5 hours, or overnight, if desired. Slice onions ¼ inch thick and green pepper into ¼-inch rings. Alternate cubes of beef on six metal skewers with onion slices, green pepper rings and mushroom caps. Repeat, ending with meat cubes. Place kabobs on broiler rack 3 inches from source of heat. Broil about 20 minutes, turning once. Spoon over butter or margarine before serving. Accompany with flaky rice.

BEEF AND KIDNEY PIE

1 beef kidney	2 cups boiling water
½ cup sliced onion	2 tablespoons flour
1 tablespoon cooking oil	¼ cup cold water or dry white
1 pound beef chuck, cut in	wine
1-inch cubes	½ recipe Rich American Pie
2 teaspoons salt	Pastry (see Index) or a mix
¼ teaspoon pepper	
½ tablespoon Worcestershire	
sauce	

Wash kidney and split in half lengthwise. Remove the skin, white tubes and fat. Soak kidney in cold salted water 30 minutes. Drain and cut into 1-inch cubes. Brown onion slowly in oil; add meat and brown well. Add salt, pepper, Worcestershire sauce and boiling water. Simmer 2 hours, or until very tender. Blend flour and cold water or white wine. Mix in a small amount of hot liquid from the stew; add to the gravy, stirring constantly until thickened. Transfer to a deep baking dish. Cover the top with thin piecrust. Slash in the center to let the steam escape. Bake in a moderate (375°) oven for 50 minutes.

BEEF PIES PIQUANT

2 pounds boneless sirloin of beef, in ½-inch cubes	1 teaspoon caraway seeds
½ cup butter or margarine	1 teaspoon salt
1 cup peeled chopped onion	1 teaspoon Tabasco
1 cup diced celery	Pastry-Piquant

Brown beef in 2 tablespoons butter in skillet, 15 to 20 minutes. Remove beef and liquid from skillet. Melt remaining butter in skillet; add onion and celery; brown lightly. Add beef with liquid, caraway seeds, salt and Tabasco. Remove from heat; cool slightly. Spoon into Pastry-Piquant-lined individual pie pans (or disposable aluminum pans) 4¼ inches in diameter. Top with pastry; seal edges with fork. Cut cross in top with paring knife for steam escape. Bake 45 minutes in hot (400°) oven, or until crust is golden brown.

Pastry-Piquant:

3 cups sifted flour	2 eggs, slightly beaten
1 teaspoon salt	¼ cup cold water
1 cup shortening	1 teaspoon Tabasco

Sift flour with salt. With pastry blender chop shortening into flour until fine flakes are formed. Stir in eggs. Combine water and Tabasco; sprinkle over pastry mixture and mix lightly. Form into ball; chill while preparing meat filling. Divide pastry into 12 equal portions; then, on lightly floured board, roll ¼ inch thick. Use as directed.

RANCHER'S BEEF PIE

2 pounds lean beef stew meat	2 tablespoons oil
1 teaspoon garlic salt	1 (10½-ounce) can beef broth
½ teaspoon dill, rubbed between the fingers	½ cup water
	4 carrots
1 teaspoon paprika	3 celery stalks
½ teaspoon chili powder	12 very small white onions
2 tablespoons flour	Herb Crust

Spread beef on a board. Combine garlic salt, dill, paprika, chili powder and flour. Sprinkle over meat; rub meat with this seasoned flour until well coated. Cut meat in bite-sized pieces. Remove meat and brown slowly and well in oil in heavy skillet. Remove to large saucepan. Add beef broth and water. Cover and simmer 45 minutes. Pare carrots and cut into diagonal chunks; cut celery in 1-inch pieces. Peel onions. Parboil vegetables 5 minutes; drain and add to meat. Cover again and continue cooking until meat and vegetables are just tender. Turn into a 10×6-inch baking pan. Cover with Herb Crust. Bake in hot (425°) oven for 25 minutes, or until crust is crisp and richly browned.

Herb Crust: Combine 1½ cups sifted all-purpose flour, ¼ teaspoon ground rosemary and ½ teaspoon ground thyme. Cut in ½ cup shortening. Add 3 to 4 tablespoons cold milk, just enough to hold pastry together. Roll to fit top of baking pan as directed. Place over meat filling, crimp edges and cut a few slits in top crust to allow steam to escape during baking.

FRENCH-STYLE POT-AU-FEU WITH VEGETABLES

4 pounds shin or shank of beef
2½ teaspoons salt
½ teaspoon pepper
¼ cup flour
¼ cup cooking oil
½ teaspoon sugar
½ teaspoon powdered
   rosemary
2 bay leaves
4 whole cloves
3 quarts boiling water
1½ pounds carrots, peeled
   and quartered
1½ pounds turnips, peeled
   and sliced
12 medium-sized onions,
   peeled
12 medium-sized white
   potatoes, peeled
1½ cups thin-sliced celery
1 pound cleaned spinach or
   kale, cut across in 2-inch
   lengths

Rub meat all over with mixture of salt, pepper and flour. Measure cooking oil into 6-quart kettle and heat. Add meat; slow-brown all over. Add sugar, rosemary, bay leaves, cloves and water. Cover. Simmer 2½ hours, or until beef is almost tender. Add carrots, turnips, onions and potatoes. Cover. Continue to slow-boil 40 minutes. Strain off the broth. (Keep meat and vegetables warm.) Add celery and spinach or kale to the broth. Cover. Simmer 20 minutes to serve as a soup. Slice half the meat. Center on platter. Surround with half of the vegetables. Pass prepared horseradish, pickles or pickled beets. Serves 10 to 12.

French-Style Pot-au-Feu Dinner Planned Over: Keep the remaining pot-au-feu and broth refrigerated up to two days and serve it in a different way. For example: Cut the beef remaining from the pot-au-feu into bite-sized pieces. In a deep skillet that can go-to-table, brown beef lightly in 2 tablespoons fat. Cut remaining pot-au-feu vegetables into 1-inch dice; dust with 2 tablespoons flour and add to the skillet. Pour in the remaining broth (this should be 2 cups). Add 1 cup mashed canned tomatoes. Bring to a slow boil. Edge with small dumplings made by the recipe on a package of biscuit mix. Cover. Simmer 20 minutes. Uncover. Strew minced *fresh* parsley over the meat. Dust the dumplings with paprika.

RAGOÛT

4 medium-sized white
potatoes, peeled and sliced
5 medium-sized onions,
peeled and sliced
6 medium-sized carrots, peeled
and sliced
2½ teaspoons salt
½ teaspoon pepper
½ teaspoon thyme

4 slices bacon, cut in short
strips
1½ pounds chuck steak,
thin-sliced, cut in 2-inch
squares
1 cup drained canned
tomatoes
½ cup dry wine
Boiled barley

Season vegetables. Put bacon in casserole. Arrange meat, vegetables and tomatoes in layers. Cover closely. Bake at 350° almost 2 hours; ½ hour before ragoût is done, add wine. Cover; finish baking. Turn the ragoût onto a platter; edge with barley shaped into balls.

GREEK STEW

2 pounds fillet of beef, cut in
1-inch cubes
4 tablespoons each butter and
cooking oil
3 medium onions, peeled and
sliced
⅔ cup burgundy wine or
undiluted canned beef broth

1 (1-inch) stick cinnamon
6 whole cloves
3 sections garlic, peeled and
crushed
1 stick celery
½ cup seasoned tomato sauce

Sauté beef until lightly browned in 2 tablespoons each butter and oil. Sauté onions separately in remaining butter and oil. Combine beef and onions; add wine or beef broth, spices, garlic and celery. Simmer 5 minutes; add tomato sauce; cover and simmer 20 minutes. If too dry, stir in ¼ cup water. Remove cinnamon stick and serve.

BEEF STEW MAINE WOODS

2 pounds lean stewing beef
2 ounces salt pork
1½ tablespoons brown sugar
2 teaspoons salt
¼ teaspoon pepper
8 cups boiling water

8 small carrots, scraped and
  halved
6 medium-sized onions, peeled
2 cups coarse-diced celery
6 white potatoes, peeled and
  diced

Cut beef in 1-inch dice and salt pork in cubelets. Put pork in heavy 3-quart saucepan; fry until fat runs freely. Into meat, stir brown sugar mixed with salt and pepper. Add meat to salt pork and fat and slowly caramelize and brown it. Add boiling water; cover; simmer 2 hours. At end of 1 hour, add carrots, onions and celery. The last 30 minutes add potatoes.

BEEF AND MUSHROOM STEW, FRENCH STYLE

3 pounds boneless chuck, cut
  into 2-inch cubes
2½ cups beef stock or
  consommé, homemade or
  canned (if desired substitute
  ½ cup red wine)
¼ cup peeled chopped onion
2 tablespoons chopped parsley
2 tablespoons olive or salad oil
½ teaspoon salt
¼ teaspoon ground thyme
¼ teaspoon ground black
  pepper

1 bay leaf, crumbled
2 medium-sized carrots, peeled
  and shredded
½ cup flour
¼ pound diced salt pork
¼ cup butter or margarine
½ pound fresh or 1 (6- to
  8-ounce) can sliced
  mushrooms
8 small whole onions, peeled

Place meat in a Dutch oven or large saucepan with beef stock, onion, parsley, olive oil, salt, thyme, black pepper and bay leaf, making a marinade. Stir in carrots. Refrigerate 12 hours to marinate. Remove meat and drain reserving marinade. Coat meat with flour; set aside. In large skillet, fry salt pork to render (cook out) fat; add butter. Stir in meat and brown it on all sides.

Bring reserved marinade to boiling point; add browned meat. Cover and simmer 2 hours, or until meat is tender. Meanwhile, rinse, pat dry and slice fresh mushrooms, or drain canned mushrooms. Add (with liquid) to stew with whole onions. Cover and simmer 45 minutes more, or until onions are fork-tender. Serve hot. Serves 8.

SPANISH BEEF STEW

1 section garlic, peeled	1 teaspoon salt
¾ cup peeled minced onion	⅛ teaspoon pepper
1 green pepper, cored and minced	1 teaspoon sugar
¼ cup butter or margarine	1½ quarts water
1½ pounds round of beef, diced	1 (No. 3) can tomatoes
1½ teaspoons powdered meat tenderizer	½ cup rice
	½ cup dry red wine
	¼ cup pitted olives, halved
	Hot crisp toast or seed rolls

Crush garlic. Add to onion and green pepper, and sauté until softened in butter. Add beef and mix in meat tenderizer; slightly brown meat. Transfer all to large kettle. Then add salt, pepper, sugar, water and tomatoes; cover, bring to boiling point; boil 10 minutes, then simmer over low heat about 1¾ hours, or until meat is almost fork-tender. Stir in rice; cover and simmer 30 minutes longer. Add wine and olives; serve in soup plates with plenty of toast or seed rolls.

BEEF STROGANOFF

1½ pounds lean beef (no fat)	1 tablespoon flour
2 tablespoons butter or margarine	½ pint sour cream
½ pound or 1 (4-ounce) can mushrooms	Salt
1 tablespoon butter	Paprika
	Rice

Any cut of beef can be used. The better the beef, the better the Stroganoff. Top round steak is very good. Cut the beef across the grain and then into little pieces, about 1 inch long and half the width of a pencil. Place 2 tablespoons of butter or margarine, into a fry pan; heat and add the beef. Cook slowly with pan covered for 15 minutes, turning the meat occasionally. Then add mushrooms which have been cut into small pieces, and cook 10 minutes longer. Add additional butter if the pan becomes dry.

When mushrooms and meat are cooked, place them in top of double boiler. In a fry pan, add 1 tablespoon of butter to flour and stir in sour cream. Pour this sauce into beef and mushrooms in double boiler and cook 5 to 10 minutes. Season to taste. Serve with rice.

SUKIYAKI

An American favorite originating in Japan, where sukiyaki is classed as a "saucepan" food. It is cooked entirely in clear broth in a large shallow saucepan over charcoal (you can use a deep electric skillet), then placed in the center of a table large enough to seat six guests, yet narrow enough for them to reach the saucepan or skillet easily for individual cooking.

Ingredients Per Person:

2 ounces thin-sliced raw fillet
  of beef
⅓ cup sliced leeks or scallions
½ cup fine-shredded Chinese
  cabbage
½ cup thin-sliced medium-
  sized mushrooms

½ cup thin-sliced celery
1 heaping tablespoon
  vermicelli in 1-inch lengths
8 sprigs water cress or spinach
  or other greens

Broth: A combination of canned condensed beef broth with half the quantity of water and single-strength chicken broth, combined, about 2 quarts.

Meat and Other Ingredients: Prepare in advance and arrange in layers on plates in portions.

At-Table Cooking: Bring broth to rapid boil. Add vermicelli at one side. Using long-handled kitchen fork, each person adds his beef and vegetables, and simmer-boils them about 3 minutes. A second person follows at once.

If saucepan or skillet is large enough, up to 4 persons can cook at one time. Stir and lift out the foods with chopsticks or tongs. So good and so much fun!

Veal

Wonderful recipes for veal dishes, which had their beginnings in France, Germany, Switzerland or Italy, have been welcomed in all fifty United States. The white firm meat is delicious and may be broiled, simmered, roasted, stewed or sautéed and, because it is young, immature meat, it lends itself to a variety of interesting seasonings.

All recipes are for six servings unless otherwise stated.

BLANQUETTE OF VEAL

A classic French favorite, this choice dish has been gratefully adopted by Americans.

3 pounds shoulder or breast of veal	3 tablespoons butter
1 teaspoon seasoned salt	3 tablespoons flour
4½ cups boiling water	1 egg yolk
1 carrot, peeled and sliced	1⅔ cups sour cream
½ onion, peeled and sliced	¾ tablespoon lemon juice
2 whole cloves	⅛ teaspoon nutmeg
2 sprigs parsley	1 tablespoon minced parsley
½ bay leaf	White potatoes

Cut veal into 18 small portions. Place in heavy saucepan; add salt and boiling water. Bring to boiling point; add carrot, onion, cloves, parsley sprigs and bay leaf. Cover; simmer until veal is tender, about 1½ hours. Remove meat; strain off broth. There should be 1½ cups. Melt butter in saucepan; stir in flour and, when smooth, slowly stir in broth drained from veal. Stir-cook until boiling. Beat egg yolk with fork; to it add sour cream. Stir into boiling sauce. Cook, stirring, 1 minute. Add lemon juice, nutmeg and minced parsley. Place hot veal in center of heated large platter; pour sauce over all. Arrange parslied white potatoes at each end.

BRAISED VEAL CHOPS

2 tablespoons butter or bacon
   fat
¼ cup minced onion
4 generous-sized veal chops
Salt
Pepper

2 tablespoons flour
1 teaspoon beef extract
Boiling water (part white wine
   if desired)
1 cup sour cream

In heavy fry pan, melt the butter; add the onion and cook till softened. Dust the chops with salt, pepper and flour; brown in the fat. Add enough beef extract to enough boiling water to cover the bottom of the pan to the depth of about ¼ inch; cover and simmer 30 minutes. Remove chops; keep warm. Add sour cream to pan, stir over low heat till hot. Spoon sauce over chops. Serves 4.

VEAL CHOPS CAPRICE

1 teaspoon paprika
¼ teaspoon salt
1 tablespoon flour
4 large loin veal chops, well
   trimmed

2 tablespoons olive oil
4 slices natural Gruyère or
   Swiss Emmentaler cheese

Combine paprika, salt and flour, and work into the chops. Sauté chops in olive oil until well browned on each side. Lay them in a large shallow casserole with a slice of cheese over each; place in broiler oven 4 inches from heat until cheese is melted and lightly browned. Serves 4.

VEAL CHOPS CORDON BLEU

6 large thick veal chops
Seasoned salt
6 (2-inch) squares thin-sliced
   Swiss cheese
6 small thin slices prosciutto
   or smoked ham

2 tablespoons vegetable oil
1 tablespoon flour
½ teaspoon seasoned salt
2 tablespoons canned bouillon
Sprigs of parsley

Order chops split, making deep pockets. Dust inside with sea-soned salt. In each pocket tuck 1 slice each cheese and ham. Press edges together. Brush with vegetable oil. Dust with the flour and additional seasoned salt. Place chops ½ inch apart in oiled baking pan. Add bouillon. Bake 40 to 45 minutes in mod-erate (350°) oven. Turn once. If necessary to brown both sides more, broil 1 to 2 minutes. Garnish with parsley.

VEAL CHOPS SPANISH

6 thick veal chops (any cut)	¼ cup minced parsley
1½ teaspoons salt	¾ teaspoon cornstarch
1 teaspoon paprika	1 cup dry white wine or
3 tablespoons olive oil	chicken bouillon
¼ cup minced onion	2 tablespoons sour cream
2 sections garlic, peeled and crushed	

Dust chops with salt and paprika; brown over moderate heat in oil. Transfer to casserole. Add onion, garlic and parsley to oil; cook until pale golden. Spoon over veal chops; dust with corn-starch. Add wine or chicken bouillon; cover. Bake 1½ hours in moderate (350°) oven. Remove from oven; stir in sour cream; do not cook further.

VEAL CUBES-ON-NOODLES

1½ pounds lean veal (any cut)	1½ quarts boiling water
1½ teaspoons meat tenderizer	2 teaspoons seasoned salt
3 tablespoons flour	¼ teaspoon pepper
¾ teaspoon sugar	2 teaspoons chicken bouillon powder
3 tablespoons butter or margarine	Grated rind of ½ small lemon
1 large mild onion, peeled and sliced	1 (8-ounce) package thin egg noodles cooked by package directions

Cut veal in ½-inch cubes. Mix meat tenderizer and flour; coat cubes with this. In 2-quart heavy saucepan, melt sugar and butter together. Add onion; slow-fry until color turns. Add veal cubes and continue to slow-fry, turning often until lightly browned all over. Add water, seasoned salt, pepper, bouillon powder and lemon rind. Cover. Simmer 1½ hours, or until fork-tender; stir occasionally. Serve in border of buttered thin egg noodles.

VEAL BIRDS

2 pounds lean veal cutlets, ¼ to ⅓ inch thick
¼ cup flour
1 small onion, finely chopped
2 tablespoons butter
¾ cup bread crumbs
¾ cup chopped celery
1 cup chopped veal trimmings and sausage meat, equal portions

1 teaspoon poultry seasoning
¼ cup stock or water
1 egg, beaten
3 tablespoons butter
½ cup cream
½ cup stock
Salt and pepper

Cut veal into 4-inch squares, then pound with wooden mallet. Dredge one side with flour. Lightly brown the chopped onion in 2 tablespoons butter and remove from the stove. Add bread crumbs, celery, chopped veal and sausage, poultry seasoning and stock or water, and the beaten egg. Mix all together well and let stand 10 minutes. Divide stuffing so each piece of veal will have a share. Wrap each piece around its portion of stuffing, keeping the dredged side outside. Fasten each roll with small skewers, toothpicks or tie with string. Brown each bird well in the additional 3 tablespoons of butter, turning so each side is browned. Add the cream and the stock. Cover tightly and let simmer for approximately 40 minutes. If desired, gravy can be thickened with additional flour or by adding more cream. Season to taste with salt and pepper.

VEAL BOLOGNESE

2 pounds veal cutlets, sliced thin
1 teaspoon seasoned salt
1 egg, lightly beaten
1 cup seasoned bread crumbs
2 tablespoons olive oil
2 tablespoons butter
½ pound mozzarella cheese
1 cup tomato sauce
12 slices fresh orange

Pound cutlets until very thin. Dust with seasoned salt. Brush with egg; cover with crumbs. Let stand 10 minutes to firm coating. Pan-fry until golden in olive oil and butter. Top with mozzarella cheese. Dot each cutlet with 1½ teaspoons tomato sauce; cap with slice of orange. Broil until lightly browned, about 2 minutes.

VEAL CUTLETS PARMIGIANA

6 medium-sized veal cutlets (about 2 pounds), cut ⅜ inch thick
1 cup sifted flour
2 eggs, well beaten
1 teaspoon seasoned salt
2 cups fine dry bread crumbs
¾ cup olive or salad oil or use equal parts each
¼ pound thin-sliced Parmesan cheese
Tomato sauce (homemade or canned)

Dust veal cutlets with flour. Brush all over with eggs, beaten with seasoned salt; then dust with bread crumbs, patting them over and in. Set aside at least 10 minutes to "set" coating. Heat oil in good-sized fry pan until cubelet of bread fries golden in 1 minute. Fry cutlets over medium heat until golden brown. Transfer to broiler pan or to shallow heat-resistant casserole that can go-to-table. The cutlets should not touch each other. Top cutlets with sliced cheese. Place about 4 inches from source of heat for 2 minutes, or until cheese melts. Pass hot well-seasoned tomato sauce.

VEAL ROLLS WITH SOUR CREAM

2 pounds veal cutlets, sliced thin	⅓ teaspoon salt
1 section garlic, peeled	Pepper to taste
1¼ cups soft white bread crumbs	1 onion, peeled and minced
1 tablespoon minced parsley	3 tablespoons flour
6 ripe olives, pitted and chopped	3 tablespoons olive or salad oil
	1 cup water
	1 cup thick sour cream

Pound veal cutlets until very thin, and cut in 4-inch squares; rub them over with the cut side of a section of garlic; next make a stuffing by mixing crumbs, parsley, ripe olives, salt, pepper and minced onion, and moisten slightly with water. Place 1 tablespoon of stuffing on each cutlet. Roll up and fasten together with wooden toothpicks; roll in flour and brown in oil. Transfer to casserole; add water, cover and bake 1 hour, or until tender, in a moderate (350°) oven. Stir in sour cream 10 minutes before veal is done.

VEAL SAUSAGE BIRDS

2 pounds veal cutlets, sliced thin	¼ teaspoon vinegar
6 small smoked pork sausages	1 tablespoon minced parsley
1 good-sized onion, peeled and sliced	½ teaspoon crushed dried tarragon
3 tablespoons butter	¼ teaspoon powdered thyme
1½ teaspoons salt	1½ cups hot water
¼ teaspoon pepper	¼ cup dry red wine

Cut the veal into six servings. Pound until thin. Roll around the pork sausages; fasten with picks. Brown all over with the onion in the butter in a good-sized fry pan. Add the remaining ingredients; cover. Simmer 2 to 2½ hours, or until fork-tender.

VEAL SCALLOPINI

2 pounds tender veal, sliced
thin
1 teaspoon salt
¼ teaspoon pepper
½ teaspoon garlic powder

½ cup butter
1 (6-ounce) can mushrooms
⅓ teaspoon beef extract
⅓ cup Marsala wine or dry
vermouth or beef broth

Pound veal slices with wooden mallet or edge of saucer until thin, flat and round. Trim if necessary for symmetrical shape. Mix together and rub in seasonings. Melt butter in large fry pan. Add veal. Drain mushrooms and add; sauté 5 minutes; add liquid from mushrooms, beef extract and wine or broth. Cover. Simmer 7 minutes, or until fork-tender. Use liquid as sauce. To thicken, boil rapidly 1 minute after removing veal.

VEAL SAUTÉ WALDORF

1½ tablespoons flour
1 teaspoon salt
¼ teaspoon pepper
⅓ teaspoon ground marjoram
2 pounds veal cutlet, cut in 6
portions
½ cup butter
Juice of 1 large lemon

2 ripe medium-sized avocados,
cubed
½ cup California dry sherry
or Madeira wine
½ pound vermicelli or thin
spaghetti (cooked by
package directions)

Mix first four ingredients. Rub all over veal portions. Melt butter in 10-inch fry pan. Fry veal in it until done, about 4 minutes, or until fork-tender. Remove veal and keep hot. Add lemon juice to pan drippings. Heat; add avocado cubes (reserve a few for garnish). Cover; steam 3 minutes. Stir with fork for even cooking. Add wine and simmer 3 minutes more. Serve veal slices overlapping on a bed of vermicelli. Pour over the sauce. Garnish with reserved avocado cubes.

Note: If desired, the wine may be omitted and ½ cup undiluted canned beef broth used instead.

VEAL FRICANDELLES

1 cup enriched bread crumbs	¼ teaspoon thyme
½ cup milk	¼ cup minced parsley
1 pound chopped raw veal	Flour as needed
1 can deviled ham	Bacon fat
1 teaspoon onion juice	Water or beef or chicken stock
1 teaspoon salt	Spaghetti or spinach, cooked
¼ teaspoon pepper	

Simmer crumbs and milk 3 minutes. Combine with veal, ham, onion juice, salt, pepper, thyme and parsley. Form into egg-shaped cakes. Roll in flour. Brown in bacon fat. Pour in water or stock to half cover. Simmer 1 hour. Serve on spaghetti or spinach. Serves 4.

ROAST LEG OF VEAL GRUYÈRE

½ cup minced, peeled onion	Leg of veal, boned and rolled
2 tablespoons butter	(about 5 pounds)
2 teaspoons salt	½ cup grated Gruyère cheese
¼ teaspoon pepper	½ cup dry bread crumbs
¼ teaspoon powdered thyme	¼ cup melted butter or
1 cup dry white wine	margarine
1 cup beef bouillon	3 tablespoons bouillon

Sauté the onion in 2 tablespoons butter until yellowed. Add salt, pepper, thyme, wine and bouillon; bring to rapid boil. Drain and pour liquid over veal. Cover. Marinate at least 2 hours. Drain and save any remaining marinade. Place veal on rack in roasting pan. Insert meat thermometer in thickest part. Pour in marinade; baste veal with it 3 times while roasting. Allow altogether 20 minutes to the pound in moderate (350°) oven, or until the meat thermometer registers 175°. Thirty minutes before completion, remove from the oven. Spread veal evenly with mixture of cheese and crumbs moistened with additional melted butter. Return to oven.

When done, turn off the oven heat; add 3 tablespoons additional bouillon to pan. Let veal stand 15 minutes in oven to set. Serve with pan gravy.

MINCED VEAL À LA ZURICH

1½ pounds tender veal
1½ teaspoons salt
1½ teaspoons paprika
1½ teaspoons flour
½ cup butter
2 teaspoons minced onion or
   scallions

⅓ cup dry white wine
¾ cup brown sauce
  (homemade or canned)
1 tablespoon butter

Cut veal into small narrow strips about 2 inches long. Add seasonings and flour; toss with fork. Stir-fry rapidly 2 minutes in half the butter. Add ¼ cup remaining butter and onion or scallions; sauté until light brown. Stir in wine. Simmer 5 minutes, or until half evaporated. Stir in brown sauce and additional butter.

OSSO BUCO (Braised Veal Shanks)

2 tablespoons butter or
   margarine
2 tablespoons olive oil
3 veal shanks, split
1 teaspoon salt
¼ teaspoon pepper
½ cup peeled diced carrot
½ cup diced celery
¼ cup peeled chopped onion
¼ section garlic, peeled and
   crushed

2 cups boiling water
4 tablespoons tomato paste
1 teaspoon beef bouillon
  powder
6 small carrots, peeled and
  halved
6 small onions, peeled and
  halved
1 pound thin noodles, cooked
Butter
Minced parsley

In large heavy skillet or chicken fryer, heat butter and oil. Meantime rub veal all over with salt and pepper. Brown on both sides in heated oil. Add diced carrot, celery, onion and garlic. Continue sautéing until vegetables are limp. Add water, tomato paste and bouillon powder. Cover; simmer 30 minutes. Add carrots and onions. Continue to simmer covered about 30 minutes longer, or until both vegetables and veal are fork-tender. Serve with noodles cooked by package directions, seasoned with butter and minced parsley.

VEAL STEW

1 ounce European dried
    mushrooms
½ cup hot water
Flour to coat
2½ pounds boneless stewing
    veal cut in 1-inch cubes
3 tablespoons butter or
    margarine

2 large onions, chopped
1 section garlic, crushed
2 cups water
2 chicken bouillon cubes
½ teaspoon salt
Generous sprinkling pepper
2 tablespoons minced parsley

Put mushrooms to soak in ½ cup hot water. Lightly flour veal and brown in butter over medium heat. Remove. Add onions and garlic and sauté a few minutes. Add water, bouillon cubes and bring to a boil, stirring until cubes dissolve. Add mushroom liquid, salt, pepper and meat. Chop mushrooms and add together with parsley. Cover, lower heat and simmer 2 to 2½ hours, or until meat is fork-tender. Adjust seasoning as desired.

WIENER (VEAL) SCHNITZEL

2 pounds leg of veal, sliced ¼
    inch thick
1½ teaspoons salt
⅓ teaspoon pepper
¼ cup flour
¼ cup milk
1 egg, beaten
1½ cups fine dried seasoned
    bread crumbs

2 tablespoons butter or
    margarine
2 tablespoons cooking oil
6 thin slices lemon
6 small sardine fillets or
    anchovy fillets (optional)
6 thin slices lemon
Parsley

Cut veal into 6 pieces suited to individual service. Sift together salt, pepper and flour. Dust all over the slices of veal. Add milk to beaten egg, and dip in veal slices; then cover all over with a coating of crumbs. Slow-fry until tender and golden brown in butter and oil. Top each lemon slice with sardine or anchovy fillet. Place atop each sautéed "schnitzel." Use additional lemon slices with parsley as platter garnish.

Lamb

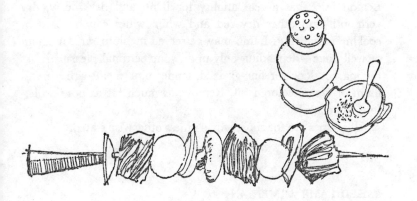

Lamb that has been carefully seasoned and cooked to bring out the real flavor can't be surpassed. Especially compatible spices and herbs are thyme, marjoram, mint, bay leaf and cumin. Lemon juice has a real affinity for lamb and dry sherry, dry vermouth and other dry red and white wines can be used in cooking or saucing. Lamb may be served medium rare, medium or well done—depending only upon your personal pleasure! (At the market, look for fine-grained, tender pink meat with a minimum of cream-colored fat. Remove as much fat as possible before you cook.)

All recipes are for six servings unless otherwise stated.

BAKED LAMB ARMENIAN

3 pounds breast of lamb, cut in pieces for serving
3 tablespoons lemon juice
⅞ cup apple juice
1 medium-sized onion, peeled and minced
1 section garlic, peeled
1 green pepper, seeded and minced
1 teaspoon salt
½ teaspoon coarse black pepper
½ teaspoon oregano

Place lamb in single layer in shallow baking pan. Pour lemon and apple juice over meat; let stand 1 hour at room temperature; turn pieces 3 times. Drain off and reserve liquid. Place lamb fat side down in pan. Bake 1 hour in moderate (375°) oven. Remove from oven and pour off all fat from pan. Turn lamb fat side up. Add remaining ingredients to reserved liquid; pour over meat. Return to oven and continue baking for 30 minutes, or until lamb is tender and browned; baste 3 times with mixture in pan.

BRAISED LAMB RIBLETS

2 pounds lamb riblets
1 tablespoon melted butter or
    margarine
½ cup sliced celery
2 large onions, peeled and
    sliced

2 cups vegetable juice cocktail
2 tablespoons flour
1 tablespoon vinegar
Salt and onion salt to taste
Pepper to taste

Sauté lamb riblets in butter in large fry pan until well browned on all sides; drain off drippings. Add celery, onions and 1¾ cups of vegetable juice cocktail; cover and simmer over low heat 1 hour, or until lamb is fork-tender. Stir together flour and remaining vegetable juice cocktail. Gradually add flour mixture to lamb; cook over low heat, stirring constantly, until thickened. Add vinegar, taste, mix in salt, onion salt and pepper as needed. Serves 4 to 6.

Accompany with green beans, whipped potatoes and a crispy salad of Chinese cabbage.

AFRICAN BREDE

5 medium-sized onions, peeled
3 pounds boneless lamb stew
    meat, cut in cubes
3 tablespoons olive or cooking
    oil
4 teaspoons salt
3 cups hot water
2½ tablespoons flour
⅓ cup cold water

2 (9-ounce) packages frozen
    peas
1 (1-pound) package or 2
    (9-ounce) packages frozen
    french fries
⅓ cup thin-sliced chili peppers
Black pepper to taste
1 teaspoon thyme
½ teaspoon ground cumin

Chop 1 onion. Brown lamb pieces in oil in covered heavy kettle; stir as needed to brown meat evenly. Add onion, 2 teaspoons salt and hot water. Cover; bake or simmer 1½ hours, or until meat is tender. Measure flour into cup; add cold water, all at once, and stir until smooth. Add to stew; stir until slightly thickened.

Cut remaining onions into eighths. Add to stew. Cover and bake or simmer 15 minutes, or until onions are crisp-tender. Fold in peas, frozen french fries and peppers. Dust over remaining salt, pepper and spices. Cover; bake or boil 15 minutes, or until vegetables are thoroughly heated.

CASSOULET

1 (1-pound) package navy beans	1 bay leaf
2½ quarts water	6 Italian sausages
¼ pound diced salt pork	1½ pounds shoulder of lamb
1½ teaspoons salt	1 pound shoulder of pork
6 onions, chopped	½ teaspoon pepper
2 tablespoons chopped parsley	2 tablespoons shortening
½ teaspoon thyme	1 clove garlic, crushed
	1 (8-ounce) can tomato sauce

Soak navy beans overnight in 1 quart water, in large heavy kettle. Add 1½ quarts water, salt pork, ½ teaspoon of the salt, 1 onion, herbs and bay leaf. Cook 20 minutes. Pierce and brown Italian sausages. Add to beans. Cook slowly until beans are tender. Bone and cut meat into bite-sized pieces. Season with remaining 1 teaspoon salt and the pepper, and brown in shortening in heavy saucepan along with 5 onions. Pour off fat, add bones, garlic and tomato sauce. Cover and bake 1½ hours in 325° oven.

Remove bones from meat mixture. Drain liquid from beans and save. Arrange beans and meat in alternate layers in a 4-quart casserole. Pour over this the gravy from meat mixed with bean liquid. Put back in 325° oven, and bake another hour. Serve in the casserole. Serves 6 to 8.

LAMB CREOLE

5½ pounds lamb shoulder and neck
1 quart water
3 teaspoons salt
8 whole black peppers
¼ teaspoon fresh ground pepper
1 teaspoon paprika
Flour to dredge
3 tablespoons salad oil
2 cloves garlic, crushed
1 cup chopped onion
½ pound mushrooms, sliced
1 cup chopped sweet peppers (half red, half green if available)
1 (8-ounce) can tomato sauce
2 tablespoons chopped parsley
⅛ teaspoon thyme
¼ cup Marsala
1 tablespoon cornstarch

Have butcher cut lamb into ¼-inch thick chops and slice thin cutlets from neck. Remove fat and bones from chops. Put remainder of the neck and bones in a pot with the water; add 1 teaspoon of the salt and whole black peppers; boil until tender. Save any bits of meat that can be removed from bones. Strain broth and skim fat from top. Sprinkle 2 remaining teaspoons salt, pepper, paprika over meat, then coat with flour. Brown in 2 tablespoons of the salad oil in fry pan. Transfer to a 3-quart casserole. Add remaining salad oil to fry pan and sauté garlic, onion, mushrooms and sweet peppers. Add 3 cups of lamb broth, tomato sauce, parsley, thyme and Marsala. Add small pieces of meat that have been cut from the bones. Bring mixture to a boil. Pour over lamb in casserole. Salt to taste. Cover and bake in 350° oven for about 1 hour. Thicken with cornstarch. Serves 8 to 10.

IRISH LAMB STEW

3 to 4 pounds shoulder of lamb
4 cups water (about)
2 teaspoons salt
½ teaspoon pepper
6 large carrots, peeled and cut into eighths
6 small onions, peeled
2 pounds potatoes, peeled and quartered
Parsley (optional)

Have the meat cut into medium-sized pieces, cover with the cold water and bring slowly to boiling point. Skim, and simmer for 1½ hours. Add the salt, pepper, carrots, onions and potatoes, and continue to simmer until the potatoes and the meat are tender—about ½ hour longer. Arrange the meat in the center of the platter, the potatoes around it, and garnish with the carrots and onions. A little chopped parsley may be sprinkled over the top if desired.

LAMB CURRY WITH RAISINS

1 tablespoon curry powder
1 tablespoon butter or margarine at room temperature
1 medium-sized onion, peeled and thin-sliced
2 medium-sized stalks celery, sliced crosswise ¼ inch thick
1½ pounds boneless lean lamb, cut in 1-inch cubes

1 (14-ounce) can chicken broth or 1¾ cups water and 2 teaspoons chicken broth powder
½ teaspoon garlic salt
1½ tablespoons cornstarch
2 tablespoons water
½ cup dark seedless raisins
Rice à la Middle East (see Index)

Stir curry powder, butter, onion and celery together in heavy 2-quart saucepan. Cover; stir-cook over moderate heat 3 minutes, or until vegetables are wilted. Add lamb, broth and garlic salt. Tight-cover; simmer 1 to 1½ hours, or until lamb is tender. Stir cornstarch with water; stir in raisins. Stir into cooking lamb. Simmer-boil 15 minutes longer. Serve hot with Rice à la Middle East.

Note: For extra tenderness, dust lamb after cubing with 1½ teaspoons powdered meat tenderizer.

LAMB PILAFF CASSEROLE

3 pounds boned lamb shoulder
2 onions, peeled and
 fine-chopped
3 (6-ounce) cans tomato paste
3¼ cups hot water
1 teaspoon mint flakes

2 teaspoons salt
¼ teaspoon pepper
¼ teaspoon powdered bay
 leaf
2 cups uncooked rice

Remove excess fat from lamb. Cut meat into bite-sized pieces. Place in heavy saucepan. Slow-fry until fat remaining on lamb begins to melt. Add onions; slow-fry until turning color. Mix together lamb, onions, tomato paste, water, mint and seasonings. Transfer to a 4-quart casserole. With big fork stir in uncooked rice. Bring to rapid boil. Cover. Bake 1 hour in moderate (350°) oven, or until rice is tender and absorbs nearly all the liquid. Uncover to brown.

LAMB-VEGETABLE RAGOUT

2½ pounds stewing lamb
3 large tomatoes, peeled and
 quartered
10 small onions, peeled
1 garlic clove, peeled and
 crushed
1 lemon
⅓ cup olive oil

1½ cups canned beef broth
2 bay leaves
1 sprig thyme
1½ teaspoons each salt and
 pepper
1 (1-pound 2-ounce) can ceci
 beans (chick-peas)

Cut meat into 2-inch cubes. Prepare tomatoes, onions and garlic. Cut 4 ¼-inch strips peel from lemon. Heat oil in stew pan. When very hot, put in meat and onions; brown lightly on all sides. Heat and pour in beef broth; simmer 5 minutes. Add tomatoes, garlic clove, bay leaves and thyme, strips of lemon peel, salt and pepper. Cook uncovered 10 minutes; then cover; simmer over a low flame for 45 to 50 minutes, or until meat is nearly done. Twenty minutes before serving, drain ceci beans and stir in. Cover and finish cooking. Serve piping hot.

SHEPHERD'S PIE

1½ pounds lean shoulder of
 lamb, cubed
Flour
1 teaspoon salt
¼ teaspoon pepper
2 tablespoons shortening
2 onions, peeled and chopped
½ clove garlic, crushed
Marjoram

Thyme
2 potatoes, peeled and diced
2 carrots, peeled and thinly
 sliced
6 small onions, peeled
1 cup peas
3 or 4 stalks celery, diced
Mashed potatoes

Dredge lamb with flour seasoned with salt and pepper. Brown in shortening with chopped onions, garlic and herbs. Add water to cover and simmer until nearly tender. Add vegetables, except mashed potatoes, and cook until tender, about 20 minutes. Skim off fat. Thicken juices with a thin flour and water paste. Pour into 2-quart casserole. Frill with mashed potatoes. Bake in hot (450°) oven until brown. Serves 4.

SHISH KEBOB

Part I:

2 pounds boned tender leg of
 lamb
1 cup dry red wine
Juice of 2 lemons
¼ cup olive oil
2 medium-sized onions, peeled
 and minced

1 raw carrot, peeled and sliced
1 teaspoon crushed cardamom
 seed
1 section garlic, peeled
1½ teaspoons salt
¼ teaspoon pepper
1 bay leaf

Cut lamb into 1½-inch cubes. Mix together all remaining ingredients making marinade. Add lamb; cover; refrigerate 4 hours.

Part II:

Meantime, make ready the following items:

4 medium-sized tomatoes, quartered	6 mushroom caps
16 slices medium-sized peeled onion	4 small lamb kidneys
16 2-inch squares green pepper	¼ pound butter for basting
	1 teaspoon salt
	Wild and white rice, cooked

Remove meat from marinade; scrape off any spice or vegetable pieces, and run lamb onto 4 long skewers, alternating meat with similarly sized pieces of tomato, onion, green pepper, mushroom caps and squares of lamb kidney. Melt butter for basting. Broil 15 to 20 minutes in hot broiler; turn often to brown all sides, basting with melted butter. Dust over 1 teaspoon salt. Serve very hot on a bed of fluffy wild and white rice mixture. Serves 4.

BAKED LAMB OR VEAL CHOPS

6 shoulder lamb or veal chops, ¾ inch thick	¼ teaspoon seasoned salt
1 teaspoon powdered meat tenderizer, unseasoned	Broiled Tomato Halves (see Index)
¼ teaspoon onion powder (optional)	

Rub chops with meat tenderizer, onion powder and seasoned salt. Brown on both sides in chops' own fat in large fry pan that can go into oven. When lightly browned, bake at 350° to 375° 25 to 30 minutes, or until fork-tender. Turn once. Serve with Broiled Tomato Halves.

BARBECUED LAMB CHOPS

¼ cup cider vinegar	¼ teaspoon pepper
1 cup chili sauce	1 teaspoon oregano
2 tablespoons sugar	6 loin lamb chops (or any cut)
1 teaspoon salt	

Combine and mix first 6 ingredients in a rather low bowl. Add lamb chops; cover; let stand to marinate (season) 1 hour. Drain chops but save marinade. Broil 5 minutes on each side, brushing often with marinade until done. Heat remainder for sauce.

LAMB CHOPS JARDINIÈRE

3 sweet potatoes, boiled
1 pound fresh or 2 (10-ounce) packages frozen whole green beans, cooked
6 large cauliflowerettes, cooked
⅓ cup vegetable oil
Salt and pepper to taste
6 good-sized lamb chops, cut 1 inch thick

1 teaspoon seasoned salt
1 teaspoon fine-crushed mint flakes
Seasoned crumbs
Parsley
Mint Sauce Piquant (see Index)

Cook all the vegetables in advance. Peel and slice the sweet potatoes lengthwise. Brush the potatoes and vegetables with the oil. Dust with the salt and pepper. Remove excess fat from the chops and rub in the seasoned salt and mint flakes. Brown lightly in a little oil. Cover with foil; bake 10 minutes at 350°. Transfer to a big heatproof platter. Broil the chops 5 minutes.

Surround with sections of sweet potatoes, beans and cauliflowerettes; dust the latter with seasoned crumbs. Broil 3 minutes to lightly brown the vegetables. Garnish with the parsley. Pass Mint Sauce Piquant.

LEMON LAMB CHOPS

6 thick lamb chops
1 teaspoon salt
¼ teaspoon pepper

6 slices lemon
6 slices onion
Brown sugar

Broil chops about 7 minutes on one side. Season with salt and pepper and turn over. Season the uncooked side. Place a slice of lemon and a slice of onion on each chop. Sprinkle with brown sugar. Broil until brown. Salt and pepper lightly.

LAMB CHOPS À L'ORANGE

6 lamp chops cut ½ inch
  thick (any cut)
4 tablespoon soy sauce
1½ teaspoons ground ginger
½ teaspoon garlic salt
¼ teaspoon pepper
½ teaspoon sugar
½ cup orange juice
2 oranges cut into 6
  lengthwise wedges
Orange Sauce
4 cups flaky hot rice

Remove excess fat from chops. Brown chops lightly on both sides in their own remaining fat. Arrange in single layer in oblong baking dish. Combine soy sauce, ginger, seasonings, sugar and orange juice. Spoon over chops. Marinate in refrigerator 2 hours or more, turn over once. Cover; bake 1 hour, or until fork-tender, in moderate (350°) oven. About 10 minutes before completing, add orange wedges and replace cover. To serve garnish with orange slices; pour over Orange Sauce. Accompany with flaky rice.

Orange Sauce: Pour pan drippings from chops into bowl and skim or siphon off fat from surface of drippings with meat baster. Then measure drippings. Add ¼ teaspoon grated orange rind, and water or bouillon to make 1½ cups. Bring to boiling point. Mix 1 tablespoon cornstarch smooth with 1 tablespoon cold water. Gradually stir into drippings; boil 2 minutes, or until thickened. Season to taste with salt and pepper.

MIXED GRILL

6 lamb chops
6 slices tomato, ½ inch thick
6 teaspoons bread crumbs
3 teaspoons butter
2 teaspoons salt
½ teaspoon pepper
6 pork sausages or slices of
  bacon
6 large mushroom caps
6 lamb kidneys or small pieces
  of calf's liver or chicken liver
Flour

Broil chops for about 7 minutes. Turn. Broil 7 minutes more. Add the tomato slices topped with the bread crumbs and butter.

Season with salt and pepper. Sauté the sausages or bacon until nearly cooked. Drain most of fat from pan. Sauté together mushroom caps and kidneys, or liver, which have been lightly dusted with flour, for about 10 minutes. Adjust seasoning.

LAMB DIVAN

2 tablespoons butter
2 tablespoons flour
1 cup milk
1 cup grated processed
  American cheese
½ teaspoon salt
¼ teaspoon celery seed
¼ teaspoon dry mustard
⅛ teaspoon pepper

½ teaspoon Worcestershire
  sauce
1 pound cooked lamb, sliced
1 (10-ounce) package frozen
  broccoli, cooked
1 medium-sized tomato, sliced
¼ cup grated processed
  American cheese

Melt butter in saucepan; blend in flour. Gradually add milk, stirring constantly, and cook until thickened. Add 1 cup grated cheese, salt, celery seed, mustard, pepper and Worcestershire; stir until cheese is melted, making a sauce. Arrange layers of lamb, broccoli and tomato slices in 1½-quart shallow baking dish. Pour sauce over all; bake 15 minutes in moderate (350°) oven. Dust additional grated cheese on top; bake 5 minutes longer.

BAKED LAMB DUMPLINGS

1 recipe Rich American Pie
  Pastry (see Index) or a mix
3 cups chopped cooked lamb
¾ cup thick brown gravy
¼ teaspoon marjoram

⅓ cup fried fine-chopped
  onion (or canned fried
  onion)
Milk

Roll pastry into oblong, scant ¼ inch thick. Cut in 4-inch squares. Combine lamb, gravy, marjoram and onion; place heaping tablespoon on each pastry square. Fold pastry up and over, twisting and pinching it on top. Be sure all seams are pressed together. Brush with milk; bake 25 minutes in hot (425°) oven. Accompany with creamed vegetable.

LAMB-EGGPLANT CASSEROLE

4 cups small cuts cooked lamb or other meat
2 cups canned tomato, mashed
1 cup gravy or beef bouillon
1 onion, peeled and fine-chopped
½ teaspoon oregano or basil

3 tablespoons flour
½ teaspoon sugar
¼ teaspoon pepper
1 eggplant (about 1 pound)
2 tablespoons vegetable oil
1 teaspoon seasoned salt

Mix first eight ingredients. Slow-stir-heat atop range. Meantime, peel eggplant and slice ¼ inch thick. Cut in half-slices. Sauté until softened (about 5 minutes) in oil. Add seasoned salt. Oil 2½-quart casserole. Layer in meat and eggplant, ending with latter. Bake 30 minutes in moderate oven, or until browned.

LEFTOVER CASSEROLE

½ cup rice
2 to 2½ cups diced leftover lamb or other roast meat
2 onions, chopped
½ cup minced celery
1 cup minced green pepper
1 clove garlic, crushed

3 tablespoons shortening
2 cups chopped tomatoes, fresh or canned
½ teaspoon salt
⅛ teaspoon pepper
4 dashes hot pepper sauce
¼ teaspoon mace or nutmeg

Cook rice in boiling salted water. Drain. Mix lamb or other meat with the rice. Gently sauté onions, celery, green pepper and garlic in the shortening. Add tomatoes and mix together with meat and rice. Season with salt and pepper. Add pepper sauce and mace or nutmeg. Pour into a casserole and bake 20 minutes in moderate (350°) oven.

Note: This casserole may be made with other leftover meats—chicken, turkey, beef or veal.

CASEROLE OF MINCED LAMB

4 cups minced cooked lamb
2 cups crushed, thick, canned
  tomatoes
½ cup gravy or ½ cup
  bouillon
1 teaspoon salt
⅛ teaspoon pepper
½ teaspoon dried mint flakes
1 cup peeled sliced onion
2 tablespoons butter or
  margarine

3 tablespoons flour
3 tablespoons cold water
1 teaspoon beef bouillon
  powder
4 cups fluffy, whipped instant
  mashed potatoes
1 tablespoon butter
¼ cup minced parsley
  (optional)

Combine lamb, tomatoes, gravy and seasonings. Sauté onion until almost tender in the 2 tablespoons butter; add to meat. Stir in flour, mixed smooth with cold water. Add bouillon powder. Thoroughly oil 2½-quart low casserole or baking dish. Spoon in lamb-tomato mixture; cover, bake 35 minutes in moderate (350°) oven. Edge generously with whipped mashed potatoes. Dot with remaining butter. Bake 10 minutes longer, or sufficiently to brown slightly. Or put under broiler to brown, but watch it! Serve dusted with minced parsley.

BRAISED LAMB CALIFORNIA

3 tablespoons flour
1½ teaspoons salt
¼ teaspoon pepper
4 to 5 pounds shoulder of
  lamb, boned and rolled
2 tablespoons bacon drippings
  or other fat
½ cup peeled fine-chopped
  onion
½ cup scraped chopped
  carrots

½ cup cleaned chopped celery
1 section garlic, peeled and
  minced (optional)
1 cup dry white wine or ½
  cup each orange juice and
  cranberry juice cocktail
1 tablespoon lemon juice
1 cup boiling water
1 bay leaf
4 peppercorns

Mix flour and seasonings together, then dust mixture over lamb. Heat bacon drippings in Dutch oven or heavy 4-quart saucepan; add lamb and slow-brown all over, allowing about 20 minutes. Add remaining ingredients; cover. Simmer (turning occasionally) about 2 hours, or until meat is fork-tender. Drain off and save liquid; strain and make gravy from it. Slice lamb and overlap on heated platter. Serve with a gravy. Serves 8 to 10.

POT-ROAST ROLLED SHOULDER OF LAMB

4 to 5 pounds shoulder of lamb, boned and rolled
1½ teaspoons salt
¼ teaspoon pepper
2 tablespoons vegetable oil
1 onion, peeled and minced
½ cup each diced turnip and celery

3 cloves
1½ teaspoons salt
½ teaspoon pepper
1 teaspoon Worcestershire sauce
½ tablespoon cornstarch
1½ tablespoons cold water

Order lamb boned and rolled. Dust with salt and pepper. Brown in oil. Add remaining ingredients up to cornstarch; snug-cover. Simmer 3 hours, or until lamb is fork-tender. Remove lamb. Strain off broth. Refrigerate about 15 minutes, then remove excess fat. Add sufficient water to broth to make 1½ cups. Stir cornstarch in 1½ tablespoons cold water; stir with broth until boiling rapidly. Serves 8.

ROAST LEG OF LAMB GRATINÉ

5 to 7 pounds leg of lamb, well trimmed
1½ teaspoons garlic or onion powder
2 teaspoons salt

½ teaspoon pepper
¾ cup dry sherry or canned beef bouillon
¾ cup fine dry bread crumbs

Order lamb well trimmed. Combine seasonings and rub all over lamb. Place lamb on rack in roasting pan. Roast in hot (450°) oven, until well browned. Reduce heat to 350°. Continue to roast until fork-tender, allowing 20 minutes to the pound, or until a meat thermometer registers 180°. While lamb is roasting, baste it 3 times with ½ cup dry sherry or bouillon. Within half an hour of finishing, remove meat; cover it evenly all over with the fine dry bread crumbs. Return lamb to oven, finish roasting it. When done, turn off heat and add remaining sherry or beef bouillon to roasting pan. Close oven door and let lamb stand 15 minutes to set and create pan gravy. Serves 8 to 10.

BOUQUET OF HERB-ROASTED LAMB

5½ pounds leg of lamb,
    boned and rolled and netted
    by butcher
2 teaspoons salt
¼ teaspoon pepper
½ cup butter
½ teaspoon bouquet garni or
    mixed herbs

¼ teaspoon garlic salt
¼ teaspoon grated lemon
    rind
½ teaspoon powdered ginger
Water cress

Dust lamb with salt and pepper. Make ½-inch deep incisions in between netting at various intervals across top of boned leg. Mix remaining ingredients except water cress into a paste; spread two thirds over netted top of lamb. Place on rack in shallow roasting pan and roast in slow (325°) oven 35 minutes per pound (about 3 hours), or until meat thermometer registers 180°. Spread 3 times with remaining paste. When lamb is done, place it on serving platter and let "set" 10 minutes. Cut netting lengthwise on upper side and peel down carefully in one piece. Garnish with water cress. Save pan drippings, remove fat and make a gravy. Serves 8 to 10.

HERBED ROAST LAMB

5 pounds leg or shoulder of lamb, boned and rolled
1 teaspoon salt
¼ teaspoon pepper
¼ cup butter or margarine at room temperature
¾ cup fine fresh white bread crumbs
1 tablespoon minced white portion scallions or onion
1 section garlic, peeled and crushed
¼ teaspoon crushed dried thyme leaves
2 tablespoons minced parsley
¼ cup dry white wine or sharp apple cider
⅓ cup bouillon
Salt and pepper to taste

Rub lamb all over with salt, pepper and butter mixed. Place on a shallow roasting pan. Roast 45 minutes in a hot (400°) oven. Turn once. Meantime, mix crumbs, scallions, garlic, thyme and parsley. Press in thin layer over top and sides of lamb. Continue roasting at 350° for 50 minutes (180° by a meat thermometer). Crumbs should be lightly browned. Let lamb stand 15 minutes in warm place, then slice thin. Meantime, stir wine or apple cider and bouillon into roasting pan. Scrape up all loose particles. Bring to brisk boil; simmer 5 minutes. Season to taste with salt and pepper. Strain if necessary. Spoon over the lamb. Serves 8 to 10.

ROAST LEG OF LAMB LONGCHAMPS

6 to 7 pounds leg of lamb plus lamb bones
2 teaspoons salt
¼ teaspoon pepper
¼ cup shortening
2 medium-sized onions, peeled and coarse-chopped
2 carrots, peeled and coarse-chopped
Few celery leaves, chopped
1 bay leaf
¼ teaspoon powdered thyme
¼ teaspoon powdered oregano
2 cups beef broth

Have the butcher include all bones trimmed from lamb. Rub meat with salt and pepper. Next, heat shortening in roasting pan, add bones and leg of lamb (fat side up). Roast 30 minutes in 375° (or moderate) oven. At this point, distribute around lamb all chopped vegetables mixed with herbs. Continue roasting 35 to 40 minutes longer, basting occasionally with lamb drippings. This amount of roasting produces pink lamb (best for flavor and moistness and the way the French cook it), but if you are of the well-done school, roast 20 minutes longer.

Transfer lamb to heated platter and keep hot. Pour broth into roasting pan. Simmer it on top of stove about 10 minutes. Strain into saucepan, taste and correct seasoning; bring it to boil. Skim off all fat, then pour into warm sauce boat. Serves 10.

ROLLED ROAST SHOULDER OF LAMB

Order a shoulder of lamb boned, but not rolled. Remove as much fat as practical from exterior. Rub interior with 1 teaspoon seasoning salt. Fill with Vegetable Crumb Stuffing. Roll up; tie snugly in six places. Brown in hot (450°) oven, then roast at 350° allowing 20 minutes to the pound, or until meat thermometer registers 180°. When done, brush the lamb all over with English mustard; dust evenly with 1 cup fine dry bread crumbs mixed with 1 tablespoon minced parsley and ⅛ teaspoon garlic salt.

Vegetable Crumb Stuffing:

4 cups herb crumb stuffing (packaged)	1 (1-pound) can mixed vegetables and liquid
1 onion, fine-chopped	½ teaspoon ground thyme

Mix ingredients; let stand 15 minutes to soften. If necessary add a little hot water.

ROSEMARY-ROASTED LAMB

5 to 6 pounds leg of lamb or   ¼ teaspoon pepper
   boned rolled shoulder   Herb-Seasoning Base
2 teaspoons salt

Rub lamb all over with salt and pepper. Place on rack in roasting pan. Roast 20 minutes in hot (450°) oven, or until well
browned; reduce heat to 350°. Remove from oven and brush
thoroughly with Herb-Seasoning Base. Continue to roast until
fork-tender, when meat thermometer registers 180°. Allow 20
minutes to the pound. During this time brush generously 3 times
with Herb-Seasoning Base. Serves 8 to 10.

Herb-Seasoning Base: Combine and mix ¼ cup olive oil, 1½
tablespoons wine vinegar, ½ teaspoon ground cumin seed and 1
teaspoon fine-crushed dried rosemary.

LAMB SHANKS GREEK STYLE

6 small lamb shanks   ½ teaspoon powdered mint
2 tablespoons flour   2 tablespoons lemon juice
2 tablespoons margarine   1¼ cups hot water
1 onion, peeled and chopped   1 envelope beef broth powder
1½ cups canned tomatoes   1 pound green beans, shredded
1½ teaspoons salt   6 medium-sized white potatoes,
¼ teaspoon pepper   peeled and chopped
¼ teaspoon ground cinnamon

Ask butcher to remove bones from lamb shanks, and use them
as a basis for soup stock another day. Remove excess fat from
lamb shank sections. Split them lengthwise in half, and dust
with flour. Melt margarine in low 4-quart kettle. Add onion,
then lamb shanks. Slow-sauté 20 minutes, or until light brown.
Add tomatoes, salt, pepper, cinnamon, powdered mint, lemon
juice, the hot water and beef broth powder. Cover. Simmer 1
hour. Add beans and potatoes. Simmer 30 to 35 minutes more,

or until vegetables and lamb are fork-tender. Add a little more water if necessary.

Place lamb shanks in center of large deep platter. Surround with potatoes and green beans; pour over meat gravy. Serve piping hot.

BRAISED LAMB SHANKS

6 lamb shanks	2 tablespoons Worcestershire
2 tablespoons flour	sauce
½ cup shortening	½ cup vinegar
1 cup catsup	¼ cup brown sugar
1 cup water	2 teaspoons dry mustard
2 teaspoons salt	1 cup sliced onion
Generous sprinkling pepper	Fluffy rice

Ask butcher to crack shanks. Dust with flour and brown in shortening in Dutch oven. Drain off excess fat. Combine other ingredients except rice and pour over meat. Cover and simmer about 2 hours, until lamb is tender. Baste occasionally while meat is cooking. Cook uncovered 15 minutes longer. Serve over fluffy rice.

LAMB STEAKS OR CHOPS SEVILLE

2½ pounds lamb steaks or	2 tablespoons olive oil
chops, cut ½ inch thick	1½ teaspoons salt
⅓ teaspoon garlic salt	¼ teaspoon pepper

Rub steaks or chops with garlic salt; brush with oil. Dust with salt and pepper. Broil 15 minutes 3 inches from source of heat, turning when well browned. When done, meat should be deep pink inside. Grind fresh black pepper over meat. Pass bottled meat sauce of choice.

Pork

The most novice cook knows at least one fact about pork: it must be cooked thoroughly and never even tasted when it is raw! Except for this little warning, pork is a desirable meat—it's plentiful and has a superb flavor. Ham, pork chops and loin roasts have long been popular but my mailbag tells me that spareribs and other tasty pork dishes are finding new widespread favor. Watch for a good buy and try a recipe you've never served before.

All recipes are for six servings unless otherwise stated.

HAM CASSEROLE

4 onions, sliced	1 teaspoon salt
¼ cup olive oil	2 (No. 2) cans lima beans
½ green pepper, chopped	2 cups diced ham
Pinch of cayenne	3 tomatoes, sliced
½ teaspoon sugar	¼ cup grated Parmesan cheese

Sauté onions in oil until they're light brown. Add green pepper, cayenne, sugar, salt and drained beans. Mix for a few minutes in the pan. Put diced ham in bottom of ungreased casserole and cover with the bean mixture. Place sliced tomatoes on top and sprinkle with Parmesan cheese. Bake uncovered in 350° oven for ½ hour. Brown under broiler if desired.

BAKED HAM AND EGGPLANT

1 large eggplant (about 1½ pounds)
1 teaspoon salt
¼ teaspoon pepper
1½ teaspoons flour
Vegetable oil as needed
¼ cup small slices cooked ham (fat removed)

1¼ cups grated American cheese
2 (8-ounce) cans tomato sauce
½ pound mozzarella cheese, sliced
¼ cup grated American cheese

Wash eggplant but do not peel; cut crosswise in ½-inch slices. Dust with salt, pepper and flour mixed. Slow-sauté in vegetable oil until barely tender and slightly browned. Drain on paper towels.

Oil 2-quart shallow baking dish that can be used as serving dish. In it, arrange layer of ⅓ of the eggplant. Over this spread ⅓ of the sliced ham, ⅓ of the grated American cheese, and ⅓ of the tomato sauce. Repeat this process twice. Top with sliced mozzarella cheese and the additional grated American cheese. Bake 30 minutes in a moderate (350°) oven, or until lightly brown.

HAM AND EGGS HAWAIIAN

6 ripe bananas
½ cup butter
6 slices canned pineapple, drained
1 dozen eggs
Salt and pepper

2 pounds smoked ham, sliced
½ cup brown sugar
2 tablespoons butter
¼ cup water
Buttered toast

Peel and split bananas; fry in good-sized skillet in ¼ cup of butter. Remove to heated platter. In same fry pan, slightly fry pineapple slices and remove to warm platter. Add remaining ¼ cup butter to same fry pan and fry or scramble eggs, seasoning to taste with salt and pepper. Keep warm. Fry ham in another fry pan; add to platter. In saucepan, make a heavy syrup by boiling together for 3 minutes the brown sugar, additional 2 tablespoons butter and the water. Spoon 1 tablespoon of this syrup over bananas, pineapple and ham. Serve with buttered toast.

IOWA HAM-LOAF RING-AROUND WITH CHERRY SAUCE

1½ pounds ground ham (or smoked picnic shoulder)	2 eggs, beaten
	½ cup milk
1¼ pounds ground fresh pork	Brown Sugar Glaze
1½ cups soft bread crumbs	Cherry Sauce
½ cup chopped onion	

Thoroughly mix together ground meats, crumbs, onion, eggs and milk. Lightly oil a 6½-cup ring mold. Press meat mixture into mold for shaping. Then invert on shallow baking pan and remove ring mold. Bake ham ring 1 hour at 350°. After 30 minutes of baking, brush loaf with Brown Sugar Glaze and return ring to oven for remaining 30 minutes. Baste 4 times during this last period. Serve with Cherry Sauce in a bowl in center of ring. Serves 10 to 12.

Brown Sugar Glaze: Blend together ½ cup brown sugar, 1 tablespoon prepared mustard, 2 tablespoons vinegar, 1 tablespoon water.

Cherry Sauce: Heat or use cold: 1 can prepared cherry pie filling. For a different zesty taste, add 1 tablespoon horseradish and mix thoroughly.

HAM SLICE/SWEET POTATO BAKE

2½ pounds tenderized ham, cut in 1-inch-thick slices	1 cup orange juice
	1 cup apple juice or cider
1 large can vacuum-pack sweet potatoes	¾ cup raisins
	½ tablespoon sugar
½ tablespoon vegetable oil	(preferably brown)

Cut excess fat from sliced ham. Place ham in oiled large low casserole. Surround with sweet potatoes; brush with vegetable oil. Pour fruit juices over and around. Strew with raisins and sugar. Bake 30 minutes in moderate (350°) oven. If necessary, slide under broiler 1 minute to brown. Do not overcook.

ORANGE-GLAZED BAKED HAM

Bake a 10- to 12-pound whole smoked ham, bone in, uncovered, at 325° for 20 minutes to the pound, or until a meat thermometer registers internal temperature of 155°. While ham is baking, make glaze by combining and simmering together for 5 minutes:

1 tablespoon grated orange rind	¼ cup light corn syrup
1½ cups fresh orange juice	¼ teaspoon each ground cinnamon and nutmeg
¼ cup sugar	5 whole cloves

Half an hour before ham will be done, remove from oven. Pare off rind. Score (cut) fat in diamond pattern making diagonal cuts 1 inch apart. Stud each "diamond" with additional whole cloves. Spoon glaze generously over ham. Return it to oven and bake 25 minutes more; brush twice with remaining orange glaze. Turn off heat. Let ham stand in warm oven 20 minutes before carving. Serves 12 to 15.

TENNESSEE HAM

1 (10-pound) ham, country style	¼ to ½ cup cider or apple juice
1 cup dark molasses	Cloves
1½ cups brown sugar	Fruit preserve
1 cup meal or fine-crushed cracker crumbs	

Completely cover ham in cold water; allow to soak overnight. Take out and remove any hard surface. Put ham in suitably sized pot with fresh water, skin side down, add molasses. Cook in a slow (225°) oven, allowing 25 minutes to the pound. Allow to cool in liquid. Pull skin off carefully. Sprinkle with paste made of brown sugar, meal or cracker crumbs and sufficient liquid to make the paste. Score ham; stick a clove in each square. Bake slowly in moderate (350°) oven for 1 hour. Decorate platter with thin ham slices cut from the roast ham, rolled into cornucopias and filled with fruit preserve. Serves 12 to 15. *Note:* The fruit preserve should be tart, such as wild plum or grape jam. Serves 12.

ROAST HAM VIRGINIA

1 (8- to 10-pound) country-style or tenderized ham or
1 (6¾-pound) ready-to-serve ham
1 quart sweet cider
1 teaspoon whole cloves
1 teaspoon celery seed
1 (2-inch) stick cinnamon
6 peppercorns

¾ cup dry red wine
½ cup apricot purée
1 egg yolk
¼ cup fine dry bread crumbs
Whole cloves
Water cress (optional)
Cumberland Sauce (see Index) or bottled ham sauce

If the ham is country style, add the sweet cider and spices with boiling water to cover; simmer 3 to 4 hours, or until tender; then glaze and bake, as indicated below. If the ham is tenderized, or canned and ready to serve, observe package directions.

In general, if tenderized, place on a rack in a baking pan; bake 22 to 25 minutes to the pound, or until a meat thermometer registers 160°. During the first hour baste 4 times with the sweet cider previously boiled 10 minutes with the spices and the wine.

If canned and ready to serve, remove the ham to a baking pan; bake 14 minutes to the pound, or until the meat thermometer registers 130°. Baste with the spiced cider and wine.

Pare off the ham rind if left on. Brush the fat surface with the apricot purée blended with the egg yolk. Dust with the bread crumbs. Decorate with a pattern of whole cloves. Return to the baking pan. Brown in the oven; allow 30 minutes at 350°.

If the ham bone has been left in, pare away the meat and trim the bone with a bouquet of water cress. Pass Cumberland Sauce. Serves 12.

ORANGE-GLAZED SMOKED PORK BUTT WITH POTATOES

1 (2½-pound) smoked pork butt
½ cup frozen orange juice concentrate, thawed

12 small white potatoes, peeled
Mustard (optional)

Simmer-boil smoked pork butt 2 hours, or until tender; then drain. Place in baking pan. Lightly brush pork all over with orange concentrate. Surround with potatoes. Spoon over any fat that has dripped from smoked pork butt. Bake 35 minutes, or until potatoes are fork-tender and browned. Serve as is, or accompany with mustard.

Note: For a change, use cranberry sauce, melted, in place of orange concentrate.

PORK CHOPS BAKED WITH APPLE SLICES

4 small loin pork chops, cut ½ inch thick
½ teaspoon salt
⅛ teaspoon pepper
¼ teaspoon powdered sage
1 tablespoon flour

½ apple, peeled, sliced thin
1 teaspoon sugar
1 tablespoon butter
3 tablespoons hot water or beef bouillon

Place chops in shallow 1-quart baking dish. Dust with salt, pepper, sage and flour; lay apple slices on top. Dust with 1 teaspoon sugar. Dot with butter. Place in hot (450°) oven, for 10 minutes. Bake at 350° 25 minutes longer. Baste with hot water or beef bouillon.

Small canned or frozen cooked potatoes may be baked with meat; if fresh ones are used, peel and cut in halves or quarters. Serve in baking dish. Serves 2.

BROILED PORK CHOPS WITH POTATO SLICES

6 (½-inch-thick) large pork chops (any cut)	⅓ cup flour or ½ cup wheat germ
1 small bay leaf	4 unpeeled large potatoes, sliced lengthwise
Boiling water	
3 tablespoons vegetable oil	Vegetable oil
1 teaspoon seasoned salt	Seasoned salt

Place the pork chops and bay leaf in a saucepan. Half-cover with the boiling water. Cover. Simmer 30 minutes, when water should mostly evaporate. Drain and dry the chops. Brush with the 3 tablespoons oil; dust with the 1 teaspoon seasoned salt. Lightly coat with the flour or wheat germ. Arrange on a broiler.

Brush the potato slices with additional oil, then dust with additional seasoned salt. Add to the broiler. Place 4 inches from the source of heat. Broil 12 to 15 minutes, or until both the chops and the potatoes are golden brown. Turn once using tongs. The chops will be thoroughly cooked, tender and moist; the potatoes will have an enticing bake-fried flavor.

BRAISED APPLE-STUFFED PORK CHOPS

1 cup packaged herbed stuffing crumbs	1 (10½-ounce) can condensed beef broth
1 cup fine-chopped peeled cored tart apples	1¼ cups water
½ cup apple juice or cider	Juice of ½ lemon
6 thick loin or rib pork chops	1 (8-ounce) can small onions, drained
1½ teaspoons seasoned salt	
2 tablespoons flour	1 teaspoon cumin seeds (optional)
2 tablespoons margarine	

Combine and mix crumbs, apples, apple juice or cider. Cut slit in each pork chop to make a pocket. Fill with crumb stuffing. Press edges together. Dust all over with seasoned salt and flour mixed. Slow-brown on both sides in margarine. Add beef broth and water. Cover and bake about 50 minutes in moderate (325 to 350°) oven, or until fork-tender. When almost done, add lemon juice and onions, which should be well drained. If desired, add cumin seeds when chops are half-braised.

PORK CHOP/ONION CASSEROLE

6 good-sized pork chops	1 teaspoon bouillon powder
2 tablespoons cooking oil	¾ cup hot water
2½ cups peeled sliced onions	¼ cup sherry
1 teaspoon seasoned salt	1 bouillon cube
½ teaspoon sage	Minced parsley
½ cup hot water	

Cut all possible fat from chops; brown them lightly in the oil; remove. Add the onions and seasonings to the fat in the fry pan. Stir in ½ cup hot water and bouillon powder; cover. Steam-fry until the water evaporates. Place chops in slightly oiled low baking dish. Top with the fried onions. Pour in the additional water mixed with sherry and bouillon cube. Cover. Bake at 350° for 1 to 1½ hours, or until the chops are fork-tender. Garnish with minced parsley.

BAKED CURRIED PORK CHOPS

1 teaspoon seasoned salt	2 tablespoons cooking oil
1½ teaspoons curry powder	1 (10½-ounce) can
2 tablespoons flour	condensed beef broth
6 (1-inch-thick) pork chops, fat trimmed (any cut)	1 can measure hot water

Mix together seasoned salt, curry powder and flour; rub into pork chops, covering all sides. Lightly brown chops in cooking oil. The oil should be absorbed.

Gradually pour in from the outer edge of the fry pan the beef broth and can measure of hot water. Cover and simmer-cook 40 minutes. Turn chops twice for even cooking.

BROILED BREADED PORK CHOPS

4 pork chops, cut 1 inch thick	Juice of 1 lemon
2 eggs, beaten	¼ cup grated Parmesan cheese
6 tablespoons sifted dry bread crumbs	1 tablespoon prepared mustard
	1 garlic clove, split
Salt and black pepper	⅓ teaspoon crushed red
2 tablespoons olive oil	pepper or a dash of Tabasco
3 tablespoons butter, melted	

Dip chops into beaten eggs, then into bread crumbs; do this twice. Then sprinkle a little salt and black pepper over chops. Preheat broiler. Place chops in lightly greased broiler pan 8 inches from source of heat. Broil slowly for 10 minutes. Mix all other ingredients to make basting sauce. Discard garlic. Spoon half the sauce over chops. Cook slowly for 20 minutes longer. Turn chops over and spoon remaining sauce over them. Cook slowly for about 30 minutes more. Check for doneness. Serves 4.

PORK CHOPS FARCI

6 thick loin pork chops	1 teaspoon ground cumin seed
12 pitted tenderized prunes	½ cup dry sherry or 2
2 tablespoons butter or oil	tablespoons sherry extract
1 teaspoon salt	and 6 tablespoons water
¼ teaspoon pepper	

Remove excess fat from chops. Cut a slit in each to make a pocket; fill with 2 prunes; press together. Brush all over with butter. Dust with salt, pepper and cumin seed. Brown on both sides in an iron or other ovenproof fry pan. Add sherry. Cover. Slow-bake 50 minutes at 325°, or until fork-tender.

GOURMET PORK CHOPS WITH CHIVES

6 pork chops, cut 1 inch thick
¾ cup white wine
⅓ cup honey
1 teaspoon salt
⅛ teaspoon pepper

⅓ cup frozen chopped chives
⅓ cup diced green pepper
1½ teaspoons cornstarch
1 teaspoon water

Trim fat from chops. Arrange in layer in baking pan. Combine wine, honey, salt and pepper. Pour over chops and marinate 1 hour or more. Bake uncovered 1 hour at 300°, basting with marinade to glaze. Cover with chives and green pepper. Continue baking about 30 minutes more, or until tender. Remove to heated platter. Thicken sauce in pan with cornstarch moistened with water.

Note: All alcohol evaporates from wine while cooking, leaving only pleasant flavor.

PORK CHOPS LOUISIANA

6 large pork chops
¼ cup flour
1 teaspoon salt
⅛ teaspoon pepper
2 onions, peeled and sliced
1 green pepper, shredded with
  seeds left in

1 cup canned tomato, mashed
  rather liquid
¼ teaspoon powdered garlic
2 cups boiling water
½ teaspoon instant bouillon

Remove excess fat from chops. Place fat pieces in heated fry pan; cook until fat runs. Rub flour, salt and pepper into chops. Sauté in fry pan until golden brown; then set chops aside. Add onions and green pepper to fry pan. Sauté until color turns. Stir in remaining ingredients; bring to a boil. Add chops. Cover. Simmer 35 to 40 minutes, or until they are fork-tender and liquid mostly evaporated.

SKILLET SWEET-SOUR PORK CHOPS

6 pork chops (any cut)
2 tablespoons cooking oil
1 onion, peeled and chopped
1 cup tomato juice
¼ cup cider vinegar

2 tablespoons soy sauce
1 tablespoon sugar
¾ teaspoon salt
¼ teaspoon pepper
5 cups coarse-cut cabbage

Trim excess fat from chops and discard. Brown chops in large frying pan in oil. Combine and add remaining ingredients except cabbage. Cover; cook over high heat until steaming freely. Then lower heat and simmer 30 minutes, or until chops are fork-tender. Add cabbage; cover; cook 10 minutes more. Remove chops. Toss cabbage in pan sauce. Serve very hot.

CROWN PORK ROAST WITH CORN STUFFING

Have the butcher make a crown roast from a strip of loin containing 10 to 12 ribs. Ask him to remove the backbone for easier carving. Place with rib ends up in a roasting pan. Cap rib ends with aluminum foil to prevent excess browning. Roast uncovered at 350° about 35 minutes per pound—or until meat reaches 170° internal temperature with the meat-cooking thermometer. An hour before the meat will be done, fill the center of the crown with Corn Stuffing. Bake any extra corn stuffing in an oiled casserole along with the meat. To serve the crown pork roast, remove foil caps from ribs and replace with paper frills. Accompany with pickled crab apples and parsley. Serves 8 to 12.

Corn Stuffing:

1 (12-ounce) can whole-kernel corn, drained (about 1½ cups)
1 (16-ounce) can cream-style corn (about 2 cups)
1 egg, beaten
1 cup soft bread crumbs

¼ cup fine-chopped peeled onion
¼ cup fine-chopped green pepper
1 tablespoon chopped pimiento
1½ teaspoons salt
⅛ teaspoon pepper

Combine all ingredients; fill center of a crown pork roast. Return to oven for 1 hour, or until the roast registers 170°.

WINE-ROASTED LOIN OF PORK

4 pounds loin of pork	½ teaspoon garlic powder
2 teaspoons salt	1 teaspoon crushed cumin seed
¼ teaspoon pepper	1 cup dry white wine

Order bones of the pork cracked for easy carving. Place pork in large bowl. Pierce pork with skewer in several places. Combine and rub in seasonings; pour over wine. Cover; refrigerate 6 hours or up to 24 hours. Turn 3 times to marinate evenly.

Transfer meat to a rack in roasting pan. Start in hot (450°) oven, roast 20 minutes, or until beginning to brown. Then reduce heat to 350°. Continue to roast until pork is fork-tender; a meat thermometer should register 185°. Baste twice with extra wine. Serves 8.

GREEN-PEPPERED PORK

The perfect solution to the leftover pork problem. Delicious.

4 tablespoons butter or margarine	4 sweet green peppers, cored and minced
3 medium-sized onions, peeled and minced	4 cups cubelets cold roast pork
3 tablespoons flour	1 (8-ounce) package egg noodles, cooked
1½ pints boiling water	
2 teaspoons beef bouillon powder	

Melt margarine; add onions; slow-fry until color begins to turn, about 2 minutes. Add flour and cook until slightly browned. Gradually stir in hot water. Add bouillon powder, then peppers and pork. Simmer 10 to 15 minutes. Serve poured over the noodles.

ORANGE ROAST PORK

1 large can frozen orange juice
  concentrate
Water
2 cloves garlic, crushed
1½ teaspoons salt
1 teaspoon freshly ground
  pepper

1 teaspoon rosemary or savory,
  rubbed fine
Fresh pork shoulder (about 6
  pounds)
½ cup tart jelly

Mix orange juice with equal amount of water, combine with
next four ingredients, pouring over pork. Marinate covered 12
hours or more, turning from time to time. Remove pork, reserving marinade. Roast on rack in 325° oven, allowing 40
minutes to the pound, or until meat thermometer registers
185°. Baste often with marinade. Before serving, simmer remaining marinade with ½ cup tart jelly such as currant or beach
plum, if available, or orange marmalade for 10 minutes. Strain
and serve sauce with pork. Serves 8 to 10.

ROAST SUCKLING PIG

Suckling pig (about 6 weeks
  old)
1 tablespoon baking soda
1 tablespoon and 2 teaspoons
  salt
2 minced anchovies
1 tablespoon powdered sage
10 cups fine, day-old bread
  crumbs
½ cup melted butter
2 teaspoons salt
½ teaspoon pepper
½ cup minced onion

½ pound chopped mushrooms
¼ cup butter
2 eggs, beaten
1 quart dry white wine
¼ cup butter
½ cup flour
½ teaspoon pepper
Juice of ½ lemon
1 (1-pound) loaf enriched
  bread
Cube of butter
Gravy for Suckling Pig

Order the pig completely dressed and cleaned; this includes removing the eyes; wax from the ears. The head is left on. Scrape

the pig. Scrub in plenty of cold water containing 1 tablespoon baking soda. Rinse and dry. Rub 1 tablespoon salt all over the interior and 2 teaspoons salt over the exterior.

Make a stuffing by combining the anchovies, sage, crumbs, ½ cup melted butter, 2 teaspoons salt, ½ teaspoon pepper, onion, the mushrooms sautéed in ¼ cup additional butter, the eggs and 1 cup of the wine. Sauté and stir for 5 minutes. Fill the interior of the pig with this stuffing. Sew up the opening with heavy thread, or skewer together with poultry picks and white string. Skewer the front feet forward and the hind feet backward. Force the mouth open and insert a block of wood 2 inches thick. Massage all over with a mixture of ¼ cup butter, ½ cup flour, ½ teaspoon pepper and lemon juice. Cover the ears with buttered paper.

Place the pig on a rack in an open roasting pan; bake in a hot (450°) oven, until beginning to brown. Then pour the remaining wine into the pan. Reduce the heat to 325°, and roast about 3 hours, or 30 minutes to the pound. Baste generously with the wine from the pan every half hour. When half roasted, cut the loaf of bread in halves lengthwise and place underneath the pig. When roasted, remove both pig and bread from the pan. Rub the pig with a cube of butter in a piece of cheesecloth until the skin shines. Make Gravy for Suckling Pig from the pan liquid.

For a grand entrance, place the pig on a large platter, a half loaf of the bread on each side. Put a small polished red apple or a lemon in the pig's mouth. Deck the neck with a lei of strung cranberries or garland of parsley sprigs, studded with cranberries or sprays of barberries. You might add earrings and a big fat bow on the tail! If for a Christmas celebration, garnish the platter with holly; for late fall use barberries with their frost-turned leaves. Serves 10 to 12.

Gravy for Suckling Pig: Skim the fat from the liquid in the roasting pan. Measure the liquid. Add enough consommé to make 2 cups. Stir in 1 fine-minced anchovy, 1 tablespoon minced parsley and the grated rind and juice of ½ lemon. Bring to a boil. Blend 1½ tablespoons flour with 2 tablespoons cold water and ½ teaspoon Angostura bitters and stir in. Simmer 3 minutes.

JELLIED PIGS' KNUCKLES

1 large onion stuck with 2 cloves
1 section garlic, crushed
½ bay leaf
1 tablespoon salt
12 peppercorns, crushed
Sprig of parsley
1 teaspoon crushed thyme leaf

1 stalk celery
1 cup dry white wine or ¼ cup vinegar
8 pigs' knuckles, brushed and washed
6 cups water or to cover
Sauce Vinaigrette (see Index)

In deep saucepan, combine all ingredients except pigs' knuckles, and cover with water. Bring to boil and simmer 20 to 25 minutes. Add pigs' knuckles, bring to boil again; cover, and simmer over low heat 2 hours, or until meat is fork-tender. Do not overcook and do not cook too fast or you will break the skin and destroy eye appeal of the knuckles. Remove knuckles from broth. Strain broth and boil it down one third. Correct seasoning. Arrange pigs' knuckles in deep serving dish. Ladle broth over knuckles; cool. Refrigerate several hours or until broth has jellied. Serve with Sauce Vinaigrette or mustard mayonnaise. Serves 8.

BARBECUED SPARERIBS

4 pounds spareribs
2 onions, peeled and minced
½ cup tomato catsup
½ tablespoon sugar
1 tablespoon Worcestershire sauce

1 tablespoon vinegar
4 drops Tabasco
½ teaspoon chili powder
1 cup water
½ teaspoon salt
⅛ teaspoon pepper

Place spareribs overlapping in good-sized flat baking pan. Mix together remaining ingredients and spoon over meat. Bake in a

400° oven, basting frequently, about 1¼ hours, or until meat is tender and well browned. Accompany with baked white or sweet potatoes, baked apples and baked peeled small white onions cooked in the same oven.

SPARERIBS CALIFORNIA

4 pounds spareribs
½ cup fresh lemon juice
2½ tablespoons soy sauce
¼ teaspoon ground ginger
½ cup brown or ¾ cup
   brownulated sugar
1 cup fresh orange juice

¼ cup flour
1 cup chunks peeled
   California orange
1 medium-sized onion, peeled
   and sliced
1 small green pepper, seeded
   and sliced

Put spareribs on rack in baking pan and brown in very hot (450°) oven allowing 30 to 40 minutes. Meanwhile, combine and mix fresh lemon juice, soy sauce, ginger, sugar and fresh orange juice; stir in flour. Bring to boil; simmer 5 minutes. Stir in orange chunks, onion and green pepper to make sauce. Drain fat from baking pan. Spoon sauce over spareribs. Bake uncovered in moderate (325°) oven for 1 hour, or until fork-tender. Baste 4 times.

SPARERIBS ORIENTAL STYLE

4 pounds spareribs
½ cup soy sauce
4 scallions, chopped
1 section garlic, peeled and
   minced
1 tablespoon sugar
1 tablespoon sherry
½ cup water

1 (43-ounce) can mushroom
   chow mein divided pack
   (purchased)
½ head lettuce, shredded
1 tablespoon butter
Sliced fresh tomato and
   cucumber (optional)

Separate spareribs into one-bone portions and place in large fry pan. Combine soy sauce, scallions, garlic, sugar, sherry and water; pour mixture over ribs and simmer 45 minutes, turning occasionally. During last few minutes of simmering process, separate divided-pack cans of mushroom chow mein sauce and chow mein vegetables. Heat mushroom sauce. Drain and rinse chow mein vegetables, mix with shredded lettuce and sauté in butter until vegetables are just heated through. Arrange bed of hot chow mein vegetables on a serving platter, and top with spareribs combined with heated mushroom sauce. Garnish with sliced tomato and cucumber if desired.

PORK AND VEGETABLE CHOP SUEY

1½ cups peeled small-diced carrots
1½ cups frozen peas
5 tablespoons peeled minced onion
1 teaspoon salt
2¼ cups boiling water
½ teaspoon cooking oil
1 pound lean fresh or cooked pork, small-diced

2¼ cups thin-sliced celery
1½ cups corn kernels, fresh or canned
1 chicken bouillon cube
3 tablespoons cornstarch
½ cup cold water
1½ teaspoons soy sauce
Flaky rice

Add carrots, peas, onion and salt to boiling water. Boil 7 minutes, or until almost tender. Meantime put cooking oil in large preheated fry pan. Add pork. Sauté until golden brown. Add celery, corn kernels, bouillon cube, cooked vegetables and their liquid. Simmer 10 minutes. Mix cornstarch with cold water and soy sauce and stir in. Cook-stir until boiling all over. Serve on flaky boiled rice.

PORK STEAK SWISS

2 pounds pork steak, sliced ½ inch thick
1½ tablespoons flour
½ teaspoon salt
⅛ teaspoon pepper
¼ teaspoon thyme
2 tablespoons fat (any kind)

1 cup hot water or bouillon
1 small onion, peeled and chopped
½ cup thin-sliced celery
1 large sweet pepper, seeded and chopped

Cut steak in 6 serving portions. Pound with meat mallet or edge of saucer to flatten. Mix flour, salt, pepper, thyme and rub into meat. Melt fat in fry pan. Brown pork steak on both sides in it. Add hot water or broth. Mix onion, celery and sweet pepper; spread over steak. Cover; simmer 1½ hours, or until fork-tender. Add more water if needed. Make gravy from pan liquid.

FRESH PORK RAGOUT WITH VEGETABLES AND BLACK OLIVES

A one-dish entree ready in 1 hour.

2 pounds fresh pork, cut in 1-inch cubes, fat trimmed off
1½ tablespoons olive oil
1½ teaspoons salt
¼ teaspoon pepper
½ teaspoon freeze-dried shallots (optional)
1 large onion, peeled and thin-sliced
¼ teaspoon garlic powder
1 bay leaf
¼ teaspoon thyme
¼ teaspoon allspice
1 teaspoon paprika
1 tablespoon flour
1 cup dry white wine
1 (10½-ounce) package frozen mixed vegetables, thawed
⅓ cup pitted black olives
8 medium-sized white potatoes, peeled and halved

Sauté pork until golden in olive oil. Add salt, pepper, freeze-dried shallots and onion. Sauté until onion looks translucent. Add garlic powder and bay leaf, thyme, allspice and paprika. Continue to sauté until onion becomes golden. Stir occasionally. Stir in flour; continue to sauté until light brown. Add wine. Boil 5 minutes; stir in mixed vegetables and olives. Top with potatoes and cover. Simmer 35 minutes or bake at 350° until vegetables and pork are fork-tender.

Ground

These dishes are versatile and appeal to almost everyone. They are flavorful, adaptable to skillet or casserole and invaluable when there isn't time for elaborate preparations, when trying to use up leftovers or when the food budget has been stretched to the breaking point.

All recipes are for six servings unless otherwise stated.

CHILI CON CARNE WITH SAUSAGE

3 tablespoons butter	1 (No. 2½) can tomatoes
1 onion, peeled and fine-chopped	1 tablespoon sugar
	1 bay leaf
2 sections garlic, peeled and crushed	1 teaspoon salt
	6 cloves
½ green pepper, fine-chopped	¼ teaspoon ground basil
½ pound chopped raw beef	2 tablespoons chili powder
½ pound hot Italian sausage (skin removed)	1 (1-pound) can red kidney beans, drained

Melt butter in 2½-quart saucepan; add onion, garlic and pepper; sauté until lightly browned. Add beef; cook, mashing with fork, until it breaks into small pellets and is gray in color. Fry sausage in separate pan. Drain off fat; chop sausage and add to beef mixture. Stir in tomatoes, sugar and seasonings. Bring to boil; reduce heat and simmer uncovered 1 hour, or until mixture reaches desired thickness. Add red kidney beans 10 minutes before chili will be done. Serves 4.

CHOPPED BEEF SAVORY

2 cups peeled fine-chopped
   onion
1 section garlic, mashed
¼ cup butter or margarine
½ teaspoon sugar
1½ teaspoons salt
⅛ teaspoon pepper

½ teaspoon ground basil
1 (1-pound 12-ounce) can
   tomatoes
1 pound chopped beef
½ cup coarse bread crumbs
Grated Cheddar cheese
   (optional)

Fry onion and garlic until yellowed in butter or margarine; add sugar. Stir salt, pepper and basil into tomatoes. Oil a 3-pint baking dish. Spoon layer of seasoned tomatoes in bottom; strew with ⅓ of fried onion, then layer of ⅓ of the chopped beef, well broken up. Continue until all is used. Strew top with bread crumbs, and cheese if used. Cover; bake 30 minutes in moderate (350 to 375°) oven; uncover, bake 15 minutes more.

DEEP-DISH CHOPPED BEEF PIE

3 tablespoons cooking oil
1 large onion, peeled and
   fine-chopped
1½ pounds chopped beef
1 (8-ounce) can tomato sauce
1 cup water
1 teaspoon beef bouillon
   powder
½ teaspoon salt

⅛ teaspoon pepper
1 bay leaf
1 recipe rich baking powder
   biscuits or 1 package ready-
   to-bake refrigerated biscuits
1 teaspoon powdered sage
1 tablespoon minced parsley
Milk

Heat oil in 10-inch fry pan. Add onion; slow-sauté until golden. Add beef; stir with kitchen fork until well separated. Stir in tomato sauce, water, bouillon powder, salt, pepper and bay leaf. Simmer 15 minutes; remove bay leaf. Transfer to an oiled, shallow 2-quart baking dish.

Meantime, prepare biscuits, adding sage and parsley to flour. Roll dough ½ inch thick; cut in 2-inch rounds. If refrigerated biscuits are used, dust with sage and parsley. Top meat mixture with biscuits; brush them lightly with milk. Bake 25 minutes, or until browned in hot (400°) oven.

MEAT CASSEROLE PIE

Corn Meal Pastry Crust:

1 cup sifted flour	⅓ cup shortening
½ cup enriched corn meal	¼ cup cold water
½ teaspoon salt	

Sift together flour, corn meal and salt. Chop in shortening until mixture resembles coarse crumbs; sprinkle on water by table-spoonfuls, stirring lightly with a fork until barely dampened (if necessary add 1 extra tablespoon cold water). Form into a ball.

Meat Filling:

1½ pounds good-quality ground beef	1 (6-ounce) can tomato paste
¼ cup peeled fine-chopped onion	¾ teaspoon salt
1 (8-ounce) can tomato sauce	¼ teaspoon pepper
	1 (15½-ounce) can cut green beans, drained

Mash ground beef with fork. Thoroughly mix in next five ingredients. Lightly mix in green beans.

Turn pastry onto lightly floured surface. Divide dough in half; roll half to form 13-inch circle. Fit loosely into 9-inch pie plate. Trim so pastry extends ½ inch beyond the rim. Fill with meat mixture. Roll remaining dough to form 12-inch circle; cut 3 slits in center to allow for steam escape. Adjust pastry over filling. Trim so pastry extends ½ inch beyond rim. Fold top and bottom pastry together; flute edges. Bake about 30 minutes in hot (400 to 450°) oven. Serve hot, cut in wedges.

Garnish and accompaniment might be celery sticks, bread-and-butter pickles and whole ripe olives.

BEST EVER HAMBURGERS

2 eggs	1 tablespoon Worcestershire
1⅓ pounds chopped chuck	sauce
¼ teaspoon minced parsley	1½ teaspoons salt
½ cup chopped onion	Generous sprinkling freshly
3 tablespoons pickle relish	ground pepper
3 tablespoons chili sauce	

Beat eggs and mix thoroughly with remaining ingredients. Shape into 6 patties. Broil in preheated broiler about 3 inches from heat, approximately 4 to 5 minutes each side, or until of desired doneness, or pan-fry the hamburgers in butter or margarine.

CHOPPED BEEF/MUSHROOM PATTIES

¼ pound mushrooms	¼ teaspoon onion powder
1½ pounds twice-ground	1 egg
beef	½ cup undiluted evaporated
1 teaspoon seasoned salt	milk
¼ teaspoon cinnamon	Oil
¼ teaspoon pepper	2 teaspoons butter
¼ teaspoon oregano	Brown Sauce (see Index)

Remove stems from mushrooms and chop stems fine. Reserve caps. Combine stems and next eight ingredients in order given; mix thoroughly. Shape into 8 thin flat patties. Let stand 15 minutes to become thoroughly merged. Brush all over with oil. Line a broiler pan with aluminum foil. Place patties on this 2 inches apart. Broil 6 minutes 4 inches from source of heat, turning once. Turn reserved mushroom tops upside down, and add ¼ teaspoon butter to hollow of each mushroom top. Place 1 atop each patty. Continue to broil 7 to 8 minutes more, or until mushrooms are golden brown. Serve with Brown Sauce or a gravy made from the drippings in the broiler pan. Serves 8.

PLANKED CHOPPED BEEF PATTIES

1½ pounds chopped raw beef
1 medium-sized onion, peeled
  and minced
1 medium-sized sweet green
  pepper, seeded and minced
1½ teaspoons seasoned salt
¼ teaspoon pepper
¼ cup milk
2½ tablespoons tomato paste
2 tablespoons butter or
  margarine

¼ cup hot water
1 tablespoon butter
¼ cup red wine or cranberry
  juice cocktail
3 canned pimientos, halved,
  drained
Baked Potatoes Duchesse (see
  Index)
Parsley

Mix beef thoroughly with onion and green pepper. Add and mix in seasonings, milk and tomato paste. Form meat into 6 thin round flat patties; fry on both sides quickly in 2 tablespoons butter, 7 minutes altogether. Meantime, combine water, additional butter and wine or cranberry juice cocktail. From side of pan slowly pour mixture over and around beef patties; simmer 5 minutes. Transfer to 6 oiled heated individual planks. Top each with half a pimiento. Edge planks with Baked Potatoes Duchesse; slip them under low flame broiler 2 minutes to brown. Garnish with parsley.

Note: If inconvenient to plank the patties, serve them on buttered toast; pour pan drippings over all.

LAMBURGERS

½ cup milk
¾ cup soft bread crumbs
1½ pounds twice-ground lean
  lamb
1½ teaspoons salt
¼ teaspoon pepper
¼ teaspoon ground cinnamon
½ teaspoon powdered or
  2 tablespoons minced peeled
  onion
1 egg

2 tablespoons flour
2½ tablespoons cooking oil
1½ cups meat broth mixed
  with ½ tablespoon lemon
  juice
⅓ cup fine-chopped pimiento-
  stuffed olives
6 full-sized slices toast
3 pimiento-stuffed olives,
  halved

Combine milk and bread crumbs in a 1-pint saucepan. Cook-stir over moderate heat until boiling. In a 2-quart bowl, combine and mix the lamb, salt, pepper, cinnamon, onion and egg. Mix until quite smooth. Shape into 6 flat patties about ¾ inch thick. Dust over the flour. Heat cooking oil in large skillet. Reduce heat. Add patties; slow-brown on both sides. Slowly pour in broth and lemon juice; add chopped stuffed olives. Simmer-cook 6 minutes; turn patties once. Arrange lamburgers on the toast and pour around the gravy. Top each burger with half an olive.

STUFFED LAMB PATTIES

3 pounds ground lamb
2 tablespoons minced onion
1 teaspoon salt
¼ teaspoon pepper

16 slices bacon
8 pitted prunes, drained
Orange sections

In a large bowl, mix together lamb, onion, salt and pepper. Fry 8 slices bacon until crisp. Stuff prunes with the crumbled bacon. Shape lamb into 8 patties. Lay a prune in the center of each patty. Wrap a slice of bacon around each patty and secure with toothpicks or small skewers. Flatten patties. Broil about 4 inches from heat, 10 minutes on each side. Garnish with orange sections. Serves 8.

VEAL PATTIES WITH PAN GRAVY

6 veal patties, ready-to-cook,   1 teaspoon seasoned salt
   from meat counter   ½ cup hot water
¼ cup soft margarine   ½ teaspoon beef broth powder

The veal patties should be about 4 inches in diameter and ½ inch thick. If they are not on sale at meat counter, purchase 1½ pounds veal and have it put through food chopper twice. This will produce an equivalent amount. Shape the patties yourself. Heat margarine in large skillet; add veal patties with seasoned salt. Slow-brown 10 minutes on one side; then turn and brown reverse side 10 minutes. Remove patties to warm platter. Add hot water to skillet, pouring it in from the side to avoid spattering. Stir in beef broth powder. Boil rapidly and pour over patties on platter.

CHOPPED BEEF/SALAMI BALLS IN ONION GRAVY

¼ pound salami   1 large egg
1½ pounds chopped beef   1 cup fine dry bread crumbs
½ cup undiluted evaporated   2 tablespoons oil
   milk or ½ cup half and half   1 (10½-ounce) can onion
1½ teaspoons seasoned salt   soup
1 tablespoon instant minced   ½ soup can hot water
   onion   ¼ teaspoon oregano
¼ teaspoon Tabasco
½ cup plain white bread
   crumbs

Ask the butcher to add the salami to the beef before chopping and put through chopper twice. Combine chopped meats with next six ingredients in the order given. Mix thoroughly until smooth; set aside 10 minutes for the crumbs to swell. Shape into 12 balls.

Roll lightly in additional bread crumbs. Heat oil in large skillet that can go-to-table. Brown meat balls all over in it. Add onion soup, then the ½ soup can hot water and oregano. Simmer-cook 40 minutes. Turn meat balls 3 times for even cooking. Serve in onion gravy.

MEAT BALLS IN TOMATO SAUCE

1½ pounds good-quality chopped beef or lamb	¼ teaspoon pepper
	½ cup blanched pine nuts
1 large onion, peeled and grated	3 tablespoons flour
	¼ cup butter for browning
1 teaspoon chopped parsley	2 medium-sized tomatoes, skinned and chopped fine, or ¼ cup tomato paste and 1 cup water
2½ slices whole wheat bread, soaked in water to cover, squeezed dry	
2 eggs, slightly beaten	Cooked rice or spaghetti
1½ teaspoons salt	

Combine chopped beef, onion, parsley, soaked bread, eggs, salt, pepper and pine nuts. Mix thoroughly. Shape into balls the size of a walnut. Dust with the flour. Heat butter in 10-inch skillet; add meat balls and brown all over. Add tomatoes or tomato paste and water. Simmer 25 minutes. Serve with hot cooked rice or spaghetti.

SCANDINAVIAN MEAT BALLS AU GRATIN

May be prepared in advance, refrigerated, then baked 45 minutes at 350°.

½ cup milk	½ pound ground lean pork
¾ cup soft bread crumbs	3 tablespoons butter
1 egg	¼ cup flour
1½ teaspoons salt	2 cups milk
⅛ teaspoon pepper	1 teaspoon salt
¼ teaspoon nutmeg	1 cup shredded Cheddar cheese
¼ cup minced onion	
2 tablespoons butter	Parsley-Cooked Rice
1½ pounds ground lean beef	

Add ½ cup milk to crumbs; let stand. Add egg, 1½ teaspoons salt, pepper and nutmeg; beat with fork until well mixed. Sauté onion in 2 tablespoons butter until color changes. Add meat and onion to crumb mixture; mix with fork. Form into 1-inch balls. Brown in additional butter; remove as they brown. Mix flour into drippings. Stir in 2 cups additional milk; add 1 teaspoon salt and cheese; stir until cheese melts. Add meat balls; stir carefully to avoid breaking them. Pour meat with sauce in center of casserole lined with Parsley-Cooked Rice. To complete: Bake 20 minutes in moderate (350°) oven.

Parsley-Cooked Rice: Into 4 cups hot cooked rice, toss 2 tablespoons minced onion, lightly sautéed in 2 tablespoons butter, and ¼ cup minced fresh parsley.

SWEDISH MEAT BALLS

1 egg	¼ teaspoon allspice
¾ pound chopped fresh beef	1 cup fine soft bread crumbs
½ pound chopped fresh veal	⅓ cup dehydrated skim milk
2 tablespoons peeled grated onion	1 cup lukewarm water
1½ teaspoons salt	Butter or margarine for browning
¼ teaspoon ground pepper	

Break the egg into a 3-quart bowl; beat slightly. Add the beef, veal, onion, salt, pepper, allspice, bread crumbs and skim milk. Mix well. Add the water. Stir and beat vigorously until smooth, creamy and very thick. Refrigerate 1 hour. Form into walnut-sized balls. Brown evenly in butter or margarine, turning occasionally. Then continue to cook slowly about 7 minutes. Accompany with barbecued beans or toast with or without gravy made from the residue in the pan. Serves 4.

CANNELON OF BEEF

⅓ cup soft enriched bread
  crumbs
⅓ cup hot water
2 pounds chopped chuck
4 sprigs fresh parsley
1½ teaspoons salt

¼ teaspoon pepper
1 onion, peeled and sliced
⅓ teaspoon ground nutmeg
1 large egg, beaten
6 slices bacon, scalded

Mix crumbs and water. Next put beef through chopper with parsley, salt, pepper, onion and nutmeg. Mix in egg and crumbs. Let stand 10 minutes. Shape into oblong roll. Place on rack in small roasting pan. Place bacon atop loaf. Bake 40 minutes in moderate (375°) oven, or until both bacon and loaf are well browned. Accompany with spaghetti, which is served with mushroom sauce.

FAIL-SAFE MEAT LOAF

2 eggs
1 medium-sized onion,
  quartered if blender is used
½ cup mushroom or beef
  gravy
1 scant teaspoon salt
Generous sprinkling pepper
¼ cup white wine
1 beef bouillon cube
½ teaspoon savory

½ teaspoon basil
1 tablespoon Worcestershire
  sauce
2 tablespoons parsley
1 section garlic, peeled
1½ pounds ground chuck or
  round
¾ to 1 cup seasoned stuffing
  crumbs

In blender, combine all ingredients except meat and stuffing crumbs. Buzz until smooth. Pour over crumbs and stir until crumbs soften a bit. Add meat and mix thoroughly. Form into a loaf. Bake at 375° 1½ hours until brown and crusty.

If you haven't a blender, combine ingredients as stated but beat eggs, mash garlic, grate onion and dissolve bouillon cube in warmed wine. Proceed as above.

If you really like a decidedly "herby" flavor, increase quantities of savory and basil to 1 teaspoon each.

FOUR-MEATS LOAF

1 pound ground beef
¼ pound ground fresh pork
¼ pound ground veal
1 sausage, skinned and mashed
1 egg
¼ cup wheat germ

½ cup milk
1½ teaspoons seasoned salt
¼ teaspoon pepper
1 teaspoon ground thyme
Spiced Glazed Parsnips (see Index)

Put meats through chopper twice. Combine with remaining ingredients except parsnips in order given. Mix and work together with big spoon until smooth. Pack into an oiled 5×9-inch loaf pan. Bake 1 hour in a moderate (350 to 375°) oven. Let stand in pan 5 minutes before serving to improve flavor. Unmold on heated large platter; surround with Parsnips.

MEAT LOAF ITALIAN STYLE

2 pounds chopped chuck or round
1 cup fresh bread crumbs
1 cup any good-quality marinara sauce
2 eggs, lightly beaten
2 medium-sized onions, peeled and fine-chopped
1 teaspoon salt

1 heaping teaspoon meat extract
1 tablespoon fine-minced fresh basil or 2 tablespoons fine-minced fresh parsley
1 large section garlic, peeled and mashed
¼ teaspoon ground cloves
¼ teaspoon ground pepper

Combine above ingredients and mix *thoroughly*. Form into a loaf and bake in a moderate (375°) oven 1½ hours until brown and crusty.

UPSIDE-DOWN MEAT LOAF

¾ cup packaged bread stuffing
½ cup milk
⅓ cup catsup
1 medium-sized onion, peeled
  and chopped
1½ pounds ground beef
¾ teaspoon salt

Few grains pepper
Few drops Tabasco
½ teaspoon Worcestershire
  sauce
3 or 4 canned cling peach
  halves
⅓ cup red currant jelly

Empty measured stuffing into large bowl. Combine milk and catsup; pour over stuffing; let stand 15 minutes, or until stuffing is soft. Add remaining ingredients except peaches and jelly; mix thoroughly until all ingredients are well blended. Arrange peach halves, cut side down, in greased loaf pan; cover with meat mixture. Bake at 350° for 1 hour. Unmold on serving platter. Fill centers of peach halves with currant jelly.

Variety Meat

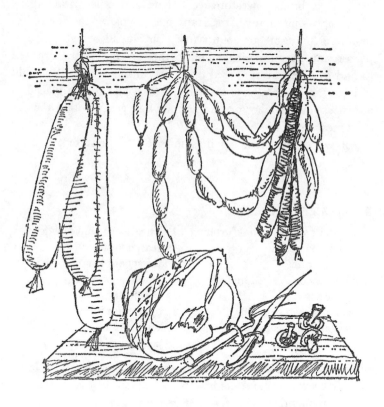

A main dinner dish each week based on one of the variety meats will give a nice change and will help to control that meat bill. Protein-vitamin, mineral-rich variety meats include liver, kidneys, tripe, brains, sweetbreads, tongue and other vital organs of animals that many Americans once bypassed as foods. As more and more of our countryfolk visit abroad or eat in European restaurants in their own cities, they are pleasantly surprised to find excellent dishes based on variety meats. Some, if not all, of these meats are always available. And if an order is placed in advance, your butcher or market man can easily obtain the desired meat for you!

All recipes are for six servings unless otherwise stated.

BARBECUED FRANKS

2 pounds skinless frankfurters
3 tablespoons butter or margarine
2 tablespoons peeled minced onion
½ teaspoon garlic salt
1¼ tablespoons table mustard
½ teaspoon salt
1½ teaspoons chili powder
½ teaspoon sugar
2 tablespoons lemon juice or 1 tablespoon vinegar
½ cup water
1 cup tomato juice
Baked beans or Rice Jambalaya (see Index)

Slash each frankfurter not quite through, diagonally in 6 places. Lightly brown frankfurters in 1½ tablespoons of the margarine; reserve remainder. Mix together remaining margarine and all other ingredients except baked beans or Rice Jambalaya. Add the resulting mixture to frankfurters. Turn them over and cover. Simmer about 8 minutes. Serve with baked beans or with Rice Jambalaya.

BROILED STUFFED FRANKFURTERS

Split each frankfurter almost in half lengthwise. Pack in a choice of desired stuffing; brush all over with cooking oil. Broil as usual. The following stuffings are enough for 4 average-sized frankfurters.

Cheddar Cheese Stuffing: Combine ½ pound grated sharp processed Cheddar cheese with 2 tablespoons grated fresh onion and ¼ cup chopped pimiento-stuffed olives.

Spinach Stuffing: Combine 1½ cups well-drained, seasoned, chopped, cooked fresh or frozen spinach with 1 tablespoon dry bread crumbs and 1 tablespoon catsup. After stuffing, dust frankfurter tops with ¼ cup Parmesan cheese and broil.

Baked Bean Stuffing: Mash 1½ cups well-drained baked beans (homemade or canned), and mix with ½ tablespoon each pickle relish, chow-chow and snappy pepper relish.

FRANKFURTERS PIQUANT

Melt 2 tablespoons butter or margarine over medium heat. Add 1 pound skinless frankfurters and 1 small onion, peeled and chopped. Slow-fry until the onion is tender. Mix ¼ cup wine vinegar, ¼ cup water and 1 tablespoon table mustard. Add to the frankfurters. Cover and simmer 10 minutes. Remove the frankfurters. Mix in ¾ cup dairy sour cream and ½ cup sweet pickle relish. Add the frankfurters and reheat. Serve with flaky boiled potatoes or mashed potatoes. Or serve each frankfurter on a toasted halved frankfurter roll, the sauce spooned over; sliced tomato on lettuce the garnish. Serves 4 to 6.

RITZY SLUMGULLION

Just right for three couples to enjoy at a picnic cooking area. The food is precooked and then divided into three empty coffee cans, sealed with the plastic tops or with foil, then reheated, with foil coverings, at mealtime. Also great for a teen-age party.

4 slices bacon, cut in small
squares
1 medium onion, peeled and
chopped
1 (1-pound) can tomatoes
2 (1-pound) cans red kidney
beans, drained
1 (12-ounce) can kernel corn,
drained

1 (3-ounce) can broiled
mushrooms, with liquid
1 (10¾-ounce) can beef-
flavored mushroom gravy
2 tablespoons chili powder
½ pound sharp Cheddar
cheese, grated
2 (12-ounce) cans frankfurters

Fry bacon crisp. Drain on absorbent paper; set aside. Cook onion in 2 tablespoons of bacon drippings until soft but not brown. Add next six ingredients. Bring to boiling point. Add cheese. Stir until cheese melts. Cut frankfurters in thirds. Add with bacon bits to other ingredients. Bring to serving temperature. Fill into 3 (1-pound) coffee cans. When ready to serve, heat on grill. If can tops are plastic, replace with aluminum foil before putting on grill. Pass sliced canned brown bread and plenty of delicious coffee as accompaniments.

TOAD IN THE HOLE

1 cup sifted flour
2 large eggs, beaten
1½ cups milk
½ teaspoon salt

Generous sprinkling pepper
1 pound link or brown-and-
serve-type sausages

Have milk and eggs at room temperature. Combine flour, eggs and ¾ cup of the milk, beating until smooth and bubbles form. Stir in remaining milk, salt and pepper and mix well. Cover. Cook sausages. Drain. In an 8-inch square or a 10×6-inch baking pan, heat 2 tablespoons of drippings until sizzling hot. Pour ½ of the batter into the pan, quickly arrange sausages over it, then pour in the remaining batter. Bake at 375° for 40 minutes, or until puffed and golden.

RABBIT PIE

¼ cup butter or margarine	Salt and pepper to taste
¼ cup peeled chopped onion	3 cups coarse-cut cooked
½ cup seeded chopped green	rabbit meat (broiled or
pepper	roasted fresh or frozen
¼ cup sifted flour	rabbit)
2 cups hot rabbit broth (or	Pastry for Savory Pies
water with 4 chicken	
bouillon cubes)	

Heat butter or margarine in large fry pan. Add onion and green pepper; slow-sauté 5 minutes. Stir in flour; cook until mixture bubbles. Pour in broth gradually, stirring constantly. Cook until thick and smooth, stirring often. Add salt and pepper to taste. Stir in rabbit meat. Bring to rapid boil. Pour into buttered shallow 3-pint baking dish or pan. Roll out Pastry for Savory Pies and cut 3 slits in center for steam escape. Fit to top of dish or pan, crimping edges of crust. Bake pie 15 to 20 minutes in a hot (425°) oven, or until crust browns and sauce bubbles.

Pastry for Savory Pies:

1 cup sifted flour	⅓ cup lard
½ teaspoon salt	2 tablespoons cold water

Sift flour and salt together; cut in lard with pastry blender or chopping knife. Mix in just enough water to hold ingredients together.

VENISON STEW WITH POTATO DUMPLINGS

3 pounds venison shoulder	6 peppercorns
4 tablespoons butter	2 cloves
4 tablespoons flour	1 bay leaf
1½ teaspoons salt	Juice of ½ lemon
2 cups stock or bouillon	½ cup red wine
4 cups hot water	Potato Dumplings
1 small onion, peeled and sliced	

Rinse meat with cold water; wipe dry. Cut in serving-sized pieces. Heat butter in deep kettle. Stir flour smoothly in and cook until browned. Add salt, stock and hot water; stir and mix well. Add onions, peppercorns, cloves, bay leaf and lemon juice. Bring to boil and let boil 5 minutes. Put in meat. Cover pot; boil gently 1½ hours. Add wine and mix with gravy in pot; continue cooking 15 minutes. Serve with Potato Dumplings.

Potato Dumplings (Kartoffelklösse) :

2 pounds raw medium-sized potatoes (about 6)	1 teaspoon minced parsley
4 slices white bread	2 eggs, well beaten
1 teaspoon salt	¼ cup flour
¼ teaspoon pepper	1½ quarts boiling salted water
1 onion, peeled and grated	

Wash, peel and grate potatoes. Soak bread in a little cold water for 5 minutes; squeeze out as much water as possible. Mix bread, salt, pepper, onion and parsley. Add potatoes and eggs; mix well; form into balls; roll lightly in flour; drop into the boiling salted water. Cover pot tightly; boil 15 minutes. Serve with venison. The dumplings can also be served with beef, chicken or game.

BARBECUED HASH

¼ cup peeled chopped onion
¼ cup chopped green pepper
2 tablespoons oil
3 cups chopped cooked beef, pork or veal
1½ cups peeled chopped cooked potatoes

1 cup broth or water
2 tablespoons catsup
3 tablespoons chili sauce
½ tablespoon Worcestershire sauce

Sauté onion and green pepper in oil until golden brown. Add meat, potatoes and broth or water. Stir in catsup, chili sauce and Worcestershire, and transfer to a 7×11-inch oiled pan or oblong baking dish. Bake about 45 minutes, or until browned in a hot (400°) oven.

QUINTET OF BOILED MEATS

1 (3-pound) smoked tongue, not cooked
½ cup peeled sliced onions
¾ cup peeled, quartered carrots
¾ cup sliced celery
4 sprigs parsley
1 pound slice round of beef, ½ inch thick

1 pound rolled breast of veal
1 (2½-pound) broiler fryer, halved
2 sausages, Polish or Italian
½ teaspoon black pepper
Parsley sprigs
Sauce Piquant or canned tomato sauce, heated

In a large (6-quart) kettle, place tongue; add *cold* water to cover. Bring to boiling point; drain. Cover with fresh *boiling* water. Add vegetables and parsley. Simmer-boil 1 hour. Remove any froth from surface of liquid. Add beef and veal. Simmer-boil 1 hour. Add chicken, sausages and pepper. Simmer-boil 1 hour longer. The meats should all be tender. Taste broth; if necessary, add salt. Drain, and reserve broth.

Slice and add meats, and section the chicken (use half of each for 1 dinner). Center on large platter. Garnish with parsley sprigs. Pass Sauce Piquant. Makes enough for 2 meals.

Sauce Piquant:

3 tablespoons vegetable oil	½ cup meat broth
1 tablespoon wine vinegar or garlic vinegar	½ teaspoon table mustard
1 (8-ounce) can tomato sauce	3 hard-cooked egg yolks, mashed

In saucepan, combine first four ingredients. Bring to boiling point. Stir-cook over low heat 3 minutes. Mix together mustard and egg yolks; stir into cooking sauce. Serve hot.

BRAINS AND SWEETBREADS

Do you like sweetbreads? They are expensive; but here is an interesting fact: Brains cost only a fraction as much, and when properly cooked, they have a similar smooth, firm texture and may be used interchangeably with sweetbreads in many dishes. So you can substitute cooked brains for sweetbreads in using your own favorite recipes. The basic preparation for both brains and sweetbreads is the same.

BASIC PREPARATION FOR BRAINS AND SWEETBREADS

First, soak 1 pound of brains or sweetbreads in cold water for 1 hour. Change water twice during this time. Then drain; place brains in saucepan; cover with 1 quart boiling water; add 1 teaspoon salt and 1 tablespoon vinegar and slow-boil 20 minutes. Drain; cover with cold water to firm the meat, then drain again. Remove any excess fibers and divide into sections or slice to use as desired.

FRIED BRAINS OR SWEETBREADS

Dust prepared brains or sweetbreads with flour seasoned with salt and pepper; sauté in butter or margarine. Serve with crisp bacon, or with Spanish sauce, or hot Tartar Sauce (see Index).

SWEETBREADS SPANISH

3 pairs sweetbreads or 6 frozen sweetbreads
3 cups boiling water
¾ teaspoon salt
3 tablespoons cider vinegar
6 scallions, chopped with 1 inch green tops
3 tablespoons Spanish olive oil
3 small tomatoes, peeled and seeded, or 3 tablespoons tomato paste

1 medium carrot, peeled and grated
1½ cups chicken broth or bouillon
6 large mushroom crowns
1 teaspoon butter
1 teaspoon olive oil

Add sweetbreads to the water with salt and vinegar, which tends to firm and keep them white when cooked. Slow-boil until tender, about 30 minutes; if frozen, cook 15 minutes longer. Rinse at once with cold water. If fresh, remove tubes and membranes. Slice the sweetbreads in halves crosswise. Sauté the scallions in the oil until the color turns. Add the tomatoes; cook until soft. Add the carrot and chicken broth; cook 5 minutes. Rub the sauce through a food mill or buzz in a blender. Then boil down until one-third reduced and thickened. Spoon into 6 individual low casseroles. Place a half sweetbread in each casserole. Top each with a mushroom crown and brush with the combined melted butter and additional olive oil. Heat 20 minutes in a moderate (350°) oven.

Note: Can be prepared in advance for final quick cooking.

BASIC PREPARATION FOR KIDNEYS

Remove all fat. Wash the kidneys; remove the tubes, gristle and all white centers or "eyes" as they are called. Soak the kidneys 30 minutes in cold water to cover, containing 1 teaspoon salt and 1 tablespoon of vinegar to 1 quart. Drain; rinse under running water.

ENGLISH BEEF KIDNEY PUDDING

Short Biscuit Pastry
1 pound diced chuck steak or
   thin-sliced flank steak
3 veal kidneys
½ cup enriched flour

1 teaspoon salt
⅛ teaspoon pepper
1 cup cold water
1 teaspoon bouillon powder
Brussels sprouts

Prepare Short Biscuit Pastry. Roll ⅓ inch thick and line a 3-pint bowl, allowing pastry to drop over edge. Thin-slice or dice steak; prepare kidneys as directed above; cut in bite-sized pieces. Mix together flour and seasonings; roll two meats in this until all flour has been used. Place in pastry-lined bowl. Add water with bouillon powder dissolved in it. Moisten edges of pastry; fold up over meat, enclosing it completely. Put plate in good-sized saucepan. Stand pudding on it; pour boiling water to ½ inch the depth of bowl. Cover; boil steadily 3 hours. If necessary to add more water, be sure it is boiling, as cold water would tend to make the pastry heavy. Turn out on platter. Serve surrounded with buttered Brussels sprouts.

Short Biscuit Pastry:

2 cups sifted flour
2½ teaspoons baking powder
½ teaspoon salt

⅓ cup lard or shortening
¾ cup cold water
2 tablespoons margarine

Sift together dry ingredients. Add shortening; chop in with pastry blender until the mixture looks flaky. Slowly mix in water with fork. Transfer to floured surface. Press dough together; dust with flour; roll scant ½ inch thick. Stir margarine until creamy. Spread to within ½ inch of the edge of dough. Fold over and press edges together. Then lightly roll again scant ½ inch thick.

KIDNEY STEW

1 beef kidney or 6 lamb kidneys	⅔ teaspoon salt
3 cups water	⅙ teaspoon pepper
2 medium-sized onions, peeled and sliced	2 tablespoons flour
	1 teaspoon dry mustard
6 slices bacon or salt pork, diced	Toast or boiled rice

If beef kidney is used, cut from the central tough fiber; if lamb kidneys, remove the thin skin and split the kidneys lengthwise into halves. Soak them for 1 hour in lukewarm water slightly salted, drain and put them into a saucepan with cold water and bring slowly to boiling point, discard this first water and add the 3 cups of cold water; bring slowly to boiling point again, skim, add the onions and the bacon or salt pork; simmer until the kidneys are tender—lamb kidneys will take about 1 hour, beef kidneys 1½ to 2 hours. Add salt and pepper when half done, thicken with the flour and mustard rubbed smoothly with a little cold water. Cook for 5 minutes and serve with a garnish of toast or boiled rice. If the oven is being used for other cooking, the kidneys may be baked instead of stewed, using the same recipe.

BEEF KIDNEYS AND MUSHROOMS BRITTANY

2 beef kidneys	⅛ teaspoon pepper
½ bay leaf	1 (5-ounce) can sliced mushrooms
1½ cups water	
1 cup any California dry red wine	1 tablespoon minced chives
	½ pound broad high-protein noodles
2½ tablespoons butter or margarine	
	4 cups boiling salted water
2 tablespoons flour	2 tablespoons butter or margarine
¾ teaspoon salt	

Soak beef kidneys 1 hour in cold water. Remove the strings and membranes and thin-slice the meat. Add the bay leaf to the water and pour in wine. Cream together butter or margarine and flour. Add a little of the boiling wine mixture, and when smooth return it to the sauce until boiling all over. Add salt and pepper. Add the kidneys; cover and simmer until tender, about 30 minutes. Add mushrooms and chives. Continue to simmer 15 minutes longer. Meantime cook noodles in boiling water, which they will absorb. Season with additional butter or margarine, and use to line a heated deep platter. Pour over the kidney-mushroom mixture and serve very hot.

LIVER, BACON, TOMATO-SLICE PLATTER

16 slices bacon	Pinch of pepper
1½ pounds sliced calf, lamb, beef or pork liver	8 slices tomato
	2 tablespoons milk
⅓ cup all-purpose flour	⅓ cup seasoned bread crumbs
½ teaspoon crushed dry dill	12 small sprigs parsley or water
½ teaspoon salt	cress

Pan-fry bacon until crisp or, better still, bake-fry it in moderate (350°) oven. Reserve fat to use as needed in preparing remaining foods for platter.

Order liver with the skin removed. Stir together flour and dill; dust over the liver. Season with salt and pepper. Let stand 10 minutes. Sauté 8 to 10 minutes in bacon fat over moderate heat, or until browned.

The tomatoes should be firm and not quite ripe. Slice ½ inch thick. Brush with milk and dip into seasoned bread crumbs. Let stand at least 10 minutes to set the crumbs. Sauté in reserved bacon fat.

Top liver slices with bacon and parade them smartly down the center of the platter. Surround with sautéed tomato slices, separating them with small sprigs of parsley or water cress.

BAKED LIVER SLICES

1 tablespoon flour
1 teaspoon seasoned salt
½ teaspoon ground sage
1¾ pound beef liver, skinned
  and thin-sliced

1½ tablespoons cooking oil
Sage-Crumb Topping

Mix together flour, seasoned salt and sage. Cut liver into 6 servings. Rub flour mixture all over each side. Brush a 7×11-inch low baking pan with 1 tablespoon oil. Put in liver slices; brush over remaining oil. Bake 10 minutes at 350°; then spread with Sage-Crumb Topping. Return pan to oven and bake 20 minutes more, or until topping is golden brown.

Sage-Crumb Topping:

1½ tablespoons cooking oil
1 tablespoon each minced
  celery, onion and green
  pepper
2 cups fine soft white bread
  crumbs

¾ teaspoon ground sage
½ teaspoon seasoned salt
¼ cup milk or meat broth, or
  enough just to moisten

Heat oil in 9-inch fry pan. Add minced vegetables; slow stir-fry until color turns. Then add crumbs, sage and seasoned salt; fry-stir until crumbs are light brown. Stir in milk or broth. Spread this topping over liver slices, and finish as directed in previous recipe.

LIVER CREOLE

1½ pounds calf's or beef liver, skinned

3 tablespoons flour

4 tablespoons margarine or chicken fat

¾ teaspoon salt

⅛ teaspoon pepper

1 (1-pound) can tomatoes

2 green peppers, seeded and shredded

2 medium-sized onions, peeled and sliced

¼ cup sliced celery

⅛ teaspoon garlic powder

6 cups cooked converted rice (2½ cups raw rice)

Parsley spriglets (optional)

Order liver skinned and sliced ½ inch thick. Dust with flour, making a light coating all over. Then fry quickly, about 8 minutes, in margarine or chicken fat, adding salt and pepper as it cooks. Remove liver and set it aside to keep warm. Into pan in which liver was cooked, put tomatoes, green peppers, onions, celery and garlic powder; stir together. Cook-stir often until tender and blended, about 10 minutes. This is the Creole sauce.

On heated large platter, make border of hot, cooked converted rice. Center this with liver; top with Creole sauce. Garnish with parsley spriglets if desired.

LIVER IBERIAN

You can cook this in advance and reheat at dinnertime.

1½ pounds beef liver

1¼ teaspoons salt

⅓ cup flour

5 tablespoons olive oil

1 medium-sized onion, peeled and coarse-chopped

¾ cup tomato juice

1 tablespoon paprika

½ teaspoon table mustard

¾ cup water or beef broth

Juice and grated rind of 1 small lemon

Order liver skinned and sliced ¼ inch thick. Cut into bite-sized pieces. Stir salt and flour together; dust over liver. Sauté in oil until lightly browned on both sides. Keep heat moderate. Remove. Add onion to pan. Sauté until tender. Add remaining ingredients; simmer 10 minutes, or until smooth. Add liver to sauce. Cover. Simmer 20 minutes.

LIVER LYONNAISE

1½ pounds liver, skinned and sliced ½ inch thick (any kind)
3 tablespoons melted butter or margarine
1 teaspoon salt
¼ teaspoon pepper
2½ cups sliced onions, fried
1 tablespoon vinegar
½ teaspoon seasoned salt
Parsley sprigs

Slash sliced liver 8 times ½ inch deep at the edge so it will not "curl" while cooking. Brush with melted butter. Rub broiler rack with fat; place liver on it. Broil slowly about 7 minutes, seasoning with salt and pepper and turning when half done. Meantime prepare the onions; add vinegar and seasoned salt. Overlap liver slices on warm platter. Surround with the onions. Garnish with parsley.

OVEN-BRAISED LIVER

1 pound beef liver
¼ cup flour
1 teaspoon salt
½ cup fat or oil
1 pint beef or chicken broth

Skin liver and cut in 1-inch pieces. Roll in flour and salt sifted together. Brown in fat or oil. Place liver in a 7×11-inch baking pan. Pour broth over liver. (If desired, use 1 cup tomato purée and 1 cup broth or water.) Bake uncovered 45 minutes in moderate (350°) oven. Accompany with noodles, grits, mashed potatoes or rice.

CHICKEN LIVERS SAUTÉ ON BROILED HAM SLICES

12 chicken livers
¾ teaspoon seasoned salt
2 tablespoons flour
1½ tablespoons butter

1½ tablespoons cooking oil
6 thin round slices broiled
   smoked ham
Parsley

Rinse chicken livers with cold water, then drain on paper towels. Mix together seasoned salt and flour; coat the livers with this mixture. Heat butter and oil in a 10-inch skillet. Add the livers; sauté gently until well browned, turning often. Meantime broil ham and set aside.

To serve, arrange 2 livers atop each slice of broiled ham. Garnish with parsley.

OXTAIL STEW

2 oxtails, cut into joints
Flour as needed
3 tablespoons fat
4 cups chicken or beef stock or
   4 cups water and 4 bouillon
   cubes
1½ teaspoons salt
¼ teaspoon pepper

1½ cups peeled and sliced
   carrots
½ cup peeled and sliced onion
1½ cups diced turnips
½ cup chopped green
   pepper
¼ cup red California wine
Buttered noodles

Roll oxtail joints in flour; brown in fat. Add stock and seasonings. Cover; simmer 3 hours, or until tender. Add vegetables; simmer 1 hour. Add wine and simmer 5 minutes. Serve in a border of buttered noodles.

BEEF TONGUE NEW STYLE

1 (3-pound) "ready-to-eat" smoked beef tongue
3 large bay leaves
Horseradish sauce or brown mustard sauce

Put beef tongue in a 4-quart kettle. Cover with cold water and slowly bring to a rapid boil. Thoroughly drain off water, then pour in boiling water to cover tongue. Add bay leaves. Cover and simmer-boil 2 hours. Most of the salt is cooked out, leaving the delicate smoked flavor. Serve hot with horseradish sauce or brown mustard sauce. Every morsel of the tongue can be used and not a bit wasted.

TONGUE MOLDED IN ASPIC

1½ envelopes unflavored gelatin
1 cup cold water
1 (10½-ounce) can condensed beef broth
2 teaspoons vinegar
3 drops Tabasco

2 cups cubed cooked tongue (home cooked or canned)
¾ cup fine-chopped celery
3½ tablespoons pickle relish
2 tablespoons minced green onion
Crisp salad greens

Sprinkle gelatin on cold water to soften. Place over low heat; stir until gelatin dissolves. Remove from heat; stir in broth, vinegar and Tabasco. Refrigerate 30 minutes, or until slightly thickened. Fold in cubed tongue, celery, pickle relish, onion; pour into a 5-cup mold or loaf pan first rinsed with cold water. Refrigerate 6 hours, or until firm. Unmold on platter. Garnish with crisp salad greens.

TRIPE CREOLE

2 pounds tripe
2 cups tomato sauce
1 green pepper, minced

½ teaspoon onion juice
Boiled rice

Soak tripe in cold water for 24 hours. Cover with fresh water and bring to a boil. Lower heat and cook ½ hour. Drain and cut into 1½-inch squares. Heat in the sauce to which the minced pepper and onion juice have been added. Simmer 15 minutes over hot water (double boiler); serve with a border of boiled rice.

Poultry

For generations in this country, chicken was the most elegant among the entrees. Chicken and more chicken—that was a homemaker's dream. But chicken was expensive. To devise or learn more ways to make it "go further" was an important facet of poultry cookery. At last there was a break-through. Chicken production was brought out of the small farm-growing class and has become a gigantic scientific industry.

Today chicken is just as "elegant" but is much kinder on the budget. Recipes have been gathered from round the world and many have become favorites in this country. These include Chicken Marengo, Chicken Paella (see Index) and chicken recipes from Persia, Sweden, Japan and the Caribbean. Some are quick, simple, easy to prepare, others call for longer cooking—all are a real treat.

All recipes are for six servings unless otherwise stated.

ARROZ CON POLLO

2 (3-pound) broiler-fryers
½ cup peeled chopped onion
1 section garlic, peeled and crushed
2 tablespoons minced parsley
1½ teaspoons salt
2 tablespoons butter
¼ cup olive or salad oil
½ teaspoon oregano
¼ cup chopped bacon
¼ cup chopped ham scraps
2 onions, peeled and sliced
1 section garlic, peeled and crushed
3 green peppers, seeded and diced

2 tablespoons butter
1 (1-pound) can tomatoes
2½ cups chicken broth or 2½ cups water and 2 teaspoons broth powder
2½ cups uncooked long-grain rice
½ teaspoon fine-crushed saffron
3 teaspoons capers
3½ cups cooked green peas
6 canned asparagus tips
1 (2½-ounce) can pimientos
2 hard-cooked eggs, chopped fine

This dish consists of three parts: chicken, sauce and rice. Order chickens sectioned as for fricassee. Combine in fry pan with ½ cup chopped onion, crushed garlic, parsley, salt, butter and oil, oregano, bacon and ham. Simmer-sauté until chicken is lightly browned; turn often.

To make sauce, put additional onion and garlic with green peppers and additional butter in second fry pan. Simmer-sauté until lightly browned. Add tomatoes; simmer 20 minutes. Rub through sieve into chicken.

To chicken broth add rice and saffron. Stir and bring to boiling point. Stir in chicken. Transfer to a 3-quart low casserole. Cover. Bake 30 to 35 minutes in very hot (425 to 450°) oven, or until the rice is bite-tender and flaky. With fork, gently stir in capers.

Decorate with a border of peas, asparagus tips and strips of pimiento, and chopped egg smartly heaped in center. Serves 8.

CALIFORNIA BAKED CHICKEN

2½ pounds sectioned chicken parts
1½ teaspoons salt
¼ teaspoon pepper
¼ cup butter or margarine
2 teaspoons freeze-dried shallots

½ cup dry white wine or sparkling white grape juice
¼ cup medium-chopped parsley

Clean chicken as necessary. Rinse and pat dry. Dust with salt and pepper. In square or rectangular baking dish, put butter and shallots. Place in oven and set at 350°. When butter melts and shallots are light brown, dip in chicken pieces and turn them over. Arrange in one layer in pan, or casserole, skin side up. Pour wine over chicken; dust with parsley. Bake 1½ hours, or until chicken is fork-tender, crisp and golden brown. The wine will be practically evaporated.

CRISP BARBECUED CHICKEN

3 broiler-fryer chickens, halved
   or quartered
½ cup butter or margarine
½ cup lemon juice
2 tablespoons soy sauce

½ teaspoon Tabasco
2 teaspoons barbecue
   seasoning
2 cups medium-fine soft bread
   crumbs

Wash and dry chicken. In a ½-pint saucepan, combine butter, lemon juice, soy sauce, Tabasco and barbecue seasoning; heat until butter melts. Brush both sides of chicken pieces with sauce. Broil on grill over medium-hot coals about 15 minutes on each side, brushing with more sauce when chicken is turned. When lightly browned and almost done, brush again with the sauce; roll in the bread crumbs and continue broiling until the chicken is fork-tender and the crust is crisp; turn often.

BROILED DRUMSTICKS À LA MODE

1½ teaspoons seasoned salt
½ cup melted butter or
   margarine
⅛ teaspoon each ground
   savory, rosemary, tarragon
   and thyme
2 tablespoons lemon juice
1 tablespoon wine vinegar

6 or more chicken drumsticks
   as desired
½ cup minced fresh parsley
Buttered flaky rice
Parsley sprigs or butter-broiled
   mushroom caps, each
   centered with a pitted ripe
   olive

Two hours or more in advance, combine and mix salt, butter, seasonings, lemon juice, vinegar in a 1-quart shallow bowl to make marinade. Put in drumsticks; turn over to coat with marinade. Cover. Turn again in 1 hour.

Arrange drumsticks on broiler rack. Brush over part of remaining marinade. Broil 40 minutes 4 inches from source of heat. Turn several times; the use of tongs makes this easy. When ready to serve dust over the minced parsley. Mound rice in center of warm, large platter. Stand drumsticks around it, bone ends up. Garnish edge of platter with parsley sprigs or mushroom caps.

LEMON-BAKED CHICKEN

2 (2½-pound) ready-to-cook broiler-fryers, quartered
¼ teaspoon fine-crushed thyme leaves
1½ teaspoons fine-crushed dry tarragon leaves
1½ teaspoons seasoned salt
2 medium-sized lemons

Rub quartered broiler-fryers all over with herbs and seasoned salt. Arrange in 1 layer in well-oiled small roasting pan. Squeeze over the juice of 1 lemon. Bake uncovered for 40 minutes at 400°. Turn over the chicken. Squeeze over juice of remaining lemon. Continue to bake 20 minutes or more, or until chicken is fork-tender and lightly browned. Serve as is or accompany with a sour cream sauce, homemade or from a mix.

CHICKEN À LA KING BAKED WITH HAM DEVILED EGGS

Ham Deviled Eggs (see Index)
⅓ cup butter or margarine
¼ cup minced green pepper
⅓ cup flour
1 cup chicken broth
1 cup milk
½ teaspoon salt
⅛ teaspoon ground pepper
1 teaspoon fine-grated onion
1½ cups large-diced cooked chicken
1 pimiento, diced
1 (4-ounce) can sliced mushrooms
2 tablespoons sherry wine or
2 tablespoons water and
1 teaspoon sherry flavoring

Prepare Ham Deviled Eggs (in advance if desired).

Melt butter or margarine; sauté green pepper till tender. Remove green pepper, add flour; stir over low heat until uniformly thickened. Add broth and milk gradually; bring to boil. Simmer over low heat 1 to 2 minutes. Add seasonings, chicken, green pepper, pimiento and mushrooms; heat thoroughly. Add sherry. Transfer to long shallow casserole (about 11 inches). Cover; bake 20 minutes in a hot (400°) oven, or until bubbly. Place

Ham Deviled Eggs atop chicken à la king to heat during last 5 minutes of baking; cover with foil so they don't brown.

CHICKEN ASPIC GOURMET

Aspics that look so tempting are not complicated to prepare and attain a professional look even when made by an inexperienced cook.

1 (3-pound) broiler-fryer chicken	2 bay leaves
3 cups water	1 teaspoon salt
1 medium-sized onion, peeled and sliced	⅛ teaspoon pepper
2 celery stalk tops	2 chicken bouillon cubes
	2 egg whites with egg shells

Place chicken in deep kettle. Add next seven ingredients; cover. Bring to a boil; simmer 40 minutes, or until tender. Remove chicken; strain broth and refrigerate. Cool; remove chicken skin; slice meat from breast; remove any meat from bones. Skim chicken fat from broth; add water to make 4 cups. To clear or clarify broth: To each quart of cold, strained broth or soup stock, add 2 egg whites with egg shells crushed and mixed together. Bring to a boil in a saucepan; then strain through a sieve lined with several layers of cheesecloth.

To Prepare Molds:

8 stuffed olive slices	3 cups cooked chicken
8 slices cooked boned ham	3 envelopes unflavored gelatin
2 (4½-ounce) cans liver pâté (4 slices to each can)	4 cups clarified chicken broth
	Chicory

Center 1 olive slice in each of 8 (1-cup) molds. Cover each slice with a slice of ham, cut to fit molds. Top ham with 1 slice liver pâté. Fill each mold evenly with chicken pieces. Dust gelatin on cold chicken broth. Heat and stir-cook 3 minutes, or until gelatin dissolves. Cool. Pour into molds. Chill 4 hours, or until firm. Unmold. Garnish with chicory. Serves 8.

BATTER-DIPPED CHICKEN

No phase in cookery has been the subject of more controversy than the frying of chicken. Here's a method ready to stand up against any contender. It's crisp, crunchy, with a corn meal batter, and it can be prepared hours in advance, ready for dipping and frying 5 minutes before dinner is served.

   2 (2½-pound) frying chickens, sectioned

Place chicken pieces, skin side up, in oiled large shallow baking pan. Bake in moderate (350°) oven about 40 minutes.

Batter Dip:

¾ cup enriched corn meal	½ teaspoon paprika
¾ cup sifted flour	¼ teaspoon pepper
1 teaspoon poultry seasoning	1 egg
1 teaspoon salt	1 cup milk

Sift together dry ingredients into a deep 1-quart bowl. Add remaining ingredients; beat with rotary beater for 2 minutes.

   Dip cooked chicken into batter; drain; dust lightly with additional corn meal. Fry in hot deep fat (375°) for 2 to 3 minutes or until golden brown. Drain on absorbent paper.

CHICKEN AU JUS

1 (4- to 5-pound) stewing chicken	¾ teaspoon crushed tarragon leaves
1 teaspoon garlic salt	½ teaspoon pepper
1 teaspoon salt	

Clean chicken as necessary. Wash, drain; blot on absorbent paper towels. Mix seasonings; dust chicken generously inside and sparingly outside. Fit chicken into deep casserole. Cover, or seal with aluminum foil. Set on rack in deep pan. Add water to half depth of casserole. Simmer 4 hours or until fork-tender. Cool slightly. Remove skin; reserve. Skim off fat from juices in casserole. Slice chicken; serve with pan gravy. Accompany with saffron rice.

Note: In some parts of Europe they make tasty chitterlings from the skin of chicken. Cut skin into 1-inch squares, and slow-sauté in oiled pan until crisp brown. Season with salt and pepper to taste. Use as garnish to sliced chicken.

CHICKEN BONNE FEMME

2 (2½-pound) chickens	18 small mushroom caps
½ pound butter	18 pearl onions
½ pound diced salt pork	2 teaspoons salt
18 new potatoes (small, size of walnut)	¼ teaspoon pepper
	½ cup chopped fresh parsley

Cut each chicken into 6 pieces (breasts and legs cut in two at joint). Heat butter. Add salt pork and sauté until lightly browned. Remove salt pork and reserve. Put chicken parts in same casserole, and sauté on both sides until lightly colored. Then add peeled raw potatoes, mushroom caps, pearl onions and reserved salt pork. Season with salt and pepper, and cook slowly covered for 35 to 40 minutes. Toss ingredients every 10 minutes so that they do not stick on bottom of pan.

When done, place chicken in serving casserole; surround chicken with accompanying vegetables. Pour over some of cooking fat. Dust with freshly chopped parsley.

CHICKEN CACCIATORE (AMERICANIZED)

⅓ cup flour	2 stalks celery, chopped
2 teaspoons salt	1 section garlic, minced
2 (3-pound) chicken fryers, sectioned	1 (15½-ounce) can spaghetti sauce with mushrooms
5 tablespoons olive or salad oil	¾ cup chicken bouillon
1 medium onion, fine-chopped	

Mix flour and salt; rub over chicken. Heat oil. Add vegetables; cook until limp. Remove and set aside. Add chicken to fry pan and brown well. Return vegetables to pan. Pour spaghetti sauce and bouillon over chicken. Cover; cook gently 45 minutes, or until fork-tender.

CHICKEN CROQUETTES

The success of any kind of croquettes depends upon the seasoning; otherwise they tend to be bland, or even blah! This recipe can be used to make croquettes of many different kinds—fish, meat or vegetable. The quantity is always 2 cups. Chicken croquettes, an old American stand-by, are made as follows:

3 tablespoons butter	2 tablespoons chopped parsley
⅓ cup flour	1 tablespoon sherry
1 cup milk	Flour
½ teaspoon salt	1 egg mixed with 1 tablespoon
Generous sprinkling pepper	water
1 egg yolk	Bread crumbs
2 cups minced chicken	Oil for deep frying
2 tablespoons finely chopped onion	

Prepare first five ingredients as for basic White Sauce (see Index). Remove from heat and add egg yolk; mix well. Add chicken, onion, parsley, sherry. Spread in greased pan and chill, covered with foil. Form into shapes 1×1×2½ inches. Roll in flour, dip in egg mixed with water, then roll in bread crumbs to coat completely. Let rest 1 hour. Fry in deep fat 375°, or until bread cube browns in 1 minute.

CHICKEN CUTLETS KIEV

2 sticks butter, melted, chilled	Rice, buttered, wild or white
6 chicken breasts (young)	Curry or ginger
1 teaspoon salt	Fresh Mushrooms Sauté (see
¼ teaspoon pepper	Index)
2 egg whites	Lemon wedges
½ cup flour	Water cress
¼ cup cold water	
1½ cups white bread crumbs, sifted	

Cut the sticks of butter into three portions each. Shape in rolls 2 inches long and ½ inch thick; freeze. Halve the chicken breasts; remove the skin, and fillet. Leave on the collarbone. Trim ragged edges from the meat. Cover the fillets with waxed paper; flatten with a meat mallet or edge of a saucer. Dust with salt and pepper. Place a frozen butter roll on each. Fold the chicken meat around into oval form; fasten firmly with wooden picks. Be sure the butter is completely covered so it will not melt out when cooking. Brush the edges with unbeaten egg white, to seal. Roll in the flour. Slightly beat together the egg whites and cold water and coat the chicken. Cover all over with the bread crumbs. Chill 10 minutes.

Meantime half fill a heavy deep (2½-quart) saucepan with corn oil (or use an electric fryer). Heat to 375°, or until a small cube of bread browns in 1 minute. Dip in a frying basket. Place the cutlets (not touching) in it. Gently lower in the chilled suprêmes, fold side up. Fry until golden brown. Remove with a large perforated spoon. Place fold side up in a pan. Bake 10 minutes in a hot (400°) oven. Remove the picks.

Serve atop curried or ginger rice to absorb the melted butter from the cutlets. Garnish with Fresh Mushrooms Sauté, lemon wedges and water cress.

Smithfield Ham Chicken Cutlets Kiev: Follow the preceding directions with this exception: Work in ½ cup Smithfield ham spread when making the butter rolls.

Cornish Game Hen Cutlets Kiev: Thaw frozen Cornish game hens, fillet the breasts, and use in place of chicken in preparing Cutlets Kiev; or purchase frozen cutlets ready to cook.

CHICKEN CURRY

Basic Indian Curry Sauce (see Index)
1 (3-pound) all-purpose chicken, steamed and cut into bite-sized pieces
½ cup yogurt or heavy cream
1 teaspoon ground poppy seeds or 1½ teaspoons ground blanched almonds
2 tablespoons packaged coconut, sugar removed*
Ceylon Rice (see Index)

Make the Basic Indian Curry Sauce but use chicken broth instead of water and omit the beef broth powder. Add chicken to sauce; heat 20 minutes. Stir in yogurt or heavy cream, poppy seeds or blanched almonds and coconut. Bring to boil; serve with Ceylon Rice.

* To de-sugar coconut: Add ¼ cup water to 2 tablespoons packaged flaked coconut. Bring to boil; drain and rinse with cold water.

FRIED CHICKEN WITH GRAVY

½ cup dry bread crumbs
½ teaspoon crushed rosemary
1 teaspoon salt
Dash pepper
1 broiler-fryer, completely sectioned
1 egg, beaten
½ cup corn oil
1 tablespoon cornstarch
1½ cups milk

Combine dry bread crumbs, rosemary, salt and pepper. Dip chicken pieces in egg. Coat with crumb mixture. Heat corn oil 3 minutes in large, heavy skillet over medium heat. Add chicken and brown on all sides. Reduce heat to low. Cover and cook 30 minutes, or until chicken is fork-tender. Remove cover; cook 10 minutes more. Remove and drain on paper toweling. Keep warm.

Pour drippings from the skillet into a cup. Measure 2 tablespoons drippings back into the skillet. Mix in cornstarch. Place over low heat. Gradually stir in milk. Stirring constantly, bring to a boil and boil 1 minute. Serve with chicken. Serves 4.

CHICKEN WITH HAM BÉCHAMEL SAUCE

1 onion, peeled and chopped
3 tablespoons butter
8 ounces egg noodles, cooked
   by package directions
½ pound fresh mushrooms
4 cups cooked and diced
   chicken

2 cups cooked and diced ham
Sauce Béchamel (see Index)
1 cup light cream
1 cup grated Cheddar cheese

Sauté onion in butter until limp; remove onion and reserve. Cook and drain noodles and reserve. Wash and slice mushrooms. Brown mushrooms in onion-flavored butter. Add onion, chicken, ham, half the Sauce Béchamel, and half the cream. Add remaining sauce and cream to cooked noodles. Layer chicken mixture and noodles alternately in a buttered 2½-quart casserole. Top with cheese. Bake 25 minutes at 350°.

CHICKEN FRICASSEE

1 (5-pound) stewing chicken,
   cut up
2 onions, quartered
2 whole cloves
1 small carrot, diced
1 stalk celery with leaves, sliced
3 sprigs parsley
1 clove garlic, minced
1 bay leaf

½ teaspoon thyme
2 teaspoons salt
3 tablespoons butter or
   margarine
2 tablespoons flour
1 cup evaporated milk, light
   cream or half and half
Salt and pepper to taste
Parsley for garnish (optional)

Put chicken, onions, cloves, carrot, celery, parsley, garlic, bay leaf and thyme into a large kettle. Add salt, and water to cover. Bring to a boil and simmer, covered, 2 to 2½ hours or until chicken is tender. Remove to hot platter, keep warm in oven. Strain broth and remove fat. Melt butter in saucepan, stir in flour and gradually add evaporated milk or light cream mixed with 1½ cups reserved broth. Cook, stirring, until thickened.

Add additional salt and pepper to taste. Pour sauce over chicken and garnish with chopped parsley.

HERBED CHICKEN LAYER CASSEROLE

1 (3-pound) broiler-fryer, sectioned	1 cup canned corn kernels, drained
1½ teaspoons seasoned salt	1 cup bouillon
⅓ cup salad oil	2 tablespoons butter or 3 strips smoked bacon, diced and scalded
6 cups packaged herbed poultry stuffing	
2 onions, peeled and fine-chopped	

Rub the chicken all over with the seasoned salt and brown in the oil. Meantime, prepare the herbed poultry stuffing using packaged herbed crumbs or following a standard recipe. Add the onions and corn kernels. Alternately layer the chicken sections and the stuffing in an oiled, low 3-quart casserole. Pour in the bouillon. Cover. Bake 1½ hours in a moderate (375°) oven; uncover the last 20 minutes. At this point, dot with butter or strew with smoked bacon. Return to the oven to brown.

CHICKEN WITH LIME BAKE

2 fresh limes	4 tablespoons cooking oil or margarine
2 (2½- to 3-pound) broiler-fryers, sectioned	2 tablespoons brown sugar
⅓ cup flour	½ cup chicken broth
1½ teaspoons salt	½ cup dry white wine
1 teaspoon paprika	6 sprigs fresh mint
¼ teaspoon garlic powder	1 avocado, peeled and sliced

Grate peel of limes and set aside. Squeeze lime juice over chicken parts. In plastic bag, mix flour, salt, paprika and garlic powder. Put in chicken parts; close bag and shake to coat chicken parts evenly. Remove and fry until golden brown in cooking oil or margarine. Place chicken parts in single layer in roasting pan. Mix together grated peel of limes and brown sugar. Add broth and wine; pour mixture over chicken. Bake 1 hour in a moderate (350°) oven. Serve on warm large platter. Garnish with mint and avocado slices. Serves 8 to 10.

Note: Two tablespoons bottled lime juice may be used if fresh limes are unavailable. The wine evaporates in cooking, leaving only the flavor.

MARINATED CHICKEN BAKE

2 (2½-pound) broilers, quartered

The Marinade:

⅓ cup corn oil
⅓ cup fresh lemon juice
1½ teaspoons fine instant
    onion
⅓ teaspoon garlic powder

3 teaspoons crushed dried
    tarragon
2½ teaspoons salt
¼ teaspoon pepper
½ cup white wine (optional)

Line good-sized baking pan with double duty foil. In it, arrange chicken quarters, skin side down. Heat together all remaining ingredients. When boiling, pour over chicken. Cover with foil. Refrigerate at least 2 hours, up to all day to develop full flavor. To cook, drain off excess marinade from the chicken; reserve for basting and seasoning other foods. Spoon 1 tablespoon marinade over chicken. Cover with foil. Bake 30 minutes in moderate (350°) oven. Uncover and turn chicken. Bake uncovered for 30 to 40 minutes more, or until the chicken is golden brown. Serves 8.

GOLDEN CHICKEN PILAFF

1 teaspoon crushed saffron
2 tablespoons cold water
2 cups long-grain rice (not washed)
1 tablespoon each butter and olive oil
1 teaspoon salt
5 cups chicken broth
¼ cup chopped small onion
¼ teaspoon instant garlic
1 large green pepper, seeded and cut in squares
1 cup sliced mushrooms
4 tablespoons butter (preferably whipped)
1 cup cooked shredded green beans
1 (3-pound) cold cooked chicken, cut into bite-sized pieces
2 (2-ounce) cans pimientos, cut in squares
1 cooked or canned artichoke heart, diced (optional)
1 tablespoon chopped parsley

Combine saffron and cold water. Let stand 5 minutes. In heavy 3-quart saucepan slow-sauté rice in butter and oil until color turns. Add salt and chicken broth; strain in liquid from saffron. Cover tight. Place over high heat. When boiling vigorously, reduce heat to a simmer-boil. Simmer rice 15 minutes, then uncover. Meantime, sauté onion, garlic, green pepper and mushrooms 6 minutes in additional butter. Stir into rice with 2-prong fork. Add green beans and chicken. Cover. Add a little heated broth if too dry. Slow-heat 20 to 25 minutes over boiling water. Transfer to heated uncovered low casserole. Garnish with pimientos, heated artichoke heart and parsley.

CHICKEN MARENGO

1 (2½-pound) broiler-fryer, cut up
¼ cup oil
½ cup chopped onion
1 section garlic, peeled and minced
½ teaspoon crushed marjoram
¼ teaspoon crushed tarragon
1 teaspoon salt
¼ teaspoon pepper
½ cup dry white wine or chicken broth
1 (3-ounce) can sliced or chopped mushrooms
2 tomatoes, peeled
2 tablespoons chopped parsley

Brown chicken slowly in hot oil. Add onion, garlic and herbs; cook 5 minutes. Season with salt and pepper. Add wine and liquid drained from mushrooms. Scrape bottom of pan to loosen browned bits. Cover and cook over low heat until chicken is tender, about 40 minutes. Skim off fat. Cut tomatoes into eighths and add with mushrooms to chicken. Continue cooking covered for 5 minutes. Garnish with parsley. Serves 4.

CHICKEN NORMANDY

1 (3-pound) frying chicken, cut in serving pieces
¾ teaspoon salt
¼ cup butter or margarine
1 medium-sized onion, peeled and thin-sliced
2 tablespoons minced celery
2 tablespoons chopped parsley
2½ cups apple slices or 1 (1-pound 4-ounce) can sliced apples, drained
⅛ teaspoon thyme
½ teaspoon salt
⅛ teaspoon nutmeg
2 tablespoons heavy cream or undiluted evaporated milk
1 tablespoon salt
3 quarts boiling water
8 ounces spaghetti
Butter, salt and pepper to taste

Dust chicken with ¾ teaspoon salt. Melt butter. Add chicken and sauté over medium heat, until golden brown on all sides. Remove chicken from skillet. To drippings in skillet add onion and celery. Sauté over medium heat, stirring occasionally, 5 minutes. Add chicken, parsley, apple slices, thyme, ½ teaspoon salt and nutmeg. Cover; simmer over low heat 40 to 45 minutes; stir occasionally. Stir in cream just before serving.

Meanwhile, add 1 tablespoon salt to rapidly boiling water. Add spaghetti gradually so that the water continues to boil. Cook uncovered until bite-tender; stir occasionally. Drain in colander. Season with butter, salt and pepper. Serve chicken surrounded by spaghetti.

CHICKEN OLIVETTE

¼ cup butter or margarine
1 cup sour cream
½ cup milk
1½ cups grated Swiss cheese
2 tablespoons chopped
  pimiento
1 tablespoon instant minced
  onion
½ teaspoon salt
½ teaspoon nutmeg

⅛ teaspoon pepper
2¼ cups hot cooked noodles
  (¼ pound when uncooked)
1 cup canned pitted
  California ripe olives
1 (10-ounce) package frozen
  chopped broccoli
2½ cups cubed cooked
  chicken
½ cup buttered bread crumbs

Combine butter, sour cream, milk, cheese, pimiento, onion, salt, nutmeg and pepper. Stir-cook over low heat until cheese melts, making sauce. Mix together drained noodles, olives, cut into wedges, defrosted broccoli, chicken and cheese sauce. Turn into a 1½-quart baking dish. Dust with bread crumbs. Bake 40 minutes in moderate (350°) oven.

CHICKEN WITH ORANGE SAUCE

4 oranges
3 tablespoons slivered orange
  peel
2 (2½-pound) broiler
  chickens, completely
  sectioned
1 teaspoon salt
1 teaspoon paprika

⅓ cup butter or margarine
3 tablespoons flour
½ teaspoon salt
¼ teaspoon pepper
1 tablespoon brown sugar
½ teaspoon ground ginger
½ pound cooked noodles
  (hot)

Squeeze the juice of 3 oranges. Sliver rinds to make 3 tablespoons; add to juice with water to make 2¼ cups; reserve. Dust chicken pieces lightly with 1 teaspoon salt and paprika; brown in butter in large skillet. Remove chicken. Stir flour, additional ½ teaspoon salt, pepper, brown sugar and ginger into drippings in skillet. When smooth, add reserved orange liquid and stir-cook until mixture thickens and comes to a boil. Add chicken pieces.

Cover; simmer 45 minutes, or until fork-tender. Section remaining orange. Add to chicken the last 5 minutes cooking time. Serve over hot noodles.

CHICKEN PAELLA

1 (3- to 4-pound) all-purpose chicken, sectioned (save giblets)
1 tablespoon salt
½ teaspoon pepper
½ cup olive oil or chicken fat
½ cup sliced onion
1 section garlic, peeled
¼ teaspoon oregano
3 cups white rice, uncooked
½ pound dry sausage (Spanish preferred)
8 cups boiling water
4 envelopes beef broth powder

½ pint shucked clams
12 shrimp, shelled and browned
8 clams in the shell, well scrubbed
1½ pounds whole green beans, cooked
8 canned artichoke hearts
2 pimientos
4 tomatoes, halved, broiled and dusted with oregano
Romaine or chicory
Amontillado sherry (optional)

Clean, wash, drain and blot chicken on absorbent paper toweling; rub all over with salt and pepper. Heat oil in heavy large kettle; add chicken; sauté until yellowed. Then add onion, garlic, oregano and rice. Stir-fry until golden. Coarse-chop chicken giblets and stir in. Slice sausage ⅛ inch thick and add. Pour in 7½ cups of the boiling water; add beef broth powder dissolved in remaining water; cover. Simmer 50 minutes. Add shucked clams. Transfer to a 4-quart casserole. Halve shrimp; press into rice. Place clams in the shell around edge. Cover top of casserole with aluminum foil. Bake-steam 15 minutes, until clams open.

Garnish with whole cooked green beans, the artichoke hearts, heated and butter-seasoned, and strips of pimiento. Edge casserole platter with broiled tomatoes, alternating with crisp Romaine or chicory. Amontillado sherry completes this symphony of taste. Serves 8.

SAVORY ROAST CHICKEN AND GRAVY

1 (3- to 4-pound) roasting
   chicken
2 teaspoons seasoned salt
¼ teaspoon garlic powder
1 tablespoon paprika
1½ cups chicken broth or
   1½ cups hot water and
   1 teaspoon chicken broth
   powder

1 cup peeled medium-chopped
   onion
1 cup peeled thin-sliced
   carrots
1 cup ¼-inch-thick sliced
   celery
Chicken Gravy

Clean chicken as necessary. Wash with tepid water; drain. Dry on absorbent towels. Rub all over, inside and out, with a mixture of seasoned salt, garlic powder and paprika. Truss. Place chicken on its back in a roasting pan or heavy, large, ovenproof skillet. Pour in chicken broth (should cover bottom of pan). Roast in a hot (400°) oven, about 1½ hours, or until well browned and a pick inserted near thigh joint comes out clean, with no rosy fluid. While roasting, turn chicken on its side every ½ hour and baste with pan drippings. Add onion, carrots and celery last 30 minutes.

Chicken Gravy: Remove vegetables left in roasting pan and rub through a sieve, making a purée. Skim fat from drippings in pan. Into drippings stir 2 tablespoons flour and cook-stir until flour is golden brown. Stir in puréed vegetables and 1¼ cups hot water with 1 teaspoon chicken broth powder. Cook-stir until boiling. Season to taste with salt and pepper. Stir in ¼ cup dairy sour cream, if desired; heat but do not boil.

CHICKEN ROSEMARY

2 (2½- to 3-pound) broiler-fryers	4 thin slices carrot
2 teaspoons powdered rosemary	1 stick (½ cup) butter or margarine
2 teaspoons salt	2½ tablespoons flour
¼ teaspoon pepper	¾ cup dry white wine or
2 slices peeled onion	⅔ cup orange juice and
	½ tablespoon lemon juice

Wash, drain and blot chickens on absorbent paper towels. Dust interior of each with 1 teaspoon rosemary, 1 teaspoon salt and ⅛ teaspoon pepper, and add to interior of each bird, 1 slice onion, 2 slices carrot and 6 pats butter. Fasten vents together with toothpicks and lace with white cord; fasten neck skin onto back. Tie legs together, wings to body with white string. Rub all over with remaining butter mixed with flour.

Rest each bird on its side on rack in baking pan. Roast in hot (425°) oven until beginning to brown. Then cover loosely with aluminum foil. Reduce heat to 350°, continue to roast 40 to 50 minutes, or until fork inserted near the leg joint draws a clear liquid not tinged with pink. Meanwhile, baste 3 times with wine or orange and lemon juice. When half done, turn on the other side and brush with butter. Remove the foil the last 15 minutes. When done, turn off heat; let stand in oven 15 minutes before carving.

SESAME OVEN-FRIED CHICKEN

2 (2½-pound) frying chickens, cut up	3 teaspoons salt
4 tablespoons melted butter or margarine	¾ teaspoon ground black pepper
½ cup toasted sesame seeds	Pinch of garlic powder
	1⅓ cups sifted flour

Brush chicken pieces with melted butter or margarine. Put sesame seeds, salt, pepper, garlic powder and flour in stout paper bag. Add chicken and shake bag to coat well with mixture. Place on foil-lined baking pan. Bake 50 to 60 minutes in hot (400°) oven, or until golden brown.

CHICKEN TARRAGON EN CASSEROLE

1 (3½-pound) all-purpose chicken
3 tablespoons flour
1½ teaspoons salt
2 teaspoons paprika
3 thin slices fat salt pork, cut in squares
3 cups boiling water or chicken broth

½ cup converted rice
½ teaspoon crushed dry tarragon
2 green peppers, seeded and minced
1 cup well-mashed canned tomatoes
Lemon wedges
Parsley sprigs

Wash, drain and dry the chicken. Section as for fricassee. Stir together the flour, salt and paprika. Coat each chicken piece with this. Place the chicken in a casserole in layers alternating with the salt pork. Add the boiling water or broth. Bake-simmer in the oven or over low heat 1½ hours, or until the chicken is almost tender. Add the rice, tarragon, green peppers and tomatoes. Continue cooking 40 minutes, or until the rice is tender. Serve in the casserole. Garnish with the lemon wedges and parsley.

CHICKEN TWO-CRUST PIE

1 recipe Rich American Pie Pastry (see Index) or a mix
1 teaspoon fine dry bread crumbs
5 cups coarse-chopped cooked boned chicken

2 tablespoons minced onion, sautéed in butter
2 cups thick well-seasoned chicken gravy
Milk
Parsley

Line a 9-inch pie plate with pie pastry rolled a scant ¼ inch thick. Dust bottom with 1 teaspoon bread crumbs, lightly pressing them in. Mix chicken, onion and gravy to make a thick filling. Spoon evenly into pastry-lined pie plate. Roll remaining pastry and cover top. Press edges together with tines of fork.

Slash center for steam escape. Brush top lightly with milk to help brown the crust. Bake 35 minutes in hot (375 to 400°) oven. Cool slightly. Serve while still hot, cut in wedges. Garnish with parsley.

CHICKEN POTPIE

It was my Grandmother Bailey who first introduced me to old-time Chicken Potpie. "A very good way to make chicken serve more people," she remarked, "and if you can get skillful enough to turn it upside down on a platter and dress it with a little parsley from the garden, you have what Grandpa calls an eating picture."

½ cup small-diced fat salt pork	⅓ cup flour
2 (2½-pound) broiler-fryers, sectioned	¾ cup heavy cream or undiluted evaporated milk
6 cups boiling water	Short Biscuit Pastry
1 onion, peeled and chopped	1 hard-cooked egg, sliced (optional)
1 cup diced celery	Parsley
3 teaspoons seasoning salt	
1 bay leaf	

Heat a heavy 3-quart saucepan. Add the salt pork and sauté until the fat runs. Add the sectioned broiler-fryers; sauté until browned; turn often. Pour in the water gradually; add the onion, celery and seasonings; cover and simmer top-of-range or in the oven until tender. Gradually stir the flour into the cream and stir until smooth. Stir into the cooked chicken. Bring to a boil.

Roll the pastry ¼ inch thick. Cut two thirds into strips 2 inches wide and with them line a slightly oiled 2½-quart round baking dish or casserole with straight sides; pinch the pastry strips together. Pour in the prepared chicken. Fit a round pastry "cover" over the top; press the edges together with the tines of a fork. Bake 35 minutes, or until golden brown in a hot (400°) oven. Serve as is with a top garnish of sliced hard-cooked egg and parsley. Or go old-fashioned and cool the pie 5 minutes; then run a knife around the top to loosen the crust. Place a big deep round platter on top and quickly invert the pie as you would an upside-down cake. Stick a parsley sprig in the top. Surround with creamed peas to complete a one-dish entree.

Short Biscuit Pastry:

1½ recipes baking powder biscuit dough (homemade or from a mix)
3 tablespoons butter or margarine at room temperature

Roll the biscuit dough ¼ inch thick on a floured surface. Spread to one-half inch of the edge with 1½ tablespoons butter. Press the edges together. Roll out lightly again. Spread with remaining butter; fold and roll out as described. Use as directed.

CHICKEN VERONIQUE

A chicken casserole with fresh green seedless grapes.

2 (2½- to 3-pound) broiler-fryers
3 tablespoons vegetable oil
3 tablespoons butter
2 teaspoons frozen chives
¼ cup white wine or dry sherry
1 cup sweet or sour cream
1½ cups seedless green grapes

Cut chicken into serving pieces. In skillet, sauté chicken unfloured, in combined oil and butter until lightly browned. Add additional oil if needed. Lower heat, cover and simmer 30 minutes. Transfer pieces to buttered shallow casserole.

To fat and juices in skillet, add frozen chives and wine. Let bubble for 5 minutes. Scrape all crusty portions from skillet and reduce heat. Stir in sweet or sour cream and seedless green grapes. Stir well and pour over the chicken. Cover and bake 30 minutes at 325°. Remove the cover for the last 10 minutes of baking. Serves 6 to 8.

COQ AU VIN

2 (2½-pound) broiler-fryers, sectioned
1 teaspoon salt
¼ teaspoon pepper
⅓ cup diced bacon, scalded
3 tablespoons butter
12 small onions, peeled
12 medium-sized mushrooms, sliced
3 scallion bulbs or shallots, peeled and minced
1 section garlic, peeled and crushed
2 tablespoons flour
1 bay leaf
½ teaspoon thyme
½ teaspoon marjoram
1 tablespoon minced parsley
1 pint dry red wine

Dust broiler-fryer sections with salt and pepper. Fry bacon until golden; remove. Add butter to fry pan. Brush chicken with combined fats. Line large baking pan with aluminum foil and in it arrange chicken sections with a little space between. Pour over half the remaining fat. Bake 35 minutes, or until golden. Turn once. Transfer to low 2½-quart casserole that can be served at the table. Meantime, add onions, mushrooms, scallions and garlic to fat in fry pan. Brown slightly. Stir in flour, bay leaf, herbs and parsley. Gradually add wine. Stir until boiling. Pour into casserole. Top with bacon bits. Cover. Bake at 350° for 35 minutes, or until fork-tender. Serves 6 to 8.

CHICKEN OR TURKEY HASH

3½ cups medium-hashed cooked chicken or turkey meat
1 cup light cream
½ cup White Sauce made with cream or ½ cup heavy cream
½ teaspoon salt or to taste
⅛ teaspoon white pepper (optional)
Simplified Mornay Sauce
½ cup grated Parmesan cheese

Combine and heat chicken or turkey meat and light cream. Stir in White Sauce and seasonings. Place in serving dish. Spread with Simplified Mornay Sauce, dust with grated Parmesan cheese and brown under broiler or in hot oven.

Simplified Mornay Sauce: Melt 2 tablespoons butter or margarine. Stir in 3 tablespoons flour. Gradually add 1 cup water, 2 teaspoons chicken broth powder and ¾ cup light cream. When boiling, stir into 1 beaten egg yolk. Return to heat and cook-stir 1 minute. Add ⅓ cup grated Parmesan cheese or Cheddar cheese and ½ tablespoon butter or margarine. Cook-stir 1 minute—do not boil.

GEORGIA COUNTRY CAPTAIN

2 (1½- to 3-pound) broiler-fryers	¼ cup flour
1½ teaspoons seasoned salt	2 tablespoons curry powder
⅛ teaspoon pepper	½ cup tomato paste
½ pound lean bacon, fine-chopped	2 cups chicken broth
1 cup medium-chopped celery	2 cups light cream
1 medium-sized onion, peeled and fine-chopped	Salt and pepper to taste
1 section garlic, peeled and crushed	Currant Rice
	½ cup toasted slivered almonds

Rub chicken all over with salt and pepper. Roast 1½ hours in moderate (350 to 375°) oven, or until golden brown and fork-tender. Cool. Remove meat from bones and cut it in good-sized pieces. Meanwhile, prepare the sauce.

In heavy 2-quart saucepan, sauté bacon, celery, onion and garlic until vegetables are lightly browned. Smooth-stir in flour, curry powder and tomato paste. Gradually stir in chicken broth. Cook-stir until boiling. Simmer 45 minutes uncovered, stirring occasionally. Pour preceding mixture through sieve, pressing down with the back of a spoon to extract all juices from the bacon and vegetables. Stir in cream and roast chicken meat. Season to taste with salt and pepper. (If a hotter curry is desired, at this time add 1 teaspoon additional curry powder, stirred smooth in 1 teaspoon cold water.) Heat to serving temperature. Serve with Currant Rice; garnish with slivered almonds.

Currant Rice: Cook 1½ cups converted rice following package directions with these exceptions: Add ½ cup dried currants when half cooked. When done, stir in 2 tablespoons butter cut in bits.

ORIENTAL CHICKEN

4 whole chicken breasts
½ teaspoon salt
1 (3- or 4-ounce) can sliced mushrooms
2 teaspoons cornstarch
4 tablespoons water
3 tablespoons soy sauce
¼ teaspoon Tabasco
⅛ teaspoon powdered ginger

6 tablespoons salad oil
6 scallions, sliced
1½ cups diagonally sliced celery
1 (5-ounce) can water chestnuts, drained and sliced
1 (1-pound) can bean sprouts, drained
Cooked rice

Remove skin from chicken. Remove chicken meat from bones. Cut into thin strips. Dust with salt. Drain mushrooms. Combine liquid with cornstarch, water, soy sauce, Tabasco and ginger; reserve. Heat oil in skillet or electric fry pan. Add chicken; stir-cook over high heat until chicken looks white, about 3 to 5 minutes. Add scallions and celery; cook 1 minute more. Add reserved soy sauce mixture, drained sliced mushrooms, water chestnuts and bean sprouts; cook-stir 3 minutes longer. Serve with rice. Serves 4.

SMOTHERED CHICKEN

2 (2½-pound) broiler-fryers
2 tablespoons flour
1 teaspoon salt
¼ teaspoon pepper
1 teaspoon paprika
½ cup fine-chopped celery with leaves

1 onion, peeled and sliced
4 tablespoons butter or margarine
1 cup hot water or chicken broth
1 cup half and half

Arrange chicken in single layer in large low casserole. Combine and dust over flour, salt, pepper and paprika. Add celery and onion; dot with butter. Bake uncovered 20 minutes in moderate (375°) oven. Add water, bake 20 minutes longer. Add half and half; cover and bake 10 minutes.

STEWED CHICKEN WITH BISCUIT TOPPING

¼ cup butter or margarine
6 tablespoons flour
3 cups chicken broth, well seasoned
Salt and pepper (optional)
1 (3-pound) broiler-fryer, boiled and cut into bite-sized pieces

1 standard recipe rich baking powder biscuit or a biscuit mix or biscuits ready-to-bake (refrigerator case)
3 cups drained cooked green peas (frozen)

Melt butter or margarine; remove from heat. Stir in flour. When smooth, gradually add broth; stir until boiling. Taste; add salt and pepper if needed. Stir in chicken (no need to remove skin). Pour bubbling hot into buttered 2-quart shallow baking dish that can go-to-table. Top with rounds of baking powder biscuits a scant ½ inch apart. Bake 30 minutes at 400°. Serve in baking dish; ring edge with green peas.

CHICKEN BREASTS POLYNESIAN STYLE

4 large chicken breasts
Boiling water to cover (about 1 quart)
1 teaspoon salt
⅛ teaspoon white pepper
Pinch of garlic powder
2 tablespoons butter or margarine
¼ teaspoon rosemary
1 (14½-ounce) can pineapple slices, drained; save syrup

¼ cup dry sherry or 1¼ teaspoons sherry extract and 2¾ cups water
4 teaspoons wine vinegar
½ teaspoon Worcestershire sauce
4 drops Tabasco
1 tablespoon cornstarch
1 tablespoon water

Remove bones and skin from chicken. Place bones and skin in saucepan; cover with hot water; boil 30 minutes to make a broth. Meantime combine salt, pepper and garlic powder and dust over chicken. Heat butter and rosemary together in 10-inch skillet; add chicken breasts and slow-brown on both sides. Measure ¼ cup of cooking broth. Add syrup drained from pineapple, sherry, vinegar, Worcestershire and Tabasco. Pour over chicken. Bake 20 minutes in moderate (350°) oven. Add pineapple slices; bake 5 minutes more. Remove chicken and pineapple to heated serving platter. Mix cornstarch with 1 tablespoon cold water; stir into liquid remaining in skillet. Cook-stir until mixture thickens and clears, making a sauce. Strain over chicken. Serve at once accompanied with servings of rice mixed with a few sautéed chopped nut meats or dry-roasted peanuts. Serves 4.

COLONIAL DUCK CASSEROLE

2 ducks	6 beef bouillon cubes
2 teaspoons salt	5 cups boiling water
¼ teaspoon pepper	1 teaspoon mint flakes
1 teaspoon mixed Italian herbs	¾ cup port wine
5 tablespoons butter	2 cups green peas, fresh, or
5 tablespoons flour	1 can peas, drained

Clean, wash, drain and blot the ducks on absorbent paper towels. Cut in sections for serving. Rub all over with the seasonings. Roast 30 minutes in a moderate (350 to 375°) oven. Blend the butter and flour; gradually stir in the bouillon cubes dissolved in the hot water. Stir in the mint flakes and wine. Transfer the duck to a casserole. Cover. Bake 1 hour, or until fork-tender. Half an hour before completion, stir in the peas; finish cooking. Garlic toasts or assorted warm crisp bread sticks the accompaniment.

In colonial tradition, Duck Casserole would be accompanied by hominy croquettes and quick-cooked young cabbages dressed with parslied sour cream, and, to complete the savor, a glass of Madeira. Serves 8.

FRENCH DUCK-RUTABAGA RAGOUT

1 (5-pound) duck	½ cup apple cider or white
Fat for browning	wine
2 teaspoons salt	12 small white onions, peeled
2 stalks celery	3 cups diced rutabaga
2 sprigs fresh parsley	½ teaspoon sugar
1 small bay leaf	1 tablespoon flour
½ teaspoon whole black	1 tablespoon water
peppers	½ teaspoon crushed thyme
½ cup stock or water	leaves

Wash the duck and cut into sections. Brown in fat in a heavy-bottom skillet. Reserve 1 tablespoon fat. Place the duck in a 3- to 4-quart casserole. Add the salt, celery, parsley, bay leaf, black pepper, stock or water and the cider or wine. Cover; bake 1 hour in a moderate (350°) oven. Meantime brown the onions and rutabaga in the reserved duck fat. Dust with the sugar to aid browning. Mix the flour with the water until smooth. Stir into the mixed vegetables. Add to the cooking duck. Add the thyme 10 minutes before completion.

OVEN-FRICASSEED DUCK A LA MODE

2 (4- to 5-pound) frozen	¼ teaspoon pepper
ducklings, thawed	3 tablespoons flour
1 cup cider vinegar	3 tablespoons cold water
2 cups cider or apple juice	Beef or chicken bouillon
3 onions, peeled and minced	(optional)
2 teaspoons whole allspice	Rice Pilaff with Saffron (see
2 medium-sized bay leaves	Index)
1½ teaspoons salt	

Place ducklings in deep bowl. Pour over vinegar and cider or apple juice. Stir in onions, allspice and bay leaves. Refrigerate at least 8 hours, turning the ducklings several times to marinate thoroughly. Drain. Dust with salt and pepper. Roast in hot

(425°) oven, until well browned, basting occasionally with some of spiced liquid. Siphon or spoon off fat from liquid in roasting pan at the end of 1 hour. Reduce heat to 350°. Roast 20 minutes to the pound. When done, set aside to keep warm. Remove excess fat from pan liquid. Stir in flour smoothed with cold water. Bring to boil; simmer 3 minutes. If too thick, thin with a little beef or chicken bouillon; strain. Serve with Rice Pilaff with Saffron. Serves 8.

DUCK PLATTER HONG KONG

2 cups diced roast duck
½ cup bamboo shoots
½ cup mushroom slices
2 tablespoons oil
1½ cups beef or chicken broth
2 tablespoons soy sauce
1 teaspoon sugar
½ teaspoon ground ginger
½ teaspoon garlic powder
2 tablespoons dry sherry or
  2 tablespoons sherry
  flavoring

½ tablespoon cornstarch
1 tablespoon cold water
6 small slices sautéed Virginia
  ham
6 hot individual flaky rice
  molds
Water cress

Slightly sauté the duck and vegetables in the oil. Add the broth, seasonings and sherry. Cover. Simmer 1 hour. Mix the cornstarch with the cold water. Add to the duck; cook-stir 3 minutes. Arrange the ham slices on a large heated platter. Unmold the rice on these. Spoon over the duck. Garnish with the water cress.

ROAST DUCK WITH CHERRIES

1 (5-pound) duckling
Salt
Lemon juice
1 section garlic, cut
1 (1-pound) can pitted Bing
  cherries

2 tablespoons white or cider
  vinegar
2 tablespoons sugar
2½ cups Brown Sauce (see
  Index)

Rub duck with salt, lemon juice and cut garlic. Roast at 350° on one side for 30 minutes. Turn and roast on the other side another 30 minutes, pouring off fat. Turn duck breast side up and roast for another 1 to 1½ hours, continuing to pour off fat.

Meanwhile, drain liquid from cherries and simmer it for 10 to 15 minutes. Return cherries to liquid—do not boil. In a saucepan, combine vinegar and sugar; simmer, watching carefully, until caramelized. Careful—do not burn! Add Brown Sauce, cherries and liquid, and bring to a boil. Pass sauce with carved duck. Serves 4.

ROAST DUCK A L'ORANGE

1 (5-pound) frozen Long Island duckling, thawed	Lemon juice
	1 section garlic, cut
Salt	

Rub duck with salt, lemon juice and cut garlic. Roast at 350° on one side for 30 minutes. Turn and roast on the other side another 30 minutes, pouring off fat. Turn duck breast side up and roast for another 1 to 1½ hours, continuing to pour off fat. Serves 4.

Orange Sauce:

2 tablespoons butter	1 teaspoon Angostura bitters
2 tablespoons flour	2 tablespoons currant jelly
1 orange, grated rind and juice	Water chestnuts (or plain chestnuts)
½ cup additional juice	
1 cup dry white wine	½ cup hot water
Salt	

Melt butter, add flour, then rind, juice, wine, salt, bitters and jelly. Bring to a boil, stirring constantly. Add chestnuts. Simmer 3 to 4 minutes. Set aside.

Remove duck when done, pour off fat and liquid from pan into jar. Refrigerate. Meanwhile, add ½ cup hot water to pan, to scrape up bits. Add this to sauce. When fat can be removed from jar, add remaining liquid to sauce. Carve duck, lay pieces in casserole, cover with sauce. Heat to serve.

POT-ROASTED DUCK WITH OLIVES

1½ tablespoons butter or margarine
2 thin slices bacon, cut in 1 inch squares
1 (4- to 5-pound) frozen duckling, thawed
¼ cup peeled chopped onion
1 section garlic, peeled and crushed
¼ teaspoon black pepper
2 cups boiling water or chicken or beef stock
1 medium-sized bay leaf
¼ cup chopped celery
¼ cup chopped parsley
1½ teaspoons salt
2 tablespoons instant flour
¾ cup stuffed olives, sliced

Combine butter and bacon in fry pan; in same pan, slow-fry duckling all over. When almost browned, add onion. Finish browning. Transfer duckling and onion to a deep 4-quart casserole; add remaining ingredients, except instant flour and olives. Cover; slow-bake 3 hours, or until fork-tender in moderate (350°) oven. Remove duckling from casserole. Stir the instant flour into casserole and stir-boil to thicken gravy. Let duckling stand in a warm place 10 minutes, then carve. Arrange on warm large serving platter; pour hot gravy over and around. Top with sliced olives. Serves 4.

ROAST GOOSE

1 (10-pound) goose
2 teaspoons salt
¼ teaspoon pepper
2 tart apples
1 large orange
6 prunes, soaked
2 tablespoons butter
1 cup hot water
¾ cup dry white wine
Salt and pepper to taste
Prune Gravy (you will need 10 additional prunes)

Prepare the goose by washing, drying and blotting on absorbent paper towels. Dust the interior generously with salt and pepper. Instead of stuffing, fill the interior with the apple cut in quarters, the orange sliced with the rind, and the prunes. These fruits are used for flavor only, and are not to be served. Close the vent with picks laced together with white string. Fasten the skin of the neck down over the back. Tuck in the tips of the wings and fasten close to the body with white cord. Tie the ends of the legs together with white cord. Place on the side on a rack in a roasting pan; roast 1 hour in a hot (425°) oven, or until browned. Turn the goose on the other side; reduce the heat to 350°, and continue to roast 1 hour longer. In all, allow 20 minutes to the pound. Baste every 15 minutes with a mixture of the butter, hot water, and wine, seasoned with additional salt and pepper.

Prune Gravy: Skim the fat from the liquid in the pan; measure the liquid. Add enough canned chicken consommé to bring the amount to 2 cups. Stir in 3 tablespoons flour blended with ¼ cup cold water. Stir-cook until boiling rapidly. Add 1 teaspoon gravy seasoning and 10 plumped, halved, pitted, unsweetened prunes.

PHEASANT IN CREAM

1 pheasant	2 tablespoons chopped onion,
¼ cup flour	browned (optional)
¾ teaspoon salt	¼ to ½ cup sour or heavy
⅛ teaspoon pepper	cream
Cooking fat	
1 (3½-ounce) can mushrooms	
(optional)	

Cut pheasant in pieces. Mix flour with seasonings. Dredge pieces of pheasant in this flour and dry them on a rack about 30 minutes. Heat ¼ inch layer of cooking fat in skillet to 340 to 360°. Brown pheasant pieces evenly and slowly in heated fat. Avoid crowding meat in skillet and turn as necessary, using tongs to avoid piercing the coating. Allow 15 to 20 minutes for browning. Remove browned pieces from skillet and place one layer-deep in shallow casserole. If desired, add mushrooms and chopped onion previously browned in fat in skillet. Drizzle 1 to 2 tablespoons sour or heavy cream over each of browned pheasant pieces in casserole.

Bake in 325° oven 45 to 60 minutes, or until fork-tender. Do not cover a young bird. An older bird may be baked covered until fork-tender, then uncovered 15 to 20 minutes to recrisp. If needed, turn once or twice during cooking so that pieces cook and crisp evenly. Add more cream if meat gets dry. Serves 4 to 6.

ROAST CORNISH GAME HENS

6 (1-pound) Cornish game hens	2 tablespoons butter
4 teaspoons seasoned salt	2 tablespoons flour
½ teaspoon powdered rosemary	1 cup heated chicken bouillon or dry white wine
12 thin slices each carrot and celery	Bouquet of parsley or water cress
3 tablespoons minced onion	6 cups cooked wild rice or 6 potatoes, oven-browned
3 tablespoons butter or margarine	

Wash, drain and blot hens on paper toweling. Mix salt and rosemary, and dust over the interior of each bird. Into each, put 2 slices each carrot and celery, and ½ tablespoon each minced onion and butter. Fasten vents with poultry picks; pin the neck skin down on the backs. Stir together additional butter and flour, and massage over the birds. Lock the wings together; tie the legs together with white cord. Rest birds on one side on a rack in a baking pan. Bake in hot (425°) oven, until birds begin to brown. Baste with chicken bouillon or wine. Turn birds over on other side. Roast 35 to 40 minutes at 350°, or until a fork inserted near the leg joint draws clear liquid not tinged with pink. Baste 3 times with the bouillon. When half roasted, turn the breast sides up to brown. When done, remove cord and poultry picks.

Arrange game hens on large round platter, legs pointing toward the center; fill the center with a bouquet of parsley or water cress. In the spaces between the birds, place large spoonfuls of wild rice or small oven-browned potatoes. Canned small onions rolled in warmed dairy sour cream make an excellent accompaniment.

TURKEY WITH HONEY-LEMON BASTING SAUCE

Prepare a (10- to 12-pound) ready-to-cook turkey as usual, and truss. Prepare Honey-Lemon Glazing Sauce for basting. Meantime, fold a sheet of heavy-duty aluminum wrap double-thick, and turn up the edges all around about 1 inch. Miter (match together) the corners to make a firm "pan." Put pan on the grill rack over the fire and place the turkey in the pan. Brush with the Honey-Lemon Glazing Sauce. Cover turkey loosely with a single sheet of foil. Just drape it over the bird. Close the cover of the grill, adjust vents half open and roast 2½ to 3 hours. One hour before roasting is finished, remove the foil cover, baste the turkey again with the sauce and continue cooking, basting twice for a fine glaze. Serves 10 to 12.

Honey-Lemon Glazing Sauce:

½ cup butter or margarine	Grated rind of 1 lemon
1 cup honey	1 teaspoon salt
½ cup lemon juice	Fresh-ground black pepper

TURKEY (OR CHICKEN) À LA KING

⅓ cup corn oil margarine	1 cup light cream or half and half
½ pound fresh mushrooms, sliced	2 cups diced cooked turkey or chicken
¼ cup cornstarch	½ cup chopped pimiento
1 teaspoon salt	2 tablespoons dry sherry
¼ teaspoon white pepper	½ teaspoon Worcestershire sauce
¼ teaspoon dry mustard	Rice or noodles, cooked
Dash of cayenne pepper	
1½ cups turkey or chicken stock	

Melt margarine in saucepan. Add mushrooms. Cook over low heat until tender, stirring occasionally, about 5 minutes. Stir in cornstarch, salt, white pepper, dry mustard and cayenne pepper. Remove from heat. Gradually stir in turkey stock and light cream, stirring until smooth. Stirring constantly, cook over medium heat until mixture thickens, comes to a boil and boils 1 minute. Add turkey, pimiento, sherry and Worcestershire sauce. Heat 5 minutes. Serve over rice or noodles.

Note: The alcohol in the sherry evaporates while cooking, leaving only the appetizing flavor.

TURKEY IN THE SNOW

1 teaspoon chopped onion
¾ cup sliced fresh mushrooms
¼ cup butter or margarine
5 tablespoons flour
1½ cups hot chicken broth
1 cup heated milk
2 cups diced cooked turkey
¼ cup chopped green pepper
¼ cup chopped pimiento
½ cup grated Parmesan cheese
1 envelope packaged mashed potatoes
½ cup water
½ teaspoon salt
½ cup milk
2 tablespoons butter

Sauté onion and mushrooms in butter or margarine for 5 minutes. Stir in flour and gradually broth and milk. Cook-stir until mixture thickens and comes to boil. Fold in turkey, green pepper, pimiento and cheese. Meantime, prepare packaged mashed potatoes, with water, salt, milk and butter, following package directions. Pour creamed turkey into buttered 2-quart casserole. Around edge, spoon mashed potatoes. Bake 20 minutes in moderate (350°) oven, or until potato is lightly browned.

TURKEY (OR CHICKEN) DIVAN

6 stalks cooked broccoli (trimmed)	1½ cups White Sauce (see Index)
1½ tablespoons melted butter or margarine	3 egg yolks
2 tablespoons grated Parmesan cheese	1½ tablespoons sour cream
	½ teaspoon salt
2 tablespoons dry sherry	⅛ teaspoon pepper
6 slices cooked turkey or chicken, cut ½ inch thick	2 tablespoons grated Parmesan cheese
	1½ tablespoons dry sherry

Rub a 7×11-inch baking dish with butter. Arrange trimmed cooked broccoli crosswise on bottom. Sprinkle over melted butter, the 2 tablespoons grated Parmesan cheese and the 2 tablespoons dry sherry. Cover broccoli with sliced turkey or chicken. Beat together White Sauce, egg yolks, sour cream, salt and pepper. Spoon this over sliced turkey. Dust over the additional Parmesan, and sprinkle with the additional sherry. Bake about 15 minutes at 350°.

TURKEY SCALLOP

2 cups diced roast turkey	Salt (optional)
2 cups canned cream of celery soup	3 cups toasted ½-inch bread cubes
¼ cup diced green pepper	¼ cup crumbled blue cheese
⅛ teaspoon nutmeg	

Combine turkey, soup, green pepper and nutmeg. Taste; add salt if needed. Place all but 1 cup of bread cubes in buttered 3-quart casserole. Add creamed turkey mixture. Dust with cheese, then top with remaining bread cubes. Bake 40 minutes at 350°, or until sauce bubbles through topping.

POULTRY STUFFINGS

Stuffings originally had one primary purpose, that of introducing interesting seasonings to meat, poultry or fish, through direct contact with the interior of the bird. When the stuffing is baked separately in a pan, instead of in the meat, it is called a "dressing," and a little extra spice or herb seasoning is rubbed into the cavities of the poultry. In general, allow a generous cup of crumbs for each pound of dressed bird.

To Bake Stuffing Separately: Pack lightly 2 inches deep into a pan rubbed with drippings from the roasting bird. Punch a few holes in the stuffing with a long-pronged fork. Spoon over 2 tablespoons drippings from the roasting bird to give flavor and richness. Bake 1 to 1½ hours. The following stuffings are proportioned for 3- to 4-pound birds. For a capon, prepare double the quantity; for a 12-pound turkey, triple the amount, etc.

Moist Crumb Stuffing: Combine 2 cups (4½-ounces) plain or onion-seasoned bread croutons or 3½ cups crumbs from decrusted day-old enriched bread, ¼ cup melted butter or margarine, ¾ teaspoon salt, ¼ teaspoon pepper, 2 teaspoons poultry seasonings, 1 tablespoon minced or instant onion and 1 tablespoon minced parsley or ½ tablespoon parsley flakes. Mix in ½ cup hot canned chicken or mushroom broth. Add 1 egg, beaten.

Dry Crumb Stuffing: Follow the preceding recipe with these exceptions: Fry the crouton or crumb mixture lightly in the melted butter and use 2 tablespoons dry sherry or cranberry juice cocktail.

Smoked Ham or Liver Pâté Stuffing for Chicken: Make up a Moist or Dry Crumb Stuffing, and mix in 1 (4½-ounce) can smoked ham or liver pâté.

Sausage Stuffing: Prepare Moist or Dry Crumb Stuffing. Mix in ½ pound slightly fried and drained sausage meat and ½ cup minced celery.

Oyster Stuffing: Make up Dry Crumb Stuffing and fold in ½ pint oysters cut in halves (or thirds if very large).

POTATO STUFFING

3 cups hot mashed potatoes
 (about 8 medium-sized)
1 cup stale bread crumbs
½ cup fat salt pork or bacon
 fat

1 onion, peeled and minced
1 teaspoon poultry seasoning
1½ teaspoons salt
¼ teaspoon pepper
1 egg

Have the potatoes freshly boiled, mash until smooth, add the other ingredients and beat together. Set aside until cold before using as a stuffing for duck or goose.

VEGETABLE CRUMB STUFFING

4 cups packaged herb crumb
 stuffing
1 onion, peeled and fine-
 chopped

1 (1-pound) can mixed
 vegetables and liquid
½ teaspoon ground thyme
Hot water (optional)

Mix ingredients; let stand 15 minutes to soften. If necessary add a little hot water.

Vegetables

Vegetable dishes have assumed importance in meals whenever menu planners consider the problem of obesity—which has been so common in our country. Low-calorie vegetables purchased in season also help a family to get more mileage from their dollar. The nutritional aspects of vegetables should not be overlooked either: spinach and other greens are important sources of vitamin C, which is needed for healthy gums and body tissues. Yellow vegetables are important sources of vitamin A, so essential to proper growth, normal vision and a healthy condition of the skin. In addition, all vegetables contain valuable minerals. The beneficial effects of these elements are often lost when the vegetables are improperly prepared or cooked. Never let fresh vegetables stand in cold water but prepare them just before cooking whether you peel, dice, julienne or just cut them up. Cook in the smallest possible amount of water, and keep covered when cooking. When they're barely fork-tender, they're done!

All recipes are for six servings unless otherwise stated.

BOILED ARTICHOKES

Wash artichokes. Cut off stems at base and remove small bottom leaves. Trim tips of leaves and cut off about 1 inch from top. Stand artichokes upright in deep saucepan; add 1/4 teaspoon salt for each artichoke and add 2 to 3 inches boiling water to pan. Cover and boil gently 35 to 45 minutes, or until base of artichokes can be pierced easily with a fork. Remove artichokes to platter, turning them upside down to drain. If they are to be stuffed, gently spread leaves and remove "choke" (thistle portion) from center of artichokes with metal spoon.

ARTICHOKES WITH LEMON SAUCE

6 Boiled Cooked Artichokes (see Index)
¼ cup butter or margarine
1 tablespoon cornstarch
¾ cup water
¼ cup lemon juice
1 teaspoon crushed, grated lemon peel
2 tablespoons chopped chives

While artichokes are cooking, melt butter. Mix in cornstarch. Gradually add water and cook over low heat, stirring constantly, until thickened and clear. Stir in lemon juice, lemon peel and chives, and simmer 5 minutes. Serve lemon sauce with hot artichokes.

ASPARAGUS LOAF ELEGANTE

2 (1-pound) bunches cooked asparagus
¼ cup butter for mold
1½ tablespoons butter
4 tablespoons flour
1 cup milk
½ cup ground tender veal
1 teaspoon salt
¼ teaspoon pepper
Pinch of nutmeg
1¼ cups inch-long lengths cooked asparagus
4 eggs, well beaten
18 radish roses with green leaves
Mousseline Sauce

Cut tips from 2 bunches of cooked asparagus in 3-inch lengths. Select a quart mold about 3 inches deep (or 5×9-inch loaf pan), cover it thickly with ¼ cup butter; cover the bottom of the mold with waxed paper. Line sides with tips, pointing green tips downward; arrange a design of the tips on the bottom of the mold from the remaining tips. Chill.

Make a sauce by melting additional butter, slowly stirring in the flour and milk, until the mixture boils. Add ground veal, seasonings and additional cut-up asparagus; when boiling, stir this mixture into the beaten eggs. Spoon carefully into the mold. Set mold in a pan and surround with boiling water. Bake 35 minutes or until firm when tested with a toothpick, in an oven so slow that the water will not noticeably boil. Remove from the water. Cool 5 minutes. Loosen the top edges with a knife and unmold on a warm platter.

Garnish with radish roses with their green leaves. Serve with Mousseline Sauce.

Mousseline Sauce: Just before serving, to 1 recipe Hollandaise Sauce (see Index) add ½ cup whipped cream. Makes 1¼ cups.

BOSTON BAKED BEANS

1 quart navy or pea beans	½ teaspoon pepper
½ teaspoon baking soda	½ cup chili sauce (optional)
⅓ cup molasses	2 slices onion, minced
½ teaspoon mustard	½ pound fat bacon or salt
2½ teaspoons salt	pork

Soak the beans overnight. In the morning drain and rinse and boil in water to cover, containing baking soda. When the skins are loose drain again, rinse with cold water to firm the beans, and mix with the molasses, mustard, seasonings and the onion; place in the bottom of the bean pot the sliced pork or bacon, the rind of which has been scored or cut through in squares; add beans with water to cover, put on the lid and bake steadily in a slow (325°) oven for 4 hours. Uncover, draw the pork or bacon to the top, add more water if necessary, and cook uncovered until the beans are done and the pork is brown—about 1½ hours longer. Serves 8 to 10.

SWEDISH BEAN POT

6 cups canned baked beans	½ cup brown sugar
1 large apple, cored and chopped	¼ cup sweet pickle relish
	1 tablespoon table mustard
⅓ cup raisins	¾ cup catsup
½ cup chopped onion	6 strips fried bacon, crumbled

Mix all ingredients. Turn into casserole; cover. Bake at 250° for 1½ hours.

BEANS BRETONNE

2 cups navy beans
1 chicken bouillon cube
1 (6-ounce) can tomato paste
1 onion, fine-chopped
1 clove garlic, peeled and
    minced

1 (4-ounce) jar pimientos,
    drained and chopped
2 tablespoons cooking oil

Soak and simmer beans (see Index—Boston Baked Beans), using a proportionate amount of water. Drain beans and put them in bean pot or casserole, reserving liquid. Dissolve bouillon cube in 1 cup of bean liquid; combine with tomato paste, pour over beans. Add remaining ingredients and enough bean liquid to cover beans. Cover pot or casserole and bake in slow (250°) oven 2 hours or longer. Serves 8.

CAPTAIN JOHN'S BEANS

2 pounds navy beans
3 quarts boiling water
12 strips bacon
½ cup molasses
3 tablespoons minced onion
3 teaspoons salt

¾ teaspoon pepper
1 teaspoon dry mustard or
    1½ teaspoons Dijon
    mustard
1 cup dry sherry or light rum

Pick over the beans. Wash and rinse. Cover with boiling water; let stand 50 minutes. Boil covered for 50 minutes in the same water. Fry the bacon until half done and set aside. Pour the fat into a 4-quart casserole. Stir in the beans with the liquid to cover. Add the molasses, onion and seasonings. Cover. Slow-bake 5 hours in a slow to moderate (325°) oven, adding boiling water if becoming dry. Stir in the sherry or rum. Transfer to individual bean pots. Top with the bacon cut in half-inch lengths. Brown about 14 minutes in a hot (425°) oven.

Accompaniments are sliced baked Virginia or canned ham and a tossed, canned artichoke-lettuce or tomato and water-cress salad, with an herb French dressing. Ready at hand, to drink before or during the meal, a planter's punch. Serves 8 to 10.

BAKED DRIED LIMA BEANS

4 cups dried lima beans	2 tablespoons cider vinegar
3 teaspoons salt	½ teaspoon Tabasco
2 quarts boiling water	1 teaspoon dry mustard
½ cup light molasses	2 medium-sized onions, peeled
½ cup chili sauce	and thin-sliced

Rinse lima beans with cold water. Drain. Place in deep 4-quart kettle. Add salt and 2 quarts boiling water; cover. Let stand 50 minutes. Then simmer 2 hours, or until fork-tender, adding more water if necessary. Drain beans; reserve 1 cup of liquid. To it add molasses, chili sauce, vinegar, Tabasco and mustard. Mix well. Layer drained beans and sliced onion in 3-quart casserole. Pour over molasses mixture. Bake uncovered 2 hours in slow (325°) oven. Serves 8 to 10.

Baked Lima Beans with Meat: When arranging beans for baking in casserole, layer with sliced onion and in addition 2 cups diced cooked ham or 1 (12-ounce) can diced luncheon meat.

HARVARD BEETS

2 (1-pound) cans beets, whole or sliced	3 tablespoons sugar
	2 whole cloves
1 tablespoon cornstarch	1 teaspoon salt
3 tablespoons mild vinegar	1 tablespoon butter

Drain the beets, reserving juice. In saucepan mix together ½ cup reserved juice, cornstarch, vinegar, sugar, cloves and salt. Cook-stir until thick and clear. Remove cloves. Add beets and butter. Mix. Heat through to serve.

INDIVIDUAL CHEESE AND BROCCOLI PIES

2 (10-ounce) packages pie
  pastry mix
¾ cup grated Parmesan cheese
2 (10-ounce) packages frozen
  chopped broccoli
2½ cups shredded sharp
  Cheddar cheese (about
  ½ pound)

1½ tablespoons flour
9 slices bacon
12 ¼-inch-thick slices tomato
4 eggs
1½ cups evaporated milk,
  undiluted
1¼ teaspoons seasoned salt

Combine pie pastry mix with Parmesan cheese; make up pastry according to package directions. Chill. Cook broccoli, following package directions; drain well. Mix grated Cheddar cheese with 1½ tablespoons flour. Fry bacon until crisp; drain on paper towels. Sauté tomato slices in bacon drippings 3 minutes and drain. Divide pastry into 6 equal portions; roll each to line an individual pie plate. Fit in pastry; flute edges. Using half the Cheddar cheese-flour mixture, spoon equal amounts into each pastry shell. Divide broccoli evenly on top; crumble a slice of bacon over each. Spread with last of Cheddar cheese-flour mixture; crumble on remaining bacon. Beat eggs light in a small bowl. Stir in milk and seasoning. Ladle ½ cup over ingredients in each pie plate. Top each with 2 tomato slices. Bake 15 minutes in a hot (425°) oven; reduce heat to 325°; cover with aluminum foil. Bake 15 minutes more.

MONTEREY BROCCOLI

1 (1-pound) bunch fresh
  broccoli
1½ tablespoons butter or
  salad oil
1 tablespoon whole mustard
  seeds

1 small section garlic, peeled
1 tablespoon water
Broccoli Anchovy Sauce

Wash broccoli. Divide flowerettes and cut stalks in ¼-inch diagonal slices. Heat butter in medium-sized skillet. Add stalk slices, mustard seeds and garlic. Cover; steam about 5 minutes; shake occasionally. Add flowerettes and water. Cover and continue steaming another 5 minutes. Shake pan twice. Drain, and serve accompanied with Broccoli Anchovy Sauce, or toss broccoli with sauce.

Broccoli Anchovy Sauce: Into a ½-pint bowl measure ¾ cup mayonnaise, ¾ cup sour cream, 1½ teaspoons anchovy paste and 6 drops Tabasco. Mix until smooth. Use as directed above.

POACHED BRUSSELS SPROUTS

1 cup chicken broth or bouillon	2 (10-ounce) packages frozen Brussels sprouts
1 tablespoon dry vermouth	Lemon Butter
Dash each of white pepper and nutmeg	

Bring broth, vermouth and pepper and nutmeg to a boil in saucepan. Add Brussels sprouts; cover and cook 5 to 8 minutes, or until just tender. Drain. Serve with Lemon Butter.

Lemon Butter: Cream ½ cup butter or margarine with ¼ teaspoon grated lemon peel. Beat in 1 tablespoon lemon juice.

LADY CABBAGE

6 cups fine-shredded white or green cabbage, packed	⅛ teaspoon pepper
1 teaspoon salt	1 tablespoon butter or margarine or sour cream (optional)
¼ teaspoon ground nutmeg	

Put shredded cabbage in a 3-pint saucepan. Add salt, nutmeg and pepper. Pour in boiling water to ⅓ depth of cabbage. Boil rapidly uncovered for 7 to 9 minutes, or until cabbage looks translucent and is just bite-tender. Drain, and season further with butter or sour cream if desired. The flavor is delightful as is.

BABY CARROTS AND RAISINS

18 small carrots (about 2 pounds)	1 tablespoon sugar
3 tablespoons butter or margarine	1 cup seeded raisins

Scrape carrots, trim off tops and root ends. Boil carrots until tender. Drain off water; dry carrots on paper towel. Heat butter in saucepan, and stir in sugar. Add carrots and spoon butter over them. Add raisins, stirring to distribute evenly.

BRAISED CARROTS AND ONIONS

1 pound mild onions	½ teaspoon salt
1 pound carrots	2 tablespoons hot water
2 tablespoons butter or margarine	

Peel onions; slice very thin crosswise. Peel carrots; cut crosswise in thin rounds. Melt butter in top of double boiler; add onions, carrots, salt and water. Stir until well mixed. Cover; steam-cook over boiling water 45 minutes, or until both carrots and onions are fork-tender.

DOROTHY BAILEY'S CREAMED CARROTS

2 cups sliced carrots	½ cup grated Cheddar cheese
1 cup diced celery	2 tablespoons butter
½ teaspoon salt	½ cup cracker crumbs
1 cup White Sauce (see Index)	

Cook vegetables in small amount of water with salt until just tender. Drain, add White Sauce in which cheese has been melted. Place in small casserole. Melt butter, add crumbs, cook-stir over medium heat until golden brown. Sprinkle buttered crumbs over vegetables in casserole. Heat in 350° oven 15 minutes.

HOT CAULIFLOWER VINAIGRETTE

1 medium-sized cauliflower	1 section garlic, peeled and
2½ cups boiling water	minced
2 teaspoons salt	⅛ teaspoon cayenne pepper
4 tablespoons olive oil or butter	3 tablespoons cider or wine
3 tablespoons peeled fine-chopped onion	vinegar

Remove outer leaves from cauliflower; wash; cut in 6 sections. Place in broad saucepan. Add water and salt. Cover; steam-boil 15 to 20 minutes, or until barely fork-tender. Drain. Heat oil; add onion, garlic and pepper; sauté until color turns. Stir often. Add vinegar and cauliflower; heat.

CAULIFLOWER WITH CABBAGE

1 quart fine-shredded crisp green cabbage	⅓ cup minced green pepper
1 teaspoon salt	1 tablespoon butter or margarine
¼ teaspoon dry mustard	
2 cups very small raw cauliflowerettes	

Half-cover cabbage with boiling water, add salt and boil rapidly 7 minutes. Stir in mustard. Add cauliflower and green pepper; continue to cook 5 minutes longer. Drain off any excess liquid. Season with butter or margarine.

CAULIFLOWER SECTIONS WITH CHEESE SAUCE AND BACON

1 medium-sized head cauliflower, cut in 6 wedges	6 slices bacon, crisp-cooked
1 teaspoon salt	6 full slices white bread
Cheese Sauce (see Index)	Parsley

Wash cauliflower. Trim off all but tiny green leaves. Cut out tough under-center. Place in 2-quart saucepan; add salt and water to depth of 2 inches. Cover; boil until fork-tender, about 25 minutes. Drain. Meantime, prepare the Cheese Sauce; crisp-fry bacon, and toast the bread. To assemble, place one cauliflower wedge on top of each piece of toast. Spoon over each 2 tablespoons Cheese Sauce, and top with a piece of crisp bacon. Parsley is the garnish.

FRESH CORN ON THE COB WITH GUACAMOLE

Remove husks from corn. Allow 1 or 2 ears per serving. Cut off tips and brush off silk. Place corn in a kettle with boiling water and salt, using 1 teaspoon salt to 1 quart water. Cover and bring to boiling point. Boil 5 to 6 minutes or until the milk in corn is just set (try it with a sharp knife). Remove from water and serve at once with Guacamole Butter.

Guacamole Butter: Cut 1 ripe medium-sized avocado in half. Remove pit and scoop out avocado pulp. Mash, put through sieve and measure (there should be ¾ cup). Add and mix in 2 teaspoons fresh lemon juice, 1 teaspoon fresh onion juice, ½ teaspoon salt, ⅛ teaspoon ground black pepper and 1 tablespoon catsup. Use instead of butter as a spread over boiled hot corn on the cob.

CREAMED CORN

6 ears fresh corn	⅛ teaspoon ground black
¾ cup boiling water	pepper
½ cup milk	½ teaspoon sugar
2½ tablespoons butter or	1¼ tablespoons flour
margarine	2 tablespoons cold water
1½ teaspoons salt	

Shuck corn and remove silk. Cut corn kernels off cob; scrape ears with bowl of a tablespoon to remove all juice and pulp left on cob. Turn kernels and pulp into saucepan; add boiling water, milk, butter, salt, pepper and sugar. Slowly bring to boiling point. Cover and cook 10 minutes, or until corn is bite-tender, stirring occasionally. Mix flour with cold water, and stir into creamed corn. Cook 1 minute more, stirring constantly.

FRESH CORN CRUMB PIE

½ cup soft bread crumbs
6 strips bacon, cut in halves
3 eggs
1½ cups fresh corn, cut off
    the cob (about 3 large ears)

¾ cup milk, heated
1 teaspoon salt
⅛ teaspoon ground pepper
2 tablespoons butter or
    margarine

Butter a 9-inch pie plate; spread bread crumbs over bottom and sides. Broil bacon until almost done and arrange on pie plate. Set aside. Beat eggs slightly. Stir in corn, milk, salt, pepper and butter or margarine. Turn into bacon-lined plate. Bake in slow (325°) oven, 1 hour and 10 minutes, or until knife inserted near center comes out clean.

GRANDMA COGSWELL'S STEWED FRESH CORN

3 cups milk, heated
4 large ears fresh corn
1½ teaspoons salt
⅛ teaspoon ground black
    pepper

6 pats butter
Chopped fresh parsley

Heat milk in double boiler. Meantime, husk corn; remove silk. Slit each row of kernels lengthwise with sharp knife. Cut a thin layer of corn from cob; repeat, cutting 2 more layers. Now, scrape cob with bowl of tablespoon to extract all juice from cob. Add corn to milk in double boiler; cook 30 minutes, or until slightly thickened and hot. Stir in salt and pepper. Serve in soup bowls, a pat of butter floating over each. Garnish with parsley.

CORN PUDDING

4 eggs, slightly beaten
4½ tablespoons corn oil
1 tablespoon sugar
1½ teaspoons salt
Dash pepper
1½ tablespoons peeled fine-chopped onion
1 (1-pound 1-ounce) can cream style corn (about 2 cups)

½ cup fine dry bread crumbs (scant)
1¼ cups scalded milk
2½ tablespoons crumbled crisp bacon
Paprika

Mix together all ingredients except the paprika. Pour into an oiled 1½-quart baking dish. Sprinkle with paprika. Set into a pan containing 1 inch hot water. Bake in a moderate (350°) oven until a knife inserted in center of pudding comes out clean, about 1 hour and 10 minutes.

GREEN CORN PUDDING SOUFFLÉ

A main dish treat for luncheon, brunch or a light dinner.

2 cups fresh corn kernels cut from cob
1 teaspoon sugar
1½ teaspoons salt
⅛ teaspoon ground black pepper

3 eggs, lightly beaten
2 tablespoons butter or margarine
2 cups milk
3 tablespoons chopped chives
Fresh parsley

Combine corn, sugar, salt and pepper. Add eggs and mix well. Add butter or margarine to milk; heat until butter melts. Mix with corn and egg mixture. Stir in chives. Turn into buttered 1-quart casserole. Place in pan with 1½ inches of hot water. Bake 1 hour in preheated slow (325°) oven, or until knife inserted in center comes out clean. Garnish with fresh parsley.

OLD-FASHIONED SUCCOTASH

2½ cups milk, heated
3 cups fresh green corn kernels
1½ cups cooked green lima
beans, cranberry beans or
dried kidney or lima beans
1½ tablespoons butter or
margarine at room
temperature

1½ tablespoons flour
½ teaspoon salt
⅛ teaspoon pepper

Heat milk in double boiler. Add corn kernels. Cook 15 minutes; add beans. Smooth-mix butter and flour; stir in 2 tablespoons of the hot milk; return to cooking corn. Cook 5 to 10 minutes, stirring occasionally, or until thickened. Add seasonings.

BAKED STUFFED EGGPLANT

Select medium-sized eggplants, boil for 20 minutes, then cut in halves crosswise, scoop out the pulp to within ½ inch of the edge, mash and add to it an equal quantity of fried bread crumbs, 2 tablespoonfuls minced green pepper, ½ teaspoon salt, and ⅛ teaspoon pepper, ½ cup of either chopped nutmeats, chopped smoked salmon or cooked minced ham. Heap into the shell, cover with buttered crumbs and bake about 20 minutes longer.

Stuffed Eggplant, Caribbean:

Proceed as for Baked Stuffed Eggplant but instead of the above fillings add the following to the mashed eggplant pulp.

1½ teaspoons salt
¼ teaspoon pepper
1 green pepper, seeded and
minced
1 tomato, chopped
1 tablespoon chopped onion
1 cup chopped cooked fresh
pork
1 cup chopped cooked beef

1 cup chopped cooked smoked
ham
2 tablespoons melted butter or
margarine
1 teaspoon herb blend
1 teaspoon Angostura bitters
1 cup dry bread crumbs
¼ cup melted butter

Combine first eleven ingredients, combine with the mashed eggplant pulp, lightly spoon and pack into the eggplant shells. Cover with dry bread crumbs mixed with melted butter. Place 1 inch apart in a large baking pan; add water to a depth of ¼ inch. Bake 30 minutes in a moderate (375°) oven, or until lightly browned. Serve ½ eggplant per person.

FRIED EGGPLANT

2 (1-pound) eggplants
1 tablespoon flour
1 teaspoon salt
⅛ teaspoon each pepper and ground cumin seed
Oil for frying

Wash eggplants. Slice off ends; then slice into ½-inch-thick slices. Dust with mixture of flour, salt, pepper and ground cumin seed. Fry in just enough oil (preferably olive oil) to prevent sticking, until brown on both sides. Drain on crumpled paper towels. Serve hot.

EGGPLANT PARMIGIANA

2 (1-pound) eggplants
3 teaspoons salt
½ cup flour
⅓ cup olive oil
1¼ pounds ripe tomatoes, peeled and sliced
¾ teaspoon fresh ground black pepper
¾ pound mozzarella cheese, thin-sliced
¾ cup grated Parmesan cheese
3 tablespoons butter or margarine

Peel and wash eggplants. Cut crosswise in ½-inch slices. Dust with 2 teaspoons of the salt. Cover. Let stand 1 hour at room temperature; drain. Dry on paper towels. Dust all over with flour. Heat 2 tablespoons oil in skillet; lightly brown eggplant in it on both sides. Place half the slices in well-buttered 2½-quart baking dish. Cover with ½ the tomatoes; dust with pepper and remaining salt. Next place ½ the mozzarella and ½ the Parmesan cheese in layers over tomatoes. Add another layer of eggplant slices and remaining tomatoes and cheese. Dot with butter; sprinkle over remaining oil. Bake 25 to 30 minutes in moderate (350°) oven. Cool slightly, but serve quite warm.

GARDEN OF EDEN EGGPLANT

4 large tomatoes, peeled and
quartered
1 large eggplant, peeled and
coarse-diced
2 green peppers, peeled,
seeded and coarse-diced
1 cup tart applesauce

2 tablespoons butter
Salt, pepper and paprika to
taste
½ cup buttered bread crumbs
½ cup grated Parmesan or
Cheddar cheese

Boil tomatoes until juicy. Add eggplant. Cook gently 30 minutes, or until the eggplant is fork-tender; mash. Add green peppers. Continue cooking until mixture is quite thick. Stir often. When peppers are tender, add applesauce and butter, salt, pepper and paprika to taste. Transfer to low 2-quart casserole. Mix buttered crumbs and grated cheese; spread over top. Brown in a hot (400°) oven.

WALNUT EGGPLANT STEAKS

1 (2-pound) eggplant
1½ teaspoons seasoned salt
½ cup flour
3 eggs

½ cup cold water
1 cup fine white bread crumbs
1 cup fine-chopped walnuts
Corn oil for frying

Wash the eggplant; cut in crosswise slices 1 inch thick. Cut the slices in half; dust with the salt and flour. Dip into the eggs slightly beaten and diluted with the water. Then coat with the mixed crumbs and the fine-chopped walnuts. Fry until golden in 1 inch of corn oil, hot enough to brown a cubelet of bread in 1 minute. Drain on absorbent paper toweling. Serve with a pickle relish.

STUFFED GREEN PEPPERS AMERICANA

6 medium-sized green peppers	1 cup sliced cooked celery
1 cup shredded American cheese	½ teaspoon salt
1 cup cooked French fresh snap beans	⅛ teaspoon ground black pepper
1 cup cooked rounds peeled fresh carrots	2 cups White Sauce (see Index)

Wash green peppers; cut off tops and scoop out seeds. Parboil peppers 10 minutes in 1 inch boiling salted water. Remove from water and drain. Mix together remaining ingredients, and fill the green pepper shells with the mixture. Bake 50 minutes in preheated moderate (350°) oven.

BAKED MEAT-STUFFED GREEN PEPPERS

6 medium-sized green peppers	2 cups diced cooked lamb or beef
1 section garlic, peeled and crushed	1 teaspoon salt
¼ cup small-diced onion	½ teaspoon oregano
2 tablespoons salad oil or bacon fat	¼ teaspoon ground black pepper
1 cup fine soft bread crumbs	

Wash green peppers; slice off tops; remove seeds. Boil 5 minutes in water to cover, with ½ teaspoon salt. Remove and drain upside down. Sauté garlic and onion in oil or bacon fat until limp. Blend in crumbs, meat and seasonings. Spoon into green peppers. Place in baking dish. Add ¼ inch hot water. Bake in a moderate (350°) oven for 30 minutes. Delicious served hot, just as good when cold.

SPRING GREENS

All leafy green vegetables must be thoroughly cleaned to remove soil and/or insect life. First, cut wilted leaves from the greens, then the roots. Separate the leaves if in clusters (as dandelions or spinach); wash in tepid water three times or until all grit has been removed. Then rinse thoroughly. All plain cooked greens may be included in the main course at luncheon or dinner. If prepared with a tart sauce, such as vinaigrette, they are particularly good with fish. If cooked with pork or bacon, use in a light luncheon menu.

Steamed Greens (including spinach, beet tops, lettuce and wild greens of mild flavor): Prepare as previously directed. Dust 2 quarts greens with 1 teaspoon salt; place in a utensil, transfer to a steamer and steam until tender—from 30 to 35 minutes. Chop; season each 3 cups with 1 tablespoon butter, $\frac{1}{2}$ teaspoon salt, $\frac{1}{8}$ teaspoon pepper and pinch of honey or sugar; a pinch of nutmeg or powdered onion may be added to spinach; sorrel, which is slightly acid in flavor, may be cooked with any bland-flavored greens. Drain all greens after cooking. Chop medium-fine with a chopping knife. A little minced mint may be added to beet greens or to coarse-shredded, cooked lettuce greens.

Boiled Greens (including spinach, beet tops, lettuce and wild greens of mild flavor): Place the greens in a saucepan with water barely covering the bottom. To 3 quarts greens, add 1 teaspoon salt; season as for Steamed Greens. Close-cover; simmer 12 to 25 minutes, stirring occasionally. Garnish, if desired, with sliced hard-cooked egg, juliennes of pickled beets or pickled carrots.

Boiled Greens of Pronounced Flavor (including dandelions, milkweed, mustard greens, turnip leaves and chicory): Follow previously given preparations before cooking. Place greens in boiling water; boil 5 minutes and discard water. Add fresh boiling water to half cover, containing 1 teaspoon salt to the quart; gently boil until tender—15 to 20 minutes. Drain, chop and season as for Steamed Greens.

Creamed Greens on Toast: Combine 1½ cups White Sauce (see Index) with 1 quart chopped cooked greens and serve plain or on toast. For a light entree, top each serving with a poached egg.

PLANTATION PLATTER OF MIXED GREENS WITH POTATOES

½ pound fresh kale	1½ teaspoons salt
½ pound fresh turnip greens	½ teaspoon sugar
½ pound fresh spinach	¼ teaspoon ground black
2 tablespoons bacon drippings	pepper
2 cups small-diced uncooked	Dash cayenne
potatoes	6 strips crisp bacon
¼ cup boiling water	Cream-Mayonnaise Sauce

Wash greens in warm water. Rinse 4 times in cold water; set spinach aside. Measure bacon drippings into 3-quart saucepan. Add kale, turnip greens, potatoes, boiling water, salt and sugar. Cover; cook 15 minutes. Add spinach and cook 5 minutes, or until spinach is wilted. Add black pepper and cayenne. Toss lightly; be careful not to crush potatoes. Top with strips of crisp bacon. Pass Cream-Mayonnaise Sauce.

Cream-Mayonnaise Sauce: Prepare 1½ cups medium-thick White Sauce (see Index). While boiling hot, beat in ½ cup thick mayonnaise and ½ tablespoon each lemon juice and minced chives. Serve hot.

KOHLRABI À LA CRÈME

3 medium-sized kohlrabi	½ cup milk
½ teaspoon salt	¼ teaspoon salt
¾ cup small-curd cottage	⅛ teaspoon pepper
cheese	

Remove leaves, wash and quarter kohlrabi globes, drop into boiling water; add salt. Cook 18 to 20 minutes or until fork-tender. Drain. Remove peel, and put kohlrabi in blender. Add small-curd cottage cheese, milk, salt and pepper. Buzz 2 minutes, or until smooth. Reheat.

BRAISED LETTUCE ITALIAN STYLE

2 firm heads iceberg lettuce, washed and quartered
½ cup boiling water
¾ teaspoon salt
3 tablespoons olive oil

½ cup fine soft bread crumbs
3 tablespoons grated Parmesan cheese
Pinch of ground black pepper

Place lettuce in large saucepan with boiling water and ½ teaspoon of the salt. Cover; cook 2 minutes, or until wilted. Drain. Arrange in shallow baking dish. Sprinkle with olive oil, then with bread crumbs mixed with cheese, remaining ¼ teaspoon salt and black pepper. Bake in preheated very hot (450°) oven for 15 minutes. Serve hot as a combined vegetable and salad.

MEXICALI STUFFED LETTUCE

1 large head iceberg lettuce
1 teaspoon unflavored gelatin
2 teaspoons cold water
4 ounces cream cheese or Neufchâtel cheese
1 packet onion soup mix
1 tablespoon salad oil

½ teaspoon salt
1 tablespoon chili sauce
1 tablespoon lemon juice
1 cup drained cooked or canned kidney beans
½ cup corn chips, crushed

Remove core of head of lettuce. Rinse lettuce with heavy stream of cold water. With knife, hollow out center of lettuce head. Turn it upside down, and drain thoroughly. Add gelatin to cold water; place over boiling water to dissolve. In electric mixer bowl, mix together cream cheese, onion soup mix, oil, salt, chili sauce, lemon juice and dissolved gelatin. Fold in beans and half the corn chips. Pack into hollow of lettuce. Cover and refrigerate 1 hour or more. Serve cut in slices. Garnish with remaining corn chips.

LENTIL KEDGEREE

1 pound green lentils	1 (1-inch) piece stick
1 teaspoon salt	cinnamon
2 quarts boiling water	3 sections garlic, peeled and
1 teaspoon whole cloves	minced
¼ teaspoon ground mace or	1 large onion, peeled and sliced
nutmeg	2 tablespoons cooking oil
Seeds from 12 cardamoms	1 cup uncooked rice
2 bay leaves	6 lemon wedges

Pick over lentils and rinse with cold water. Place in a deep 4-quart saucepan. Add salt and boiling water. Cover. Let stand 50 minutes. Tie all spices and garlic in a square of cheesecloth for easy removal, and add to lentils. Bring to boil and boil 1 hour.

Meantime, fry onion in oil until tender and add to lentils. Stir in rice and slow-cook 30 minutes longer. Remove spices. Serve very hot with lemon wedges and accompany with browned sausages.

FRESH MUSHROOMS SAUTÉ

1 pound fresh mushrooms	Pinch each of pepper and
2 tablespoons butter	nutmeg
1 tablespoon vegetable oil	Toast rounds (optional)
¼ teaspoon salt	

Wipe mushrooms all over with a clean damp cloth. Cut off ends of stems. Thin-slice mushrooms profile fashion. Heat butter and oil in a medium fry pan. Add the mushrooms. Dust with the seasonings. Slow-sauté 7 minutes, turning occasionally with a spatula. Cook only until the color turns and they are a golden beige. Serve on toast rounds if desired. Serves 4.

MUSHROOMS EN CASSEROLE

1 pound fresh mushrooms
2½ cups crumbs of decrusted white bread
½ cup butter or margarine (½ stick)
1 teaspoon grated fresh onion or ¼ teaspoon instant onion
¼ teaspoon ground nutmeg
½ teaspoon salt
⅛ teaspoon pepper
3 cups heated beef or chicken broth
¼ cup fine dry bread crumbs
2 tablespoons melted butter or margarine

Dice mushroom caps; thin-slice stems crosswise. Rub a 3-pint shallow casserole with butter. Lightly sauté white bread crumbs in butter. Place crumbs in casserole, alternating with layers of mushrooms mixed with seasonings. Heat broth and pour over contents in casserole. Dust with dry crumbs stirred with melted butter. Bake 35 minutes in moderate (350 to 375°) oven, or until mushrooms are fork-tender. Serve at once.

MUSHROOMS PAPRIKA

1 cup sliced onion
3 tablespoons butter or margarine
5 cups sliced fresh mushrooms (about 1 pound) or 2 (6- or 8-ounce) cans sliced mushrooms
2 tablespoons dried parsley flakes
1 tablespoon paprika
1 teaspoon salt
⅛ teaspoon ground black pepper
Pinch of ground cayenne pepper
1 cup sour cream
6 slices enriched bread, toasted

Sauté onion in butter until golden. Add mushrooms and seasonings. Cook slowly 5 minutes or until mushrooms are tender, stirring frequently. Add sour cream and heat, but *do not boil*. Serve over toast.

OVEN-FRIED ONIONS

Oven-frying saves fuel, reduces food shrinkage, saves time and uses comparatively little fat. To oven-fry onions: peel and slice crosswise ¼ inch thick. Brush generously with cooking oil, then dust lightly with flour, salt and pepper. Pour in enough cooking oil so that it barely covers bottom of a large iron or ovenware fry pan; add ½ tablespoon water and heat through. Into this, place onion slices. Bake-fry about 20 minutes. Turn once with tongs when barely browned on bottom. Drain on absorbent paper toweling.

SPICED GLAZED PARSNIPS

6 medium-sized fresh parsnips
2 tablespoons butter or
   margarine
2 tablespoons light brown
   sugar

⅛ teaspoon salt
¼ teaspoon ground cloves
3 tablespoons orange juice

Wash parsnips; cook in the skins in boiling water to cover 30 minutes, or until fork-tender. Lift out of water and cool. Remove skins, cut parsnips in half lengthwise; set aside. Melt butter in large skillet. Stir in sugar, salt, cloves and orange juice; heat. Add parsnips and slow-sauté 5 minutes, or until hot and glazed.

BLACK-EYED PEAS

1 pound dried black-eyed peas
2 medium-sized onions, peeled
   and diced
1 strip of salt pork, ½ to ¾
   by 4 inches

5½ cups water
Salt to taste
Crushed red pepper

Pick over the peas and wash in running cold water. Soak peas 3 hours in cold water. Drain and place in saucepan with onions, salt pork and water. Cover; cook slowly 2 hours. Season to taste

with salt, and red pepper (not too much). Remove pork before
serving. Serves 6 to 8.

HOPPING JOHN (A modern adaptation)

This old southern dish made with dried peas was popular during
the days of food scarcity after the Civil War. At that time, people
really had to skimp in their kitchens. Cupboards and pantries,
once well stocked with preserved vegetables, homemade jellies
and the like, were bare. Livestock and poultry had disappeared,
either appropriated by the troops or released to wander away.
Crops and gardens had been raided, trampled and laid waste.
This was a period when the hard-pressed Southerners had to rely
on crops that could be planted with little expense while produc-
ing edible food in a short time. Soon dried peas and beans became staples in most kitchens. The dish then, as now, was high
in protein and continues to maintain its popularity today.

1 (10½-ounce) can condensed
  onion soup
1 soup can water
¼ teaspoon salt
½ teaspoon Tabasco
1 (10-ounce) package frozen
  black-eyed peas

1½ cups cooked ham strips
2 tablespoons salad oil
1½ cups water
1½ cups packaged precooked
  rice

Pour onion soup in 2½-quart saucepan. Add water, salt and
Tabasco; bring to boil. Stir in black-eyed peas. Cover and simmer 40 to 45 minutes, or until peas are tender. Sauté ham
strips in oil. Add additional water, rice and ham strips to black-
eyed peas mixture. Continue to simmer 5 minutes, or until rice
is tender.

BAKED POTATOES DUCHESSE

Prepare 1 quart hot fluffy mashed potatoes (12 medium-sized
potatoes), fresh or packaged. Beat 2 large eggs until light with
¼ teaspoon onion powder, pinch of ground nutmeg and salt to

taste. Butter a 3-pint baking dish. Pile in the potatoes, leaving the surface rough. In a 375° oven bake 20 minutes, or until golden brown. Serves 8.

FLAKY BOILED POTATOES WITH PARSLEY

6 white potatoes
3 tablespoons melted butter
3 tablespoons parsley

Peel potatoes; barely cover with boiling water; add ½ teaspoon salt. Cover, and boil slowly and steadily about 35 minutes, or until the potatoes are tender when pierced with a fork. Drain off the liquid, and use in diluting condensed soup or making gravy. Gently shake the pan containing the potatoes over the low heat until they look flaky. Roll potatoes in the melted butter and parsley. Serve at once.

POTATO CROQUETTES

3 cups hot mashed potatoes
  (about 9 medium-sized
  potatoes)
1 egg yolk
Pinch of cayenne
Pinch of nutmeg

1 tablespoon minced parsley
1 teaspoon onion juice
Egg wash*
1½ cups fine dry bread
  crumbs
Vegetable oil for deep frying

Combine first six ingredients; beat thoroughly. Shape into balls containing 1 tablespoon each. Chill. Roll in egg wash, then roll lightly in crumbs. Let stand 10 minutes to set coating. Fry in deep 375° fat, hot enough to brown a bit of bread in 40 seconds. Drain on crumbled paper towels. Makes 8 to 12.

* To make egg wash, slightly beat 1 egg; stir in ½ cup milk.

JILL'S ROAST POTATOES

Have baking pan with ¼ to ½ inch of roast drippings in it, sizzling hot, in oven. Select 1 good-sized baking potato for each serving; try for uniform size. Peel and parboil 15 minutes; drain and carefully blot on paper toweling. With tongs, place in drippings in baking pan—if you have a roast cooking, you may place potatoes directly in the drippings in the roasting pan. Check in 15 minutes; if deep, golden brown, turn and cook another 15 minutes, turn again until deep golden brown and crusty. Test for doneness. Drain on paper toweling. A perfect accompaniment to roast beef or lamb.

SESAME-BAKED POTATOES

Roll warm fresh boiled white potatoes in melted butter. Dust all over with plenty of sesame seeds, about 1½ teaspoons to a potato. Place in an oiled low pan. Bake 30 minutes in a moderate (375°) oven, or until golden brown.

STUFFED WHITE POTATOES

Allow a large potato for each person served. Bake the potatoes, and when done cut the top off lengthwise and scoop out all the pulp. Add to 2 cups of pulp 3 tablespoons of hot milk or cream and 1 tablespoon of butter. Season with 1 teaspoon salt and ⅛ teaspoon pepper, and beat until creamy. Pile into the shells and brown quickly in the oven.

BASILED NEW POTATOES WITH PEAS

12 small new potatoes	½ teaspoon crushed dried basil
½ teaspoon salt	leaves
½ cup butter or margarine	⅛ teaspoon ground black
2 tablespoons flour	pepper
1 cup reserved potato water	1 cup cooked fresh or frozen
and milk (combined)	green peas
½ teaspoon salt	

Wash and scrape potatoes. Place them in saucepan with boiling water to cover. Add ½ teaspoon salt. Cover, bring to boiling point and boil 20 minutes, or until potatoes are tender. Drain, saving potato water to use in making the following white sauce. Melt butter or margarine. Blend in flour. Cook ½ minute, or until bubbly. Pour potato water into 1-cup measure and finish filling with milk. Add to butter-flour mixture. Mix well. Stir-cook until thickened. Add additional ½ teaspoon salt, basil, pepper and peas. Heat 2 minutes. Pour sauce over potatoes.

BROILED LONG POTATO SLICES

4 Idaho potatoes
1½ tablespoons cooking oil
Seasoned salt

Thin-peel potatoes. Cut in lengthwise slices, ½ inch thick. Brush with cooking oil; dust with seasoned salt. Line broiler or low pan with aluminum foil. Place slices on it. Broil 3 inches from source of heat about 20 minutes, or until fork-tender and browned; turn at once. This method produces combined bake-fried flavor with the use of very little oil. Serves 4.

FRENCH FRIED POTATOES

Large raw potatoes   Salt
Frying fat   Pepper

Select large potatoes if possible, pare and cut into thick slices, then cut lengthwise as broad as they are thick. Allow them to stand in ice-cold water for 1 hour, drain, pat dry with a cloth, and cook a few at a time until golden brown in deep fat (325°), hot enough to brown a piece of bread in 1½ minutes. Drain on crumpled soft paper, sprinkle generously with salt and pepper, and serve immediately.

FRIED POTATOES WITH GREEN PEPPERS

¼ cup cooking oil
4 cups peeled thin-sliced raw
   white potatoes, cut in half-
   moons
¾ cup seeded shredded green
   pepper

¼ cup peeled thin-sliced onion
1 teaspoon cumin seed
1½ teaspoons salt
⅛ teaspoon pepper

In a 10-inch skillet, heat oil. Add potatoes and slow-fry 3 minutes. With kitchen fork, gently add green pepper, onion, cumin seed, salt and pepper. Continue to slow-fry until green pepper and onion are softened and cumin seed and potatoes are slightly browned.

SARATOGA CHIPS

Pare medium-sized potatoes; cut in paper-thin slices crosswise, crisp in ice water, drain, and plunge into deep fat (375°) hot enough to brown a bit of bread in forty counts, and fry until brown. Drain on crumpled paper. Dust with salt when ready to serve.

OVEN FRENCH FRIES

2 pounds medium-sized white potatoes
½ cup cooking oil
1 teaspoon salt

Pare potatoes; cut into thick lengthwise slices; then cut into strips as broad as they are thick. Rinse thoroughly in cold water; drain, and dry on paper toweling. Heat cooking oil 3 minutes in medium-sized roasting pan in a 425° oven. Remove pan; spread and stir potatoes in it making one layer. Return pan to oven. Bake 25 to 30 minutes, stirring occasionally with kitchen fork to coat potato slices with oil to insure even browning. When done, remove potatoes from pan, and drain on crumpled paper toweling. Dust with salt.

BAKED WHITE POTATOES WITH TASTY TOPPINGS

Scrub medium-sized baking potatoes and cut out any blemishes. Grease lightly with butter, margarine, drippings or salad oil. (This keeps the skin soft enough to eat.) Bake in a very hot (425°) oven for 15 minutes. Then reduce heat to 375°, and bake until potatoes feel tender when pressed, about 30 to 40 minutes longer, according to size.

To serve baked potatoes, cut top open in form of a cross, press pulp up from the bottom of the potato, put on a pat of butter and dust with paprika. Top with any of the following:

Deviled ham topping: Mix the contents of 1 (2¾-ounce) can deviled ham with 1 tablespoon minced green pepper and ¼ tablespoon tomato catsup, and heat.

Sour cream chives topping: Season ½ cup sour cream with 3 tablespoons minced fresh or frozen chives, or use freeze-dried chives; add salt and pepper to taste and 4 drops Tabasco.

Bacon topping: Bake or sauté 6 strips bacon until crisp. Crumble, mix in 1 tablespoon minced parsley.

DIANE'S MASHED POTATOES

6 medium-sized potatoes, peeled and quartered	¼ teaspoon nutmeg
4 cups boiling water	1 medium-sized onion, chopped
½ teaspoon salt	1 (3-ounce) can sliced mushrooms
2 tablespoons hot milk	
3 tablespoons butter	2 tablespoons fine-chopped parsley
1 teaspoon salt	
Generous sprinkling pepper	

Cook potatoes in water with salt added 20 minutes, or until tender. Mash, beat in hot milk with 2 tablespoons of the butter, 1 teaspoon additional salt, pepper and nutmeg. Sauté onion and mushrooms in remaining tablespoon of butter about 5 minutes. Add with parsley to mashed potatoes; mix thoroughly.

ALL-AMERICAN SWEET POTATO LOAF

⅓ cup butter or margarine
¼ cup fine-chopped onion
¼ teaspoon ground allspice
4 cups peeled boiled mashed sweet potatoes (about 12 medium-sized potatoes)
¾ cup medium-chopped walnut meats

2 large eggs, beaten light
1¾ teaspoons salt
¼ teaspoon ground black pepper
½ cup chopped pitted dates
1 cup fine dry bread crumbs

In small skillet melt butter; add onion. Cook over moderate heat until translucent. Stir in allspice. In 2-quart bowl combine sweet potatoes, walnut meats, beaten eggs, salt and pepper. Stir in onion mixture. Stir together dates and bread crumbs and add. Oil a 9×5×3-inch loaf pan. Spoon in sweet potato mixture. Bake 1 hour in moderate (350°) oven. Cool 10 minutes in pan. Loosen edges with knife and unmold onto platter; serve cut in 1-inch slices. This makes 8 servings.

SOUTHERN CANDIED SWEET POTATOES

6 sweet potatoes
¼ cup butter or margarine
½ cup dark corn syrup
2 tablespoons water

¼ cup brown sugar
1½ tablespoons lemon juice
Grated lemon rind

Wash potatoes and cook in boiling water 15 minutes. Remove from heat; cool. Peel potatoes, cut in half lengthwise. Place all ingredients except potatoes in heavy skillet. Arrange potatoes on top, cut sides down. Cook over very low heat, basting occasionally, about 1 hour, or until potatoes are tender and well glazed.

If desired, potatoes may be placed in a shallow baking pan, covered with remaining ingredients, and baked for 15 to 20 minutes in a moderate oven.

SWEET POTATO RHUMBA

4 cups hot boiled smooth-
   mashed sweet potatoes
   (about 12 medium-sized
   potatoes)
¼ cup butter or margarine
½ cup half and half
½ teaspoon ground nutmeg
½ teaspoon salt

2 tablespoons sugar (optional)
1 teaspoon rum extract
   (optional)
1 tablespoon melted butter or
   margarine
1 tablespoon grated orange
   rind

Combine first seven ingredients. Beat until fluffy. Turn into well-buttered 6-cup casserole. Brush top with melted butter or margarine. Dust with grated orange rind. Bake in hot (400°) oven for 35 minutes, or until top is browned. Serves 8.

DICED RUTABAGAS WITH BASIL LEMON-BUTTER

2 tablespoons butter or
   margarine
1 tablespoon fresh lemon juice
1 teaspoon salt
¼ teaspoon crumbled basil
   leaves

Pinch of black pepper
3 cups diced cooked rutabagas,
   hot
2 tablespoons minced fresh
   parsley

Melt butter or margarine; add lemon juice, salt, basil and black pepper. Mix well and pour over and into the hot, diced cooked rutabagas. Dust parsley over top. Cover; let stand 5 minutes.

FRESH SPINACH LOAF

2 pounds fresh spinach
¾ cup soft enriched bread
   crumbs
1 small onion, peeled and
   chopped
3 tablespoons butter or
   margarine
⅓ cup flour

¾ cup milk
2 eggs, separated
1 teaspoon salt
1 teaspoon sugar
¼ teaspoon crumbled dried
   rosemary
½ teaspoon black pepper

Wash spinach. Cook covered in its own liquid 7 minutes, or until bite-tender. Drain; save liquid. Chop spinach medium-fine. Stir in crumbs. Sauté onion in butter; blend in flour. Gradually add milk. Stir-cook until thick and boiling. Add spinach. Beat egg whites until stiff, yolks until creamy. To spinach add yolks, salt, sugar, rosemary and pepper. Fold in beaten egg whites. Transfer to buttered 8×8-inch loaf pan. Bake 1 hour in moderate (350 to 375°) oven, or until pick inserted in center comes out clean. Let stand 10 minutes. Unmold on serving platter. Cut in squares or slices.

WILTED LEAF SPINACH

3 pounds fresh leaf spinach	1 teaspoon salt
½ cup heavy cream or ¼ cup fresh butter	⅛ teaspoon pepper
	Pinch of ground nutmeg

Carefully wash the spinach leaves but do not detach from the main stems. Heat the cream or butter; in it slowly sauté the spinach leaves until well wilted, turning often with a fork and dusting with the seasonings.

SPINACH-MUSHROOM CASSEROLE

2 packages chopped frozen spinach	1 tablespoon flour
	1 tablespoon butter
1 (10½-ounce) can cream of mushroom soup	3 eggs, separated
	1 hard-cooked egg, chopped
⅛ teaspoon nutmeg	½ cup chopped mushrooms, sautéed in a little butter
½ teaspoon salt	
⅛ teaspoon pepper	

Thaw and drain spinach; reserve liquid. Combine spinach, soup and seasonings in a blender. Buzz 2 minutes. Smooth flour and butter together until pasty. Stir in spinach liquid. Heat-stir until thickened. Remove from heat. (May be done in advance.) To finish, beat yolks until creamy and whites until stiff. Stir yolks into spinach; stir-heat 1 minute. Fold in egg whites. Transfer to buttered casserole. Stand this in pan; pour in hot water to almost half fill. Bake 30 minutes in a moderate (325 to 350°) oven. Garnish with hard-cooked egg and mushrooms.

SPINACH PARMESAN

2 pounds fresh spinach	½ cup grated Parmesan cheese
¼ teaspoon sugar	4 drops Tabasco
½ teaspoon salt	Salt and pepper to taste
2 tablespoons dairy sour cream	

Wash spinach. Place in kettle with sugar and salt, but no water; close cover. Cook 7 minutes, or until spinach leaves wilt and stems are tender. Drain off any liquid. Chop spinach medium-fine. Stir in sour cream and Parmesan and stir-heat until well combined. Add Tabasco, salt and pepper to taste.

BAKED ACORN SQUASH

Wash, cut in halves lengthwise, and scrape out seeds and pulp. Dust with salt and pepper, dot with butter and bake 45 minutes at 375°. Allow ½ squash per person.

ACORN SQUASH WITH CEREAL PORK STUFFING

2 good-sized acorn squash	1 chicken bouillon cube
½ pound ground lean pork	½ teaspoon salt
¼ cup peeled chopped onion	¼ teaspoon curry powder
2 tablespoons butter or	⅛ teaspoon pepper
margarine	1 cup oven-toasted rice cereal
½ cup water	

Wash and dry squash; cut in half lengthwise and remove seeds and pulp. Place cut side down in a baking pan, with water ¼ inch deep. Bake 20 minutes in hot (400°) oven. Sauté pork and onion in margarine until pork loses pink color. Add water, bouillon cube and seasonings; simmer 10 minutes. Stir in cereal. Turn squash cavity side up. Fill squash with cereal mixture. Cover with aluminum foil, crimping it to the edges of the pan. Bake 20 minutes at 400°; remove the foil and bake about 10 minutes or until tender and lightly browned. Cut each section in halves, making 8 servings.

GLENN McCASKEY'S SQUASH THING

4 butternut or acorn squash,
   halved and seeded
8 tablespoons butter
½ teaspoon salt
1 teaspoon cinnamon
¼ teaspoon nutmeg
¼ teaspoon allspice
1 tablespoon maple syrup per
   ½ squash
¾ cup brown sugar
Pinch of pepper

Mix above ingredients—except squash—in saucepan over low heat until sugar is dissolved. Set squash in shallow pan; surround with 1 inch boiling water. Pour sugar-syrup mixture into hollows in squash. While baking in a 350° oven, brush warmed mixture over neck or edges of squash several times. Bake for 1 hour, or until easily forked. Serves 8.

CHEESED SUMMER SQUASH

2 pounds medium-sized
   summer squash
¼ cup milk
1½ teaspoons salt
¼ teaspoon pepper
⅛ teaspoon garlic powder
¾ cup fine dry bread crumbs
¼ cup vegetable oil
1 cup well-seasoned thick-
   stewed tomatoes
1½ cups grated sharp
   American Cheddar cheese

Peel squash if skin seems tough, then slice ⅛ inch thick. Dip into milk, a slice at a time. Dust with salt, pepper and garlic powder. Cover with crumbs. Let stand 10 minutes to set coating. Sauté in oil until lightly browned on both sides. Rub low 3-pint baking dish with oil. Arrange squash in it, slices barely overlapping. Spoon over tomatoes. Cover with cheese. Bake in moderate (375°) oven, or until squash is fork-tender.

SPICED ACORN SQUASH WEDGES

2 medium-sized acorn squash
½ teaspoon ground cinnamon
½ teaspoon salt
¼ teaspoon ground black
  pepper

Pinch of ground cloves
2 tablespoons brown sugar
2 tablespoons butter or
  margarine
¼ cup boiling water

Wash squash; peel and cut into wedges; remove seeds and stringy portion. Place in shallow baking dish. Combine next five ingredients and dust over squash. Dot with butter or margarine. Add water to pan. Cover and bake 35 minutes in moderate (375°) oven, or until squash is fork-tender. Remove cover and brown under broiler.

STUFFED PATTYPAN SQUASH

2 (¾-pound) pattypan
  squash
3 large ears fresh corn, cooked
1½ cups day-old bread
  crumbs
⅓ cup diced green pepper
3 tablespoons peeled diced
  onion

¾ cup diced fresh tomato
2 teaspoons salt
⅛ teaspoon ground black
  pepper
½ cup chopped pecans or
  walnuts

Wash squash; place whole in saucepan with boiling water to cover. Put on lid; boil 15 minutes, or until half done. Remove from water. Drain. Cool. Cut a slice from top of each; discard seeds of squash. Cut corn from cobs and mix with crumbs, green pepper, onion, tomato, salt and black pepper. Spoon into hollows of squash. Place in baking pan. Pour in hot water to depth of ¼ inch. Bake 30 minutes in moderate (350°) oven. Dust with nut meats. Bake 10 minutes more, or until they are lightly browned.

BAKED TOMATO HALVES

3 good-sized tomatoes
¼ teaspoon seasoned salt
2 tablespoons cooking or olive
  oil

3 tablespoons grated Parmesan
cheese

Wash tomatoes, cut out stem ends; do not peel; cut in halves. Dust with salt. Heat oil in 7×11-inch pan. Put in tomatoes, cut side down. Bake 20 minutes in slow oven. Then turn over, dust with Parmesan cheese and bake 10 minutes more.

STEWED FRESH TOMATOES NEW ENGLAND STYLE

Scald 3 pounds ripe tomatoes with boiling water, drain; remove skins and stem ends. Cut in coarse dice. Place in a 3-quart saucepan with 1½ teaspoons sugar, 1 teaspoon salt or to taste, and ⅛ teaspoon pepper. Boil rapidly uncovered until very soft; add 1 tablespoon butter. If desired, stir in ½ cup coarse dry white bread crumbs.

BROILED TOMATO HALVES

Wash 6 medium-sized tomatoes; cut out stem ends. Halve tomatoes crosswise. Brush cut sides with melted butter or margarine. Dust with very little brown sugar, salt, fresh ground black pepper and powdered oregano. Oil cups of a 12-compartment muffin pan (2¾-inch cups). Spoon ½ teaspoon water into each compartment. Add to each a half tomato, cut side up. Slow-broil at 350 to 375° for 20 minutes 4 inches from source of heat. The steam from the water cooks the tomatoes through.

TOMATOES AND HOMINY

4 tablespoons butter or margarine	6 medium-sized tomatoes
1¼ cups dry hominy grits	Salt and pepper
1 teaspoon salt	1 egg, beaten
4 cups water	12 small slices American cheese

Melt butter in saucepan. Add grits and slow-fry to a light brown. Add salt and water. Cover, boil 40 minutes. Wash tomatoes. Dry and cut out stem ends. Do not peel. Cut tomatoes in half. Place on a pan, dust over with salt and pepper, and broil for 10 minutes. Stir egg into the hominy. Transfer to an oiled, shallow dish that will withstand heat. Make slight hollows in the hominy; nest the broiled tomatoes in them; dust with salt and pepper. Top tomatoes with small slices of sharp cheese. Place under broiler 6 inches from the heat until cheese melts.

FRIED TOMATOES

Select firm tomatoes, do not remove the skins. Cut in half-inch slices, dust with salt and pepper and a trace of sugar. Dip in flour and sauté in butter, vegetable fat or savory drippings until brown. Serve as a garnish to meat, or as a supper or luncheon dish on toast, with a white or egg sauce.

Tomatoes Fried in Deep Fat: Prepare the tomatoes according to Fried Tomatoes; after dipping in flour cover them with beaten egg, as in making croquettes, then with fine dry bread crumbs. Place in a frying basket and fry in deep fat (350°) hot enough to brown a bit of bread in 60 counts. Serve plain or dust with sugar.

GRILLED TOMATOES AU GRATIN

3 large tomatoes, washed
½ cup grated process cheese
1 tablespoon milk
1 tablespoon melted butter or
   margarine

6 drops Tabasco sauce
½ teaspoon seasoned salt
Paprika

Cut tomatoes in half, crosswise. Combine cheese, milk, butter, Tabasco and seasoned salt. Arrange tomato halves, cut side up, in large foil-lined pan. Spread equal amounts of cheese mixture over top of each tomato. Dust with paprika. Heat in moderate (350°) oven for 5 minutes or over warm coals on outdoor grill for 10 minutes, or until cheese melts and tomatoes are hot.

TURNIPS SWEDISH STYLE

3 cups peeled sliced cooked
   turnips
1 small onion, peeled
¼ cup mild vinegar
1 cup boiling water
½ teaspoon sugar

1 tablespoon flour
1 tablespoon butter or
   margarine
½ teaspoon salt
⅛ teaspoon pepper
2 egg yolks

Arrange cooked turnips in overlapping slices on deep medium-sized serving platter. Pour over a sauce made as follows: Combine onion, vinegar and water; boil 20 minutes. Mix together sugar, flour and butter; stir into boiled mixture. When mixture boils again, stir in seasonings, and beat-stir hot sauce into egg yolks. Do not reboil. Use at once.

BAKED-STUFFED ZUCCHINI

8 small-sized zucchini
1 cup soft bread crumbs
½ cup grated Parmesan cheese
1 teaspoon peeled minced
   onion
1 egg, slightly beaten

2 tablespoons salad oil
½ teaspoon thyme
¼ teaspoon instant meat
   tenderizer
Garlic salt (optional)

Peel zucchini and trim off ends; cook zucchini 15 minutes in boiling salted water. Drain and cool. Cut zucchini lengthwise in half. Scoop out pulp; drain thoroughly and reserve. Mix pulp with bread crumbs, half the grated Parmesan, onion, egg, oil, thyme and meat tenderizer. Taste, and add garlic salt, if desired. Pile mixture into zucchini shells; arrange in oiled skillet. Dust zucchini with remaining Parmesan. Bake 30 minutes at 350°. Remove with pancake turner or broad spatula. Serve hot. Serves 8.

LOUISIANA YAM-APPLE MEDLEY

Its bright orange flesh tells you it's a "yam" and not a "sweet potato."

2 (1-pound) cans Louisiana yams, drained and sliced
1 (1-pound 4-ounce) can sliced apples, unsweetened
½ cup coarse-chopped pecans
¼ cup firm-packed brown sugar
½ teaspoon cinnamon
2 tablespoons melted butter or margarine

Arrange yams and apple slices in a 2-quart casserole. Mix together pecans, brown sugar and cinnamon; sprinkle on top. Drizzle butter over all. Bake uncovered in a moderate (375°) oven for 20 minutes, or until hot. Baste frequently.

BRANDIED YAMS

Peel 4 medium-sized yams and slice 1 inch thick. In a saucepan combine 1 (6-ounce) can tangerine juice concentrate, 1 cup water and ½ teaspoon salt. Add the yams. Cover and simmer-boil over a low heat for 30 minutes, or until tender. Add 2 tablespoons brandy and keep hot 5 minutes more. Serves 4.

Salads

The exciting thing about salads is their versatility. They may be prepared and served as appetizers, garnishes, accompaniments to main dishes or as main dishes themselves.

When preparing tossed green salads use crisp iceberg-type lettuce if your plans call for advance preparation and refrigeration. If tossed right before the meal the soft-leafed Boston lettuce is ideal for absorbing the dressing.

Make use of wood, ceramic, silver or glass bowls. They add variety to any table and provide an inviting accent note for the endless color combinations of green or vegetable salads.

All recipes are for six servings unless otherwise stated.

APPLE SLAW

½ cup small-diced red apple
4 cups fine-shredded crisp green cabbage
¼ cup coarse-chopped nut meats (any kind)
½ cup raisins

½ cup dairy sour cream
¾ teaspoon salt
Pinch of pepper
3 drops Tabasco
½ teaspoon sugar
1 tablespoon cider vinegar

Combine first four ingredients; toss with dressing made by smooth-stirring together remaining ingredients. Cover; chill; serve within 30 minutes. It is nice as is or in nests of lettuce leaves.

ARTICHOKE HEARTS PARISIAN

6 fresh-cooked or canned artichoke hearts
½ cup French dressing (not sweet)
6 cherry tomatoes

3 cups fine-shredded crisp lettuce
1 sliced hard-cooked egg
6 pitted ripe olives

Put artichoke hearts in bowl; pour over French dressing. Refrigerate to marinate 1 hour or more. Cut cherry tomatoes in halves from top to bottom. Reserve 6 halves. Add remainder to marinated artichoke hearts. Arrange individually as follows: First a bed of shredded lettuce on each plate. Top each with marinated artichoke heart and half a cherry tomato. Finish each with slice of hard-cooked egg and pitted ripe olive.

BAR HARBOR SALAD

2 cans Maine sardines
½ cup plus 2 tablespoons
  mayonnaise
1 tablespoon lemon juice
1 teaspoon Dijon-type mustard
Generous sprinkling pepper
Salt (optional)
4 hard-cooked eggs, chopped
4 cups diced cooked potatoes

¾ cup fine-minced celery
¼ cup fine-minced onion
1 section garlic, fine-minced
2 tablespoons fine-chopped
  parsley
Lemon wedges (optional)
Sliced olives or pimiento
  strips (optional)

Thoroughly mash and blend with fork 2 cans sardines, drained; mayonnaise, lemon juice, mustard and pepper. Taste for salt, add if needed. Carefully mix with eggs, potatoes, celery, onion, garlic and parsley. Garnish with lemon wedges and sliced olives or pimiento strips if desired.

NEW BEET SALADETTES

2 pounds medium-sized red
  beets
4 quarts water
6 anchovy fillets, minced
2 garlic cloves, mashed

¼ cup olive oil
½ cup wine vinegar
½ teaspoon black pepper
Salt to taste

Wash beets. Boil in their skins in water. (If you have a roast on, wrap beets in aluminum foil and bake in oven for about 1½ hours, or until cooked. This will give beets more flavor than the usual boiling.) When cooked, skin and slice. Place in bowl and cover. Combine remaining ingredients, adding salt to taste, and pour over warm beets. Cover. Cool, then refrigerate. Serve as a first course or as a salad.

RED-AND-WHITE CABBAGE PATCH SALAD

2 cups well-crisped, fine-shredded red cabbage
2 cups well-crisped, fine-shredded green cabbage
½ cup small-cut, red-skinned apple

1 teaspoon grated onion
French dressing or French onion dressing to moisten (about ½ cup)

Combine two cabbages, apple and grated onion. Add French or onion dressing. Toss.

TANGY CAESAR SALAD

1 head iceberg lettuce
8 slices bacon, cooked crisp and crumbled
¾ cup olive oil
¼ cup lemon juice

1½ cups white bread croutons
6 tablespoons Caesar salad mix
1 egg, slightly beaten
1 cup cherry tomatoes
¼ bunch water cress

Tear lettuce into salad bowl. Add next six ingredients; toss lightly. Garnish with tomatoes and water cress.

CAESAR SALAD DRESSING MIX

Time-saving homemade mix for the popular Caesar salad.

Combine 1½ teaspoons garlic salt with ½ teaspoon each dry mustard, crushed oregano, pepper. Add 1 cup grated Romano or Parmesan cheese or a blend of the two. Mix thoroughly. Store in an air-tight jar, no refrigeration necessary. This recipe makes about 1 cup, or enough for 3 family-sized salads, figuring 1 tablespoon mix per person.

CHEF'S SALAD

1 head lettuce	6 ounces white meat of chicken
1 head romaine	6 ounces baked ham
1 head chicory	6 ounces tongue
1 head escarole	6 ounces Swiss cheese
4 small or medium tomatoes, cut in quarters	6 sprigs water cress
	French garlic dressing

Chop coarsely the heads of lettuce, romaine, chicory and escarole. Mix together and divide equally into 6 wooden bowls. Place tomato quarters on top of greens. Cut chicken, ham, tongue and Swiss cheese in narrow strips. Place on top of salad and garnish with water cress. Serve with French garlic dressing.

CHICKEN SALAD

3 slices pineapple, diced	¼ cup dairy sour cream
3 cups diced cooked chicken	2 teaspoons lemon juice
2 cups bias-sliced celery	Salt and pepper to taste
2 tablespoons chopped pimiento	1 cup toasted, blanched almonds
2 tablespoons diced preserved ginger	Salad greens
½ cup mayonnaise	3 or 4 pickled crab apples, halved

Combine first five ingredients. Mix mayonnaise, sour cream and lemon juice. Pour over chicken; toss well; season. Add ⅔ cup almonds (save remainder for topping); chill. Heap in low serving bowl; border with salad greens. Top with almonds and pickled crab apples.

CHICKEN-KIDNEY BEAN SALAD BOWL

3 cups coarse-chopped cooked
chicken
2 cups cooked or canned
kidney beans, drained
¾ cup fine-chopped sweet
pickle
1½ cups sliced celery, strings
removed
2 tablespoons peeled minced
onion

3 hard-cooked eggs, diced
1½ teaspoons salt
½ cup mayonnaise
1 teaspoon table mustard
1½ teaspoons liquid from
sweet pickle
Crisp tender chicory leaves
and tomato wedges

Combine all ingredients except chicory and tomatoes. Toss lightly and refrigerate at least 1 hour. Then heap into salad bowl and edge with chicory and tomato wedges.

COLESLAW

4 cups fine-shredded crisp cabbage
½ cup French or sour cream dressing
1½ tablespoons minced parsley, chives or scallions

Whatever the kind of slaw, the cabbage must be fine-shredded. Rinse with cold water, put in a bowl, cover closely and refrigerate 30 minutes or more to crisp. To the cabbage, add the dressing and seasoning.

Radish Coleslaw: Add ½ cup thin-sliced radishes to above.

Herbed Coleslaw: Add ½ tablespoon minced basil or dill to above.

Carrot Coleslaw: Add ½ cup coarse-grated raw carrots to above.

Apple Coleslaw: Add ½ cup small-diced apple to above.

Creole Coleslaw: Put together with French garlic dressing. Add ¼ cup each chopped sweet green pepper and celery and 1 teaspoon minced fresh thyme.

STUFFED CUCUMBER-CHEESE SALAD

4 cucumbers (about 8 inches long)
½ teaspoon salt
3 (3-ounce) packages cream cheese, softened
2 tablespoons minced onion
3 tablespoons fine-chopped green pepper
3 tablespoons fine-chopped sweet red pepper
1 teaspoon salt
⅛ teaspoon pepper
1 teaspoon paprika
2 tomatoes, cut into wedges
Lettuce
Mayonnaise

Wash cucumbers, score with a fork and cut in half lengthwise. Scoop out seeds, leaving centers hollow, and sprinkle inside with ½ teaspoon salt. Drain. Combine cream cheese, onion, green and sweet red pepper, additional salt, pepper and paprika. Mix well and pack into cucumber cavities. Wrap in foil. Refrigerate several hours or overnight. Slice and serve with tomato wedges on lettuce with mayonnaise. Serves 8.

FROZEN FRUIT SALAD

1 teaspoon unflavored gelatin
1 tablespoon cold water or orange juice
1 cup mild-seasoned mayonnaise
1½ cups heavy cream, whipped stiff
⅔ cup drained canned crushed pineapple, scalded and cooled
¾ cup each hulled halved firm ripe strawberries, peeled seeded halved Tokay grapes, peeled halved Thompson seedless grapes and diced firm orange pulp
½ cup minced well-drained maraschino cherries
Shredded tenderized figs
Lettuce hearts
Fresh fruits

Stir gelatin into cold water or juice; melt over hot water. Stir in mayonnaise. Fold into whipped cream. Stir in fruits. Transfer

to freezer tray that has first been rinsed with cold water. Freeze
steadily at lowest temperature until firm, about 2 hours. Stir
once at end of 15 minutes, again at end of 30 minutes. Slice;
serve with a garnish of delicate lettuce hearts and colorful fresh
fruits.

GREEK SALAD

3 cups fine-shredded white
    cabbage
1 large green pepper, seeded
    and shredded
1 cup fine-shredded peeled
    carrot
1 cup Dutch Maätjes herring,
    cut in tidbits

½ cup sharp vinegar
1 cup water
½ cup olive oil
½ teaspoon salt
⅛ teaspoon pepper
Hearts of lettuce

Combine first four ingredients. Beat together vinegar, water, oil,
salt and pepper. Pour into salad ingredients and toss; refrigerate
24 hours. Serve on lettuce.

GREEN GRAPES SALAD À LA WALDORF

1½ cups Thompson seedless
    grapes
1 cup diced unpeeled pitted
    nectarines
1 tablespoon fresh lemon juice
½ teaspoon sugar
1 cup thin-sliced celery

¼ cup chopped pecans or
    walnuts
¼ cup mayonnaise
12 lettuce leaves
6 clusters Thompson green
    seedless grapes

Combine grapes, nectarines, lemon juice and sugar. Mix lightly.
Add celery, nuts and mayonnaise. Toss; arrange on lettuce. Garnish each serving with a cluster of Thompson seedless grapes.

HAM AND SWISS CHEESE SALAD

2½ cups small-diced canned
    smoked ham
1½ cups small-diced or
    shredded Swiss cheese
2 cups cooked fluffy long grain
    rice
1 tablespoon fine-grated mild
    onion

1 teaspoon salt
¾ cup Lemon-Mustard
    Mayonnaise
Crisp salad greens
French dressing
6 radish roses

Combine first five ingredients. Lightly stir in Lemon-Mustard Mayonnaise. Chill. Serve on tossed salad greens or slices of lettuce sprinkled with French dressing. Garnish with a radish rose with its tender green leaves.

Lemon-Mustard Mayonnaise: To 1 cup commercial mayonnaise stir in 1 teaspoon table mustard and 1 tablespoon fresh lemon juice.

LIMA BEAN SALAD

2 (10-ounce) packages frozen
    green lima beans
½ cup water
1 teaspoon onion salt
½ teaspoon salt
¼ teaspoon fresh ground
    pepper

4 teaspoons Italian-style salad
    dressing
1 cup chopped celery, chilled
½ cup sliced red radishes,
    chilled
½ cup mayonnaise

Combine beans, water, onion salt, salt and pepper in heavy 1-quart aluminum saucepan. Cover, place over high heat. When hot, reduce heat to low, and cook 10 minutes, stirring once with fork. Turn into good-sized salad bowl. Add Italian dressing and toss. Cover and refrigerate several hours to marinate. Toss in remaining ingredients.

MACARONI-CHEESE-TOMATO SALAD

4 cups cold cooked macaroni
½ cup thin-sliced scallions
½ cup thin-sliced celery
⅓ cup French dressing
⅔ cup diced peeled raw firm
tomatoes

½ cup coarse-grated sharp
Cheddar cheese
Mayonnaise or salad dressing
Crisp lettuce or chicory

Combine macaroni, scallions and celery with French dressing. Chill 30 minutes. Toss in tomatoes and cheese. Then add enough mayonnaise or salad dressing to mix lightly. Serve on lettuce or chicory.

SALAD NIÇOISE

1 large raw onion, peeled and
sliced paper-thin
3 medium-sized potatoes,
peeled, cooked and diced
3 medium-sized tomatoes,
skinned and cut into
eighths
2 medium-sized green peppers,
seeded and cut into
juliennes
1 heart of celery stalk, diced
small
4 tablespoons olive oil

1 tablespoon wine vinegar
½ teaspoon salt
2 (6½-ounce) cans tuna,
chilled, drained and flaked
coarse
4 hard-cooked eggs, sliced
8 stuffed green olives
8 pitted black olives
1 (2¾-ounce) can anchovy
fillets
Juice of 1 lemon
1 tablespoon chopped parsley

Prepare, combine and toss together the first eight ingredients. Transfer this mixture to a chilled salad bowl. Cover with prepared tuna, hard-cooked eggs, stuffed green olives and pitted black olives and anchovy fillets. Sprinkle over this the juice of the lemon, and over the whole dish dust the chopped parsley. Chill at least 30 minutes.

TOSSED RAW MUSHROOM SALAD

1 pound fresh mushrooms
1 cup sliced tender celery
¼ cup shredded tender celery leaves
2 tablespoons minced green onion
2 hard-cooked eggs, coarse-chopped
2 pimientos drained, cut in 1-inch strips
¼ teaspoon ground mustard
½ teaspoon salt
⅛ teaspoon fresh ground pepper
½ cup French dressing (not sweet)
Crisp romaine or any lettuce

Rinse mushrooms in very cold water; drain; dry on paper towels. Snip off ends of stems. Cut mushrooms down from crown through stems to make generous-sized bites. Place in large bowl. Toss in remaining ingredients, except romaine or any lettuce. Taste and, if necessary, add a little more ground mustard, salt and pepper. Refrigerate. Serve on lettuce leaves.

POTATO SALAD

1 pound small potatoes (new if possible)
1 small onion, peeled and grated
¼ cup olive or salad oil
1½ tablespoons sharp cider vinegar
1 teaspoon sugar
1 teaspoon salt
¼ teaspoon pepper
½ cup small-diced celery
½ cup mayonnaise
2 tablespoons minced parsley
Lettuce or water cress
1½ tablespoons minced parsley

Cook potatoes with jackets on. While they are still warm, peel and cut in ⅛-inch slices; add grated onion. Pour olive oil into vinegar; mix in sugar, salt and pepper. Add to warm potatoes. Mix with 2 forks. Try not to break the slices. Cover and chill. Then add celery. Blend with mayonnaise; add 2 tablespoons minced parsley. Arrange in salad bowl border-lined with lettuce or water cress. Garnish the top with additional parsley.

FIESTA POTATO SALAD AND DRESSING

1 tablespoon flour
1 tablespoon sugar
1½ teaspoons salt
½ teaspoon dry mustard
2 tablespoons salad oil
½ cup water
3 tablespoons vinegar
1 egg, slightly beaten

⅓ cup sour cream
4 cups sliced warm cooked
   potatoes
¼ cup peeled chopped onion
½ cup chopped dry roasted
   peanuts
¼ cup chopped green pepper
1 tablespoon chopped pimiento

In double-boiler top, combine flour, sugar, salt, dry mustard and oil. Gradually add water. Cook over medium heat, stirring constantly, until mixture thickens and begins to boil. Gradually stir vinegar into slightly beaten egg. Then stir in hot mixture. Return combined mixture to double boiler and cook over hot water 5 minutes, or until mixture thickens. Remove from heat and stir in sour cream. Cool.

Combine sliced potatoes, onion, dry roasted peanuts, green pepper and pimiento. Fold in the dressing. Refrigerate at least 1 hour.

HOT POTATO, BACON AND EGG SALAD

2 pounds small potatoes
   (preferably new)
6 tablespoons chopped green
   onion, including tender
   portion of green tops
4 slices bacon, cut in
   ½ inch squares

3 tablespoons cider vinegar
1 teaspoon sugar
2 warm hard-cooked eggs,
   fine-chopped
12 slices crisp cooked bacon

Boil potatoes, drain, peel and dice. At once, add onion with green tops. Keep warm. Slow-fry bacon squares until crisp; do not drain. Mix in vinegar and sugar. Stir into warm potato mixture. Slow-cook over low heat or in double boiler until very hot. With fork mix in hard-cooked eggs. Heap on heated platter; border with crisp cooked bacon.

RICE SALAD SPANISH

3 cups cooked long grain rice
1 shredded large green
    pepper, seeds removed
2 fresh or canned large
    tomatoes, cut up
1½ cups chopped, cooked
    fresh or drained canned
    mushrooms
3 tablespoons chopped green
    onion

2 tablespoons chopped parsley
⅔ cup olive oil
¼ cup wine vinegar
1¼ teaspoons salt
½ teaspoon pepper
1 section garlic, peeled and
    crushed
2 drained canned pimientos,
    cut in 1-inch strips

Combine first six ingredients in a salad bowl. Beat together oil, vinegar, salt, pepper and garlic. Pour into and over rice mixture; toss lightly. Garnish with pimiento strips. Chill. This is also nice when served hot!

ROAST BEEF SALAD

3 cups thin-sliced, bite-
    sized pieces roast beef
2 tablespoons slightly crushed
    well-drained capers
½ cup juliennes celery or
    green pepper
⅓ cup well-seasoned French
    dressing (not sweet)

1 teaspoon Worcestershire
    sauce or white horseradish
Lettuce
2 tablespoons chopped fresh
    or frozen chives

Combine beef, capers, juliennes of celery or green pepper, French dressing and Worcestershire or horseradish. Toss, then refrigerate 30 minutes. Edge a large, deep platter with lettuce. Center platter with mixed salad. Garnish with chives.

RUSSIAN SALAD BOWL

6 cups fine-shredded or coarse-
    grated white cabbage
6 outer stalks celery, shredded
1¾ cups diced cooked
    chicken, with cooked tongue
    or ham; or summer sausage
1 tablespoon minced parsley

½ cup sharp French dressing
Sprigs of parsley
3 hard-cooked eggs, sliced
3 tablespoons mayonnaise or
    Russian dressing
6 small slices cooked beef
    tongue

Combine cabbage, shredded celery, pieces of chicken and meat, parsley and French dressing. Toss; transfer to a low salad bowl. Border with parsley and hard-cooked eggs. Top with mayonnaise and additional tongue.

SARDINE SALADETTES

1 can large sardines
6 medium-sized lettuce leaves
Lemon-Egg Dressing

Remove sardines from can and chill. Reserve oil. Place one sardine on each lettuce leaf. Spoon over the Lemon-Egg Dressing.

Lemon-Egg Dressing: To reserved sardine oil add juice of ½ a medium-sized lemon; stir in ½ a shredded pimiento, 1 teaspoon minced parsley, ¼ teaspoon salt, ⅛ teaspoon pepper and 1 fine-chopped hard-cooked egg.

FRESH SPINACH SALAD

1 pound crisp-fresh curly
    young spinach
1½ tablespoons olive oil

Spinach Salad Dressing
2 hard-cooked eggs

Remove stems and any bruised leaves from spinach. Wash several times in tepid water; rinse with cold water to remove any sand. Drain. Sprinkle with olive oil. Cover and chill.

To serve, toss spinach with just enough Spinach Salad Dressing to coat the leaves. Sieve egg whites, then yolks over salad.

Spinach Salad Dressing:

1 egg, slightly beaten
¼ cup catsup
1½ teaspoons sugar
½ teaspoon Worcestershire sauce
½ teaspoon salt
½ teaspoon each paprika and dry mustard

1 cup olive oil
1½ tablespoons cider vinegar
1½ tablespoons lemon juice
2½ tablespoons warm water

Mix the first six ingredients. Alternately add olive oil, vinegar and lemon juice in small amounts. Beat constantly with rotary beater or use blender. Last, slowly beat in warm water.

THREE BEAN SALAD

1 can wax beans
1 can kidney beans
1 can green beans
1 green pepper, sliced thinly
½ cup diced celery

¼ cup salad oil
¾ cup cider vinegar
½ cup sugar
Salt and pepper to taste

Drain beans and put in large bowl. Add green pepper and celery and mix gently with a fork. Mix oil, vinegar and sugar, making a smooth dressing. Add to bowl of vegetables, cover, and set in refrigerator for about 8 hours. Take out occasionally and toss carefully, mixing beans well in the dressing. Add salt and pepper to taste.

SOUTHERN TOMATO ASPIC

1 pint tomato juice
½ tablespoon cider vinegar
1 teaspoon ground mustard
½ teaspoon Worcestershire
 sauce
½ teaspoon salt
⅛ teaspoon pepper
1½ envelopes unflavored
 gelatin

¼ cup cold water
½ cup thin-sliced celery
½ cup fine-chopped sweet
 pickle
Lettuce or chicory leaves
½ cup mayonnaise or salad
 dressing

Combine tomato juice, vinegar, mustard, Worcestershire, salt and pepper in a 1-quart saucepan. Simmer-boil 10 minutes; rub through a sieve. Stir gelatin into cold water; stir into hot tomato mixture. Cool; refrigerate until thickened. Stir in celery and pickle. Rinse an 8-inch square pan with cold water; pour in gelatin-tomato mixture. Refrigerate 6 hours, or until firm enough to cut in squares. Arrange each in a nest of lettuce. Garnish with mayonnaise or salad dressing.

TREMONT SALAD

1½ cups shredded apples
1½ cups diced celery
½ cup chopped toasted nut
 meats (any kind)

1 firm tomato, diced
Mayonnaise
Lettuce
Whole nut meats

Combine apple, celery, nuts and tomato with mayonnaise to blend. Serve with garnish of lettuce, additional mayonnaise, and a few whole nut meats.

TUNA SALAD

1 (13-ounce) can tuna fish
2 eggs, hard-cooked and
   chopped
1 cup small-diced celery
¼ cup fine-minced onion
¼ cup French dressing

Salad greens
¼ cup mayonnaise
Sliced stuffed olives or pickles
1 sweet green pepper, minced,
   or capers (optional)

Toss together lightly the tuna, eggs, celery, onion and French dressing. Chill. Arrange on salad greens and garnish with mayonnaise and olives or pickles. You might want to try garnishing with sweet green pepper or with capers.

SUPERB TURKEY SALAD

5 cups bite-sized chunks
   cooked turkey
2 teaspoons grated onion
1 cup coarse-diced celery
1 cup fine-chopped green
   pepper
¼ cup light cream or half
   and half

⅔ cup mayonnaise
1 teaspoon salt
⅛ teaspoon pepper
2 tablespoons vinegar
Crisp salad greens

In a 3-quart bowl, combine turkey, onion, celery and green pepper. Mix together cream, mayonnaise, salt, pepper and vinegar; toss with turkey and chill. Serve on crisp salad greens. Serves 8.

WALDORF SALAD

2 cups diced apples	Mayonnaise or salad dressing
1 cup diced celery	Lettuce
French dressing	Whole nut meats and thin
½ cup broken nut meats (any kind)	slices unpeeled apple or pimiento strips

Combine the apples and celery with enough French dressing to moisten, add the nut meats, mayonnaise or salad dressing to blend, and serve in nests of lettuce leaves with a garnish of whole nut meats and thin slices of red apple or strips of pimientos.

Salad Dressing

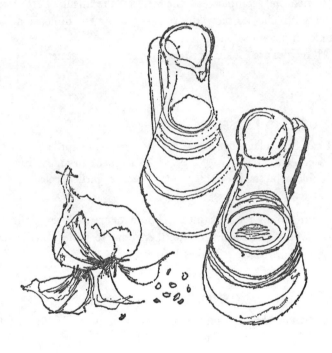

The dressing is the crowning glory to any salad. In fact, any salad is incomplete without it. It's easy to diversify the taste of the basic ingredients by varying the choice of dressing. Use ingredients that complement the rest of the meal. Tart, sweet, laced with cheese, tasty dressings add a new dimension to a simple or elegant salad plate.

All recipes are for six servings unless otherwise stated.

BASIC SALAD DRESSING

1 cup corn oil or olive oil
⅓ cup vinegar
1 tablespoon sugar
1½ teaspoons salt

½ teaspoon paprika
½ teaspoon dry mustard
1 section garlic, peeled

Measure all ingredients into a bottle or jar. Cover tight and shake well. Chill several hours, then remove garlic. Shake thoroughly before serving. Makes 1⅓ cups.

BOILED OIL MAYONNAISE

This dressing has the luxurious taste of mayonnaise at half the cost and about two thirds less calories.

2 tablespoons salad oil
2 tablespoons flour
2 tablespoons lemon juice
Boiling water
1 egg yolk, beaten

1 cup salad oil
1 teaspoon salt
1 teaspoon pepper
½ teaspoon dry mustard
1 egg white

Mix 2 tablespoons of salad oil, flour and lemon juice in measuring cup. Fill cup with boiling water; transfer to double-boiler top and cook over hot water until thickened, stirring constantly.

Beat into egg yolk and cool. Then gradually beat in additional oil and seasonings, and last, thin mixture with egg white whipped stiff. Makes 1½ cups.

REAL FRENCH SALAD DRESSING

6 tablespoons olive oil
½ teaspoon salt
⅛ teaspoon pepper

2 tablespoons wine vinegar or
mild cider vinegar

Measure above ingredients into a small deep bowl. Beat with a fork or small egg beater until well mixed. Use at once. (If dressing must stand, cover, refrigerate and rebeat before using.)

Occasionally, a little mustard is added. Garlic is generally added in the south of France. However, if you desire a subdued garlic flavor in a salad, before tossing lightly rub the salad bowl with a cut section of garlic. Epicures never add sugar to real French dressing. When mixed it should be slightly tart—a real "vinaigrette." Makes ½ cup.

CHIFFONADE DRESSING

Chiffonade Dressing is an American adaptation of Real French Salad Dressing. It is what is termed a pleasant dressing garnish for salads of fresh or cooked vegetables such as lettuce wedges, Belgian endive, sliced tomatoes, cooked asparagus or beets. It is also sometimes spooned over thin-sliced cold meat, chicken or duck, or cold poached thin fillets of white fish. The bright, chopped hard-cooked egg, pimiento and parsley form a sparkling built-in garnish.

1 recipe Real French Salad
Dressing (see Index)
Shredded pimiento
1 teaspoon minced parsley

½ teaspoon paprika
1 hard-cooked egg, fine-
chopped

Prepare Real French Salad Dressing. Add remaining ingredients. Makes about ⅔ cup.

COUNTRY DRESSING

Serve with all salads.

2 tablespoons dry mustard	1 pint mayonnaise
¼ cup table mustard	1½ teaspoons Worcestershire
¼ cup dry white wine	sauce
¼ cup wine vinegar	¼ teaspoon Tabasco
2 tablespoons lemon juice	⅛ teaspoon salt

Thoroughly mix the dry and table mustard. Gradually stir in wine, vinegar and lemon juice. Stir into mayonnaise. Add remaining ingredients; mix until well blended. Makes about 2¾ cups.

COUNTRY COLE SLAW DRESSING

½ cup sour cream	⅓ teaspoon salt
1½ tablespoons cider vinegar	⅛ teaspoon powdered dill
½ teaspoon sugar or liquid honey	

Beat together in a small bowl. Makes ½ cup.

DILL SEED SALAD DRESSING

1 tablespoon sugar	1½ tablespoons fine-chopped
1 teaspoon dry mustard	peeled onion
1 teaspoon salt	2 teaspoons dill seed, crushed
3 tablespoons vinegar	1 cup salad oil
3 tablespoons lemon juice	

Mix together sugar, mustard, salt, vinegar and lemon juice. Add onion and dill seed. Gradually beat in the oil or use a blender. Makes 1⅓ cups.

FROTHY SALAD DRESSING PIQUANT

1 teaspoon salt
1 teaspoon paprika
½ teaspoon powdered mustard
¼ teaspoon ground black
  pepper
2 teaspoons grated peeled
  onion

1 section garlic, peeled
  and crushed
2 cups salad or olive oil
¼ cup catsup
½ cup cider vinegar
2 tablespoons fresh lemon juice
1 small egg white

Combine all the ingredients. Beat until creamy and thick with a
rotary beater. Makes approximately 3 cups.

GREEN GODDESS DRESSING

⅛ teaspoon powdered garlic
2 tablespoons anchovy paste
3 tablespoons fine-chopped
  fresh or frozen chives
1 tablespoon lemon juice
3 tablespoons tarragon wine
  vinegar

½ cup sour cream
¾ cup mayonnaise
¼ cup minced parsley
Salt to taste

Combine and mix ingredients in order given. Makes 1½ cups.

HERBED ITALIAN DRESSING

½ cup corn oil or olive oil
⅓ cup wine vinegar or lemon
  juice
1 section garlic, peeled and
  halved
½ teaspoon salt

½ teaspoon crushed basil
  leaves
½ teaspoon crushed oregano
  leaves
¼ teaspoon pepper

Mix all ingredients in a half-pint jar; cover tight. Refrigerate.
Shake well before using. Makes almost 1 cup.

ROQUEFORT CHEESE DRESSING

Serve with fruit salad.

¼ cup sour cream
¼ cup mayonnaise
1 tablespoon fresh lemon
   juice

¼ cup crumbled Roquefort
   cheese

Lightly combine all ingredients. Makes ¾ cup.

SOUR CREAM DRESSING

½ tablespoon table mustard
1 teaspoon sugar
¼ teaspoon salt
⅛ teaspoon pepper

½ tablespoon lemon juice or
   vinegar
½ cup sour cream

Beat the ingredients into the sour cream. Makes almost ⅔ cup.

YOGURT THOUSAND ISLAND DRESSING

½ cup yogurt
3 tablespoons mayonnaise
2 tablespoons catsup
½ teaspoon table mustard
½ tablespoon minced parsley

½ tablespoon grated onion
¼ teaspoon salt
⅛ teaspoon pepper
¼ teaspoon paprika

Combine and thoroughly mix all ingredients. Use as a variation
with any vegetable salad. Makes ¾ cup.

Eggs

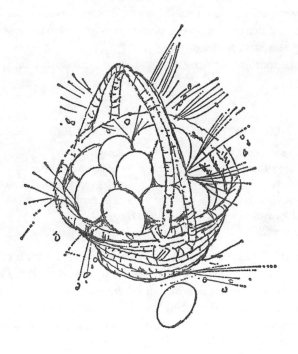

The egg—a lovely thing to look at in nature's fragile, beautifully designed package—has been part of man's diet since earliest times. Eggs are nutritious, an almost perfect food and an essential part of most well-balanced eating. Their enormous versatility makes eggs a "must" item to always have on hand. The key to excellence in any egg dish is simple: use fresh eggs, cook slowly at a low temperature.

All recipes are for six servings unless otherwise stated.

BAKED EGGS WITH RICE AND CHEESE-MUSHROOM SAUCE

½ green pepper, chopped	1 teaspoon salt
½ cup sliced mushrooms, fresh or canned	⅛ teaspoon pepper
	1 cup grated American cheese
4 tablespoons butter	3 cups cooked rice
4 tablespoons flour	8 eggs
2 cups milk	1 teaspoon paprika

Sauté green pepper and mushrooms in butter 10 minutes; add flour and stir well. Stir in milk, salt, pepper and cheese. Cook in double boiler until thick and smooth. Add half of cheese and mushroom sauce to rice, using a fork. Line well-buttered low baking dish with rice mixture, spreading evenly. Make 8 hollows with back of spoon in rice. Carefully break egg into each. Dust with paprika. Set baking dish into pan; surround with warm water; bake in moderate (350°) oven until whites of eggs are firm. Serve hot with remaining cheese and mushroom sauce. Serves 8.

BAKED EGGS IN SOUR CREAM

1 cup chopped onion	Pepper
3 tablespoons butter or other cooking fat	1 cup sour cream
	Soft crumbs, buttered
6 eggs	Paprika
Salt	

Sauté onion in butter until tender, stirring occasionally. Place in shallow, well-buttered casserole. Carefully crack eggs and drop on top of onion. Sprinkle with salt and pepper and put in a 325° oven to bake for 5 minutes. Remove from oven and gently spread sour cream over eggs. Dust with buttered crumbs. Return to oven until eggs are the desired firmness, about 10 minutes. Sprinkle paprika sparingly before serving.

EGGS BENEDICT

6 thin slices ham	6 poached eggs
Butter	Hollandaise Sauce (see Index)
½ tablespoon Madeira (optional)	Paprika
	Parsley sprigs
3 English muffins, halved, toasted and generously buttered	

Trim ham to fit muffins, sizzle in fry pan in small amount of butter, turn and add Madeira if used. Lay one slice ham on each muffin half, top each with a poached egg, and spread with the Hollandaise Sauce. Sprinkle with paprika and garnish with parsley. Serve good and hot!

CURRIED EGGS

¼ cup instant minced onion
¼ cup water
1 tablespoon curry powder
2 tablespoons coconut oil or
  melted butter or margarine
¼ cup flour
1 cup chicken bouillon
1 cup chicken bouillon or
  coconut milk

½ teaspoon salt
¼ teaspoon ground black
  pepper
¼ teaspoon ground ginger
⅛ teaspoon garlic powder
3 cups buttered cooked rice
12 hot hard-cooked eggs,
  shelled and halved
Water cress or parsley

Soften the instant onion 5 minutes with the water along with the curry powder in the coconut oil or butter or margarine. Blend in the flour. Stir in 1 cup of the bouillon. Stir-cook until beginning to thicken. Stir in the additional chicken stock or milk; cook until boiling. Add the seasonings.

Turn the rice onto a deep serving platter. Embed the eggs on it. Pour over the curry sauce. Garnish with water cress or parsley.

DEVILED EGGS

6 large hard-cooked eggs
½ teaspoon salt
Pinch of ground black pepper
2 tablespoons fine-chopped
  celery

1 teaspoon fresh lemon juice
2 tablespoons fine-chopped
  onion
3 tablespoons mayonnaise

Shell and cut eggs lengthwise into halves. Remove yolks, mash and rub through sieve. Mix with salt, black pepper, celery and lemon juice. Mix onion and mayonnaise into egg yolk mixture; mix well. Spoon into hollowed hard-cooked egg whites.

ESCALLOPED EGGS

2 tablespoons butter or
  margarine
2 tablespoons flour
2 cups milk
1 teaspoon salt
⅛ teaspoon pepper

¼ cup grated Cheddar cheese
8 hard-cooked eggs
½ cup fine dry bread crumbs
  mixed with 2 tablespoons
  melted butter or margarine
2 tablespoons sherry (optional)

Make white sauce of butter or margarine, flour, milk and seasonings; stir in cheese. Slice eggs crosswise. Oil shallow casserole; layer in half the eggs; cover with sauce and repeat. Spread with crumbs; bake 15 minutes in hot (400°) oven, or until browned. If desired, use 2 tablespoons sherry, omitting 2 tablespoons of the milk. Serves 4.

EGGS GOLDENROD

2 tablespoons butter or
  margarine
1 tablespoon minced onion
3 tablespoons flour
2 cups milk

¾ teaspoon salt
Dash pepper
6 shelled hard-cooked eggs
6 slices toast
1 tablespoon minced parsley

Melt the butter in the top of a double boiler. Add the onion and simmer until tender. Stir in the flour, milk, salt and pepper. Cook over boiling water until smooth and thickened.

Cut eggs in halves lengthwise and remove yolks. Cut whites in slivers, or chop coarsely, and add to the white sauce. Heat eggs and sauce and pour over toast. Sieve the egg yolks and sprinkle over the creamed mixture with a little minced parsley.

EGG-MUSHROOM SKILLET

½ cup (¼ pound) butter or
  margarine
3 cups sliced fresh mushrooms
½ cup peeled chopped onion

1 dozen eggs
1 teaspoon salt
¼ teaspoon pepper

Melt the butter or margarine in a 10-inch skillet, using moderate heat. Add the mushrooms and onion; spread to make an even layer. Cook 10 minutes, or until tender but not browned; stir occasionally.

Break the eggs into a quart bowl; slide into the pan atop the mushrooms and onion. Dust with the salt and pepper.

Cover; cook the eggs to desired doneness, from 5 to 7 minutes.

HAM-DEVILED EGGS

6 hard-cooked eggs, halved
1 tablespoon lemon juice or vinegar
1 teaspoon "hot" table mustard
1 teaspoon Worcestershire sauce
½ teaspoon salt
⅛ teaspoon ground pepper
2 tablespoons deviled ham
2 tablespoons mayonnaise or salad dressing

Remove egg yolks. Rub through sieve and mix with remaining ingredients until smooth. If desired, add more seasoning and salad dressing. Refill the whites.

HARD-COOKED EGGS WITH CURRIED VEGETABLES

1½ pounds new cabbage, cut in thick slices
½ pound green beans, sliced lengthwise
1 pound carrots, scraped and quartered
Curry Sauce
4½ cups cooked rice
6 hard-cooked eggs, hot and shelled
Paprika

Steam-boil together cabbage, green beans and carrots in 1½ inches salted boiling water for 20 minutes. Drain. Arrange on deep platter, cabbage in center, carrots at one end and beans opposite. Pour Curry Sauce over vegetables. Down sides of platter, arrange nests of rice. Fill with hard-cooked eggs cut in halves and dusted with paprika.

Curry Sauce: Melt 2 tablespoons butter or margarine; add 1 peeled crushed small section garlic, and 1 sliced medium-sized onion; slow-fry 2 minutes. Stir in 3 teaspoons curry powder and 2 tablespoons flour. Slow-fry 1 minute. Stir in 2 cups liquid drained from cooked vegetables, or use 2 envelopes chicken broth powder and 2 cups water. Cook-stir until boiling. Simmer 3 minutes. Season to taste with salt and pepper.

EGGS À LA SWISS

2 packages frozen French-cut green beans

2 tablespoons butter or margarine

Salt and pepper to taste

2 cups milk

2 tablespoons frozen chopped chives

1 (8-ounce) package cream cheese, cubed

2 teaspoons seasoned salt

1 teaspoon garlic spread or 1 section garlic, peeled and mashed

6 hard-cooked eggs, sliced or quartered

¾ cup shredded Swiss cheese

Chives

Cook beans until tender following package directions. Drain; toss with butter or margarine; season to taste with salt and pepper. Keep warm in heated casserole. Meanwhile, prepare cheese sauce as follows: Heat milk in a double boiler or over very low heat. Add frozen chopped chives, cream cheese, seasoned salt and garlic. Heat-stir until cheese melts. Fold in eggs and Swiss cheese; stir until eggs heat and cheese melts. Do not boil. Pour over green beans. Dust with additional chives.

EGGS FLORENTINE

1 pound fresh or 1 package frozen spinach, cooked

Salt and pepper to taste

8 eggs

Mornay Sauce (see Index)

Grated Parmesan cheese

Fine-chop the cooked spinach. Season to taste. Place in large shallow baking dish that can go-to-table. Poach eggs and arrange on top of spinach in baking dish. Pour Mornay Sauce over all and dust generously with grated Parmesan cheese before browning under broiler. Serves 4.

EGGS POACHED IN BUTTER

Butter

White pepper

Large fresh eggs

Parsley sprigs

Salt

Melt enough butter in a fry pan to cover the bottom. Do not let it brown. When bubbling, break in required number of eggs; keep them separate; they should almost float in butter. Dust sparingly with salt and pepper. Slow-fry or "poach" slowly—allow about 10 to 12 minutes. Baste occasionally with butter from pan. When done, eggs look translucent with pale brown edges. Remove with spatula to large platter. Garnish with parsley sprigs.

EGGS RANCHERO

3 tablespoons onion, chopped

1 clove garlic, minced

2 tablespoons butter or margarine

2 tablespoons chopped green pepper

Pulp of 2 green pod chili peppers

¼ teaspoon oregano

1 large tomato, peeled and chopped

Salt and pepper to taste

½ cup meat stock or water

4 eggs

4 tortillas

Cook the onion and garlic in the melted butter or margarine until golden. Add green and chili peppers, oregano, tomato, salt and pepper. Mix well. Add broth or water and cook until vegetables are tender and sauce is thickened. Fry or scramble eggs. Serve sauce over cooked eggs with tortillas warmed in a 200° oven. Serves 4.

PIPERADE

1 green pepper, thin-sliced	1 teaspoon salt
½ onion, peeled and minced	⅛ teaspoon pepper
3 tablespoons olive oil	6 eggs
1 medium tomato, peeled, seeded and chopped	6 slices toast or 6 slices sautéed ham
1 clove garlic, peeled and crushed	

Sauté the green pepper and onion in olive oil until soft. Add tomato, garlic, salt and pepper to taste. Simmer until mixture reaches purée stage, add eggs and stir only enough to mix well with vegetables. When eggs are set, serve on toast or thin ham slices which have been sautéed.

PLAIN OMELET

There are several types of omelets, the most common being the plain omelet, the puffy omelet or omelet soufflé, and the French omelet. From these basic recipes may be developed a large variety of delicious dishes. There is no better way to extend eggs than by combining vegetables or other foods with them in omelet form, such dishes being suitable for use at luncheon or supper. For breakfast, the plainer types should be chosen. However, omelets may be used either as savories or sweets, according to the ingredients with which they are combined.

6 eggs	⅛ teaspoon paprika
6 tablespoons cold water	2 tablespoons melted butter or margarine
½ teaspoon salt	

Beat the eggs slightly, yolks and whites together; add the water, salt and paprika. Melt the butter or margarine in a frying pan or omelet pan, pour in the egg mixture, stir it gently for a moment, then let it cook over a moderate heat until it begins to set. Gradually push the cooked part of the omelet toward the front of the pan, tipping the pan back so as to allow the uncooked portion to run over the pan; then as this sets repeat the process of pushing and tipping until the entire bulk of the omelet is set and it is lightly browned on the bottom. Turn on to a hot dish and serve immediately. An omelet should always be rather under- than overcooked; that is to say, while it should not "run," it should not be cooked so that the eggs become hard and tough.

Variations of Plain Omelet:

Sprinkle one of the following over the omelet as it begins to set:

½ cup minced ham
> or

½ cup minced tongue
> or

½ cup minced chicken and ¼ teaspoon grated lemon rind
> or

2 tablespoons minced dried beef
> or

½ cup cooked diced shrimps
> or

½ cup flaked cooked finnan haddie, kippered herring, smoked tuna fish or salmon

OMELET SOUFFLÉ OR PUFFY OMELET

5 eggs	5 tablespoons hot water or
¾ teaspoon salt	milk
¼ teaspoon pepper	

Separate the yolks from the whites of the eggs and beat the whites until stiff, the yolks until thick and creamy; add the seasonings and liquid to the yolks and fold this mixture into the stiffly beaten whites. Do not mix thoroughly, as the success of this omelet depends upon its puffiness, which in turn, is dependent upon the amount of air which is incorporated in it through the beating of the egg whites. Turn the omelet mixture into a clean frying pan containing a tablespoon of melted butter or margarine. Cook very gently over moderate heat until the omelet begins to solidify, then lift it around the edges with a knife so that the uncooked portion may precipitate. Allow the omelet to brown on the bottom, then set it in the oven to cook the top. Cut at right angles to the handle to form a hinge, then fold it over and turn it onto a hot platter.

Variations of Omelet Soufflé or Puffy Omelet:

Just before folding add one of the following:

1 cup diced, peeled mushroom caps and stems fried in 2 tablespoons of butter for about 10 minutes, seasoned with salt, pepper and a bit of mace

or

½ pint small oysters heated until the edges ruffle in 2 tablespoons butter

or

1 cup of shredded onions fried pale brown

or

1 cup of equal parts of creamed string beans, peas, sliced carrots and cooked asparagus tips, heated in ½ cup of White Sauce (see Index)

or

2 chicken livers which have been fried until tender in butter, then chopped and seasoned with salt, pepper and a bit of Worcestershire sauce

or

1 heaping cup of halved or sliced strawberries which have been sweetened to taste

or

Just before serving spread half of the omelet with drained crushed canned pineapple, or sweetened fresh grated pineapple at either end

or

Just before serving spread half of the omelet with any tart jelly; then fold over as usual.

FRENCH OMELET

1½ tablespoons butter	½ teaspoon salt
4 eggs	⅛ teaspoon pepper
4 tablespoons milk or water	

Melt but don't brown butter in a heavy 9-inch frying pan. Pour in mixture. At once lift up the edges with a fork, to let the uncooked portion of the mixture reach the bottom of the pan. When the omelet becomes firm, let it brown very lightly on the bottom. Slide a spatula under the omelet and fold over. Serves 4.

Variations of French Omelet:

Just before folding over do one of the following:

Sprinkle with 2 tablespoons mixed minced fresh parsley, chervil and a very little tarragon or basil (Omelette aux Fines Herbes)

> *or*

Spread with small fresh tomatoes cut in small pieces, heated in a little butter and well seasoned

> *or*

Spread with jelly, jam or preserves. Also sprinkle with grated coconut or chopped nuts if desired

> *or*

Sprinkle with grated American or Parmesan cheese

OVEN CHEESE LAYER OMELET

6 eggs, separated	½ cup grated sharp
¾ teaspoon salt	Cheddar cheese
¼ teaspoon Tabasco	Creole Sauce
3 tablespoons flour	

Preheat oven to 350°. Oil two 8-inch layer pans and place in oven to heat. Beat egg whites with salt until stiff, but not dry. Beat egg yolks; add Tabasco and flour; beat until thick and thoroughly blended. Stir in grated cheese. Fold into egg whites. Spread mixture into hot pans. Bake 15 minutes, or until pick inserted near center comes out clean. Turn one layer onto a serving platter; spread with Creole Sauce; top with second layer.

Creole Sauce: Melt 2 tablespoons butter; add ¼ cup each onion and minced green pepper; cook until the onion is limp, but not brown. Add the contents of a 1-pound can tomatoes, ¼ teaspoon Tabasco and ¼ teaspoon each salt, celery salt and garlic salt. Simmer 30 minutes.

SPANISH OMELET

Make Plain Omelet (see Index) and serve Spanish Sauce as a filling or over the omelet.

Spanish Sauce:

½ small onion, peeled and minced
1 stalk celery, minced
½ sweet green pepper, seeded and minced
½ section garlic, peeled and minced
1 tablespoon butter or margarine
1 (8-ounce) can tomato sauce
¼ cup water

Slow-fry vegetables in butter or margarine until the color begins to turn. Add tomato sauce and water. Simmer 5 minutes.

WEST COAST FRITTATA (OMELET) WITH SAUSAGES AND ARTICHOKE

1 (1-egg) omelet 6 inches in diameter, fried in olive oil only on one side
1 drained canned or cooked fresh artichoke bottom, quartered, brushed with French dressing
2 halved cooked small spicy Italian or any well-spiced sausages
Parsley sprigs

Flip omelet light side up, not folded, onto heated dinner plate to make golden background. Arrange artichoke on light top, alternating with sausage halves. Garnish with parsley. Serves 1.

SCRAMBLED EGGS

6 large eggs	⅓ cup milk
¾ teaspoon salt	2 tablespoon butter or
⅛ teaspoon pepper	margarine

Break eggs into bowl. Add salt, pepper and milk. With egg beater, beat until frothy. Melt, but do not brown, butter or margarine in a 10-inch fry pan. Pour in egg mixture. Let stand over low heat ½ minute, or just long enough to thicken without browning at all. Then with spoon, scrape it up in pan making big flakes. Continue to scrape flakes until they are cooked through, yet tender and loose in texture.

For a change from plain scrambled eggs, try one of the following combinations for a light entree.

Egg-Potato Scramble: Combine 1½ cups diced cooked white potatoes with ¼ cup medium-chopped onion, and fry until golden brown in 3 tablespoons butter or margarine. Add to scrambled egg mixture. Cook as directed.

Crouton Egg Scramble: In 3 tablespoons butter or margarine, slow-fry until golden brown 1½ cups bread cut into ¼-inch dice (or use packaged croutons). Add ¼ cup fried onion (canned if desired), and the mixture for scrambled eggs. Cook as directed.

With Oysters: On a round platter, heap scrambled eggs cooked with croutons. Surround with creamed oysters on toast. Garnish with chopped parsley.

Ham-Egg Scramble: Add to the scrambled egg mixture ½ cup small-diced cooked ham, or substitute luncheon meat or small-diced cervelat. Cook as directed.

With Tomato and Eggplant Slices Sauté: Add ½ cup grated Cheddar cheese to the mixture for scrambled eggs. Cook as directed. Heap on a good-sized platter. Ring with sautéed tomatoes and eggplant slices. Garnish with sprigs of water cress.

Vegetable-Egg-Cheese Scramble: Combine ¾ cup mixed cooked or canned vegetables with the mixture for scrambled eggs. Add ½ cup grated Cheddar cheese. Cook as directed.

SCRAMBLED EGGS GALA

8 eggs
½ teaspoon salt
1 teaspoon Worcestershire sauce
⅛ teaspoon pepper
½ cup milk or half and half
2 (3-ounce) packages chive cream cheese, small diced

1 (4-ounce) can sliced mushrooms, drained
2 tablespoons butter or margarine
1 tablespoon frozen chopped chives

Beat eggs light, blending in seasonings and milk. Add cream cheese and mushrooms. Melt butter or margarine in chafing dish or skillet. Pour in egg mixture. Cook over low heat, gently lifting eggs from bottom occasionally to allow uncooked portion to flow underneath to cook into creamy soft mounds. Serve when firmed but still moist. Garnish with frozen chopped chives. Serves 4.

SHIRRED OR BAKED EGGS

These are baked in well-buttered individual metal, glass or pottery shirred-egg dishes or "cocottes."

Rub shirred-egg dishes with butter; strew with 1 tablespoon fine soft bread crumbs. Add 1 tablespoon cream or evaporated milk. Break in 2 fresh eggs, one at a time. Dust with salt and pepper; dot with butter. Bake 10 minutes in a moderate (350 to 375°) oven, or until the eggs are cooked through and firm to preference. Serves 1.

Shirred Eggs with Cheese: Follow the directions for Shirred Eggs, adding 1 heaping tablespoon grated Gruyère or sharp Cheddar cheese, or 2 tablespoons ready-prepared Welsh rabbit or Swiss cheese fondue to each serving dish before completing. Garnish with a ribboned border of tomato sauce.

Shirred Eggs with Crab Meat: Follow directions for shirred eggs, first adding to each dish 2 tablespoons flaked fresh or canned crab meat in one recipe White Sauce (see Index) to which 1 to 2 tablespoons sherry has been added. Garnish with water cress.

SHIRRED EGGS CALIFORNIA

2 teaspoons frozen chopped chives
1 (8-ounce) can seasoned tomato sauce
½ teaspoon Worcestershire sauce
8 eggs
8 slices buttered toast, cut in triangles

Combine frozen chopped chives with tomato sauce and Worcestershire sauce. Pour ¼ cup sauce into each of 4 buttered individual shallow baking dishes. Carefully break 2 eggs into each dish. Bake uncovered 12 to 18 minutes at 350°, or until of desired doneness. Garnish with additional frozen chopped chives and toast triangles, smartly tucked in, 2 on each side of the dish. Serves 4.

SCOTCH WOODCOCK

Anchovy paste
Hot buttered toast rounds
3 tablespoons butter or margarine
3 eggs
6 tablespoons light cream or evaporated milk
1½ teaspoons minced parsley
Salt and pepper
Paprika

Spread anchovy paste lightly on toast and keep warm. Melt butter or margarine, then add eggs beaten with cream or evaporated milk. Add seasonings and flavorings. Cook gently as you would scrambled eggs, stirring until thickened. (You may want to use a double boiler.) Pour over toast and dust lightly with paprika. Serves 4.

SPANISH EGGS IN SKILLET

1½ cups chopped onion
1½ cups chopped celery stalks
2 good-sized green peppers
   with seeds, chopped
2 tablespoons bacon fat or
   margarine
¼ cup hot water
1 teaspoon vinegar

¼ teaspoon garlic salt
¼ teaspoon pepper
1¼ teaspoons salt
1 (1-pound) can tomatoes,
   drained
6 eggs
Paprika

Prepare the three vegetables. Melt fat in large 10×12-inch skillet. Add onion, celery and hot water. Cover. Steam 10 minutes, or until color turns. Add green peppers, vinegar and seasonings. Steam-fry 5 minutes more. Mash tomatoes and stir in. Bring to rapid boil.

Break eggs, singly, into cup and gently slip onto the cooking vegetables. Reduce heat to simmering. Dust eggs with paprika. Cover. Steam-cook 10 to 12 minutes, or until set and fully cooked.

Cheese

Cheese connoisseurs declare there is a cheese for every meal—and they're probably right for there are hundreds and hundreds of varieties of cheese, over two hundred of which are made in our own country. Cheese is a nourishing, body-building food, loaded with protein and rich in fat, minerals and vitamins too. Cheese used as a main dish in a menu usually replaces meat. As a cooking ingredient, cheese adds special flavor to many dishes. You'll enjoy the recipes here—but first a cautionary word: high heat and overcooking are to be avoided!

All recipes are for six servings unless otherwise stated.

BLUSHING BUNNY

1 tablespoon butter or margarine	⅔ cup stewed tomatoes, drained and puréed
1 pound Cheddar cheese	Salt (optional)
¼ teaspoon dry mustard	Toast or crackers
¼ teaspoon pepper	

Melt the butter in the upper vessel of a chafing dish or in a double boiler, cut the cheese into dice and add to the butter with the mustard and pepper. Put boiling water in the lower vessel of the chafing dish and allow the cheese to melt slowly. Add the tomatoes and salt, if needed (this depends on the saltiness of the cheese). When smooth and creamy, serve on toast or crackers.

CHEESE CUSTARD WITH OLIVES

5 slices bread	3 eggs
2 tablespoons butter or margarine	½ cup liquid from olive jar
1 cup grated Cheddar cheese	⅛ teaspoon dry mustard
½ cup stuffed olives, sliced	2 cups milk

Remove crusts from bread. Spread slices with half the butter and cut into ½-inch cubes. Place ⅓ of them in bottom of greased casserole. Cover with ⅓ of cheese and ½ the olives. Repeat two more layers of bread and cheese, with remaining olives on second layer. Dot with rest of butter. Beat eggs well, add olive liquid, dry mustard and milk. Mix and pour over casserole contents. Place in refrigerator 1 or 2 hours before baking. Cover and bake in slow (300°) oven about 1 hour, removing cover after first ½ hour. Serves 4.

CHEESE SOUFFLÉ

6 eggs, separated	¼ teaspoon pepper
4½ tablespoons butter or margarine	1½ cups milk
3 tablespoons cornstarch	1½ cups shredded Cheddar cheese (about 6 ounces)
¾ teaspoon salt	

Beat egg yolks with a rotary beater until thick and lemon-colored; set aside. Melt butter in saucepan. Remove from heat. Mix in cornstarch, salt and pepper. Gradually add milk, mixing until smooth. Stir-cook over medium heat, until mixture thickens and comes to a boil. Reduce heat; add cheese. Cook, stirring constantly, until cheese is melted. Remove from heat. Gradually stir cheese mixture into beaten egg yolks.

Beat egg whites until stiff but not dry. Gently fold combined mixture into egg whites. Pour into an ungreased 1½-quart casserole or soufflé dish. Make a shallow path in the cheese mixture all around the top of the casserole, about 1 inch from the edge, using a teaspoon. This gives a crown effect when the soufflé is baked. Place soufflé dish in a pan containing warm water 1 inch deep. Bake in moderate (350°) oven for 1¼ hours. Serve immediately.

CHEESE TRAY

Use a cheese board of polished wood or a metal tray covered with an attractive paper place mat. Include at least three kinds of cheese, with cheese knives and a scoop for serving. For instance, center the board or tray with a bright red Edam, top removed, the center portion loosened; around this, arrange sections of Cheddar, with or without caraway; Gruyère; Brie; Roquefort; cream cheese; a sliced small smoky cheese. Place pats of butter on ice in a bowl at one side. Edge the board with an assortment of Melba toast and not-sweet crackers.

A basket of fruits, if served, is placed alongside. It includes small apples and pears, of course, with seedless grapes and tangerines.

Dried fruits are delightful with soft cheeses. So sometimes pass a sectioned trayful, such as stuffed dates, prunes and soft dried apricots, tenderized figs and clusters of raisins.

COTTAGE CHEESE

Meat bill too high? Introduce a pound of cottage cheese (2 8-ounce containers) each week. Cottage cheese contains in compact form much of the nutriment of milk. It is a valuable source of protein, riboflavin and phosphorus, and contains a significant amount of calcium. All of which makes cottage cheese a real meat alternate at budgetwise cost. One-half cup, or 4 ounces, is the minimum amount to use in place of an average serving of meat.

Forms of Cottage Cheese: Cottage cheese comes in several forms: creamed country-style; Devon sour cream style; "popcorn" shape; dry (known as farmer's cheese); low-fat; baker's cheese; and special, flavored, creamed cottage cheese, such as garden, pineapple, chive, pimiento and many other forms. Cottage cheese in bulk is sold at an even lower price than in containers.

The creamed country-style and the Devon sour cream cottage cheese are used primarily as spreads, or with vegetables or salads; they may also be used in cooking. The "popcorn" and baker's types are best to use in loaves, dumplings or whenever a drier form is needed. The farmer's cheese is more concentrated and satisfying for eating as is.

If you use one pound of cottage cheese a week to cut meat costs, a second one over the same period can be used for nutritious and budgetwise dishes without becoming monotonous. Use 1 8-ounce container as a spread in place of butter or margarine, preferably with whole grain or wheat germ bread. Use 1 8-ounce container as the protein top-off for garden plates, or vegetable or fruit salads. Use 2 8-ounce containers in combination with other ingredients in preparing dinner loaves, baked stuffed vegetables or substantial main course salads; or go glamorous and make a big cheese cake for dessert with the whole pound.

COTTAGE CHEESE PATTIES

1 pound cottage cheese	1 tablespoon melted butter or
½ cup grated rye bread	margarine
crumbs	1 teaspoon crushed caraway
1 teaspoon honey or sugar	seeds
¼ teaspoon salt	Flour

Form first six ingredients into flat cakes containing 1 tablespoon each. Dust all over with flour. Let stand 10 minutes to set this coating. Slow-fry in additional butter or margarine until golden brown on both sides. Serve as is or with honeyed sour cream as a dessert. Makes 18.

ESCALLOPED BREAD AND CHEESE

This dish puffs up like a soufflé!

12 to 14 slices bread	¾ teaspoon salt
1½ pounds Cheddar cheese	¼ teaspoon pepper
4 eggs, beaten	⅛ teaspoon paprika
2⅔ cups milk	

Remove crusts from bread and cover bottom of large buttered baking dish with half of the slices. Cover bread with thinly sliced cheese; cover with remaining slices of bread. Mix eggs, milk, salt and pepper. Pour over bread and cheese. Place in refrigerator anywhere from 1 to 24 hours. Bake in a 350° oven for 45 to 50 minutes. Serve at once.

GOLDEN BUCK

1½ pounds sharp Cheddar cheese
1 teaspoon dry mustard
1 teaspoon Worcestershire sauce
⅛ teaspoon cayenne pepper
⅛ teaspoon nutmeg
¼ teaspoon paprika
⅛ teaspoon cornstarch
1 tablespoon minced onion
1 egg yolk
⅔ cup beer or dry white wine
Buttered toast
Poached eggs
Anchovy fillets
Parsley

Coarse-grate or put cheese through a food chopper. Melt over low heat in a saucepan, stirring in mustard, Worcestershire sauce, cayenne, nutmeg, paprika, cornstarch and minced onion. Slightly beat 1 egg yolk. Add to ⅔ cup beer or dry white wine; stir into the melting cheese mixture. Pour over buttered toast. Top each serving with a poached egg garnished with anchovy fillets. Sprinkle with parsley.

SWISS CHEESE SOUFFLÉ

¼ cup butter
½ cup flour
1 cup scalded milk
⅛ teaspoon salt
¼ teaspoon nutmeg
½ pound Swiss cheese, fine-grated
3 egg yolks, beaten
1 teaspoon cornstarch
3 egg whites, beaten stiff
Paper-thin diamond-shaped slices Swiss cheese

In a small saucepan melt butter. Stir in flour, then scalded milk. Add salt and nutmeg. Stir and cook about 3 minutes until thick and smooth. Cool 5 minutes. Stir in Swiss cheese; mix with egg yolks and cornstarch. Fold into egg whites beaten stiff. Half-fill a quart-sized buttered and floured baking dish. Garnish with additional cheese. Bake at 375° until doubled in height and brown, about 35 minutes. Serve at once at "the peak." Serves 3.

SWITZERLAND SWISS CHEESE FONDUE

1 section garlic, peeled
2 cups dry white wine*
1¼ pounds Swiss cheese, coarse-grated
1 teaspoon cornstarch
1 tablespoon water or wine

⅛ teaspoon ground nutmeg
Salt and pepper to taste
¼ cup Kirschwasser (optional)
1 medium loaf French bread, or 8 crusty rolls

Rub a heavy earthenware casserole with the garlic. Pour in the wine. Place over low heat. Stir when bubbling. Stir in the cheese by large tablespoonfuls, stirring always in the same direction, until beginning to bubble. Stir in the cornstarch dissolved in the water or wine; add the nutmeg and salt and pepper to taste. (In Switzerland the Kirschwasser is stirred in at this point.)

Set the fondue over an alcohol burner or electric unit to enjoy at once. This is one time when "dunking" meets with full approval. A party of six dunk from the same casserole. Just spear a piece of bread or roll through its crusty side with a long-handled fork, securing the point in the crust so the bread or roll will not slip off when dipped in the fondue. Dunk the bread in stirring motion. While you enjoy your morsel, your neighbor takes over.

* The alcohol in the wine evaporates in cooking. (Milk may be used instead; in this case, cook fondue in a double boiler.)

QUICHE LORRAINE

1 recipe Rich American Pie Pastry (see Index) or a mix
1 egg white
6 (5-inch) slices bacon, cut ⅛ inch thick
6 ounces thin-sliced Swiss cheese

3 eggs and 2 egg yolks
1 tablespoon flour
½ teaspoon salt
⅛ teaspoon nutmeg
¾ tablespoon melted butter or margarine
2 cups milk

Line a slightly oiled shallow 7×11-inch pan with the pie pastry rolled a scant ¼ inch thick. Press down edges with fork. Brush lightly with unbeaten egg white.

Pour boiling water to cover over the bacon; let stand 2 minutes; drain on absorbent paper towels; cut slices in half; broil until well browned; drain again on paper towels. Arrange bacon and cheese overlapping in pastry-lined pan.

Combine and beat eggs and egg yolks until frothy. Beat in flour, salt, nutmeg, butter and milk. Pour into pastry-lined pan. Bake 35 to 40 minutes in moderate (375°) oven, or until lightly browned, and when a pick inserted in center comes out clean. Serve warm, cut in squares or oblong pieces.

WELSH RABBIT I

1 can beer or ale	½ teaspoon salt
2 tablespoons butter	⅛ teaspoon cayenne
1 pound sharp American	½ teaspoon dry mustard
cheese, grated	Crisp crackers, or buttered
2 eggs	toast

Open the beer and let stand 15 minutes to get a bit flat. Melt the butter in the top of a double boiler or chafing dish. Stir in the cheese. Cook-stir until it begins to melt and looks stringy. Meanwhile slightly beat the eggs with the seasonings; add the beer. Gradually stir into the melted cheese. Cook-stir until the rabbit thickens; serve at once on toast or crackers.

WELSH RABBIT II

¾ pound sharp American	¼ teaspoon dry mustard
cheese	1 tablespoon butter
4 tablespoons flour	3 cups milk
1 egg	Buttered or Melba toast or
½ teaspoon salt	crisp crackers
⅛ teaspoon pepper	

In a double-boiler top combine the cheese, flour, egg, salt, pepper, mustard and butter. Stir thoroughly to blend. Place over hot water. Gradually stir in the milk. Cook, stirring occasionally, until thick and creamy; then beat with a rotary beater for super smoothness. Serve on buttered toast or crisp crackers.

Welsh Rabbit Irish: Garnish with mixed pickles.

Rabbit on Tomato Slices: Spoon over thick slices of broiled or sautéed tomato instead of toast.

Scotch Variation: Spread the toast with anchovy paste before spooning on the rabbit.

Pasta

Generally speaking the term pasta includes the entire family of macaroni products—spaghetti and noodles in all forms. All macaroni products are good wholesome foods, which properly cooked and balanced with other foods can be eaten by the whole family from small tykes to great-grandma. Macaroni products have considerable food value besides starch. Macaroni is made from high protein durum wheat and semolina; this gives it naturally a protein content of about 12 per cent. Enriched macaroni also contains a good percentage of thiamin, riboflavin, some niacin and iron. Pasta should be served instead of potatoes, not with them; or combined with meat, poultry, fish, eggs, cheese or milk as an entree for luncheon, dinner or supper. Macaroni salads replace potato salad; soups are protein enriched when macaroni or egg noodles are added. So whether you serve pasta shaped in noodle form, such as elbows, or in shapes like sea shells, little hats, stars or snails—they all add to a well-balanced diet.

All recipes are for six servings unless otherwise stated.

GEORGE'S GOULASH

4 quarts water
1 teaspoon salt
1 pound spaghetti or elbow
  macaroni
2 tablespoons shortening
1½ pounds ground beef
1 (11-ounce) can condensed
  chili beef soup

1 (10½-ounce) can condensed
  tomato soup
1 (10¾-ounce) can condensed
  vegetarian vegetable soup
1¼ cups water

Bring 4 quarts water to boil; add salt. While stirring, gradually add spaghetti or macaroni. Boil briskly 10 minutes, or until spaghetti is tender. Meanwhile, in large pot, melt shortening; add broken-up beef; fry, stirring occasionally. When meat is slightly browned, mix in soups and water. Heat. Drain spaghetti; add to soup mixture; mix well. Serves 10.

LASAGNE WITH MEAT, CHEESE AND CREAM SAUCE

1 pound ground beef	4 quarts boiling water
½ pound ground pork	¾ pound curly edge lasagne
¼ pound sausage meat	(16 pieces purchased)
1 medium-sized onion, peeled	Cream Sauce
and chopped	1 pound ricotta cheese or
2 sections garlic, peeled and	creamed cottage cheese
minced	2 cups fresh-grated Parmesan
1½ teaspoons salt	cheese
Dash of pepper	½ pound mozzarella cheese,
1½ tablespoons salt	sliced

In large skillet, sauté meats 1 minute; add onion, garlic, 1½ teaspoons salt, pepper and continue to cook until meat browns. Set aside. Add additional 1½ tablespoons salt to large kettle containing boiling water. Gradually add lasagne slowly, so that the water continues to boil. Cook uncovered about 15 minutes, stirring occasionally until tender. Drain in a colander. In bottom of 13×9×2-inch baking pan or dish, pour ⅓ of the Cream Sauce. Lay lasagne across bottom of pan, starting at middle and letting half extend over edge of pan. Repeat on three remaining sides of pan. Spread ⅓ of the meat mixture on top. Add ⅓ of the ricotta cheese in dollops, and ⅓ of the Cream Sauce. Sprinkle with ⅓ of the Parmesan cheese.

Repeat, layering the lasagne, meat, ricotta cheese, sauce and Parmesan. Finally fold the lasagne hanging from the bottom layer over the top. Add the remaining ricotta, meats and any Parmesan. Top with the mozzarella cheese. Bake 25 minutes in a moderate (375°) oven. Serves 8.

Cream Sauce: Melt 3 tablespoons butter or margarine in a saucepan. Stir in 3 tablespoons flour, 1 teaspoon salt, ¼ teaspoon pepper and ¼ teaspoon ground nutmeg. Gradually add 2 cups milk; cook, stirring constantly, until the sauce boils 1 minute. Mix ¼ cup of the sauce with 1 egg, beaten. Stir back into the remaining sauce. Add ¼ cup chopped parsley, if desired. Makes about 2 cups.

BAKED MACARONI AND CHEESE

½ pound macaroni	¼ teaspoon dry mustard
4 tablespoons butter or margarine	2 cups milk
	¾ teaspoon salt
1 tablespoon minced onion	⅛ teaspoon pepper
¼ cup flour	2 cups grated Cheddar cheese

Cook macaroni according to package directions. Drain. Meanwhile, melt the butter or margarine in the top of a double boiler. Add the onion and simmer until tender. Stir in the flour, mustard, milk, salt and pepper. Cook over boiling water until smooth and thickened. Add grated cheese and stir until melted. Combine sauce and macaroni and turn into a greased 1½-quart casserole. Bake in a moderately hot (400°) oven for 20 minutes, or until brown.

NOODLES ALFREDO

Accompaniment par excellence to Veal Scallopini.

1 pound broad noodles	2 tablespoons grated Romano cheese
½ cup butter, preferably unsalted	2 tablespoons heavy cream
½ cup grated Parmesan cheese	

Cook the noodles according to package directions. Drain. Transfer to a skillet, or for table service to a chafing dish. Add the butter and cheese; toss over low heat until the noodles are well covered and shining. Add the cream at intervals while tossing.

NOODLES WITH GREEN PEAS

½ cup chicken broth
1 (8-ounce) package frozen
green peas
2 tablespoons butter or
margarine

½ pound undrained cooked
Noodles by Flavor-saving
Method

Heat chicken broth in a 2-quart double-boiler top. Add peas. Cook until peas thaw. With fork, stir in butter and noodles prepared by following recipe. Cover, and cook 20 minutes over hot water. Serve in bowls.

Noodles by Flavor-saving Method: In 2-quart saucepan, bring 4 cups water and ½ teaspoon salt to rapid boil. Add ½ tablespoon cooking oil or olive oil. Break ½ pound medium noodles in 2-inch lengths and stir in. Boil until of desired tenderness and water is practically absorbed. Do not drain. Use as directed in recipe. For *al dente,* allow 15 minutes; for medium well done, 20 minutes; for well done, 25 minutes.

SALMON ESCALLOPED WITH NOODLES

¼ pound noodles
2 cups medium-thick White
Sauce (see Index)
¼ cup mayonnaise
1½ tablespoons minced
parsley

1 (1-pound) can salmon
¼ cup coarse bread crumbs
2 tablespoon butter or
margarine

Cook the noodles 20 minutes, or until bite-tender, in boiling salted water. Then drain. In the meantime, combine the White Sauce and mayonnaise; add the parsley. Add this to the noodles and put half of it in a layer in a buttered baking dish or casserole. Cover with a layer of the salmon flaked into bits. (The bones and skin can be used.) Make the top layer noodles. Cover with the crumbs mixed with the butter, and brown in a hot (400°) oven.

TUNA-OLIVE BAKE

1 teaspoon salt
4 cups water
8 ounces medium noodles
2 (10½-ounce) cans of cream
  of mushroom soup
1 cup water
½ teaspoon Worcestershire
  sauce

1½ cups grated sharp
  American cheese
3 hard-cooked eggs, sliced thin
⅔ cup sliced stuffed olives
2 (7-ounce) cans tuna fish
Parsley, green pepper rings
  and radish roses

Add salt to water and bring to rapid boil; add noodles. Cook
10 minutes, or until bite-tender. Heat mushroom soup with
additional 1 cup water. Do not drain. Stir until smooth. Add
Worcestershire. Remove from heat; add cheese and stir until
melted. Reserve a few egg slices and olive slices for garnish. Mix
together remaining egg and olive slices, tuna fish, noodles, and
mushroom soup. Pour into 2½-quart glass baking dish. Bake in
moderate (350°) oven for about 30 minutes. When nearly done,
put reserved egg and olive slices on top. Garnish with parsley,
green pepper rings and radish roses.

STUFFED NOODLES PARMIGIANA

8 ounces broad egg noodles
3 bouillon cubes (optional)
1 recipe Quick Italian-Style
  Meat Sauce (see Index)
1 cup grated sharp cheese

1 tablespoon butter or
  margarine
8 ounces creamed cottage
  cheese

Cook noodles in boiling water with or without 3 bouillon cubes
for seasoning. Rub a 3-pint baking dish that can go-to-table with
butter or margarine. Arrange a layer of noodles ½ inch deep in
this dish. Spread over half the recipe for Quick Italian-Style
Meat Sauce, and cover with ⅓ cup of the grated sharp cheese.
Repeat with second layer each of noodles, sauce and another
⅓ cup cheese. Top with noodles. Cover with remaining ⅓ cup

grated sharp cheese. Dot with 1 tablespoon butter or margarine. Bake 30 minutes in moderate (375°) oven. Top with cottage cheese. Brown under broiler.

NANCY'S PIZZA

1 package hot roll mix
1 tablespoon olive oil
2 (8-ounce) cans tomato sauce
1 (6-ounce) can tomato paste
¼ cup chopped green pepper
1 medium onion, peeled and chopped fine
2 sections garlic, peeled and minced

¼ teaspoon powdered oregano
¼ teaspoon powdered basil
½ cup sliced pitted olives
1 (3-ounce) can sliced mushrooms (drained)
½ pound link sausage, sliced and browned
½ pound mozzarella cheese, grated

Prepare hot roll mix according to package directions. Knead dough several times on lightly floured surface. Oil large (14×17-inch) cookie sheet. Pat out dough to fit cookie sheet, leaving a 1-inch rim around edge. Brush dough with olive oil. Combine in a bowl the tomato sauce and paste, green pepper, onion, garlic and seasonings. Spread evenly over dough. Arrange olive slices, mushrooms, sausage and grated cheese over the tomato topping. Bake in a hot (400°) oven 15 minutes, or until crust browns and the cheese melts. Serves 8 to 10.

CLAM SPAGHETTI

2 tablespoons olive or salad oil
2 tablespoons peeled minced onion
1 section garlic, peeled and minced or ¼ teaspoon garlic powder

1 (8-ounce) can tomato paste
2½ cups hot water
½ teaspoon ground thyme
2 (8-ounce) cans minced clams
¾ pound spaghetti
¾ cup grated Parmesan cheese

Heat oil; add onion and garlic. Slow-sauté 1 minute. Stir in tomato paste, water, thyme, and clams with their liquid. Simmer-boil 20 minutes. Meantime, cook spaghetti following package directions. Add clam mixture and reheat. Top with grated cheese.

MEAT BALLS WITH SPAGHETTI

3 tablespoons olive oil
1 cup chopped onion
1 section garlic, minced
½ pound chopped raw beef
½ pound pork sausage
3⅓ cups canned tomatoes
1 (6-ounce) can tomato paste
¾ cup water
½ bay leaf

¼ teaspoon dried basil
¼ teaspoon dried thyme
½ tablespoon salt
½ teaspoon pepper
1 cup ripe olives
½ pound spaghetti
3 tablespoons melted butter
Grated Parmesan cheese

Heat oil. In a 2-quart saucepan brown onion and minced garlic. Mix and shape meats into small meat balls. Brown in oil. Add tomatoes, tomato paste, water and seasonings; simmer 1 hour. Remove bay leaf; add olives cut from pits into large pieces. Simmer-cook 15 minutes. Meantime, cook spaghetti following package directions. Drain spaghetti thoroughly, and toss in melted butter. Turn meat ball filling into center of a heated platter. Surround with spaghetti. Dust with Parmesan cheese. Accompany with mixed greens and avocado slices, tossed with a wine vinegar French dressing.

SKILLET MEAT BALLS AND SPAGHETTI

1½ pounds chopped raw beef
¾ cup Parmesan cheese
⅓ cup fine dry bread crumbs
1 cup fine-chopped onion
1½ teaspoons salt
¼ teaspoon pepper
1 cup evaporated milk (not diluted)
3 tablespoons butter
1 tablespoon cooking oil
½ cup coarse-chopped green pepper

6 cups tomato juice
1 small bay leaf
¾ teaspoon ground oregano
¾ pound uncooked fine spaghetti broken into 1½-inch lengths (about 4 cups)
Grated Parmesan cheese
1 cup tomato juice or meat broth (optional)

Thoroughly mix beef, cheese, crumbs, ½ cup of the onion, ¾ teaspoon of the salt, pepper and evaporated milk. Shape into 12 balls. In an oversized "giant" skillet or heavy 10-inch kettle, heat butter and oil over medium heat. Add meat balls; turn to brown all over. Push them to the sides of skillet. Spoon remaining onion and green pepper in the center; simmer-sauté 3 minutes. Pour tomato juice over meat balls; stir in remaining salt, bay leaf and oregano. Bring to boil over high heat. Stir in spaghetti. Tight-cover skillet or kettle; turn heat low and slow-cook 25 to 35 minutes, or until spaghetti is bite-tender. (Remove bay leaf.) Stir spaghetti occasionally with kitchen fork. If more liquid is needed, add tomato juice or meat broth. Serve with additional Parmesan cheese.

CHICKEN OR TURKEY TETRAZZINI

½ pound spaghetti
2 cups Chicken Cream Sauce
½ cup or 1 (6-ounce) can sliced fresh mushrooms
2 tablespoons butter or margarine
2 cups diced cooked chicken or turkey

½ cup grated mild cheese
¼ cup fine day-old bread crumbs
3 tablespoons melted butter or margarine

Cook the spaghetti following package directions. Make Chicken Cream Sauce. Sauté mushrooms in butter or margarine. Add both to sauce. Add chicken or turkey. Transfer to buttered low 2-quart casserole. Cover with cheese and crumbs mixed with melted butter or margarine. Heat-brown in hot (425°) oven for 30 to 35 minutes.

Chicken Cream Sauce: Make a plain white or cream sauce, using 2 tablespoons each butter or margarine and flour, 1¼ cups half and half or rich milk, ¾ cup water and 1 teaspoon chicken bouillon powder.

Gravies and Sauces

Well-sauced food used to be considered too rich or too fancy for American tables, but a good gravy or piquant sauce has often turned an everyday meal into something special. The most important considerations are color and flavor. Contrasting or harmonious color will add eye appeal and stimulate the appetite.

All recipes are for six servings unless otherwise stated.

GRAVY FROM BOILED OR BRAISED MEAT

Measure the liquid left after cooking. Remove excess fat. Add water or liquid drained from cooking potatoes, if necessary, to make 2 cups and heat to boiling. Blend 3 tablespoons flour with 3 tablespoons cold water to make a smooth paste. Gradually add to the boiling liquid. Stir for 1 minute. Simmer for 2 minutes. Season to taste with salt and pepper. If the gravy is a bit flat, add a beef or chicken bouillon cube and/or ½ teaspoon gravy seasoning.

BROWN GRAVY

This is made after roasting meat or poultry. With a spoon skim off all the fat. Then scrape up all the brown particles. Pour into a cup and measure. To 4 tablespoons of drippings, blend in 4 tablespoons flour. Place in a saucepan and cook and stir until the mixture becomes golden brown. Then stir in 2 cups of boiling water or liquid drained from cooking potatoes or from canned vegetables; add 2 bouillon cubes (beef or chicken), according to the kind of meat that was roasted. Cook and stir constantly until the gravy boils briskly. Simmer 3 minutes. Season to taste with salt and pepper and ½ teaspoon each Kitchen Bouquet and

Worcestershire sauce. If carefully made, the gravy will not be lumpy. If it is—reach for the strainer.

Onion Gravy: Make Brown Gravy and add 1 cup chopped onions steam-fried until soft in 1 tablespoon butter, margarine or meat fat.

Tomato Gravy: Follow the recipe for Brown Gravy using ½ cup water and 1 (8-ounce) can tomato sauce for the liquid.

GIBLET GRAVY

Fine-chop the cooked giblets from a chicken, duck or any kind of poultry. Melt 2 tablespoons poultry fat, butter or margarine. Add 2½ tablespoons flour. Cook and stir until the flour browns. Then gradually add 1¾ cups liquid left from cooking the giblets. If there is not enough, add hot water to make up the shortage, and add 1 chicken bouillon cube. Cook and stir until the gravy is smooth and comes to a brisk boil. Add the chopped giblets and simmer 2 minutes.

PAN GRAVY

This is made from drippings after meat or poultry has been roasted, pan cooked or broiled.

Remove the meat and keep warm. Pour off juices and reserve. Return 3 tablespoons fat to roasting pan, blend in 1½ tablespoons flour and cook-stir till thick and smooth, loosening all the brown particles that have adhered to the pan. Add enough water to degreased pan juices to make 1 cup. Blend liquid into flour mixture, cooking and stirring constantly till thickened. Season to taste. If darker color is desired, add ½ teaspoon browning liquid.

REAL SAUCE À LA KING

4 tablespoons butter or margarine	¼ cup diced green pepper
4 tablespoons flour	2 pimientos, diced
½ teaspoon salt	½ cup fresh or canned sliced mushrooms
¼ teaspoon pepper	2 egg yolks
1½ cups milk	2 tablespoons dry sherry
¾ cup half and half or light cream	

Melt butter; stir in flour and seasonings. Gradually stir in milk and half and half. Add green pepper, pimientos and mushrooms. Cook 10 minutes in double boiler, stirring occasionally, until thickened. Cook-heat 10 minutes. Stir in egg yolks beaten with sherry. Use as directed in chicken, ham and other recipes which call for à la king sauce.

BARBECUE SAUCE

Melt a scant ½ cup butter or margarine. Add 2 tablespoons minced onion and 1 peeled crushed section garlic. Slow-cook until yellowed. Add 1 teaspoon table mustard, ¾ teaspoon salt, 1 tablespoon chili powder, 1 teaspoon Worcestershire sauce, 6 drops Tabasco, ¾ cup tomato juice, ¼ teaspoon sugar, 2 tablespoons lemon juice, and ⅓ cup water. Boil 10 minutes.

SAUCE BÉARNAISE

For broiled steak or fish; with venison or other game.

2 tablespoons minced shallots or onion	Salt
¼ cup mild vinegar	⅛ teaspoon pepper
½ cup dry white wine	½ cup butter
3 egg yolks	½ teaspoon lemon juice
	1 tablespoon minced parsley

Combine the shallots or onion, vinegar and wine in a small saucepan. Simmer until the liquid is reduced one half; then strain. Beat the egg yolks light with the salt and pepper. Cream into half the butter. Place over hot water. Stir-cook like a custard, beating in the remaining butter a tablespoon at a time. Beat in the lemon juice and parsley, then the wine mixture. Cook, stirring 3 minutes, or until the consistency of mayonnaise. Serve hot or cold.

SAUCE BÉCHAMEL

3 tablespoons butter	¼ teaspoon paprika
2 tablespoons flour	¾ cup light cream or half and
¾ cup chicken broth	half
½ teaspoon salt	1 teaspoon lemon juice

In top part of a 1-quart double boiler, mix together butter and flour. Gradually stir in broth. Cook-stir until boiling. Add seasonings; slow-stir in cream. Bring again to boiling point. Put over boiling water in bottom part of double boiler; cover and cook 5 minutes. Stir in lemon juice.

BROWN SAUCE

2 tablespoons butter or margarine	1½ cups boiling water
3 tablespoons flour	2 beef bouillon cubes
	½ teaspoon gravy seasoning

Melt the butter or margarine in a small saucepan and let it brown. Add flour and cook-stir until browned. Stir in 1½ cups of boiling water and add the beef bouillon cubes and gravy seasoning. Simmer until bubbling all over.

Mustard Brown Sauce: To Brown Sauce, add ½ tablespoon table mustard and 1 teaspoon lemon juice.

Mushroom Brown Sauce: Make Brown Sauce with 1¼ cups of water. When almost done, stir in the contents of 1 (2-ounce) can mushroom pieces with the liquid. Add a few grains nutmeg.

Onion or Soubise Sauce: Fine-chop enough onions to make 1 cup. Slightly fry in 1 tablespoon butter, margarine or meat fat until tender but not browned. Add 1 recipe Brown Sauce and simmer 5 minutes.

CAPER SAUCE

½ cup fresh lemon juice
¼ cup olive or salad oil

⅛ teaspoon garlic powder
¼ cup capers, drained

Combine ingredients in small saucepan; heat, but do not boil.

CHEESE SAUCE

1½ cups grated sharp
Cheddar cheese
2½ tablespoons flour
2½ tablespoons butter or
margarine at room
temperature

⅓ teaspoon salt
⅛ teaspoon pepper
¼ teaspoon mustard
2 cups milk

Mix together cheese, flour, butter and seasonings in double-boiler top. Stir in milk; cook-stir over boiling water 5 minutes, or until creamy thick.

CHICKEN LIVER SAUCE FOR BAKE-FRIED CHICKEN

¼ pound chicken livers
3 tablespoons butter or
margarine
⅛ teaspoon oregano
1 tablespoon minced onion
2 tablespoons flour

1 teaspoon liquid gravy
seasoning
1½ cups chicken broth
¼ cup light cream or
evaporated canned milk

Rinse chicken livers with hot water; drain. Cut in small pieces. Sauté in butter until slightly browned. Add oregano and onion;

sauté until yellowed. Stir in flour and gravy seasoning. Gradually stir in chicken broth. When boiling, stir in cream and heat.

CHINESE-STYLE PLUM SAUCE

2 (No. 2) cans or 2 pounds
   fresh red plums, pitted
½ cup raisins
½ cup cider vinegar
1 cup water
¾ cup brown sugar

1 teaspoon ground allspice
1 teaspoon salt
½ teaspoon ground ginger
1 teaspoon paprika
Few grains cayenne pepper to
   taste

Combine ingredients. Simmer-cook 30 minutes, or until plums are very soft. Rub through coarse sieve; simmer about 30 minutes longer until thick like marmalade.

CREOLE SAUCE

2 tablespoons butter
¼ cup each minced onion and
   green pepper
1 (1-pound) can tomatoes

¼ teaspoon Tabasco
¼ teaspoon each salt, celery
   salt and garlic salt

Melt butter, add onion and green pepper. Cook until onion is limp, but not brown. Add the contents of the can of tomatoes and seasonings. Simmer 30 minutes.

CUMBERLAND SAUCE

For smoked ham, poultry, domestic or wild duck or other game birds.

2 lemon rinds
1 medium-sized orange
1 tablespoon sugar
1 tablespoon prepared
   horseradish

½ cup currant jelly
1 tablespoon hot water
2 drops Tabasco

Grate and crush the rind of the lemons and squeeze the juice from ½ of the orange; add the sugar and horseradish. Combine the currant jelly, water and Tabasco. Stir over a low heat until the jelly slightly melts. Stir in the fruit juice mixture and heat. Serve hot.

Cold Cumberland Sauce: For cold meats and cold game dishes, follow the directions for Cumberland Sauce, adding ⅛ teaspoon powdered ginger and ½ tablespoon minced shallot, lightly sautéed in ½ tablespoon butter. Replace the water with port wine. Serve cold.

HERB SAUCE

Melt 2 tablespoons butter or margarine. Stir in 2 tablespoons flour, 1 tablespoon lemon juice, ⅓ teaspoon salt, ¼ teaspoon paprika and ½ teaspoon sugar. Add 1 cup boiling water (or use ½ cup water and ½ cup clam juice). Bring to boiling point, stirring occasionally. Add 1 teaspoon each minced fresh tarragon, basil and dill; simmer 5 minutes.

Note: If substituting powdered or fine-crushed dried herbs for fresh tarragon, basil and dill, use ¼ teaspoon each, steeped in 1 tablespoon hot water before adding.

HOLLANDAISE SAUCE

½ cup butter	2 tablespoons mild herb or
4 egg yolks	cider vinegar
2 tablespoons flour	1 tablespoon lemon juice
⅓ teaspoon salt	1 cup boiling water
⅛ teaspoon pepper	

Melt butter in double-boiler top. Beat egg yolks; mix in flour, salt and pepper. Stir in vinegar and lemon juice. Add to melted butter, stirring constantly; slowly stir in boiling water; cook-stir until thick.

Note: Do not have more than 1 inch of hot water in the double-boiler bottom; otherwise the sauce cooks too rapidly and may separate or look curdled.

MOCK HOLLANDAISE SAUCE

¼ cup instant nonfat dry milk
  crystals
¼ cup ice water

1½ tablespoons lemon juice
¾ cup mayonnaise

Mix instant nonfat dry milk crystals with ice water. Whip until soft peaks form, about 3 to 4 minutes. Add 1½ tablespoons lemon juice; continue beating until stiff peaks form, 3 to 4 minutes longer. Lightly fold into ¾ cup mayonnaise (purchased). Stir-heat to serving temperature over hot water.

MORNAY SAUCE

2 tablespoons butter or
  margarine
3 tablespoons flour
1 cup water
2 teaspoons chicken broth
  powder

¾ cup light cream
1 beaten egg yolk
⅓ cup grated Parmesan or
  Cheddar cheese
½ tablespoon butter or
  margarine

Melt 2 tablespoons butter or margarine. Stir in flour. Gradually add water, chicken broth powder and light cream. When boiling, stir into beaten egg yolk. Return to heat and cook-stir 1 minute. Add grated Parmesan or Cheddar cheese and additional ½ tablespoon butter or margarine. Cook-stir 1 minute—do not boil.

Quick Sauce Mornay: To 1 (10¾-ounce) can cream of cheese soup, stir in ½ can measure warm water and ¼ teaspoon Worcestershire. Heat-stir until smooth.

OLIVE-ANCHOVY SWEET-SOUR SAUCE

Nice with chilled shrimp, langostino or crab meat.

½ cup butter or margarine at
  room temperature
1 tablespoon sugar
½ teaspoon pepper
¼ teaspoon onion powder
1 egg, beaten

2 tablespoons vinegar
¼ cup chopped pimiento-
  stuffed olives
1 tablespoon anchovy paste
⅓ cup chopped celery
6 sliced pimiento-stuffed olives

Stir-beat the butter or margarine until fluffy. Add the sugar, pepper and onion powder; mix thoroughly. Slowly beat in the egg until smooth. Beat in the vinegar, olives, anchovy paste and celery; beat well. Garnish with the sliced olives. Makes 1½ cups.

BASIC INDIAN CURRY SAUCE

3 tablespoons butter or cooking oil
¼ cup peeled thin-sliced onion
½ cup each peeled thin-sliced carrot, diced green beans, green peas and diced celery
¾ tablespoon curry powder
3 tablespoons flour
2 cups boiling water

1 (No. 2½) can tomatoes mashed
⅛ teaspoon garlic powder
¼ teaspoon ground cinnamon
2 teaspoons beef broth powder
½ cup peeled fine-chopped tart apple
1 tablespoon fine-chopped chutney

Heat butter or oil; add the vegetables. Slow-fry about 15 minutes. Stir in curry powder. Sauté 20 seconds to develop flavor. Stir in flour, boiling water, mashed tomatoes, garlic powder, ground cinnamon and broth powder. Simmer 5 minutes. Add apple and chutney. Simmer until medium-thick, about 10 minutes more.

ITALIAN-STYLE MEAT SAUCE

3 tablespoons olive oil
1 teaspoon sugar
¼ cup peeled minced onion
1 section garlic, peeled and minced
½ cup seeded shredded green pepper
¾ pound chopped chicken livers, or ¼ pound each chopped beef, veal and pork

3 (6-ounce) cans tomato paste
3 cups hot water
1½ teaspoons salt
¼ teaspoon pepper
¼ teaspoon powdered marjoram

Heat oil; add sugar, onion, garlic and green pepper. Slow-sauté until vegetables are soft but not browned. Add chopped chicken livers or other meats, and sauté until beginning to brown; stir often with fork. Add tomato paste, hot water and seasonings. Simmer 30 minutes, or until thick. Makes about 3 cups.

Quick Mushroom Sauce: Instead of chopped meats use ¼ pound washed, fine-chopped fresh mushrooms or 2 (4-ounce) cans mushroom caps and stems.

QUICK ITALIAN-STYLE MEAT SAUCE

3 tablespoons oil	¾ pound chopped meat
1 teaspoon sugar	3 (6-ounce) cans tomato paste
¼ cup minced onion	3 cups hot water
1 section garlic, peeled and minced	1½ teaspoons salt
	¼ teaspoon pepper
½ cup shredded green pepper	¼ teaspoon marjoram

Heat oil; add sugar, onion, garlic and green pepper. Slow-sauté until vegetables are soft but not browned. Add chopped meat. Sauté until beginning to brown; stir often with fork. Add tomato paste, hot water and seasonings. Simmer 30 minutes, or until thick.

MAÎTRE d'HÔTEL BUTTER

⅓ cup butter or margarine at room temperature	3 drops Tabasco
1 tablespoon minced parsley	1 tablespoon lemon juice
½ teaspoon salt	¼ teaspoon onion juice (optional)

Cream butter in bowl; add parsley, salt, Tabasco, lemon juice and onion juice. Beat well. Refrigerate. Serve with broiled fish, steak or chops.

MINT SAUCE PIQUANT

1 teaspoon mint leaves, rubbed fine between the fingers
¼ cup Worcestershire sauce

Stir together, let rest for 30 minutes, and there it is, ready to go to the table!

MUSTARD SAUCE

2 tablespoons butter or
  margarine
2 tablespoons flour
1½ cups beef bouillon
½ tablespoon mild table
  mustard

¼ teaspoon salt
⅛ teaspoon pepper
1 teaspoon lemon juice

Melt butter; stir in flour. Stir in bouillon and mustard, and mix thoroughly. Add salt and pepper, and stir in lemon juice just before serving.

RAISIN SAUCE FROM OLD NEW ENGLAND

For smoked pork in any form.

¾ cup brownulated sugar
¾ cup hot water
¾ cup seedless raisins
3 tablespoons sharp cider
  vinegar
2 tablespoons butter or
  margarine

⅛ teaspoon nutmeg
¼ teaspoon ground cloves
¾ cup any tart red jelly
¼ teaspoon salt
⅛ teaspoon pepper
2 tablespoons cornstarch
2 tablespoons cold water

Combine brownulated sugar and hot water. Stir until sugar dissolves. Add ingredients through ground cloves. Simmer 5 minutes. Stir in jelly; stir-cook until this melts. Add salt and pepper. Mix cornstarch smooth with cold water. Stir into sauce; cook, stirring constantly, until boiling rapidly all over. Serve hot.

SAUCE RÉMOULADE

A piquant sauce to add zest to shellfish, cold meat or game of any kind. Can be made in advance.

¼ cup tart minced pickle relish
2 tablespoons strong-flavored horseradish mustard
1 tablespoon minced parsley
½ tablespoon anchovy paste
1 teaspoon minced fresh or ¼ teaspoon powdered tarragon

½ section garlic, peeled and crushed
¾ cup mayonnaise
8 drops Tabasco

Combine and mix all ingredients except the last two. Beat in mayonnaise and Tabasco.

TARTAR SAUCE

For broiled or sautéed fish fillets, shellfish or vegetables.

1 cup mayonnaise
½ tablespoon lemon juice
1 teaspoon Worcestershire sauce
1 teaspoon mustard

4 drops Tabasco
2 tablespoons tart pickle relish
½ tablespoon minced capers
½ tablespoon minced chives
1 tablespoon minced parsley

Combine ingredients in the order given.

SAUCE VINAIGRETTE

½ cup olive oil
1 tablespoon tart pickle relish
1 teaspoon minced green pepper
⅓ teaspoon salt

⅙ teaspoon ground pepper
1 tablespoon minced parsley
⅔ teaspoon grated onion
3 tablespoons mild vinegar

Into the oil, stir all the ingredients except the vinegar. Cover. Set aside to marinate at room temperature at least 1 hour. Beat in the vinegar. Use hot or cold as desired. This refreshing sauce is used for meats, fish or cooked vegetables. Garnish, if desired, with fine-chopped hard-cooked egg.

WHITE SAUCE

2 tablespoons butter or
    margarine
2 tablespoons flour

¼ teaspoon salt
Few grains pepper
1 cup milk

Melt the butter or margarine. Remove from the heat and stir in the flour and seasonings. Add a little of the milk and stir until smooth. Then place over the heat and gradually add the remaining milk stirring constantly. When briskly boiling all over, use as directed in your specific recipe. Makes 1 cup.

Thick White Sauce:

3 tablespoons butter or
    margarine
¼ cup flour

⅓ teaspoon salt
⅛ teaspoon pepper
½ cup milk

Proceed as above. Makes ½ cup. This makes a very thick white sauce suitable for a foundation for croquettes, soufflés, etc.

BUTTERSCOTCH SAUCE

1 cup light corn syrup
1 cup sugar
¼ teaspoon salt
½ cup light cream

2 tablespoons butter
1 teaspoon vanilla
2 drops vinegar

In a 1-quart saucepan, combine all ingredients except vanilla and vinegar. Cook-stir over medium heat until mixture comes to full rolling boil. Boil rapidly 5 minutes. Stir occasionally. Remove from heat and add vanilla and vinegar. Use warm. Or to reheat, place container in hot, not boiling water, until sauce thins to pouring consistency.

CHOCOLATINA SAUCE

4 tablespoons powdered cocoa	4 tablespoons honey
1/3 cup very strong hot coffee	1/3 cup white corn syrup
1/2 tablespoon butter or margarine	1/4 teaspoon vanilla

In small saucepan, mix cocoa and coffee. Add butter. Stir until boiling. Add honey and corn syrup; cook-stir until boiling all over. Add vanilla. Use hot or cold.

REGAL CHOCOLATE SAUCE

2 squares unsweetened chocolate	Pinch of salt
6 tablespoons water	3 tablespoons butter
1/2 cup sugar	1/4 teaspoon vanilla

Combine chocolate and water in saucepan. Place over low heat, stirring until blended. Add sugar and salt. Cook-stir until sugar dissolves and mixture is slightly thickened. Stir in butter and vanilla. Use cold.

HARD SAUCE

1/2 cup butter
2 cups confectioners' sugar, sifted
3 teaspoons boiling water

Cream the butter, add the sugar gradually, beating it into the butter. Add the boiling water a teaspoonful at a time and beat it vigorously into the sauce. Pile in a dish and set aside to chill before using.

Brandy Hard Sauce: Add to the above 2 teaspoons brandy.

Chocolate Hard Sauce: Reduce quantity of butter in above to 1/3 cup and add 3 tablespoons of melted chocolate.

Cherry Hard Sauce: Substitute 3 teaspoons of syrup from cherries for the water in above recipe, and when sauce is thoroughly creamed, add 2 tablespoons of coarsely chopped cherries.

Orange Marmalade Hard Sauce: Work 2 tablespoons of orange marmalade into above recipe during beating.

Spicy Hard Sauce: Add to above ⅛ teaspoon of cinnamon, ⅛ teaspoon of ground ginger and a slight grating of nutmeg.

WHIPPED DAIRY SOUR CREAM FOR DESSERTS

1 cup dairy sour cream
1 tablespoon sugar or honey

Chill ingredients, also bowl and beater before starting to whip. Combine ingredients in deep bowl. Whip slowly and steadily until fluffy and almost double in volume. Sour cream does not become stiff when whipped so it cannot be put through a pastry tube. It is a delightful topping for gingerbread, spicecake or fruit compote.

Cereal Combinations

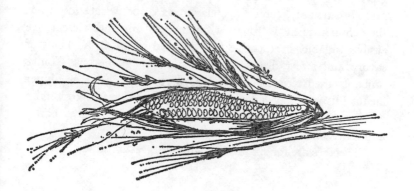

Watch a wheat field ripple as wind blows over it. Hear the corn-fields rustle in the breeze. Notice how new oats poke tiny green spears through the good earth, see the rice paddies touched with green—and you'll realize that cereals represent the upspring of life. Nutritionally, cereals are classed as carbohydrate foods but they contain needed protein, vitamins and minerals. Cereals are easily available, inexpensive and adapted to use in all kinds of savory and sweet dishes, both simple and glamorous. You've probably used rice dishes often as part of luncheon or dinner menus but you may have neglected some wonderful possibilities employing other grains too, such as corn meal, hominy, barley and rolled oats!

All recipes are for six servings unless otherwise stated.

HOMEMADE SCRAPPLE

5 cups boiling water
2 pounds fresh or leftover
  cooked pork bones
2 teaspoons salt
1 teaspoon ground sage
2 tablespoons grated onion
1 cup cold water

1 cup enriched corn meal
1 tablespoon flour
2 cups minced cooked lean
  pork
Flour for dusting
Vegetable oil

Measure hot water into a 2-quart saucepan. Add bones; simmer 1 hour; strain. Bring broth to boil. Add seasonings and grated onion. Mix cold water and corn meal and flour. Slow-stir into boiling broth. Cook 30 minutes, stirring occasionally; or steam 45 minutes in double boiler. Add cooked pork. Rinse a 10×4×2-inch loaf pan with cold water. Spoon in mixture. Cover with aluminum foil to prevent crust from forming. Refrigerate over-night before using. Keeps up to a week.

Serve the scrapple in ½-inch-thick slices. Dust with flour. Brown in vegetable oil on top of range or in oven.

CORN MEAL PUDDING

1 quart milk	2 eggs
1 cup enriched yellow corn meal	2 tablespoons milk
1½ teaspoons salt	¼ cup grated sharp Cheddar cheese
¼ teaspoon pepper	

Heat milk in double boiler. When bubbles form at edge, slow-stir in corn meal, seasonings; stir-cook constantly until thick and smooth to prevent lumping. Beat eggs with additional milk until frothy; then slow-stir into corn meal; add half the cheese. Transfer to buttered 9×5-inch loaf pan. Strew over remaining cheese. Bake 30 minutes in a moderate (350°) oven, or until light brown and firm to the touch. Cool 5 minutes; slice 1 inch thick.

CHEESE POLENTA WITH TOMATO-MEAT SAUCE

½ cup enriched corn meal	1 egg, beaten
2 cups hot milk	½ pound sharp Cheddar cheese, shredded
1 teaspoon butter	Tomato-Meat Sauce
½ teaspoon salt	

Gradually stir corn meal into milk. Add butter and salt. Cook over boiling water 15 to 20 minutes, stirring occasionally. Stir in egg and cheese together (reserve ½ cup cheese). Pour into buttered shallow 8×8×2-inch pan; chill. Cut into oblongs; place in buttered shallow baking pan. Pour Tomato-Meat Sauce over corn meal; dust with remaining cheese. Bake 15 to 20 minutes in a slow (325°) oven, or until cheese melts and oblongs are heated.

Tomato-Meat Sauce:

½ cup chopped onion
1 section garlic, peeled and
   minced
1 tablespoon butter
½ pound ground beef
1 cup sliced fresh mushrooms
½ teaspoon salt

1 (No. 2) can tomatoes
   (2½ cups)
1 (6-ounce) can tomato paste
1 teaspoon sugar
½ teaspoon oregano
Salt and pepper to taste

Sauté onion and garlic in butter until color turns. Add meat and mushrooms; cook and stir until meat loses its red color. Add salt, tomatoes, tomato paste, sugar and oregano. Simmer 30 minutes, or until thick. Season to taste with salt and pepper.

CHIVE CORN STRIPS

½ teaspoon salt
2 cups boiling water
½ cup enriched corn meal
1 tablespoon butter or
   margarine
1 cup shredded sharp
   American cheese
1½ teaspoons dried chives

⅛ teaspoon ground black
   pepper
1 egg, well beaten
1 tablespoon milk
1 cup fine dry bread crumbs
Oil for deep fat frying
Smoked ham or tongue

Add salt to boiling water; stir in corn meal and slow-boil 10 minutes. Add butter or margarine, cheese, chives and pepper. Stir until cheese melts. Remove from heat and spread in oiled 7×11½×1½-inch pan. Cool and refrigerate 2 hours, or until firm. Cut into 1×3-inch strips. Combine egg and milk and dip corn strips into mixture. Then dip strips into bread crumbs. Fry in deep fat preheated to 350° until crisp and brown. Serve with smoked ham or tongue.

HAM LAYER SCRAPPLE

1½ cups cold water
1½ cups enriched corn meal
½ teaspoon salt
¾ teaspoon dry mustard

⅛ teaspoon black pepper
3½ cups boiling water
2 cups ground cooked ham

Combine cold water, corn meal and seasonings. Slowly pour into boiling water, stirring constantly. Bring to boiling point; cover and continue cooking over low heat 5 minutes, stirring occasionally. Combine 1 cup cooked corn meal mush with ground ham. Layer corn meal mush and corn meal ham mixture alternately in oiled 8½×4½×2½-inch loaf pan, making 5 layers. Begin and end with plain corn meal mush layers. Cool slightly; cover; refrigerate several hours or overnight. Cut chilled scrapple into ½-inch slices. Fry on a lightly oiled griddle or fry pan until golden brown.

NEW MEXICAN TAMALE PIE

1 cup enriched corn meal
3 cups boiling water
1½ teaspoons salt
1 onion, peeled and diced
1 green pepper, seeded and
    diced
3 tablespoons fat (any kind)

¾ pound ground uncooked
    meat (any kind)
1 cup drained canned or
    cooked tomatoes
1½ teaspoons salt
1½ tablespoons chili powder

Stir corn meal slowly into rapidly boiling salted water in double-boiler top. Bring back to boil over direct heat. Cover; place over water boiling in the lower part of the double boiler, and cook 30 minutes, stirring occasionally. In fry pan, sauté onion and green pepper in the fat until tender. Add meat and cook about 15 minutes. Stir in remaining ingredients and heat thoroughly. Arrange alternate layers of corn meal and meat mixture in an oiled, low 3-pint baking dish, finishing with corn meal. Bake 30 minutes at 350°.

FRIED BREAKFAST OATMEAL SLICES

This dish, often called Goetta, is a kind of scrapple made of oats. The oatmeal provides vegetable protein and the sausage, ham or bacon, meat protein—a fine, nutritious combination. Make the day before—it needs a thorough chilling!

2 cups oatmeal (quick or old-fashioned), uncooked	Butter or margarine
1 teaspoon salt	Syrup
3½ cups water	
½ cup sausage meat, cooked, drained, and broken up fine, or ½ cup fine-chopped cooked ham, or 6 strips bacon, cooked, drained and crumbled	

Stir oats into briskly boiling salted water. Cook 1 minute for quick oats, 5 minutes for old-fashioned oats. Cover pan, remove from heat and let stand 5 minutes. Stir in meat. Pour into ungreased loaf pan. Cover and refrigerate several hours or overnight. Cut into ½-inch slices. Pan-fry in butter or margarine until golden brown, about 10 minutes per side. Serve hot with butter or margarine and syrup.

RAISED CALAS

1 teaspoon salt	3 eggs, well beaten
3 cups boiling water	¼ cup sugar
½ cup uncooked rice	⅛ teaspoon nutmeg
½ yeast cake, softened in ½ cup lukewarm water	½ teaspoon salt
	¼ cup sifted flour

Add salt to water and stir in rice. Cook 25 minutes, or until very soft. Drain, mash and cool to lukewarm. Add yeast; beat, cover and let rise overnight free from drafts. In the morning add remaining ingredients. Beat again and let rise about 20 minutes in warm place. Drop by tablespoonfuls into hot (360°) deep fat and fry until golden brown. Drain on paper toweling and serve hot. Makes 20 Calas.

CEYLON RICE

2 cups long grain white rice
1 teaspoon salt
4 cups cold water
1 teaspoon fine-crumbled
    saffron, soaked 5 minutes in
    1 tablespoon cold water
¼ cup slivered blanched
    almonds or pignolia nuts
¼ cup raisins
¼ cup canned crisp-fried
    onions

In a 3-quart saucepan, measure rice, salt and water. Add soaked saffron. Cover. Place over high heat. When boiling rapidly reduce heat; simmer 15 minutes. Uncover. Stir in almonds or pignolia nuts, raisins and onions. Cover again. Let stand 5 minutes. Uncover to steam-dry 5 minutes more. The rice grains will be fluffy and separate. Do not stir.

CHINESE FRIED RICE

1 cup long grain rice
¼ cup oil
2 eggs, beaten
3 cups diced cooked pork,
    chicken or shrimp; or any
    combination of all three
1 can bean sprouts, thoroughly
    rinsed and drained
4 scallions, washed and finely
    chopped
¼ cup soy sauce
1 section garlic, peeled and
    mashed
Salt and pepper to taste

Cook rice as directed on package. In fry pan, gently fry beaten eggs in 2 tablespoons oil until firm. Remove; cut in thin strips. Heat remaining oil; add meat and/or shrimp mixture, bean sprouts and scallions; cook, stirring, 3 to 4 minutes. Add rice, soy sauce mixed with garlic, salt and pepper to taste, and eggs. Mix thoroughly. Serve piping hot.

CHINESE FRIED RICE WITH HAM

⅓ cup cooking oil	1 cup fine-diced cooked ham
½ teaspoon salt	4 cups flaky white rice
⅛ teaspoon pepper	½ teaspoon sugar
2 eggs	2 tablespoons soy sauce
2 teaspoons minced onion	

In heavy 10-inch fry pan, heat cooking oil, salt and pepper. Beat eggs. Pour into fry pan and slow-fry, like a pancake, until yellowed and firm. Do not brown. Remove and slice into fine shreds. Meantime, add minced onion and diced ham to fat remaining in fry pan; slow-fry until onion is yellowed. Add rice, sugar and soy sauce. Stir constantly with fork over moderate heat, about 5 minutes, or until rice is hot. Then stir in shredded egg and reheat a moment more. Serve very hot.

FRIED RICE AND RAISINS

Melt 2 tablespoons butter or margarine in skillet. Add ½ cup raisins and stir-fry ½ minute. Stir in 4 cups cooked long grain rice and slow-sauté about 4 minutes, stirring with fork. Serve with lamb or chicken. I especially recommend it to serve with curried meat or poultry; or with baked or broiled spareribs of pork.

PORK FRIED RICE

1 pound boneless pork, cut in thin strips	1 teaspoon salt
1 clove of garlic, peeled and minced	¼ teaspoon pepper
	1 (3-ounce) can mushrooms
1 medium onion, peeled and chopped	1¾ cups water
	1 egg
1 cup uncooked rice	Salt and pepper to taste
	Soy sauce

Brown pork in large skillet with garlic and onion. Add rice and cook-stir until lightly browned. Add 1 teaspoon salt, ¼ teaspoon pepper, mushrooms with liquid and water, bring to a boil and simmer covered until rice is tender. Meanwhile, beat egg with additional salt and pepper, and fry gently in small greased skillet until firm. Turn once. Remove from skillet and cut in strips. Use to garnish fried rice. Serve with soy sauce. Serves 4.

GREEN RICE

3 tablespoons butter	2 cups long grain rice
2 tablespoons olive or salad oil	3½ cups boiling water
½ cup minced scallions	2 envelopes chicken broth
1 cup minced parsley	powder
1½ cups fine-chopped, well-drained tender raw spinach leaves	1 teaspoon salt
	¼ teaspoon white pepper
	½ cup grated Parmesan cheese

Combine butter and oil in a 3-quart saucepan and heat. Stir in scallions, parsley and spinach. Cook gently 3 minutes. Stir in rice. Add water, chicken broth powder, salt and white pepper. Bring to boil; cover. Simmer-cook 25 minutes, or until rice is bite-tender. With fork, stir in grated Parmesan cheese.

JAMBALAYA

2 slices bacon	1 cup unpolished rice
2 tablespoons minced onion	1 can shrimps or 1½ cups
1 tablespoon flour	cooked shrimps
2 cups canned tomatoes	1 teaspoon salt
1½ cups water	¼ teaspoon pepper

Cook the bacon in a large skillet until the fat flows freely. Add the onion and cook until it begins to color. Next put in the flour and when slightly browned, add the tomatoes and water. Bring to boiling point, shake in the rice gently and cook 10 minutes; then put in the shrimps, salt and pepper, cover tightly and simmer very slowly, stirring occasionally, for 1 hour. (Add more water if necessary to prevent sticking.)

MEXICAN RICE

4 tablespoons olive oil
1 pound converted rice
2 quarts chicken stock or broth
3 tablespoons canned tomato
   purée

1 whole onion, peeled and
   minced
1 section garlic, peeled and
   crushed
1 teaspoon salt

Pour oil in heavy skillet; add rice and slow-fry; stir until golden brown. Stir in remaining ingredients. Cover; cook 18 minutes, or until the rice is tender and fluffy. Serves 8.

ORANGE RICE

6 tablespoons butter or
   margarine
1⅓ cups diced celery and
   chopped tender celery leaves
3 tablespoons peeled minced
   onion
3 cups water
2 cups orange juice; or canned
   or frozen orange juice
   diluted by following
   package directions

2 tablespoons grated orange
   rind
1¼ teaspoons salt
2 cups white rice

Melt butter in a heavy 2½-quart saucepan; add celery and onion; slow-cook until onion is tender, but do not brown. Add water, orange juice, orange rind and salt. Bring to boil; add rice slowly. Cover; reduce heat; simmer 25 minutes.

PEPPER FRIED RICE

2 green onions, cut in small
   pieces
2 tablespoons butter
¼ teaspoon crushed red
   pepper
¼ teaspoon thyme

1 cup undrained, canned
   kidney beans
1 (13½-ounce) can fried rice
   with chicken or 1 (10-ounce)
   package frozen fried rice
   with chicken, thawed

Sauté onions in butter until slightly wilted; stir in red pepper, thyme, kidney beans and fried rice. Cover and cook 10 minutes over low heat, stirring frequently to separate rice and keep mixture from sticking to bottom of pan.

RICE À LA MIDDLE EAST

3 tablespoons butter or
   margarine
1½ cups rice
1½ cups orange juice
1½ cups water
1½ teaspoons salt

½ cup dark seedless raisins
½ teaspoon fine-grated orange
   peel
⅓ cup toasted slivered
   almonds
1 tablespoon chopped parsley

Combine butter and rice in a 9-inch skillet. Stir-cook over low heat about 1 minute, or until deep cream color. Stir in next five ingredients. Tight-cover; simmer 5 minutes, stirring twice. Continue to simmer 10 minutes more, or until rice has absorbed all liquid. Remove from heat; fluff rice, add almonds and parsley.

RICE FRITTERS

1½ cups cooked white, brown
   or converted rice
1 large egg
⅓ teaspoon salt
½ cup milk
1 cup sifted flour

2½ teaspoons double-acting
   baking powder
1 teaspoon melted butter or
   margarine
Cooking oil for frying

Turn rice into mixing bowl; break into loose kernels with fork. Beat and add egg, salt, milk, flour, baking powder and melted butter. In heavy deep fry pan, heat about ¼ inch of vegetable oil or enough to float fritters. Drop in batter by tablespoonfuls. Brown fast on one side, then the other; allow about 6 minutes altogether. Serve as accompaniment to meat, bacon, ham, fish or eggs; or with meat gravy; or as dessert with fruit sauce, melted jelly, syrup or honey.

RICE AND PEAS WITH MUSHROOMS

1 cup long grain rice
2 chicken bouillon cubes
1 package frozen green peas
2 tablespoons butter
1 (6-ounce) can sliced
 mushrooms

¼ cup chopped parsley
Onion salt
Pepper

Cook rice as directed on package, but add chicken bouillon cubes dissolved in ½ cup of the water, heated, and use the drained liquid from the mushrooms as part of the total cooking liquid. Meanwhile, cook peas, drain thoroughly and add to rice mixture with butter. Add drained mushrooms, parsley, onion salt and pepper to taste. Stir gently with fork. Serves 8.

RICE PILAFF WITH SAFFRON

6 tablespoons butter
1 cup long grain white rice
1 teaspoon salt
½ teaspoon pepper

⅛ teaspoon saffron
1½ cups chicken stock
2 tablespoons butter in small
 pieces

Melt the 6 tablespoons butter in a large saucepan and add the rice. Stir until all the rice is coated with butter. To this, add the salt and the pepper. Mix again and add the saffron. Mix until all the rice turns yellow. Add the chicken stock and stir. Cover the pot tight and set it over low heat to simmer slowly for about 45 minutes, or until all the liquid is cooked into the rice and the rice is tender. When the rice is cooked, remove the cover and carefully fold in the 2 tablespoons additional butter. Serve very hot.

RISOTTO

3 tablespoons olive or salad oil
2 tablespoons butter or margarine
1 small onion, peeled and minced
1 small section garlic, peeled and minced

1¾ cups long grain rice
4 teaspoons instant bouillon powder
5 cups boiling water
Juice of ½ lemon (optional)
½ cup grated Parmesan cheese

In heavy 2½-quart saucepan heat together oil and butter. Add onion and garlic. Simmer-sauté until translucent. Add rice; with fork, stir mixture gently about 1 minute, or until rice is yellowed. Dissolve half the bouillon powder in half the boiling water. Stir occasionally until liquid is absorbed by rice. Add remaining bouillon powder and water. Gently boil from 25 to 35 minutes, or until extremely thick and rice is tender but not dry. To accent flavor, stir in juice of ½ lemon if desired. Pass grated Parmesan cheese.

WILD RICE

Wild rice, a gourmet's delight, justifies its luxury price to some extent because the crop is harvested by hand in a few weeks' span in the fall. The rice is grown in marshes, ripening on thin stalks from the top down. Gathering the grain is a delicate task, as it must be gently tapped into canoes as it ripens. Each stand of rice must be harvested several times as progressive ripening continues. Even so, much of the rice is lost to wind or falls in the water, and a very small percentage of the crop is captured for processing. Most of the supply comes from Minnesota.

The long, slender, brown grain has developed a fantastic band of followers. It is served in casseroles, stews, desserts and salads, as well as with game and fowl. Wild rice has twice the protein, four times the phosphorus, eight times the thiamine and twenty times the riboflavin of white rice.

To Prepare Wild Rice: Carefully pick over the rice. Place in a sieve; wash and rinse with cold water. Cook according to package directions. Season to taste with melted butter.

Wild Rice with Ginger and Chutney: To 4 cups cooked or canned wild rice, stir in ½ cup diced drained preserved ginger, ½ cup drained chopped mango chutney and ¼ cup melted butter. Serve with poultry or game.

Wild Rice, Baked: Melt 2 tablespoons butter; add 2 peeled chopped small onions. Cook until tender, but not brown. Add 2 cups wild rice. Mix well a few minutes using a low heat. Add 4 cups chicken broth and salt to taste; bring to a boil, cover, put into the oven and bake for 30 minutes.

Quick Breads
and Yeast Breads

Quick Breads

Piping hot corn sticks, steaming popovers, muffins small and crusty, light-textured griddle cakes—these are only a few of the favorites that fall under the quick-bread heading. Of course, many of these are available in convenient commercial hot bread mixes, but when it comes to economy, variety and just plain satisfaction—there's nothing like making them yourself.

All recipes are for six servings unless otherwise stated.

APPLE BREAD LOAF

½ cup margarine or shortening at room temperature
1 cup sugar
1 large egg, well beaten
2 cups sifted flour
⅓ teaspoon salt
1 teaspoon baking soda

1 teaspoon baking powder
½ teaspoon ground cinnamon
¼ cup nut meats, chopped medium-fine (any kind)
1 cup minced unpeeled cored apple
⅓ cup sour milk

Combine margarine and sugar in a 2-quart mixing bowl. Mix and stir until creamy; add egg. Mix together flour, salt, baking soda, baking powder, cinnamon and nut meats. Stir in apple with fork so it will be well-coated with flour and other dry ingredients. Add to first mixture alternately with milk. Transfer to an oiled 5×9-inch loaf pan; bake 50 minutes in moderate (350 to 375°) oven. Cool. Wrap in foil; let stand a few hours or overnight before using. Slice thin; cut in halves. Serve with butter, or whipped cream cheese and/or currant jelly.

APRICOT CORN BREAD

1 cup enriched yellow corn meal	1 egg
1 cup sifted enriched flour	½ cup milk
¼ cup sugar	¼ cup shortening, soft
3 teaspoons baking powder	½ cup mashed, stewed dried apricots and juice

Sift dry ingredients together into a medium-sized bowl. Add egg, milk and shortening. Beat with a rotary beater until smooth, about 1 minute. Blend in apricots and juice. Do not overbeat. Transfer to an oiled 8-inch square pan; bake in a hot (425°) oven, 20 to 25 minutes.

APRICOT WALNUT BREAD

2 cups biscuit mix	1 cup walnuts, coarsely chopped
1 cup quick-cooking rolled oats	
¾ cup sugar	1 egg, well beaten
1 teaspoon baking powder	1¼ cups milk
¼ teaspoon salt	
½ cup dried apricots, cut in strips	

Stir together first five ingredients. Mix in apricots and walnuts. Combine egg and milk; add to dry ingredients and beat hard 30 seconds. Pour into a 9×5×3-inch loaf pan and bake at 350° for 1 hour. Cool in pan for 10 minutes before removing for further cooling on rack.

BANANA BREAD

1¾ cups sifted flour	⅔ cup sugar
2 teaspoons baking powder	2 eggs, well beaten
¼ teaspoon baking soda	1 cup mashed ripe bananas
½ teaspoon salt	½ cup chopped nuts
⅓ cup shortening	(optional)

Sift dry ingredients together. Beat shortening until creamy in mixing bowl. Add sugar gradually and continue beating until light and fluffy. Add well-beaten eggs and beat well. Add dry ingredients alternately with bananas, a small amount at a time, beating well after each addition. Turn into a well-greased 9×5 ×2½-inch bread pan, and bake in a moderate (350°) oven, about 1 hour, or until done. Chopped nuts may be added to the flour mixture.

QUICK BROWN BREAD

2 cups whole wheat flour
1 teaspoon salt
½ teaspoon soda
1½ teaspoons baking powder
1 egg

1 cup buttermilk or sour milk
½ cup molasses
¼ cup melted shortening or cooking oil

Mix flour, salt, soda and baking powder thoroughly in mixing bowl. Beat egg in a pint-sized measure. Add buttermilk or sour milk, molasses, shortening, and mix. Add liquid mixture to dry ingredients and stir, barely mixing. Pour into a greased 8-inch square pan. Bake 30 minutes at 350°. Serve warm. Serves 12 to 16.

Variation: Add ½ cup chopped nuts, dates or raisins to the dry ingredients. Half the nuts may be sprinkled over the top of the bread batter.

TOASTY COCONUT BREAD

2 cups sifted all-purpose flour
3 teaspoons double-acting baking powder
1 teaspoon salt
¼ cup toasted flaked coconut
¼ cup chopped toasted almonds
1½ teaspoons grated lemon rind

1 egg
¼ cup firm-packed brown sugar
1 cup canned applesauce
¼ teaspoon almond extract
¼ cup shortening, melted

Sift together flour, baking powder and salt. Add coconut, almonds and lemon rind. Combine and mix egg, brown sugar, applesauce, almond extract and shortening. Add to flour mixture, stirring only enough to dampen flour. Spread batter into an 8×4×3-inch loaf pan, which has been lined with paper, then oiled. Bake in a moderate (350°) oven about 50 minutes. Cool. Wrap in waxed paper or foil and store 24 hours before slicing.

CORN BREAD

1¼ cups enriched corn meal	1 egg
¾ cups sifted flour	1 cup milk
3 teaspoons baking powder	3 tablespoons shortening
½ teaspoon salt	

Heat oven to hot (400°). Sift together corn meal, flour, baking powder and salt. Add egg, milk and shortening. Beat with rotary beater until smooth, about 1 minute. Transfer to an oiled 8-inch square pan. Bake 20 to 25 minutes.

SLEEPY HOLLOW CORN BREAD

From Sleepy Hollow Restoration in Tarrytown, New York (Washington Irving country), comes this outstanding recipe for corn bread. Prepared with corn meal water ground between French burr millstones at Phillipsburg Manor, a reconstruction of an eighteenth-century mill on the Pocantico River, this corn bread has no equal. Made with any good quality unsifted yellow corn meal, it is still outstanding.

1 cup flour	¼ cup sugar
½ teaspoon salt	1 cup milk
4 teaspoons baking powder	2 eggs, beaten
1 cup unsifted yellow corn meal	1 tablespoon vegetable oil

Sift together the first three ingredients. Mix dry ingredients. Add milk, beaten eggs and oil. Beat well. Pour into an 8×8×2-inch greased pan. Bake 25 minutes at 375°, or until done. (Bread is done if center springs back when touched lightly with finger.)

SOUTHERN CORN BREAD

1 cup presifted flour
1 cup corn meal
1 tablespoon sugar
½ teaspoon baking soda
2 teaspoons double-acting
    baking powder

1 teaspoon salt
1 egg, beaten
1 cup sour milk or buttermilk
1 cup water
¼ cup melted bacon drippings
Butter

In mixing bowl stir together flour, corn meal, sugar, soda, baking powder and salt. Add egg, milk, water and bacon drippings. Mix and beat well. Turn into an 8×8×2-inch pan. Bake 30 minutes, or until browned in very hot (450°) oven. Serve hot, cut in squares, with butter.

SOUTHWESTERN CORN BREAD

1 (1-pound) can cream-style
    corn
¾ cup milk
1 medium-sized onion, peeled,
    minced and sautéed in
2 tablespoons bacon fat

3 eggs
1 cup yellow corn meal
½ teaspoon soda
1 teaspoon salt
Generous sprinkling pepper
1 cup grated Cheddar cheese

Thoroughly blend corn, milk, sautéed onion and eggs in mixing bowl. Stir to blend the corn meal, soda, salt and pepper, then add to first mixture, blending well. Pour half of batter into a greased 9-inch square pan, sprinkle with half the cheese, pour in remaining batter and top with remaining cheese. Bake at 375° for 45 minutes.

IRISH CURRANT BREAD

2 cups presifted all-purpose flour
5 teaspoons baking powder
2 tablespoons granulated sugar
1 teaspoon salt
1 cup fine entire-wheat flour
⅓ cup shortening at room temperature
1 cup dried currants
2½ teaspoons caraway seeds
1⅓ cups milk
1 tablespoon granulated sugar
½ teaspoon cinnamon

Sift together first five ingredients. Chop in shortening with pastry blender; add currants, caraway seeds and milk. Mix thoroughly and knead lightly, forming dough into a loaf. Transfer to an oiled 1-pound-sized bread pan; dust with additional sugar and cinnamon mixed; strew over a few extra caraway seeds. Cover; let rise 10 minutes. Bake 35 minutes in a moderate (375°) oven. Cool, wrap in foil and let stand 8 hours before slicing.

IRISH SODA BREAD

3 cups sifted flour
3 tablespoons sugar (for dough)
3 teaspoons baking powder
½ teaspoon baking soda
½ teaspoon salt
1 cup currants
1⅓ cups buttermilk
2 tablespoons sugar (for glaze)
2 tablespoons hot water

Sift flour, 3 tablespoons sugar, baking powder, soda and salt into bowl; stir in currants, then buttermilk until blended. Dough will be sticky. Turn out onto a lightly floured board; knead about 10 times. Shape into an 8-inch round loaf; place on ungreased cookie sheet. Cut a cross in top of dough with sharp knife. Bake in moderate (375°) oven for 45 minutes. Remove from oven. Dissolve 2 tablespoons sugar in hot water in a cup and brush generously over hot loaf. Bake 10 minutes longer. Serve warm.

BRAZIL NUT ORANGE BREAD

1¾ cups sifted enriched flour
1½ teaspoons baking powder
¼ teaspoon baking soda
1¼ teaspoons salt
⅔ cup sugar
2 tablespoons grated orange
   rind

¾ cup chopped Brazil nuts
1 egg, beaten
½ cup milk
½ cup orange juice
2 tablespoons butter or
   margarine, melted

Sift together flour, baking powder, baking soda, salt and sugar. Stir in orange rind and Brazil nuts. Mix together egg, milk, orange juice and melted butter; add to dry ingredients and stir only enough to dampen them. Place in an oiled 8½×3½×2½-inch loaf pan. Bake in a slow (325°) oven for 1¼ hours. Makes 1 loaf. Slice thin the day after making.

FLORIDA ORANGE BREAD

3 Florida oranges
½ cup sugar
¼ cup water
1 tablespoon butter or
   margarine
1 cup orange juice

1 egg
2½ cups sifted flour
2 teaspoons baking powder
½ teaspoon baking soda
½ teaspoon salt

Wash oranges. Remove thin rind with sharp knife; cut it into slivers with scissors. (Slice and use orange pulp in fruit cup.) Combine sugar and water. Add rind and cook-stir until sugar melts. Simmer 3 minutes and measure. There should be ⅔ cupful. Pour this into a bowl; add butter and orange juice. Beat and add egg. Into a mixing bowl sift flour, baking powder, soda and salt. Add orange mixture; stir just enough to moisten ingredients; do not beat. Batter should be somewhat lumpy. Transfer to oiled 9×5×3-inch loaf pan and bake 1½ hours in slow (325°) oven, or until pick inserted in center comes out clean. Cool on cake rack. Wrap in aluminum foil and refrigerate to "ripen" flavors. Serve the next day.

HONEY ORANGE BREAD

1 cup honey, scant
½ cup milk, lukewarm
2⅔ cups flour, sifted

1 teaspoon baking soda
1 tablespoon fine-cut fresh
   orange peel

Mix honey and lukewarm milk. Mix flour with baking soda and add with the fine-cut orange peel to the honey-milk mixture. Mix well for about 5 minutes, using a wooden spoon. Pour into greased pan which should be about half full. Place in warm place for about 15 minutes. Bake in a slow (300°) oven about 1¼ hours.

PECAN LOAF

1 cup shortening at room
   temperature
2 cups granulated sugar
4 eggs, beaten light
1½ teaspoons vanilla

⅓ teaspoon salt
3 cups sifted flour
3 teaspoons baking powder
1 cup milk
1 cup coarse-chopped pecans

Stir shortening until soft; beat in sugar and eggs; add flavoring. Sift together dry ingredients; add alternately with milk to first mixture. Arrange three alternating layers of batter and nuts in a slightly oiled and floured 5×9-inch loaf cake pan, starting with layer of batter and finishing with layer of pecans. Bake in moderate 350 to 375° oven, for 45 to 60 minutes. No icing is necessary as pecans decorate top.

SPOON BREAD VIRGINIA

1½ cups boiling water
1 cup enriched corn meal
1½ teaspoons salt
2 tablespoons butter or
   margarine

2 eggs, beaten
2 cups buttermilk
½ teaspoon baking soda
¾ cup grated sharp Cheddar
   cheese

Pour and stir water into corn meal. Beat in salt and butter or margarine. Add eggs, and buttermilk combined with baking soda.

Fold in cheese. Transfer to oiled shallow 3-pint baking dish. Bake 30 minutes in moderate (350°) oven, or until golden brown on top and a knife inserted in center comes out clean. Serve hot.

HOMEMADE MASTER BISCUIT MIX

5 pounds sifted all-purpose flour

¾ cup double-acting baking powder

3 tablespoons salt

1 tablespoon cream of tartar

½ cup sugar

2 pounds shortening which does not require refrigeration

Sift together flour, baking powder, salt, cream of tartar and sugar. Then sift 3 times more. Add shortening and chop in until mix has the consistency of corn meal. Store in covered containers at room temperature. Add necessary liquids when ready to bake. Makes approximately 24 cups mix.

Biscuits:

3 cups mix
⅔ cup milk

Mix and knead ingredients lightly. Roll ½ inch thick. Cut in 2-inch rounds and bake 10 minutes on cookie sheet in a hot (400°) oven.

Pinwheels: Roll out dough as for biscuits above into rectangle ½ inch thick. Brush with softened margarine or butter. Top with choice of pecan meats, raisins, peanut butter, sugar, jelly, spices, chopped meat or hamburger. Roll up dough like jelly roll. Use short pieces of string to cut into 1-inch biscuits as follows: Wrap string around roll and pull tight. It will cut through soft dough without mashing it or spilling contents. Place pinwheel biscuits on ungreased pan. Bake 15 to 20 minutes at 400°.

BAKING POWDER BISCUITS

2 cups flour	½ tablespoon sugar
4 teaspoons baking powder	⅓ cup shortening
1 teaspoon salt	⅔ cup milk

Preheat oven to 400°. Sift together dry ingredients, then work in shortening with the fingertips or two knives till mixture resembles fine crumbs. Add milk, stir till dough holds together. Knead on floured board about 12 strokes. Roll or pat out to ½-inch thickness. Cut with floured biscuit cutter. Bake 12 to 15 minutes, until lightly browned. Makes about 14 biscuits.

OLD-FASHIONED BEATEN BISCUITS

2 cups self-rising flour	⅓ to ⅔ cup sour milk or
1 teaspoon sugar	buttermilk
¼ cup shortening	

Preheat oven to 300°. Sift flour and sugar together into a 2-quart mixing bowl. With a pastry blender, cut in shortening until mixture resembles coarse crumbs. Mix in enough sour milk or buttermilk to make a stiff dough. Turn dough onto lightly floured surface; knead 30 seconds. Run dough through coarse blade of food grinder 6 times, or give it 300 strokes with a rolling pin. The dough should be slightly elastic, very smooth and slightly blistered under the surface. Roll out dough ½ inch thick. Dip a 1- or 1½-inch biscuit cutter in flour. Cut out biscuits. Place them on baking sheet. Pierce top of each biscuit 3 times with 2-tined fork. Bake 45 minutes, or until crisp and lightly browned. Makes 60 1-inch biscuits or 36 1½-inch biscuits.

CHEESE STICKS

2 cups sifted flour
½ teaspoon salt
¼ teaspoon baking powder
⅔ cup shortening
½ cup fine-grated sharp
   Cheddar cheese

1 egg yolk
4 tablespoons cold water
Paprika

Sift dry ingredients together. Add shortening and chop in with pastry blender until mixture looks like coarse meal. Add cheese, then egg yolk, slightly beaten and mixed with water. Mix with knife until dough cleans bowl of flour. If necessary, add few drops more water, as little as possible. On slightly floured surface, roll dough scant ¼ inch thick. Cut in very narrow finger-length strips. Dust with paprika. Bake in hot (400°) oven for 10 to 12 minutes. Do not over-bake. Serve cold, but fresh baked.

IRISH CREAM SCONES

In Ireland, scones (pronounced skuns) are a favorite bread made in different ways. When Irish oatmeal is added, they are served at breakfast or with soup; when they are "tea scones," they are usually served with jam or honey. Plain scones are often varied by adding either raisins or currants to the dough. A rich brown gloss is often given to the tops of the scones by brushing them with slightly beaten egg before baking them.

2 cups all-purpose flour
3 teaspoons baking powder
½ teaspoon salt
2 tablespoons butter

⅔ cup light cream
Milk
Butter

Sift together first three ingredients. Add butter and chop it in with a pastry blender or 2 knives. Add cream and mix to soft dough. Divide in 2 portions; roll each into a round ½ inch thick; cut across to form 4 triangular-shaped cakes; brush tops with a little milk and bake 12 to 15 minutes in a moderate 375° oven. Split, butter and serve hot.

ORANGE NUT BISCUITS

1 (8-ounce) package ready-to-bake biscuits

¼ cup frozen Florida orange juice concentrate, thawed and undiluted

3 tablespoons chopped nut meats

3 tablespoons brown sugar

Place biscuits in ungreased 9-inch round pan. Bake according to package directions. Combine orange juice concentrate, nuts and sugar. Spoon over biscuits. Lower heat; bake 4 to 5 minutes longer, or until glazed.

INDIVIDUAL PIZZAS

½ pound sliced salami

1 recipe Baking Powder Biscuits (see Index)

1 (6-ounce) can tomato paste

½ tablespoon crushed oregano

2 cups grated sharp Cheddar cheese (½ pound)

Shred salami fine with scissors or sharp knife. Roll biscuit dough on floured smooth surface to ¼-inch thickness. Cut into 12 (5½-inch) rounds. Place rounds ½ inch apart on baking sheet and flute edges making a rim. Spread centers with tomato paste; dust with oregano; top with salami and cheese. Bake 20 minutes, or until crust is browned, in a moderate (375 to 400°) oven. Serve warm. May be made in advance and reheated 10 minutes in warm (325°), not hot, oven. Makes 12 small pizzas.

WHOLE WHEAT AND WHEAT GERM DROP BISCUITS

2 cups whole wheat flour

3 teaspoons baking powder

⅓ cup dehydrated natural wheat germ

1 teaspoon salt

¼ cup shortening

1 tablespoon unsulphured molasses

1 cup whole milk

Mix together the dry ingredients. Add the shortening and chop in with a pastry blender. Mix in the molasses and milk. Oil a cookie sheet or large pan. Drop the dough on by half-tablespoonfuls, keeping the biscuits 1 inch apart. Bake 18 minutes in a hot (425°) oven. Makes about 2 dozen biscuits.

CINNAMON BUNS

4 cups enriched flour	Melted butter or margarine
1 cup granulated sugar	4 teaspoons ground cinnamon
1 teaspoon salt	1 cup raisins
6 teaspoons baking powder	¼ cup butter or margarine
4 tablespoons shortening	½ cup brown sugar
2 eggs	Brown Sugar Syrup
1¼ cups water	¼ cup chopped walnut meats

Sift flour with 4 tablespoons sugar, salt and baking powder. Cut in shortening with pastry blender. Beat eggs, add water, and stir into flour mixture making a soft dough. Transfer to a floured surface and roll into an oblong sheet ½ inch thick. Brush with melted butter, and sprinkle thickly with remaining granulated sugar mixed with cinnamon and raisins. Roll up like a jelly roll. Then cream the additional ¼ cup of butter with the brown sugar and spread on sides and bottom of a large heavy skillet or fry pan. Slice the dough into pieces 1½ inches wide, and lay close together in pan, cut edges up. Bake at 400° for 10 minutes, then reduce heat to 350° and bake about 35 minutes. Nice served in individual dishes with a Brown Sugar Syrup poured over and a sprinkling of chopped walnut meats. Makes 4 dozen.

Brown Sugar Syrup: Combine 1 cup dark brown sugar with ½ cup water in a saucepan and boil 10 minutes, or until the consistency of maple syrup.

BLUEBERRY MUFFINS

½ cup shortening
1 cup sugar
½ teaspoon cinnamon
½ teaspoon nutmeg
2 eggs, beaten
1½ cups sifted enriched flour

1 teaspoon salt
3 teaspoons baking powder
½ cup milk
1½ cups fresh or defrosted
    and drained blueberries

Thoroughly cream shortening and add sugar gradually, beating until light and creamy. Add spices and eggs and beat well. Sift flour with salt and baking powder and add alternately with milk. Fold berries into batter. Pour into 10 well-oiled heat-resistant glass custard cups, or large muffin pans. Bake 35 to 40 minutes in a moderate (375°) oven.

BACON AND CHIVE CORN MEAL MUFFINS

1 (12-ounce) package corn
    meal muffin mix
2½ teaspoons dried chives
⅛ teaspoon ground black
    pepper

1 egg, beaten
⅔ cup milk
½ cup crumbled crisp bacon

In a 2-quart mixing bowl, combine corn meal muffin mix, chives and pepper. Stir in beaten egg and milk. Continue stirring until well mixed. Fold in crumbled bacon. Turn into oiled 12-compartment (2¾ inches) muffin pan. Bake 25 minutes in preheated (400°) oven, or until done. Serve hot.

Note: These muffins replace potatoes, rice or any other starchy accompaniment. Also, they make that good bacon flavor go a long way.

GINGER GEMS

⅓ cup shortening
½ cup boiling water
½ cup molasses
⅓ cup sugar
1 egg, beaten
1½ cups sifted flour

½ cup coarse-chopped nut
  meats
½ teaspoon baking soda
½ teaspoon salt
1½ teaspoons powdered
  ginger

Melt shortening in water. Then add remaining ingredients in the order given, beating thoroughly. Transfer to oiled small muffin pans; bake 20 to 25 minutes in moderate (350°) oven. Serve warm or cold, as is, with or without butter. Makes 10 to 12 "gems" or muffins.

RICE MUFFINS

2 cups sifted flour
½ teaspoon salt
3 tablespoons sugar
3 teaspoons baking powder
1 cup cold cooked rice

1 egg
1 cup milk
3 tablespoons melted
  margarine or shortening

Sift together flour, salt, sugar and baking powder. Add rice; mix in with fork until grains are coated with flour mixture. Beat egg; add milk and stir in. Then add shortening. Blend lightly, but do not beat. Transfer to oiled 12 small-compartment muffin pan, filling each ⅔ full. Bake 25 to 30 minutes in hot (400 to 425°) oven.

GIANT POPOVERS

All ingredients at room temperature.

1 tablespoon butter
3 eggs, slightly beaten
1 cup milk
3 tablespoons melted butter or
  margarine

1 cup sifted flour
½ teaspoon salt

Preheat oven to 375°. Generously rub 6 (5½-ounce) custard cups with butter. Arrange cups on baking sheet or shallow roasting pan.

Combine eggs, milk and melted butter; beat well with beater. Gradually beat in flour and salt. Fill custard cups to within ½ inch of top. Bake at 375° for 50 to 55 minutes. Remove from oven.

Quickly cut a 1-inch slit in side of each popover to allow steam escape; immediately return popovers to oven for 10 to 15 minutes or until lightly browned. Serve at once.

Note: Cold popovers may be wrapped in aluminum foil and frozen up to 7 days. Reheat 10 minutes at 375° in foil.

CHERRY CINNAMON COFFEE CAKE

1½ cups sifted enriched flour	⅔ cup milk
¼ cup sugar	3 tablespoons oil or melted
2 teaspoons baking powder	shortening
¾ teaspoon salt	Cinnamon Streusel Topping
1 egg, beaten	½ cup cherry preserves

Sift together flour, sugar, baking powder and salt. Combine egg, milk and oil or shortening. Add to flour mixture, stirring until smooth. Add more milk if necessary to make a spreading batter. Spread batter in an oiled 9-inch round pan. Strew with Cinnamon Streusel Topping. Dot cherry preserves by ½ teaspoonfuls over the top of the batter. Bake in hot (400°) oven about 30 minutes, or until pick inserted in center comes out clean.

Cinnamon Streusel Topping:

2 tablespoons sugar	2 tablespoons butter or
2 tablespoons enriched flour	margarine
1 teaspoon cinnamon	

Mix sugar, flour and cinnamon. Cut or rub in butter or margarine until mixture is crumbly.

WARM CINNAMON CAKE

4 tablespoons shortening at
  room temperature
⅔ cup sugar
⅓ teaspoon salt
1 egg, well beaten
⅔ cup milk

1½ cups sifted flour
2 teaspoons baking powder
¼ cup sugar mixed with
  1 teaspoon cinnamon
Butter

Stir shortening until creamy; add sugar, salt and egg, then milk. Sift together flour and baking powder; beat into first mixture. Transfer to an oiled 8-inch square pan. Dust with remaining sugar and cinnamon mixed; bake 20 to 25 minutes in moderate (375°) oven. Serve warm with butter.

CRANBERRY RING COFFEE CAKE

1 (7-ounce) can whole berry
  cranberry sauce
10 tablespoons brownulated
  sugar or ½ cup firm-packed
  brown sugar
½ cup fine-chopped nut meats
¾ cup uncooked quick
  oatmeal

¼ to ½ teaspoon ground
  cinnamon
2 packages bake-and-serve
  biscuits (refrigerator case)
1 cup confectioners' sugar
½ teaspoon grated lemon rind
1 to 2 tablespoons cranberry
  juice cocktail

Combine and mix cranberry sauce, brownulated sugar, nut meats, oatmeal and cinnamon. Separate biscuits and spread 1 tablespoon cranberry mixture on each. Stand biscuits edge down in a well-buttered 9-inch ring pan, so cranberry mixture is between the biscuits. Bake in hot (400°) oven 20 to 25 minutes. Cool 5 minutes then loosen edges and turn out on rack to cool slightly. Mix confectioners' sugar and lemon rind with cranberry juice to give a good spreading consistency. Spread over coffee ring while it is still hot. Serve warm.

ROLLED WHEAT NUTMEG COFFEE CAKE

½ cup shortening	¾ cup milk
1 cup sugar	1 teaspoon vanilla extract
2 eggs	1 tablespoon grated lemon rind
1 cup flour	¾ cup rolled wheat
2 teaspoons baking powder	Topping
½ teaspoon salt	

Cream shortening and sugar. Add eggs. Sift together flour, baking powder and salt. Add dry mixture to creamed mixture alternately with milk, vanilla and lemon rind. Add rolled wheat and mix thoroughly, making a batter. Pour half of this coffee cake batter into oiled 9×13-inch pan. Sprinkle over half of the Topping. Spread on remaining batter and cover with remaining Topping. Bake 20 to 25 minutes in a 375° oven, or until toothpick when inserted comes out clean. Serve warm; cut in squares.

Topping: Combine ½ cup brown sugar, 1 teaspoon ground nutmeg, 1 cup chopped nuts, and mix together thoroughly.

OLD-FASHIONED NEW ENGLAND DOUGHNUTS

1 cup sugar	4 teaspoons double-acting baking powder
2 tablespoons butter at room temperature	1½ teaspoons salt
3 eggs, well beaten	1½ teaspoons ground nutmeg
3 cups all-purpose flour (not sifted)	1 cup milk
	Fat for deep frying

In deep measuring bowl combine sugar and butter; mix with slotted spoon until butter is evenly distributed. Beat in eggs. Sift together the four dry ingredients; add alternately with milk to butter mixture. (Batter will be thick but a little thinner than for most doughnuts.) Cover and refrigerate 1 hour. If too soft to handle, beat in 2 to 4 extra tablespoons flour. Remove ⅓ of dough at a time to a floured surface. Roll into oblong shape ½ inch thick.

Cut in 6-inch strips 1 inch wide. Pinch ends together to make circles. Gently slide them, as fast as shaped, into hot lard or other fat at 370°, hot enough to brown cubelet of bread in 1 minute. Turn when doughnuts come to surface. Cook about 3 minutes. With long-handled fork remove to drain on paper towels. Serve warm or cold. (This method of making doughnuts avoids wasting time fiddling with a doughnut cutter, then bunching up the scraps to roll and cut over again.) Makes about 3 dozen.

DOUGHNUTS AND CRULLERS

4 cups flour	4 tablespoons melted
4 teaspoons baking powder	shortening
¾ teaspoon salt	¾ cup milk
½ teaspoon ground nutmeg or	Vegetable oil for deep frying
cinnamon	Granulated or powdered sugar
⅔ cup sugar	(optional)
1 large egg	

Combine dry ingredients and sift into a 2-quart mixing bowl. Beat egg thoroughly. Stir in melted shortening and milk. Add to dry ingredients. Work with spoon to make light dough. Turn onto lightly floured surface and roll ½ inch thick. Dip doughnut cutter in flour and with it cut out the dough. Keep the little round centers to fry for extra "goodies." Slip doughnuts into vegetable oil heated to 370°, or until a cubelet of bread dropped in browns in 1 minute. As soon as doughnuts rise to top of oil, turn them with fork, so entire surface will be golden brown. Fry 3 minutes. Drain on crumpled paper toweling.

Serve as is or dusted with granulated sugar; or put 1 cup sifted powdered sugar in a good-sized paper bag, add the doughnuts, partly cooled 6 at a time; close the bag and shake until evenly coated. Makes 3 dozen 3-inch doughnuts.

Crullers: Make dough by preceding recipe. Roll to a scant ½ inch in thickness on lightly floured surface. Cut dough into strips 10 inches long and roll slightly with hands; then double and twist

2 portions of dough together, pressing them firmly so they will not untwist while frying. Fry and sugar as directed for doughnuts.

QUICK BREAKFAST PUFFS

Cooking oil or fat
1 cup biscuit mix
⅛ teaspoon salt
¼ cup cold water
¼ cup sugar
1½ teaspoons cinnamon

Heat oil or fat (about 1½ inches) to 375° in electric fry pan or heavy skillet. Stir biscuit mix, salt and water with fork to a soft dough. Drop by teaspoonfuls into hot fat; fry until golden brown and puffy, about 30 seconds. Drain on paper toweling. In paper bag combine sugar and cinnamon; shake puffs in bag to coat thoroughly. Makes about 12.

CROUTON DUMPLINGS

3 tablespoons butter or
   margarine
1 cup small cubes enriched
   white bread
2 cups sifted enriched flour
½ teaspoon salt
3 teaspoons baking powder
1 egg
1 cup milk
2 tablespoons water
2 quarts water
1 tablespoon salt
2 tablespoons butter or
   margarine

In a 9-inch fry pan, melt butter. In it, sauté bread cubes until golden brown all over. Sift together dry ingredients. Beat egg light; add milk and 2 tablespoons water. Stir into flour mixture. Add sautéed bread cubes and stir until completely covered.

Into wide saucepan, measure the 2 quarts water and 1 tablespoon salt. Bring to rapid boil. Shape dumpling mixture into walnut-sized balls. Drop them into boiling water; cover and boil 8 minutes; drain. Brown 2 tablespoons additional butter and roll dumplings in it to coat all over. Transfer into heated serving bowl.

CORN PONE

2 cups white corn meal
1 teaspoon salt
¼ teaspoon baking soda
4 tablespoons shortening or
  lard

¾ cup boiling water
½ cup buttermilk

Sift dry ingredients together. Work in shortening or lard with hands until well blended. Pour in boiling water and continue to blend the mixture. Gradually add enough buttermilk to make a soft dough firm enough to be patted into small, flat cakes. Place in a well-greased hot iron skillet and bake 35 to 40 minutes in a preheated 350° oven. Makes about 12 cakes.

CORN FRITTERS

1¼ cups sifted flour
1½ teaspoons baking powder
⅓ teaspoon salt
2 eggs, beaten light
½ tablespoon cooking oil

2 cups raw green corn kernels,
  cut and scraped from cobs
½ cup milk
Vegetable oil for frying

Sift together flour, baking powder and salt; stir into beaten eggs. Add oil and corn kernels. Stir in milk to make batter. Cover; let stand 10 minutes. Fry by tablespoonfuls for 1 minute in vegetable oil at 370°. Or sauté by tablespoonfuls in vegetable fat ½ inch deep, using a deep, heavy fry pan. Turn once. Drain on crumpled paper towels.

HUSH PUPPIES

2 cups enriched corn meal
½ teaspoon baking soda
1 teaspoon salt
¼ cup peeled fine-chopped,
  onion

1 cup buttermilk
½ cup water, scant

Mix together corn meal, baking soda, salt, onion, buttermilk and water. Let stand 30 minutes when mixture will be stiff; then, with the hands, press into small $1\frac{1}{2}\times 3$-inch oval cakes. Fry until well browned in deep fat at 350°, or hot enough to brown a $\frac{1}{2}$-inch cube of bread in 1 minute. Drain on absorbent paper towels. Serve warm. Makes about 2 dozen.

FLUFFY EGG FLAPJACKS

8 eggs, separated	¼ teaspoon nutmeg
½ cup pancake mix	½ cup sour cream

Beat the egg yolks until lemon-colored; add pancake mix, nutmeg and sour cream and continue beating until smooth. Beat egg whites stiff; gently fold into beaten egg yolk mixture. For each pancake, drop ½ cup batter onto hot, well-oiled griddle. Fry until golden brown on both sides. Makes 12 good-sized pancakes. Accompany with whipped butter and maple syrup; or with a choice of fruit sauces, such as raspberries in syrup, stewed pitted prunes or stewed frozen blueberries.

INDIAN FRY-BREAD

Modern version.

2 cups sifted flour	1 teaspoon salt
3 tablespoons baking powder	1 cup milk

Mix and sift dry ingredients together. Lightly stir in milk and add about 1 tablespoon more if necessary to make a drop batter. Drop by tablespoonfuls into 3 cups of deep hot fat at 375° and fry until golden brown on both sides. Remove with a slotted spoon, drain on absorbent paper and serve hot. Serves 8 to 10.

GRANDMA'S HOTCAKES

2 cups buttermilk
2 teaspoons baking soda
¾ teaspoon salt
½ cup dairy sour cream
2 eggs
½ cup uncooked oatmeal

1 cup plus 2 tablespoons
  unsifted flour
⅔ cup sugar
¾ teaspoon baking powder
¼ cup enriched or whole grain
  corn meal

Pour buttermilk into a 1½-quart mixing bowl. Add soda and salt. Stir in sour cream until mixture foams. Add eggs, beat with spoon until mixed in. Add oatmeal. Sift flour, sugar, baking powder and corn meal into the mixture and beat until flour lumps disappear. Heat and oil a griddle or large, heavy low fry pan. Pour on batter by large tablespoonfuls. Keep 1 inch apart. When deep brown on one side, turn to brown other side. (Watch, they scorch easily!) Accompany with syrup, honey, jam, jelly or preserves. Makes about 20.

OLD RHODE ISLAND JOHNNYCAKES

Scald 2 cups corn meal and ½ teaspoon salt with 2 cups boiling water. Mix and beat to a consistency that will drop from a spoon. Milk sometimes is added to make a drop consistency. Drop by tablespoonfuls onto a well-oiled hot griddle. When baked on one side, turn over. This is an old way of making johnnycakes. Serve hot, plain or with butter or syrup. Makes about 20.

UNCLE JOHN'S APPLE PANCAKES

First, prepare the topping; then the batter, using a basic French batter recipe.

French Pancake Batter:

3 eggs	1 tablespoon melted butter
3 tablespoons powdered sugar	⅛ teaspoon lemon, vanilla or
⅛ teaspoon salt	orange extract
1 cup sifted all-purpose flour	Apple Topping
1 cup half and half	Confectioners' sugar

Beat eggs with sugar until fluffy. Beat in salt and flour; add next three ingredients; mix until creamy. For each 8-inch cake, pour 3 not-heaped tablespoons batter onto fairly hot griddle. (Use an ungreased griddle, or grease it lightly, depending on the type.) Cook until cakes are lightly browned on one side; turn once to cook on other side. To serve, spoon Apple Topping over pancakes; dust with confectioners' sugar. Makes 6 8-inch pancakes or 12 4-inch pancakes.

Apple Topping:

4 medium apples, pared and	¼ cup butter
sliced	¼ teaspoon cinnamon
½ cup sugar	

Combine ingredients. Boil gently until apples are tender.

FRENCH PANCAKES

2 eggs	¼ teaspoon salt
1½ cups milk	1 cup sifted flour
3 drops orange extract	1 tablespoon powdered sugar
3 drops vanilla extract	2 tablespoons powdered sugar

Beat eggs very light; add milk, extracts and salt. Combine flour and 1 tablespoon powdered sugar and beat milk mixture into it, using rotary egg beater or wire whisk.

Heat heavy fry pan or griddle; oil sparingly with butter. Drop on batter by large tablespoonfuls; it will spread. The cakes will be very thin; fold over. Dust each pancake with some additional sugar, and accompany with honey or fruit syrup of any kind in its own glass container. Makes about 16.

CALIFORNIA ENCHILADAS

1 can tomato sauce with tomato bits	3 cups grated Cheddar cheese (¾ pound)
2 tablespoons chopped green chilies	1 cup chopped onion
1 (9-ounce) package frozen tortillas (1 dozen)	¾ cup chopped pitted ripe olives
	4 cups shredded lettuce

Preheat oven to 350°. Combine tomato sauce and green chilies; heat in saucepan large enough to allow for dipping of tortillas. Mix 2 cups of the cheese with onion in bowl. Prepare tortillas as package label directs, then dip in warm sauce. Place rounded tablespoon of cheese-onion mixture on each; roll up securely and place in baking dish, seam side up. Dribble over any remaining sauce, sprinkle with the rest of the cheese. Bake 15 minutes. Remove, sprinkle with chopped olives and lettuce. Allow 2 for each serving.

FLOUR TORTILLAS (TACO SHELLS)

The West and Southwest discovered tacos, dubbed the Mexican sandwich. Tacos are simply warm tortillas folded over a highly seasoned meat filling.

4 cups all-purpose flour	½ cup shortening
2 teaspoons salt	1 cup lukewarm water

Into a 2½-quart mixing bowl, sift together flour and salt. Add shortening and chop in with a pastry blender into coarse flakes.

Mix in lukewarm water. Knead until dough forms a large ball. Divide into 12 equal parts and shape each into a ball. Cover with a sheet of plastic and let stand 15 minutes. Then roll each into a round shape 8 inches in diameter. Cook on an ungreased skillet until golden brown spots form. Turn once to make tacos.

NAVAJO TACOS
Adapted.

1 pound ground beef	1 medium-sized head lettuce, chopped
1 tablespoon cooking oil	
2 teaspoons salt	2 medium-sized tomatoes, chopped, or use drained canned whole tomatoes
½ teaspoon black pepper	
2 teaspoons chili powder	
2 cups cooked or canned pinto beans	½ cup grated cheese
	1 small can green chilies, chopped
Indian Fry-Bread (see Index) or 4 flour tortillas	

Stir-brown beef in oil; add salt, pepper, chili powder and beans. Heat 5 minutes. Spread meat mixture on tops of 4 pieces of fry-bread. Spread chopped lettuce and tomatoes over meat mixture. Top with grated cheese and green chilies. Serves 4.

Yeast Breads

Here are my best yeast bread recipes: buns, rolls and coffee cake; up to the minute in method; nutritious and so-o-o good. Follow directions exactly. And don't panic when you note the amount of time some of them may take—you're not the one who is working, it's the yeast. You only knead as required! Your family will sniff with appreciation the fragrance from the baking oven and be delighted when they taste the result.

CALIFORNIA ORANGE BATTER BREAD

2 packages active dry yeast
½ cup tepid water
⅓ cup sugar
3 large eggs at room
    temperature
1¼ cups orange juice
1½ tablespoons fine-grated
    orange rind, crushed

1 teaspoon fine-grated lemon
    rind, crushed
6½ cups sifted flour
1 cup solid shortening, melted
2 teaspoons salt
Melted shortening or butter

Dissolve yeast in warm water with 1 tablespoon of the sugar; add remaining sugar; beat in eggs, orange juice, orange and lemon rind. Stir in 4 cups of the flour, beat until batter falls in sheets from spoon. Mix in the shortening and salt. Stir in remaining flour; do not add more, as this is a batter bread. Scrape down bowl and spoon. Brush dough lightly with additional melted shortening or butter. Cover; let rise 1½ hours in warm place 80 to 85°, or until doubled in size. Punch down dough. Cover; let rest 10 minutes. Divide dough in half. Place each in an oiled 8-cup (2-quart) Turk's-head mold or gelatin ring mold of same size. Brush top of dough lightly with melted butter. Let rise again until doubled in size. Bake 1 hour in moderate (350°) oven. Makes 1 full size of 2 8-inch rings.

CALIFORNIA RAISIN YEAST BREAD

This recipe makes 2 loaves and takes about 3½ hours to prepare.

2 cups milk, scalded
2 packages or cakes active dry
    or compressed yeast
½ cup tepid water
3 cups sifted all-purpose flour
1 teaspoon salt
¼ teaspoon nutmeg
½ cup sugar

¼ cup melted butter or
    margarine
2 eggs, beaten light
4 cups all-purpose flour, sifted
    before measuring
1½ cups dark seedless raisins
Melted butter or margarine

Cool milk until tepid. Add yeast dissolved in tepid water. Beat in 3 cups flour. Cover; set in warm place for about 30 minutes, or until batter looks "bubbly." Beat in salt, nutmeg, sugar, butter or margarine and eggs. Then beat in 3½ cups of remaining flour. Last, add raisins stirred to coat with ½ cup flour. Turn onto well-floured surface, and knead until dough feels elastic to touch. Replace in lightly oiled 4-quart bowl. Cover; let rise again until doubled in size.

Punch down; cut in halves; shape into loaves and place seam side down in 2 oiled loaf pans. Cover with waxed paper; set to rise until again doubled in size. Bake 40 to 50 minutes in moderate (375°) oven. When done, remove from pans; brush loaves lightly all over with additional melted butter or margarine; cool. Let stand a few hours or overnight before slicing.

CHRISTMAS FRUIT BREAD

This recipe makes 2 loaves.

¾ cup milk	4 eggs, slightly beaten
¾ cup warm water (105 to 115°)	1½ cups chopped citron
	1½ cups raisins
3 packages or cakes yeast, active dry or compressed	1½ cups chopped, candied orange peel
3¼ cups unsifted flour	¾ cup chopped, candied cherries
1½ cups sugar	
¾ teaspoon salt	1½ cups chopped walnut meats
¾ cup (1½ sticks) margarine at room temperature	¾ teaspoon lemon extract

Scald milk; cool to lukewarm. Measure warm water into large warm bowl. Sprinkle or crumble in yeast; stir until dissolved. Stir in milk and 1½ cups flour; beat until smooth. Cover; let rise about 30 minutes in a warm place, free from draft, until doubled in size. Add sugar and salt gradually to margarine, mixing well after each addition. Combine yeast mixture, margarine mixture, eggs, fruits, nuts, lemon extract and remaining flour; beat 5 minutes. Turn into 2 well-oiled 9×5×3-inch loaf pans. Cover; let rise 1 hour in warm place, free from draft. Bake in a moderate (350°) oven about 1 hour, or until golden brown and loaves shrink slightly from sides of pans.

OATMEAL BREAD

This recipe takes 5 hours to prepare, and makes 2 loaves.

1 compressed yeast cake	2 tablespoons shortening
½ cup lukewarm water	½ cup molasses
4 cups flour	1 teaspoon salt
2 cups boiling water	1 cup chopped nuts or raisins
2 cups oatmeal or rolled oats	(optional)

Crumble the yeast cake into the lukewarm water, add 2 tablespoons of the flour, and set aside to "start the yeast." Pour the boiling water over the oatmeal, add the shortening and the molasses and set aside until lukewarm; then combine the 2 mixtures, add 1 cup of the flour, beat thoroughly, cover and set aside in a warm place for 1 hour, until light and full of bubbles. Now add the remainder of the flour with the salt, knead thoroughly, place in an oiled bowl, cover and let rise in a moderately warm place until doubled in bulk—about 2 hours. Divide into 2 portions, knead slightly, place in oiled pans, cover and again let rise until doubled in bulk. Bake 40 to 45 minutes in a moderately hot (375°) oven. If desired, 1 cup of chopped nuts or 1 cup of chopped seeded raisins may be added with the flour.

VERMONT MAPLE OATMEAL BREAD

This recipe makes 2 loaves.

¾ cup boiling water	2 packages active dry yeast
1 cup hot coffee	¼ cup lukewarm water
1 cup rolled oats	2 eggs, unbeaten
⅓ cup shortening	5½ cups sifted all-purpose
½ cup maple syrup	flour or enough to make a
½ cup sugar	stiff dough
2 teaspoons salt	

In a 2-quart mixing bowl, combine boiling water, coffee, rolled oats, shortening, maple syrup, sugar and salt. Cool until luke-warm. Dissolve yeast in lukewarm water and stir into first mix-ture. Beat in eggs one at a time. Gradually add and beat in flour; mix until smooth. Add enough flour as needed to make stiff dough. Place in an oiled 3-quart bowl. Cover with plastic wrap; let rise free from drafts until doubled in size. Transfer to lightly floured smooth surface. Knead until smooth. Divide into 2 loaves. Place in 2 well-oiled 9×5×3-inch loaf pans. Let rise again until doubled in size. Bake 1 hour in moderate (350°) oven.

SOURDOUGH STARTER

Use a glass or pottery container. Never use metal or leave a metal spoon in the starter. Mix well 2 cups flour, 2 cups warm water and 1 package dry yeast or 1 yeast cake, making a batter.

Put in a warm place or closed cupboard overnight. Next morning, put ½ cup of the starter into a scalded and cooled pint jar with a tight cover, and store in the refrigerator or a cool place for future use. This is your sourdough starter. Use remaining batter immediately for hot cakes, waffles, etc.

A good starter smells like clean sour milk. The liquid separates from the batter when it stands several days, but this does not matter. If replenished every few days with flour and enough water to make more batter, the starter keeps fresh. If it is to be kept for several weeks, freeze it.

Make starter batter 1 week before you plan to bake your bread.

Sourdough Bread: Soften 1 package active dry yeast in 1½ cups warm water in a large mixing bowl. Blend in 1 cup starter batter. Add 4 cups sifted all-purpose flour, 2 teaspoons each salt and sugar. Beat 3 to 4 minutes. Cover; let rise in warm place till double (about 1½ hours). Mix ½ teaspoon baking soda with 1 cup sifted flour, and stir into dough. Add enough additional flour to make a stiff dough. Turn out on lightly floured surface and knead 8 to 10 minutes.

Divide dough in 2 portions; cover and let rest 10 minutes. Shape into 2 round or oval loaves. Place on lightly greased baking sheets and make diagonal gashes across top of dough with a sharp knife. Let rise until double (about 1½ hours). Brush surface of loaves with water just before baking at 400° for 35 to 40 minutes, or until crust is brown. Place shallow pan of water on bottom rack in oven.

HOMEMADE WHITE BREAD

This recipe makes 4 1½-pound loaves in less than 4 hours.

3 packages or cakes yeast
¾ cup warm water (100°)
3 cups milk, scalded
4 teaspoons salt
6 tablespoons sugar
¼ pound plus 1 tablespoon
   butter
3 eggs, beaten light
10 to 11 cups sifted all-
   purpose flour
½ cup salad oil

In small bowl, dissolve yeast in warm water. In large (about 5-quart) mixing bowl combine milk, salt, sugar and butter; stir until sugar dissolves. Cool. Add yeast, eggs and 7 cups flour; mix to make a thin "sponge." Cover bowl with clean towel and allow dough to rise at room temperature for 30 minutes. Stir in 3 cups more flour to form a soft dough.

Turn dough out onto a floured pastry board or other smooth surface, and knead until smooth and satiny (about 10 minutes of thorough, *spirited* kneading). The dough will probably pick up an additional cup of flour dusted on board to prevent dough from sticking to it.

Lightly brush dough with oil; place in oiled large bowl. Cover bowl again with clean towel and allow dough to rise in warm (75 to 80°) room until doubled in bulk, at least 1 hour. Punch down with *clenched fist*.

Form into 4 1½-pound loaves; place in well-greased 8×5-

inch aluminum bread pans. Cover pans with clean towel, and let loaves rise in warm room until doubled in bulk (about 1 hour). Preheat oven to 325°; place loaves in oven and bake 40 minutes. Turn loaves out of pans onto wire racks and allow to cool. Store in plastic bags. For week-long storage, keep in refrigerator; or freeze up to 6 weeks.

BABA AU RHUM

European legend has it that this elegant specialty, attributed to the French, originated with a Polish king who named it in honor of the famous Ali Baba. There are many variations of Baba au Rhum, and here is one which appeals to most palates.

1 cake yeast	½ cup currants
¼ cup lukewarm milk	⅓ cup chopped citron
2½ cups flour	½ cup plus 2 tablespoons
½ teaspoon salt	butter at room temperature
4 eggs, lightly beaten	Rum Syrup
3 tablespoons sugar	Whipped cream

Thoroughly mix yeast and milk. Sift flour and salt into large bowl, make a well, and drop in eggs, sugar, currants, citron and yeast mixture. Beat vigorously. Cover bowl and let rise about 40 minutes. Stir down dough, beat in butter. Fill buttered individual custard cups halfway; let dough rise until doubled in bulk. Bake in a 350° oven 30 minutes, or until golden brown. Cool 10 minutes. While still warm, pour Rum Syrup over cakes. Before serving, top with whipped cream. Serves 10 to 12.

Rum Syrup: In saucepan, combine 1 cup sugar, 2 tablespoons apricot jam and ⅔ cup water and bring to a boil. Boil 5 minutes. Remove. Add ½ cup rum. If preferred, any good quality syrup may be used in place of rum syrup.

KING'S CAKE

This rich, spicy and gaily frosted hot bread is enjoyed at parties throughout Louisiana. Baked into each cake is a pecan, a bean or a tiny doll wrapped in foil. When a young man wins the slice with the surprise in it, he is made king of the party. He then chooses a queen and she gives the next party. Should a girl come upon one of these treasures, she selects her king and he arranges the next gala.

2 envelopes active dry yeast
½ cup sugar
½ cup lukewarm water
2 teaspoons salt
¾ teaspoon ground nutmeg or mace
1 teaspoon grated lemon rind
⅓ cup milk, scalded
3 eggs
4½ to 5 cups sifted flour
½ cup shortening, melted

4 ounces glacé citron (⅔ cup)
4 ounces glacé orange peel (⅔ cup)
1 dried bean, a pecan, or a tiny doll
Lemon Confectioners' Sugar Frosting
Glacé citron, cherries, or orange peel or colored candies for decorating

Mix yeast and 1 tablespoon sugar into water. Beat in remaining sugar, salt, nutmeg or mace, lemon rind and milk cooled to lukewarm. Beat in eggs. Stir in 2 cups of the flour. Beat batter until it falls from a spoon in sheets. Mix in shortening, citron and orange peel; add 2 cups of the remaining flour. Turn onto floured surface; knead in remaining flour. Continue to knead until dough is smooth and satiny. Turn into an oiled 3-quart bowl. Cover. Let rise in a warm (85°) place until double in size, about 1¼ hours. Punch down; divide into 3 equal parts. Cover; let rest 10 minutes. Wrap bean, pecan or doll in foil and press into portion of the dough. Roll each portion into strips 30 inches long. Braid the strips. Shape in an oval on oiled cookie sheet. Cover; let rise until double in size. Bake in moderate (375°) oven 25 minutes, or until golden. Cool.

Cover top with Lemon Confectioners' Sugar Frosting. Decorate with glacé citron, cherries, orange peel or colored candies. Serves 14 to 16.

Lemon Confectioners' Sugar Frosting: Blend 2 cups confectioners' sugar with ¼ cup butter, ⅛ teaspoon salt. Beat in 1 teaspoon or more cream or evaporated milk till of spreading consistency. Add 1 teaspoon grated lemon rind. Beat thoroughly.

WILLIAMSBURG SALLY LUNN

1½ cups milk
1 cup (2 sticks) butter or margarine at room temperature
½ cup sugar
2 teaspoons salt

½ cup warm water (105 to 115°)
2 packages or cakes active dry or compressed yeast
3 eggs
6½ cups unsifted flour

Scald milk; cool to lukewarm. Stir butter until smooth in large mixing bowl. Gradually mix in sugar and salt. Measure warm water into warm small bowl. Sprinkle or crumble in yeast; stir until dissolved. Add lukewarm milk, dissolved yeast, eggs and flour to first mixture. Beat vigorously 2 minutes with mixing spoon. Cover; set to rise in warm place, free from draft, about 1 hour or until doubled in size. Stir down and divide dough in half. Spoon each half into an oiled 9-inch angel food cake tube pan. Cover; set to rise again in warm place, free from draft, until doubled in size, about 1 hour. Bake 30 to 35 minutes in moderate (350°) oven, or until well browned and bread does not stick to pan.

YEAST-RAISED BATTER MUFFINS

Plain or use any one of the special variations.

⅔ cup milk
2 tablespoons sugar
1½ teaspoons salt
1 tablespoon margarine
¼ cup warm water (105 to 115°)

1 package or cake active dry or compressed yeast
1 egg, beaten
2¼ cups unsifted flour

Heat milk until bubbles form at edge; stir in sugar, salt and margarine; cool to lukewarm. Measure warm water into warmed large bowl. Sprinkle or crumble in yeast; stir until dissolved; mix in lukewarm milk mixture. Add egg and flour. Beat until smooth. Cover; let rise at warm room temperature (70 to 75°), free from draft, for about 1 hour, or until doubled in size. This is the basic batter.

Spoon batter into 12 oiled 2¾-inch muffin cups to the half-full mark. Cover; let rise 30 minutes in warm place, free from draft, or until doubled in size. Bake 20 to 25 minutes in moderate (375°) oven. Serve warm, or when still fresh-baked. Makes 12.

Orange-Sugar Puffs: Spoon enough of the preceding basic yeast-raised muffin batter into 12 oiled muffin cups to half full. Cover; let rise 30 minutes, or until doubled in size, in warm place, free from draft. Bake 20 to 25 minutes in moderate (375°) oven. Remove from muffin pans; immediately roll muffins in 6 tablespoons melted butter or margarine, coating all sides; then roll in mixture of ½ cup sugar, 1 tablespoon grated orange peel and ⅛ teaspoon nutmeg.

Cheese Caraway Muffins: Stir ½ cup grated Cheddar cheese and 1 teaspoon caraway seeds into the basic batter for yeast-raised muffins. Spoon into 12 oiled muffin cups. Cover; let rise 30 minutes, or until doubled in size, in warm place, free from draft. Bake 20 to 25 minutes in moderate (375°) oven.

Herbed Onion Muffins: Lightly toss together 2 tablespoons fine-chopped onion with 1 teaspoon fine-chopped parsley and ½ teaspoon each of powdered oregano, thyme and poultry seasoning. Stir into the basic batter for yeast-raised muffins. Spoon into 12 oiled muffin cups. Cover; let rise 30 minutes, or until doubled in size, in a warm place, free from draft. Bake 20 to 25 minutes in a moderate (375°) oven.

CORN MEAL CRESCENTS

1 cake compressed or	1 cup milk, scalded
1 package dry yeast	1 egg, lightly beaten
¼ cup lukewarm water	3¾ to 4¼ cups sifted flour
¼ cup butter or margarine	¾ cup enriched corn meal
¼ cup sugar	Melted shortening
2 teaspoons salt	Melted butter

Soften yeast in lukewarm water. (Use warmer water for dry yeast.) Combine butter, sugar and salt, and pour scalded milk over it; stir occasionally until butter melts. Cool until lukewarm. Stir in egg and 1 cup of the flour. Add softened yeast and corn meal. Stir in enough of remaining flour to make a soft dough. Turn out on lightly floured surface; knead 10 minutes, or until smooth and satiny. Round dough into ball; place in an oiled 3-quart bowl; brush lightly with *melted* shortening. Cover and let rise in a warm place until double in size, about 1 hour.

Punch down dough; cover; let rest 10 minutes. Divide dough in thirds. Roll each part to form 11-inch circle. Brush lightly with *melted* butter; cut in 8 pie-shaped wedges. Roll each wedge from wide end to the point. Place on oiled cookie sheets. Bend ends of each roll to form crescent.

Cover; let rise in warm place about 45 minutes, or until nearly doubled in size. Bake in preheated moderate (375°) oven about 15 minutes. Makes 2 dozen.

HOT CROSS BUNS

Among the famous buns of England, none is more famous than the Hot Cross Buns made to sell from early morning to evening on Good Friday.

2 packages dry granular yeast
or 2 cakes compressed yeast
½ cup lukewarm water
⅓ cup sugar
½ cup milk, scalded and
cooled till lukewarm
3½ cups enriched flour
½ cup margarine, melted
1½ teaspoons salt

½ teaspoon ground cinnamon
¼ teaspoon ground allspice
3 eggs, well beaten
½ cup raisins
¼ cup fine-cut citron
1 egg white
Royal Confectioners' Sugar
Frosting

Soften yeast 3 minutes in lukewarm water and stir. Add with sugar to lukewarm milk. Add 1 cup of the flour and beat well. Beat in melted margarine, and remaining flour sifted with salt and spices. Stir in beaten eggs, raisins and citron. Cover with waxed paper. Let rise 1 hour, or until doubled in size. Punch down, let stand covered 10 minutes. Roll ½ inch thick and cut with a 2-inch floured biscuit cutter. Place 2 inches apart on oiled cookie sheet. Brush tops with slightly beaten egg white. Cover with waxed paper and let rise again until doubled in size. Bake 25 minutes in moderate (350°) oven. Cool and make cross of Royal Confectioners' Sugar Frosting on each bun. Makes 3 dozen.

Royal Confectioners' Sugar Frosting: Put 2½ teaspoons boiling water in a pint-sized bowl. Add a few grains salt and ½ teaspoon vanilla or other flavoring. Gradually stir in 1½ to 2 cups sifted confectioners' sugar, or sufficient to make frosting thick enough to spread.

ORANGE HONEY ROLLS

¼ cup frozen Florida orange
juice concentrate, thawed
and undiluted
2 tablespoons honey

1 (4- or 6-ounce) package
baked soft dinner rolls
⅓ cup raisins

Combine and mix orange juice concentrate and honey. Place rolls
on foil-lined baking sheet. Brush orange mixture over rolls. Dot
with raisins. Bake in moderate (375°) oven 15 minutes, frequently spooning over orange mixture.

PARKER HOUSE ROLLS

2 cups scalded milk
1 compressed yeast cake
2 tablespoons sugar
¼ cup melted shortening

6 cups bread flour (about)
1 teaspoon salt
Melted shortening

Scald and cool the milk, crumble the yeast cake into it, add the
sugar, and set aside for 10 minutes to "start" the yeast. Beat in
the melted shortening and half the flour and continue beating until perfectly smooth. Cover and set aside to rise in a warm place
about 1 hour, or until very light. Then add the remainder of the
flour and the salt, knead thoroughly, place in an oiled bowl, brush
over with additional melted shortening, and again set aside to rise
until doubled in bulk—1½ hours. Roll out ¼ inch thick, brush
slightly with melted shortening, cut into rounds with a biscuit
cutter, crease through the center and fold over. Place the rolls on
a flat oiled baking sheet a little distance apart, cover and allow
them to rise again for 45 minutes or until very light. Bake in a
hot (400°) oven 10 to 12 minutes. Makes about 5 dozen.

AWARD-WINNING POTATO ROLLS

½ cup sugar
2 teaspoons salt
2 cups hot potato water*
2 packages or cakes yeast,
    active dry or compressed
2 eggs, beaten

6 cups sifted all-purpose flour
    (about)
½ cup butter or margarine,
    melted and cooled
2 tablespoons melted butter

Dissolve sugar and salt in hot potato water in large mixing bowl. Cool to lukewarm (not hot). Add yeast; stir until dissolved. Stir in beaten eggs. Beat in half of flour with spoon or mixer until batter is smooth and very elastic. Beat in ½ cup of the melted butter and gradually work in remaining flour until dough is no longer sticky to touch. Knead dough until smooth and elastic, from 8 to 10 minutes. Put into oiled clean mixing bowl. Brush top with part of additional butter; cover with foil or clean towel. Let rise in warm (85 to 90°) place until doubled in size and light to touch—about 1 hour. Punch down and shape into round rolls. Place in oiled round pans, brush with leftover additional butter and cover with a clean towel. Let rise again in a warm place until doubled in size. Bake in a hot (425°) oven 10 to 12 minutes, or until golden brown. Brush with remaining butter. Makes 3 dozen.

* Hot potato water is water in which peeled white potatoes have been boiled.

DUTCH PRETZELS

1½ cups lukewarm water
1 package dry yeast
½ teaspoon sugar
4½ cups sifted flour

1 egg
1 teaspoon water
½ cup coarse salt crystals
    (about)

Mix water, yeast and sugar in a 2-quart mixing bowl. Let stand 1 hour. Stir in flour. On lightly floured surface, knead dough 7 minutes. Replace dough in bowl. Cover. Let rise until doubled in size. Cut off small pieces, about 1×2 inches, and use your hands to roll and twist dough into pretzel shapes to suit your fancy. Arrange ¼ inch apart on baking sheet. Beat egg and water together until mixed; brush over pretzels to form a glaze when baked. Dust with salt crystals. Bake 10 minutes or more according to size, or until golden brown, in moderate (350 to 375°) oven. Remove from pan and cool. How many pretzels does this make? That depends on the size. A lot, if they are small!

SOURDOUGH HOT CAKES

Place ½ cup Sourdough Starter (see Index) in a medium-size mixing bowl. Add 2 cups warm water and 2 cups flour. Beat well; cover and set in a warm place, free from draft, to develop overnight. In the morning, the batter (called a sponge) will have gained half its bulk again and be covered with air bubbles. Set aside ½ cup sponge in refrigerator for next use.

Beat the remaining sponge with a fork and add 2 eggs, 1½ teaspoons salt, 2 teaspoons baking soda, 1 tablespoon sugar and 2 tablespoons cooking oil, mixing in ingredients as listed. Drop by tablespoonfuls onto a hot, slightly oiled griddle. Turn once when bubbles form and hot cakes are lightly browned on bottom. Serve with melted butter and brown sugar or maple syrup, molasses or jelly.

Sandwiches

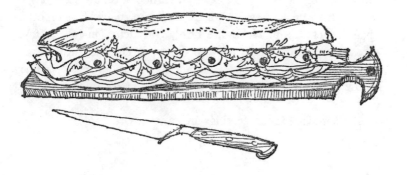

Once upon a time a sandwich was something hefty and filling to be packed for a picnic, or at the other extreme, was a dainty tidbit to be nibbled on at teatime. The sandwich family has grown so that now they are eaten at all hours, on all occasions—for lunch, supper, between meals, as a late snack. Hot or cold, open or closed, sandwiches are firmly entrenched in bills of fare across the country—in truck-stop diners, in chic restaurants and in homes like yours. It was difficult to select the most popular sandwiches but I think you'll enjoy the variety offered in this chapter.

All recipes are for six servings unless otherwise stated.

CLOSED SANDWICHES

India-Chicken: Spread slices of buttered white or cheese bread with chopped drained chutney. Put together with thin slices of lightly seasoned chicken.

Ham Sandwiches Washington State: Put buttered rye bread together with minced flavorful smoked ham blended with ¾ the quantity grated raw apple and moistened with mustard-mayonnaise, topped with thin-sliced firm tomato.

CHEESE-FILLED BOLOGNA SANDWICHES

1 (3-ounce) package cream cheese
2 tablespoons orange marmalade
¼ teaspoon prepared mustard
12 thin slices bologna
3 tablespoons soft butter or margarine
8 slices enriched bread

Combine cream cheese, marmalade and mustard; chill. For each sandwich: Spread 1 tablespoon cheese mixture over each of 2 slices bologna; stack one on top of the other, spread sides up. Top with third slice bologna. Butter the bread. Insert a bologna stack between each 2 slices buttered bread. Makes 4 sandwiches.

COTTAGE CHEESE SANDWICH SPREAD

Cottage cheese is so bland in taste that it can be used with strong seasonings as the basis for a snappy spread for sandwiches. Serve on a plate with a vegetable garnish and top off with fresh or stewed fruit and coffee or tea for a refreshing luncheon.

Cottage Cheese Anchovy Filling: Fine-chop 6 anchovies; mix into 1 (8-ounce) carton creamed or skim-milk cottage cheese. Stir in 2 tablespoons each minced radishes and pickle relish.

Cottage Cheese Tomato Filling: Fine-chop 1 good-sized peeled tomato. Stir until puréed with 1 tablespoon minced chives, ½ teaspoon snappy mustard, ½ teaspoon crushed caraway seeds and 1 (8-ounce) carton creamed or skim-milk cottage cheese.

CREOLE CHEESE SANDWICH

2 cups shredded sharp
American cheese (½ pound)
½ cup fine-diced green pepper
6 slices cooked bacon, diced
6 tablespoons chili sauce
½ teaspoon Worcestershire
sauce
6 to 8 buttered rolls or buns or
12 to 16 slices bread

Combine and mix all ingredients. Spread generously between halves of buttered rolls, buns or thick slices of French bread. Place on a baking sheet. Put in a hot (425°) oven until lightly browned. Makes 3 cups spread, enough for 6 to 8 sandwiches.

EGG-PICCALILLI SANDWICHES

⅔ cup chopped hard-cooked eggs

3 tablespoons sweet pickle relish or Piccalilli (see Index)

¼ cup mayonnaise or salad dressing

3 tablespoons butter or margarine at room temperature

8 slices raisin bread

Combine eggs, Piccalilli and mayonnaise. Butter bread. Spread 3 tablespoons filling between each 2 slices of buttered bread. Makes 4 sandwiches.

PARADISE SALMON SANDWICHES

½ cup Country Coleslaw Dressing (see Index)

1½ teaspoons lemon juice

¼ teaspoon powdered tarragon

¼ teaspoon onion salt

1 tablespoon fine-chopped green pepper

½ cup shredded American cheese

1 (7¾-ounce) can salmon, drained and boned

1 cup fine-chopped cabbage

12 slices enriched bread

¼ cup butter or margarine at room temperature

6 lettuce leaves

Combine slaw dressing, lemon juice, tarragon and onion salt. Add green pepper, cheese, salmon and cabbage; toss to blend, making a filling. Smooth-spread each bread slice with about 1 teaspoon butter. Make sandwiches, spreading ⅓ cup salmon filling and a lettuce leaf between each 2 buttered bread slices.

ROYAL CANADIAN BACON SANDWICH

1 cup canned pineapple juice

3 tablespoons table mustard

½ cup brown sugar (packed)

1 tablespoon prepared horseradish

18 (1-ounce) slices Canadian bacon

2 dozen canned French-fried onion rings, heated

12 slices wheat bread

Combine pineapple juice, mustard, brown sugar and horseradish. Add Canadian bacon slices and marinate in mixture at least 2 hours. Remove bacon from sauce; brown bacon on both sides under medium hot broiler. Sandwich 3 slices bacon and 4 onion rings between each 2 bread slices.

WESTERN SANDWICHES

For these the bread should be either cut in large rounds or cut from a round loaf and lightly buttered. For each sandwich allow 1 beaten egg, 1 tablespoon scraped or minced onion, and 3 tablespoons minced ham, cooked in butter in a small frying pan until firm like a pancake.

CLUB SANDWICH CONTINENTAL

Lightly toast 3 slices decrusted white bread. Brush generously with melted butter. Put sandwiches together with thin slices of Emmentaler cheese, smoked ham and sliced cold chicken. Press down into shape; wrap in waxed paper; chill. To serve, cut in triangles. Stick these onto long thin bamboo skewers. Thrust one end of the skewer into a small, whole tomato so it can stand up smartly. Garnish with tomato quarters, pickled onions and water cress. Pass Thousand Island dressing. Serves 1.

CINNAMON-ORANGE FRENCH TOAST

3 eggs, beaten	½ teaspoon ground cinnamon
1 cup milk	12 slices enriched bread
½ teaspoon fine-grated orange rind	Orange Butter

In shallow bowl, combine beaten eggs, milk, orange rind and cinnamon. With tongs, dip bread slices into egg mixture, one at a time, turning to coat both sides. Pan-fry bread on both sides in butter or margarine. Serve hot, each topped with 1 tablespoon Orange Butter.

Orange Butter:

½ cup soft butter or   1 teaspoon fine-grated orange
   margarine   rind
1 cup sifted confectioners'   2 tablespoons orange
   sugar   concentrate (not diluted)

Combine butter, sugar, orange rind and concentrate. Whip together until light and fluffy. Serve over Cinnamon-Orange
French Toast.

SAVORY FRENCH TOAST SANDWICHES

These sandwiches may be made in advance, wrapped in plastic
bags and refrigerated overnight to fry for breakfast.

Lightly spread 12 slices enriched white or whole wheat bread
with softened butter or margarine. Fit on thin-sliced meat loaf,
tongue, luncheon meat, chicken, turkey, Swiss or American
cheese, or spread with peanut butter. Put the slices together in
pairs. Cut in half if you like.

Dip quickly in and out of Egg Wash; fry 4 minutes, or until
golden brown on both sides, in 3 tablespoons margarine.

Egg Wash: Beat 3 eggs until frothy with ¾ cup milk. Add ¼ teaspoon salt, and a choice of ⅛ teaspoon ground cinnamon, clove
or nutmeg.

FRENCH-TOASTED SHRIMP SANDWICH

We suggest this delicious sandwich as the main dish at any casual meal—perhaps Sunday brunch after Mass or other church services.

1 pound cooked and chopped shrimp (about 2 cups)	½ cup cream cheese, softened
⅔ cup chili sauce	3 eggs, beaten
⅔ cup mayonnaise or salad dressing	3 tablespoons milk
	¾ teaspoon salt
18 slices bacon, crisply cooked	6 parsley sprigs
12 slices enriched white bread	12 ripe olives
	6 sweet pickle fans

Marinate shrimp in chili sauce 30 minutes. Add mayonnaise or salad dressing. Crumble 6 bacon slices into shrimp mixture; toss lightly. Spread bread with cream cheese. Cover 6 slices with shrimp mixture; close sandwiches, spread side down. Blend together eggs, milk and salt. Lightly butter grill or fry pan; preheat to moderate heat. Dip both sides of sandwiches in egg mixture. Grill on both sides until golden brown. Place 2 bacon slices diagonally across each sandwich and garnish with parsley, 2 olives, 1 pickle fan.

OPEN SANDWICHES

Chicken-Liver Pâté and Brisket of Beef: Spread 1 large thin slice sour-rye bread with butter and plenty of chicken liver pâté. Top with thin-sliced brisket of beef (fat removed). Garnish with whole cherry tomatoes and water cress.

Cottage Cheese: Top sliced dark or sour-dough bread, plain or toasted, with cottage cheese, then with crisp bacon, sautéed thin-sliced luncheon meat, smoked fish or canned sardines.

ALASKA KING CRAB SWISS OPEN SANDWICHES

1 (6-ounce) package frozen
   Alaska king crab meat
⅓ cup Italian salad dressing
   (not sweet)
8 large slices rye bread
¼ cup butter at room
   temperature
4 (1-ounce) slices Swiss cheese

8 thin slices tomato
½ cup sour cream
2 tablespoons chopped fresh or
   1 teaspoon ground dill weed
6 medium lettuce leaves
8 cherry tomatoes
4 lemon wedges

Defrost, drain, then flake crab meat. Stir in Italian dressing. Refrigerate at least 15 minutes. Meantime, spread rye bread with butter. Cover 4 of the slices with Swiss cheese and top with chunks of crab meat. Cover each of remaining 4 slices of bread with 2 slices tomato. Mix sour cream and dill. Place a lettuce leaf filled with 2 tablespoons of this mixture atop each tomato slice. Arrange on individual plates. Garnish with cherry tomatoes and lemon wedges. Serves 4.

DELMONICO TURKEY SANDWICHES

4 tablespoons butter or
   margarine
4 tablespoons flour
¾ teaspoon salt
¼ teaspoon prepared mustard
Dash of cayenne pepper
2 cups milk
2 cups grated processed
   American cheese (½
   pound)

4 slices toast
8 medium-sized slices cooked
   turkey
¼ teaspoon paprika
4 slices crisp bacon
2 medium-sized tomatoes,
   sliced

In saucepan over low heat, melt butter or margarine. Stir and mix in flour, salt, mustard and cayenne. Stir in milk; cook-stir until thickened, smooth and boiling. Remove from heat. Add cheese and stir until melted, making a sauce. Arrange toast in shallow 10×6-inch baking dish. Top each slice with 2 slices turkey, and pour cheese sauce over. Dust with paprika; bake 10 minutes at 450°. Garnish with crisp bacon slices and sliced tomato. Serves 4.

SWISS TOAST MOUNTAINEER STYLE

6 full slices buttered white toast	6 slices tomato
6 (¼-inch) slices cooked tender ham	Salt and pepper
	6 poached eggs
6 (⅛-inch) slices Swiss cheese	12 strips pimiento

Put buttered toast in an open low casserole or baking pan. Cover with cooked ham and cheese. Place in hot (400°) oven until cheese melts. Top with slice of tomato, dust lightly with little salt and pepper; finish with 1 poached egg. Garnish with crisscrossed strips of pimiento. Serve at once.

ASSORTED GRILLED OPEN SANDWICHES

Prepare the makings, ready to grill in a table broiler. For each person start with 1 large slice enriched white or other bread (crust on) toasted on one side. Butter the untoasted side. Top this side smoothly all the way out to the edge with the chosen topping. Grill 3 to 4 inches from the source of heat. Garnish at top or side of each sandwich, as appropriate.

HAM OR TONGUE GRILLED OPEN SANDWICH

For 6 persons, provide 6 large slices enriched bread, 3 tablespoons butter, ¼ pound thin-sliced cooked smoked ham or tongue, ¼ pound thin-sliced Swiss or Cheddar cheese, a shake of paprika. Garnish with 2 small tomatoes, cut into sections, and 6 lettuce leaves.

To assemble, completely cover the buttered untoasted side of the bread with the ham or tongue. Top with a choice of the Swiss or Cheddar cheese. Grill about 2 minutes 4 inches from the source of heat, or until hot and bubbling. Dust with paprika. Garnish each with tomato sections in a lettuce leaf.

SNAPPY CHOPPED BEEF GRILLED OPEN SANDWICH

For 6 persons, provide 6 large slices enriched white or cracked wheat bread, 3 tablespoons butter, 1 pound chopped beef (ground twice) mixed with 1 chopped peeled small onion or ½ teaspoon powdered onion, 1½ teaspoons Worcestershire sauce, 6 drops Tabasco and ½ tablespoon mayonnaise, 6 pickled artichokes, 3 small red radishes (sliced), 6 small lettuce leaves.

To assemble, toast the bread on one side and butter the untoasted side. Spread beef mixture evenly out to the edges. Grill for 4 minutes 4 inches from the source of heat. Garnish with a pickled artichoke and a few radish slices in a lettuce leaf.

LIVERWURST-ONION GRILLED OPEN SANDWICH

For 6 persons provide 6 large slices bread (enriched white or sour rye with caraway seeds), ½ pound liverwurst, 2 tablespoons butter, 1 peeled fine-chopped onion, 1 fine-chopped large mushroom, ½ teaspoon Dijon mustard, 1 teaspoon mayonnaise, 2 drained canned pimientos cut in ¼-inch strips, 6 ripe and 6 pimiento-stuffed olives.

Toast the bread on one side and butter the untoasted side. Prepare the topping as follows: Remove skin, chop and sauté the liverwurst in 2 tablespoons butter until lightly browned. Add onion and mushroom; sauté 3 minutes. Add Dijon mustard and mayonnaise.

To assemble, spread sautéed liverwurst filling evenly on the untoasted side of the bread, covering completely. Arrange pimiento strips on top. Grill about 3 minutes, or until a bubbling brown. Garnish with 1 ripe and 1 pimiento-stuffed olive.

TOASTED OPEN PEANUT BUTTER SANDWICH

Spread a full slice of caraway rye bread generously with peanut butter, either the chunky or the creamy version. Slip it under the broiler about 3 inches from the source of heat and toast the top side only. Serve steamy hot and slightly browned, with fruit and milk—refreshing and satisfying.

TUNA-CHEESE GRILLED OPEN SANDWICH

Decrust enriched bread, a good-sized slice for each sandwich. Toast on one side. Then cool and spread evenly with room-soft butter.

For 4 sandwiches, flake-fine contents of 1 (7½-ounce) can tuna, drained and seasoned with 3 drops Tabasco, 1 fine-minced drained pimiento, choice of ¼ teaspoon ground dill, or tarragon or celery salt, the juice ¼ lemon and ½ tablespoon mayonnaise or enough to make it spreadable. Smooth-spread over buttered toast out to edges. Top each sandwich with thin slice of Swiss cheese. Grill 4 to 6 inches from source of heat until cheese melts; or slip into plastic bags and refrigerate up to 24 hours until time to grill. Do not freeze. Serve piping hot with the Smooth Mushroom Sauce.

Smooth Mushroom Sauce: In blender, buzz contents 1 (10½-ounce) can condensed cream of mushroom soup, ½ cup milk, ⅛ teaspoon freeze-dried shallots or pinch each garlic and onion powder. Then heat-stir to boiling point.

TEATIME OPEN SANDWICHES

Small slices of bread cut quite thin, all with a top garnish.

Cucumber Sandwiches: Round slices buttered bread each topped with a thin slice fresh cucumber, first brushed with French dressing and dusted with coarse-ground pepper.

Curried Chicken Pâté Sandwiches: Combine and mix 1 (4-ounce) can chicken pâté with ½ teaspoon curry powder and 2 tablespoons mayonnaise to blend. Spread on oblongs of buttered bread. Garnish with pimiento dots or slices of red radish.

Egg/Green Pepper Sandwiches: Make a spread of fine-chopped, hot hard-cooked eggs, combined with 1 tablespoon each pickle relish and fine-minced green pepper, and 2 tablespoons mayonnaise to blend. Spread on rounds of whole wheat bread. Garnish with thin strips of green pepper.

Cream Cheese/Water Cress Sandwiches: Spread round or triangular slices of bread with a mixture of 3 parts cream cheese and 1 part fine-chopped water cress; mix with 2 tablespoons mayonnaise. Garnish with a leaf of water cress lightly pressed into the topping.

CAPE COD LOBSTER ROLLS

¾ cup mayonnaise
1 clove garlic, peeled and
    mashed
1 tablespoon fine-chopped
    parsley
1 teaspoon tarragon
½ teaspoon salt
2 or 3 drops Tabasco

2 teaspoons lemon juice
2½ cups bite-sized pieces
    cooked lobster meat
⅓ cup fine-minced celery
¼ cup fine-minced onion
6 hot dog rolls
Butter at room temperature

Thoroughly blend mayonnaise, garlic, parsley, tarragon, salt, Tabasco and lemon juice. Add lobster, celery and onion and blend well. Spread split hot dog rolls with soft butter and bake split side up in a 400° oven until lightly browned. Spread equal portions of lobster mixture over each.

HAWAIIAN CUBE STEAK SANDWICHES

1 tablespoon dry mustard
12 (3-ounce) cube steaks
1½ cups soy sauce

1 section garlic, peeled and
    crushed
12 sliced sesame sandwich buns

Dust dry mustard over each side of steaks; place in shallow dish. Pour soy sauce over steaks, add garlic, cover and let stand for several hours. Remove steaks from marinade and grill over medium heat. To serve, sandwich each steak between a split bun. Makes 12 sandwiches.

LOBSTER SANDWICHES FROM MAINE

Slice crisp fresh rolls lengthwise. Butter lightly. Put together with a small lettuce leaf and canned Maine lobster diced small and mixed with mayonnaise.

INDIVIDUAL OYSTER LOAVES

Homemakers in the early part of this century often used long pointed French bread-type rolls as containers in which to serve lobster Newburg, creamed shrimp or oysters in Danish Cream Sauce as in the following recipe:

12 crusty long French rolls (2 to a person)	Grated rind of ¼ lemon
	Pinch of ground nutmeg
3 tablespoons soft butter or margarine	½ teaspoon salt
	¼ teaspoon pepper
1 pint shucked or canned oysters	2 cups Danish Cream Sauce
	½ teaspoon minced parsley

Slice off tops from rolls. Hollow out interiors and make crumbs. Brush rolls inside and outside with some of the butter. Place in hot oven to brown. Fry removed crumbs in remaining butter. Cut oysters in half; then place with their liquid in saucepan with lemon rind and seasonings. With fork, stir over low heat for 3 minutes, or until edges ruffle. Add Danish Cream Sauce and stir in half the fried crumbs. Spoon into browned rolls. Garnish with remaining crumbs and parsley.

Danish Cream Sauce: Prepare 2 cups medium-thick White Sauce (see Index). Beat in 1 tablespoon mayonnaise, 1 teaspoon each lemon juice and minced parsley.

POLPETTINE HERO À LA TRATTORIA

Little Italian Meat Balls
6 (8-inch) loaves Italian bread
3 tablespoons melted butter
¾ cup brown gravy
   (homemade or canned)
¾ cup canned tomato sauce

½ tablespoon table mustard
¾ cup grated Parmesan cheese
½ pound mozzarella cheese,
   sliced
¾ cup minced fresh parsley

First shape Little Italian Meat Balls the size of small marbles, and sauté. Slice off tops of bread loaves (toast to serve as an accompaniment); hollow out loaf interiors; brush interiors with melted butter. Mix together and heat brown gravy, tomato sauce and table mustard. Spread mixture over bottom of each bread loaf. Cover with meat balls making one layer. Dust with Parmesan cheese. Top with mozzarella cheese, then with minced parsley. Bake 20 minutes in a moderate (350°) oven, or until sizzling hot.

Little Italian Meat Balls:

½ cup fine-crumbed white
   bread
1 cup water
2 teaspoons beef broth powder
1 pound twice-ground beef or
   equal parts beef, pork and
   veal
½ cup grated Parmesan cheese
2 teaspoons salt

½ teaspoon pepper
½ teaspoon ground basil
¼ teaspoon garlic powder
2 tablespoons peeled grated
   tart apple
½ cup peeled fine-chopped
   onion
3 tablespoons flour
¼ cup olive oil

Mix thoroughly all ingredients except flour and oil. Shape mixture into small marble-sized balls. Dust lightly with flour. Let stand 10 minutes to set coating. Brown all over in oil, then slow-sauté 4 minutes.

SLOPPY JOES

2 pounds ground beef
1 tablespoon oil
1 cup peeled chopped onion
1 clove garlic, mashed
2 small (3-ounce) cans
   chopped mushrooms
2 (10¾-ounce) cans
   condensed tomato soup

2 tablespoons prepared
   mustard
½ teaspoon salt
⅛ teaspoon pepper
12 buns, split and toasted

Brown beef in oil and cook with onion and garlic until tender. Stir to separate the pieces of meat. Pour off any fat. Add mushrooms, drained; soup, mustard and seasonings. Simmer-cook over low heat 10 minutes, stirring occasionally. Spoon over buns. Serves 12.

Desserts

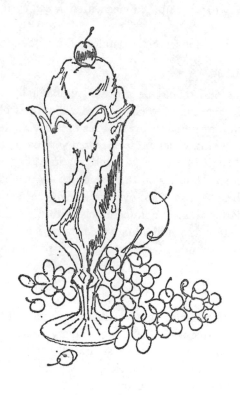

Dessert is a fitting climax to a luncheon or dinner. In fact, a meal seems unfinished without the dessert finale. Dessert is a natural energizer and—if you need a rationale—it adds a sense of well-being to wind up a dinner with a sweet, even a small portion.

All recipes are for six servings unless otherwise stated.

BAKED ALASKA

This unique dessert may be prepared individually or for service at the table. Place on a wooden board a thin layer of spongecake cut an inch larger than a brick of ice cream. On this unmold a brick of ice cream, which must be frozen very hard; cover at once with Mile High Meringue (see Index), spreading it thickly all over the cream, putting on the remainder by means of a pastry bag or tube. Place in a hot oven to brown the meringue, transfer to a platter and serve immediately with a garnish of flowers if desired. If made individually, cones of ice cream may be placed upon rounds of spongecake, the procedure being the same.

CRÊPES

Crêpes are filled pancake specialties in France. They are presented as an entree when the filling is savory, or as a dessert when it is sweet. In deluxe French restaurants, delightful entrees are made by filling crêpes with a rich, savory chicken-mushroom or crab meat and cream sauce mixture. Sometimes these are served "flambé"—flaming—in a copper skillet or chafing dish.

Another version of the French pancake, called "blinis," is served in several central European countries. The filling is of drained cooked dried fruit or sometimes slightly sweetened cream cheese or cottage cheese. They are always folded in square shape before final heating in butter in a fry pan or in a buttered baking dish in the oven. Then they are usually dusted with powdered sugar and accompanied with dairy sour cream.

Crêpes of all kinds are popular in America. Most forms of crêpes may be made in advance. A general recipe suitable for both savory and sweet crêpes is included below:

3 eggs, beaten	½ cup pancake mix
½ cup milk	Butter

Combine eggs and milk. Add pancake mix, beating with a rotary beater until smooth. Place 1 teaspoon butter in an 8-inch fry pan and heat until butter bubbles. Pour in 1 tablespoon batter and immediately tilt pan to coat bottom with thin layer. Fry until delicately browned on underside; turn and cook on other side. Continue, adding 1 teaspoon butter each time until batter is used. Fill each crêpe as desired and roll up or fold in squares. Makes 16.

CRÊPES ALASKA

In advance make 2 saucer-sized French pancakes per person. Fry in butter until pale gold. Fold in quarters; cover and set aside. At serving time heat 3 tablespoons unsalted butter. Squeeze in juice of an orange and ½ teaspoon lemon juice. Add 1 cup orange marmalade. Heat till melted. Add pancakes, turn to coat. Pancakes will glaze and slightly brown. Serve each pancake topped with a half scoop of butter pecan or vanilla ice cream.

GLAMOUR CHEESECAKE

Zweiback piecrust (see Index)	Grated rind of ½ lemon
1 pound cottage cheese	Juice of ½ lemon
½ cup heavy cream	3 grated zwieback
3 eggs, separated	Cream of tartar
¾ cup sugar	Canned stewed red cherries
⅓ teaspoon salt	(optional)

Rub a 9-inch spring form with butter or margarine; line with zwieback piecrust, packing it in. Prepare filling. Mash cottage cheese very fine with fork. Stir in cream; beat and add egg yolks; mix well. Add sugar, salt, grated lemon rind and juice and grated zwieback. Beat egg whites stiff with cream of tartar and fold in. Transfer to spring form. Bake 50 minutes in a moderate (350°) oven, or until cheese shrinks from sides of pan, is firm in center and light brown on top. Cool in pan and unmold. Serve as is or with canned stewed red cherries. Serves 8.

QUICK CHEESECAKE WITH FRUIT TOPPING

1 (10¾-ounce) package
    unbaked cheesecake mix
    containing a crust-mix
    pouch and a filling-mix
    pouch
3 tablespoons sugar
¼ cup butter or margarine,
    melted

1½ cups cold milk
2 (10-ounce) packages of
    quick-thaw frozen peaches
    and strawberries
1½ tablespoons cornstarch

First make the crust: Empty contents of crust-mix pouch into small bowl. Add sugar and butter. Mix well. Press mixture firmly with back of metal spoon over bottom and sides of an 8-inch pie plate. Refrigerate 15 minutes before filling or bake crust 8 to 10 minutes at 375° before chilling.

To make filling, measure milk into a bowl. Add contents of filling-mix pouch from package of cheesecake mix. Blend well at low speed of electric mixer or with rotary beater; then beat 3 minutes at medium speed or until very thick. Pour into chilled crust. Refrigerate while preparing glaze.

Thaw fruit as directed on package. Drain, pouring syrup in small saucepan. Stir cornstarch into syrup. Cook-stir over medium heat until mixture boils. Continue to boil 3 minutes, or until thickened. Remove from heat. Cook 5 minutes. Gently stir in fruit, carefully spoon over the top of cheesecake. Refrigerate until glaze is set. This makes an 8-inch cheesecake.

TOFFEE-BUTTERSCOTCH CREAM PUFFS

¾ cup water	⅛ teaspoon salt
6 tablespoons butter or margarine	3 eggs
¾ cup sifted enriched flour	Toffee-Butterscotch Cream Filling

Combine water and butter in a quart-sized saucepan. Bring to boil. Stir until butter melts. Add flour and salt all at once. Reduce heat. Stir-cook at low heat, 1 to 2 minutes, or until mixture is smooth and forms a soft ball. Remove from heat; cool slightly. Add eggs (unbeaten), one at a time, beating well after each addition. To bake, drop batter by rounded tablespoonfuls onto lightly oiled baking sheet, keeping batter balls 1 inch apart. Bake 30 to 35 minutes in a preheated hot (400°) oven, or until golden-brown and firm to touch. Cool on a wire rack. Cut tops off; cool shells and remove soft interior. Fill with Toffee-Butterscotch Cream Filling. Cover with the tops. Refrigerate until ready to serve. Makes 10 cream puffs.

Toffee-Butterscotch Cream Filling:

1 (3¼-ounce) package butterscotch pudding mix
4 (¾-ounce) English toffee candy bars

Prepare pudding mix following package directions. Refrigerate. Crush candy bars and fold into cooled pudding; use as directed above.

CHOCOLATE ICE CREAM ÉCLAIRS

1 package cream puff mix	3 tablespoons broken walnuts, pecans or toasted blanched almonds
1 pint rich chocolate ice cream	
1½ cups Chocolatina or Regal Chocolate Sauce (see Index)	Whipped cream rosettes (optional)
3 tablespoons chocolate sprinkles	

Make up the cream puff mix following the package directions. With a spoon or rather wide pastry tube, shape the cream puff dough into 3- or 4-inch finger lengths, leaving at least a 1-inch space between. Bake following the package directions. Cool. To fill, slit the sides. Remove any soft dough from the interior. Fill with the chocolate ice cream. Place on chilled serving plates. Spoon over the Chocolate Sauce and dust with the chocolate sprinkles and nut meats. If desired, add 2 or 3 small whipped cream rosettes for good measure.

BAKED CUP CUSTARDS

3 eggs (or 6 egg yolks)	3 cups milk, heated
½ cup sugar	1 teaspoon pure vanilla extract
¼ teaspoon salt	1½ cups hot water

Beat the eggs slightly; mix in the sugar and salt. Add the milk gradually, stirring constantly. Stir in the vanilla. Pour into lightly buttered 6-ounce custard cups. Place in a shallow pan. Pour in hot water. Bake in a moderate (350°) oven for 25 to 30 minutes, or until a knife inserted near the center comes out clean. Chill at once.

Toffee-Topped Custards: Five minutes before the end of baking time, top the custards with fine-crushed plain or chocolate-covered toffee. Chill.

Chocolate-Mint-Topped Custards: Prepare as for Toffee-Topped Custards, but use crushed peppermint candy. Chill; serve with chocolate sauce.

Pecan-Caramel-Topped Custards: Prepare as for Baked Cup Custards. Ten minutes before the end of baking time, dust with chopped pecans. Chill; serve with either caramel or butterscotch sundae sauce.

CRÈME BRULÉE

1 quart light cream or half and
  half
8 eggs

8 tablespoons granulated sugar
1 teaspoon vanilla extract
½ cup light brown sugar

Heat cream in a 2-quart double boiler. Separate eggs. Reserve whites to make a white cake or meringue shells. Beat yolks until light with granulated sugar and vanilla. Stir in cream. Pour into an 8×6½-inch oblong baking dish 1¼ inches deep that can go to the table. Place dish in a large pan; pour in boiling water to the depth of 2 inches. Cover loosely with aluminum foil. Bake 30 minutes in a moderate (325 to 350°) oven, or until a wooden toothpick inserted in center comes out dry. Cool. Refrigerate 4 hours or more.

Then sift brown sugar to remove any lumps. Spoon it lightly and evenly over top of crème in a thin layer. Place crème under broiler, 4 inches from the source of heat, which should be low (250°). Leave broiler door open; watch and do nothing else. This topping can burn fast. Broil 3 minutes, or until sugar melts to form a smooth caramel glaze. Thoroughly chill at once. Crack with spoon to serve. Serves 10 to 12.

FLOATING ISLAND

This is the traditional recipe. Some people prefer not to poach the meringues but merely to drop the beaten egg whites and sugar by spoonfuls onto the custard. In this case an attractive garnish is a hulled fresh strawberry or a bit of tart jelly on each spoonful.

2 egg whites
Salt
½ cup sugar

3 cups milk
3 eggs plus 2 egg yolks
1½ teaspoons vanilla extract

Beat egg whites with dash of salt until soft peaks are formed. Gradually beat in ¼ cup of the sugar, a tablespoon at a time, until stiff. Heat milk to simmer in a skillet. Drop egg white mixture into hot milk to form 6 meringues. Cook for about 5 minutes or until meringues are firm. Remove from milk and drain. Reserve milk for custard.

Beat eggs and yolks slightly with remaining ¼ cup sugar and additional dash of salt. Stir in the reserved slightly cooled milk, adding additional milk, if necessary, to make 3 cups. Cook-stir in the top of a double boiler over *hot* water until mixture coats a metal spoon. Remove from heat. Stir in vanilla and pour into an attractive heatproof serving bowl. Top with meringues. Serve cold.

FRENCH CUSTARD WITH CARAMEL SAUCE

1 cup granulated sugar
  (caramelized)
3 cups milk
5 eggs
½ cup granulated sugar

¼ teaspoon salt
1 teaspoon vanilla extract
⅓ cup coarse-chopped
  almonds, browned

To caramelize sugar, turn cupful of sugar into a heavy 9-inch fry pan. Place over slow heat; stir until sugar becomes lumpy, then melts to the consistency of maple syrup. Have ready the custard mold and line at once with hot caramelized sugar, tipping the mold quickly from side to side to coat it thoroughly. Take care—it's hot!

To make the custard, scald milk (heat until bubbles form at edge); beat eggs until mixed but not frothy. Beat in additional sugar, salt and vanilla. Stir into milk. Pour into caramelized-lined 3-pint mold and set in baking pan. Surround to half the depth with boiling water.

Bake 50 minutes in a slow to moderate (325 to 350°) oven, or until a pick inserted in center comes out clean. Cool and refrigerate.

Unmold onto deep round serving dish; strew almonds on top. The caramelized coating will melt while the custard is baking, forming the "built-in" sauce for the dessert.

CREAM CUSTARD

For the classic "trifle," "floating island," or any dessert based on soft custard.

1½ cups light cream	6 egg yolks
1½ cups milk	¼ teaspoon salt
6 tablespoons sugar	¼ teaspoon vanilla extract

Combine the cream and milk in a double-boiler top. Heat over boiling water until bubbles form at the edge. Beat the sugar and egg yolks together until creamy. Stir in half the heated cream mixture. Return to the double boiler; cook-stir until the custard coats the spoon. Remove from the hot water at once. Add the salt and vanilla. Beat 30 seconds with a rotary beater. Cover while cooling to prevent formation of a film. Chill.

CHOCOLATE BAKED CUSTARDS

3 eggs	1 teaspoon vanilla extract
2 tablespoons cocoa	3 cups hot milk
⅓ cup sugar	Whipped cream
¼ teaspoon salt	

Beat together eggs, cocoa, sugar, salt and vanilla. Stir-mix hot milk into egg mixture. Pour ½ cup custard mixture into each baking cup. Set in pan of hot water. Bake 25 to 35 minutes in a moderate (350°) oven, or until knife inserted near center comes out clean. Chill. Serve with whipped cream.

CHOCOLATE CRUMB CUSTARD

2 cups fine white bread crumbs	¾ cup sugar
3½ cups milk, scalded	1 teaspoon vanilla extract
2½ ounces baking chocolate squares	2 eggs, beaten
⅛ teaspoon cinnamon	Half and half or whipped cream
¼ teaspoon salt	

Stir crumbs into milk; let stand 30 minutes. Melt chocolate over hot water. Add milk mixture, and stir until smooth. Beat together cinnamon, salt, sugar, vanilla and eggs. Add to bread mixture. Transfer to a buttered 1½-quart baking dish. Place in large pan and surround with hot water to depth of 1½ inches. Bake 1 hour in a moderate (350°) oven. Serve warm with half and half or cold with whipped cream.

NORWEGIAN APPLE CUSTARD

7 good-sized cooking apples	1 cup evaporated milk
½ cup sugar	3 tablespoons sugar, additional
1 tablespoon butter or margarine	3 tablespoons flour
½ cup water	¼ teaspoon nutmeg
3 eggs, slightly beaten	Grated Apple-Honey Whip

Peel and core apples; cut into thin uniform sections. Combine sugar, butter and water. Add apple; simmer uncovered until just tender. Arrange in a low 1-quart baking dish. Chill. Combine eggs, milk, sugar, flour and nutmeg; beat together. Pour over apples. Bake 45 minutes in a moderate (325 to 350°) oven, or until a pick inserted in center comes out clean. If necessary to prevent overbrowning, cover with aluminum foil. Serve warm with Grated Apple-Honey Whip.

Grated Apple-Honey Whip:

½ cup well-chilled evaporated milk	Pinch of salt
2 teaspoons lemon juice	1 apple, peeled and grated
1 tablespoon granulated sugar	1 tablespoon strained honey

Pour evaporated milk into deep bowl. Add lemon juice. Beat with rotary beater until thickened. Add sugar and salt. Continue beating until mixture stands up in points. Stir together apple and honey, and add. Serve at once.

ZABAGLIONE

5 eggs
½ cup granulated sugar
4 tablespoons sherry or Marsala

Separate the eggs, dropping the yolks in the top of a small double boiler. Add the sugar; then, beating with an egg beater or wire whisk constantly over hot (but not boiling) water, cook until the mixture becomes fluffy; add the wine and continue to beat and cook until very light and thick. Remove from heat. Beat into the egg whites, whipped stiff and dry; transfer to small sherbet glasses and serve hot. Or, if preferred, it may be piled in glasses, chilled and served cold. Serves 4.

BAKED FIG PUDDING

1½ cups chopped dried figs
3 cups coarse, slightly dry, white bread crumbs
2½ cups milk
2 eggs, slightly beaten

½ cup sugar
¼ teaspoon salt
Grated rind and juice of ½ lemon
Hard Sauce (see Index)

Stir figs and crumbs into milk. Let stand 15 minutes. Mix in other ingredients except Hard Sauce. Pour into a buttered 3-pint baking dish that can go-to-table. Set dish in baking pan; pour in hot water to depth of 1 inch. Bake 1 hour in a moderate (350°) oven. Serve warm with Hard Sauce.

QUICK APPLE BETTY

2 tablespoons melted butter or margarine
3 cups rather dry bread crumbs or crushed corn flakes
2 cups well-sweetened applesauce, homemade or canned

¼ teaspoon ground cinnamon
¼ teaspoon ground nutmeg
1 cup half and half

Combine butter and bread crumbs or corn flakes; dust over bottom and sides of a 1-quart baking dish. Flavor applesauce with cinnamon and nutmeg and spread ⅓ of quantity in the baking dish. Cover with thin layer of crumbs or flakes, then a layer of applesauce. Continue until all ingredients are used, finishing with crumbs or flakes. Bake 20 minutes in a moderate (350 to 375°) oven, or until crumbs absorb the juice and are brown on top. Serve warm with half and half.

APPLE COBBLER

4 cups peeled sliced apples (or equal parts apples and pears)	2 teaspoons double action baking powder
1 cup sugar	⅓ cup butter or margarine
1½ cups sifted flour	1 egg, beaten
¼ teaspoon salt	¾ cup milk
¼ cup sugar	½ teaspoon vanilla extract

Combine and mix together apples and 1 cup sugar. Spread in a 7×11-inch well-buttered low baking pan. Sift together flour, salt, additional sugar and baking powder. Add butter, and chop in with pastry blender, or use two knives. Combine beaten egg, milk and vanilla and stir in, making a batter. Pour over and into the apple, leaving about 10 1-inch places uncovered to insure a "cobbled" effect when baked. Bake in a moderate (375°) oven about 50 minutes, or until the top is golden brown, and a pick inserted near the center goes in easily. Serve warm or cold in dessert dishes. Pass cream.

LAZY DAY COBBLER

1 can any kind pie filling or 1 can any kind fruit	1½ tablespoons butter, melted and cooled
1 cup plus 2 tablespoons biscuit mix	¼ cup milk
2 tablespoons sugar	1 tablespoon butter

If fruit is used, blend 1 tablespoon cornstarch with 2 tablespoons water, stir into fruit. Heat to boiling; boil gently, stirring, 1 minute. If pie filling is used, heat in saucepan till just boiling. Mix remaining ingredients except 1 tablespoon butter to form a dough. Pour hot fruit into an 8-inch square pan, dot with remaining butter, drop dough by spoonfuls onto hot fruit. Bake at 400° about 20 minutes. Serve plain, warm or cold, with ice cream, or warm or cold with any appropriate sauce—Hard Sauce (see Index) is traditional.

SPICY APPLE CRISP

5 medium-sized cooking apples, sliced	½ cup brown sugar
	½ teaspoon salt
¼ cup brown sugar	¼ teaspoon nutmeg
¼ teaspoon nutmeg	¼ cup melted butter or
1 tablespoon lemon juice	margarine
1 cup uncooked rolled oats	Ice cream or half and half or
⅓ cup flour	whipped cream

Combine apples, ¼ cup brown sugar and first ¼ teaspoon nutmeg. Arrange in a buttered 1-quart-sized shallow baking dish or deep 9-inch pie plate. Sprinkle over lemon juice. In small bowl, combine remaining ingredients except ice cream and, with fork, mix until crumbly. Spread over the apples. Bake 30 minutes in a moderate (350°) oven, until apples are fork-tender and top is brown and crisp. Serve warm with half-scoops ice cream, half and half or whipped cream.

BAKED APPLE DUMPLINGS

¾ cup shortening	⅔ teaspoons baking powder
1⅓ teaspoons salt	6 medium-sized tart apples
⅓ cup boiling water	½ cup sugar
2 cups enriched flour	½ teaspoon cloves

Measure shortening into a bowl, mix in the salt and boiling water. Sift in the flour and baking powder. Mix lightly, chill for 10 minutes. Pare apples; core them not quite to the bottom to hold in the juices. Roll pastry in 6-inch squares; center apples; fill with the sugar and spice. Fold pastry over apples; pinch edges together. Bake 35 minutes at 375°. Cool. Accompany with whipped cream garnished with candied cherries and thin slices of citron if desired.

APPLE PANDOWDY

6 tart cooking apples	¼ cup unsulphured molasses
½ cup water	2 tablespoons butter or
½ cup sugar	margarine
½ teaspoon nutmeg	1 recipe Rich American Pie
½ teaspoon salt	Pastry (see Index) or a mix

Peel and slice apples in eighths; place in a saucepan with water, sugar, nutmeg and salt. Cover. Cook over low heat until partially cooked. Pour apples into a 6×10×12-inch casserole. Dribble molasses over apples and dot with butter. Roll pastry into rectangular shape ¼ inch thick and place over apples. Cut three gashes in pastry to allow escape of steam. Bake in a hot (425°) oven for 30 minutes, or until the crust is a pretty brown.

OLD-TIME APPLE RICE

3 cups cold boiled rice	½ cup raspberry jam
½ cup sugar	¾ cup fine cookie or cake
Juice of 2 lemons	crumbs
1 teaspoon grated lemon rind	2 tablespoons melted butter or
2 cups slightly sweet	margarine
applesauce	Light cream

Mix the rice, sugar, lemon juice and rind. Layer 1 cup of the mixture in a buttered 3-pint baking dish; layer on 1 cup of apple sauce. Continue until the rice and applesauce are used. Spread with the jam; dust over the crumbs mixed with the butter or margarine. Bake 30 minutes in a moderate (375°) oven. Serve cold with light cream.

BLUEBERRY/CREAM CHEESE FLUFF

1 package black raspberry
  gelatin dessert
1 cup canned blueberries,
  drained

2 tablespoons sugar
1 (3-ounce) package cream
  cheese at room temperature
Chopped nuts (optional)

Prepare gelatin as package directs, place in refrigerator to chill. Combine blueberries with 1 tablespoon sugar. When gelatin has slightly thickened, remove about half and fold in blueberries. Turn mixture into serving bowl or mold and chill until firm. Beat remaining gelatin with sugar and cream cheese until thick and fluffy. Pour over jellied first layer. Chill. Sprinkle with chopped nuts if desired.

BLUEBERRY FLUMMERY

Quick-cooked or baked.

The trick is to have enough juicy berries so no one can guess there's bread in the finished pudding.

4 cups washed fresh or 2
  packages frozen or 2
  (1-pound) cans wild
  blueberries
1 cup sugar

6 decrusted slices white bread,
  well buttered
Nutmeg
Sweetened whipped cream or
  ice cream

Quick-cook: Combine berries and sugar; simmer-boil 10 minutes or until cooked through. In a 3-pint serving bowl arrange layers of bread and berries. Chill. Top with nutmeg-flavored sweetened whipped cream.

Baked: Layer heated berries and bread in a shallow 3-pint baking dish. Bake 20 to 30 minutes at 350°, or until well heated. Top with ice cream if you like. Serve hot or chilled.

CHERRY DUMPLINGS

⅔ cup orange juice
3 tablespoons lemon juice
1 cup light corn syrup
¼ teaspoon each ground
  cinnamon and nutmeg
2 tablespoons butter
1 (9-ounce) package pie crust
  mix

1 (1-pound) can pitted sweet
  cherries, drained
2 tablespoons sugar
2 tablespoons grated orange
  peel
1 teaspoon grated lemon peel
1 cup sour cream or whipped
  sweet cream

In saucepan, combine orange juice, lemon juice, corn syrup and spices. Simmer 5 minutes or until flavors are blended. Stir in butter. Keep warm.

Prepare pastry according to package directions. Roll out and cut into 6 8-inch triangles. Mix cherries with sugar and grated peels. Place cherries in center of each pastry triangle. Moisten edges of pastry and bring up over cherries. Pinch edges together to seal. Arrange dumplings in well-buttered 8×12-inch baking pan. Pour warm syrup over all. Bake in a 450° oven 10 minutes. Reduce heat to 375° and continue baking 15 minutes. Serve while still warm. Pass cream.

FRESH CHERRY SQUARES

¼ cup shortening at room
  temperature
¾ cup sugar
1 egg, separated
1 teaspoon vanilla
¼ teaspoon salt

1½ teaspoons baking powder
1½ cups sifted flour
½ cup milk
1 pint pitted sweet or sour
  cherries
½ cup sugar

Stir shortening till creamy; beat in sugar, egg yolk and vanilla. Sift together dry ingredients; add alternately to first mixture with milk. Fold in egg white, whipped stiff. Mix cherries with additional ½ cup sugar; transfer to oiled shallow 8-inch square pan. Pour over batter, spreading mixture higher at edges than center. Bake 35 minutes in a moderate (375°) oven. Serve with or without additional stewed cherries, cherry sauce or whipped cream cheese.

PEACH COBBLER

2 cups sliced fresh peaches*
1 cup white corn syrup
4 tablespoons shortening
6 tablespoons sugar
1 egg, beaten
½ teaspoon lemon extract

1½ cups enriched flour
2½ teaspoons baking powder
⅓ teaspoon salt
½ cup milk
Whipped or plain cream

Put a thick layer of peaches and corn syrup in a buttered baking dish. For the batter, blend shortening, sugar, egg and flavoring till fluffy. Sift together flour, baking powder, salt. Add alternately with milk; mix. Spoon batter over peaches; spread evenly; bake at 375° F about 30 minutes. In beating cream use a deep utensil; add the sugar as it thickens. The cobbler is best served warm with cream.

* When peaches are not in season, you can substitute 1 (1-lb.) can of cling peaches and ½ cup sugar instead of using fresh peaches and corn syrup.

PINEAPPLE BAVARIAN CREAM

1 cup canned crushed
  pineapple
1½ cups pineapple juice
2 tablespoons unflavored
  gelatin

½ cup cold water
⅔ cup sugar
2 tablespoons lemon juice
1 cup heavy cream, whipped

Drain crushed pineapple and add enough water to the drained liquid to make up the 1½ cups of pineapple juice. Soften the gelatin in cold water; add it with the sugar to the pineapple juice, which has been brought to a boil, and stir until both sugar and gelatin are thoroughly dissolved. Cool, add the lemon juice and as the mixture begins to congeal fold in the drained, crushed pineapple and the whipped cream. Turn into a prepared mold, chill, unmold and accompany with additional whipped cream, pineapple and a few maraschino cherries.

Strawberry Bavarian Cream: Follow the recipe for Pineapple Bavarian Cream, substituting defrosted quick-frozen or sugared fresh strawberries and juice for pineapple.

PLUM BETTY

¼ cup butter	1 cup sugar
3 cups fine soft bread crumbs	¼ teaspoon each ground
2 cups chopped unpeeled fresh	cloves, cinnamon and salt
plums	Hard Sauce (see Index)

Stir the butter into the bread crumbs. Combine the chopped plums with the sugar and seasonings. Arrange in alternate layers in buttered ramekins, crumbs making top layer. Bake 30 minutes in a moderate (350°) oven. Serve warm with Hard Sauce.

PLUM-NUT CRUMBLE

12 medium-sized fresh purple	½ cup water or any fruit juice
or blue plums	Nut Crumble
Butter or margarine	Half and half
1 tablespoon sugar	
½ cup sugar	

Wash and halve the plums; remove the pits. Rub a deep 9-inch pie plate with butter or margarine. Dust with 1 tablespoon sugar. Place the plum halves rounded side up in the plate. Dust with the ½ cup sugar; pour in the water or fruit juice. Cover with Nut Crumble. Slow-bake about 35 minutes in a moderate (350°) oven, or until browned on top. Serve warm or cold with half and half.

Nut Crumble:

⅓ cup flour
2 tablespoons any fine-chopped
nut meats
3 tablespoons butter or
margarine

⅓ cup sugar
¼ teaspoon ground cloves

Measure the ingredients into a bowl in the order given. Work together with the back of a spoon until crumbly. Use as directed.

VANILLA ICE CREAM

⅔ cup sweetened condensed
milk
½ cup water
Few grains salt

1½ teaspoons vanilla extract
1 cup whipping cream

Thoroughly blend condensed milk, water, salt and vanilla. Chill. Whip cream to custard-like consistency and fold into chilled mixture. Pour into freezing pan. Place in freezing unit. After mixture is about half frozen remove from refrigerator. Scrape mixture from sides and bottom of pan. Beat until smooth, but not until melted. Smooth out and replace in freezing unit until frozen for serving.

COUNTRY CRANBERRY SHERBET

1 envelope unflavored gelatin
¼ cup lemon juice
3 cups cranberry juice cocktail

2 cups buttermilk
1½ cups sugar
1 teaspoon ground nutmeg

Sprinkle gelatin over lemon juice; let stand 5 minutes. Place over low heat and stir until gelatin dissolves. Add remaining ingredients, stirring until sugar dissolves; pour into a freezing container and freeze until mushy. Pour mixture into bowl and beat until smooth and fluffy. Return to freezer and freeze 1½ to 2 hours.

PINEAPPLE SHERBET

Perfect on a hot day!

¾ cup sugar
Pinch of salt
1 cup water
½ cup light cream or half and half

⅓ cup lemon juice
1 (8¼-ounce) can crushed pineapple
2 egg whites
¼ cup sugar

Combine sugar, salt and water in saucepan. Bring to a boil; cook 5 minutes, or until dissolved. Add light cream, lemon juice and pineapple. Turn into ice-cube tray; freeze until firm 1 inch from edge. Beat egg whites until foamy. Add additional sugar and beat until stiff. Fold into half-frozen mixture and freeze firm, from 1½ to 2 hours. This makes about 1½ quarts.

FRESH PEACH MELBA COMPOTE

6 large scoops (balls) vanilla ice cream
3 large, fresh freestone peaches, peeled and halved
Fresh Raspberry Sauce

Scoop ice cream into each of 6 compote dishes. Cap ice cream with a peach half. Spoon Fresh Raspberry Sauce over top, and spoon 2 or 3 tablespoons at base of ice cream in each dish.

Fresh Raspberry Sauce:

2½ cups fresh raspberries
Pinch of salt
½ cup sugar

Wash berries; drain. Measure 2 cups and crush lightly (do not mash). Add salt and sugar. Stir gently. Chill 1 hour or more. Just before serving, fold in remaining whole berries.

KADAYIF

Adaptation of a favorite Near East dessert.

6 shredded wheat biscuits
½ cup chopped nut meats
1½ teaspoons cinnamon
¾ teaspoon sugar
1½ tablespoons melted butter
  or margarine

1 cup sugar
¾ cup water
¾ teaspoon lemon juice
Whipped cream

Set oven for 350°. Rub baking sheet with vegetable oil. Dip shredded wheat biscuits quickly into and out of warm water. Drain well. With point of sharp knife, cut along edge of the side seams of biscuits. Separate and place on baking sheet. Sprinkle bottom halves with nuts. Mix cinnamon sugar together; dust over nuts on each biscuit half. With broad spatula, lift top half of each biscuit onto bottom half. Brush tops with melted butter. Bake 12 to 15 minutes, or until golden brown. Meantime, mix additional sugar and water together. Cook-stir until sugar completely melts. Continue to cook, stirring occasionally until boiling. Add lemon juice. Reduce heat and boil gently 5 minutes. Remove from heat. Cool. Pour syrup over biscuits. Cool. Serve with whipped cream.

MILE-HIGH MERINGUE

2½ tablespoons cold water
3 egg whites
⅛ teaspoon salt
¼ teaspoon cream of tartar

¼ teaspoon vanilla or other
  flavoring extract
3 tablespoons sugar

Add water to egg whites. Beat until frothy with rotary hand beater. Add salt, cream of tartar and flavoring extract. Beat until stiff. Add sugar and continue beating until stiff enough to form peaks but still shiny. Use at once. This recipe makes enough meringue to top a 9-inch pie; or a round 9-inch cake or 10 small tarts. Spread lightly out to the farthest edges of pie, or whatever is to be covered. Bake 12 minutes in a slow (325°) oven, or until meringue is pale golden brown.

NEVER-FALL MERINGUE

Separate whites from yolks of enough eggs (about 5) to make ½ cup whites. Turn into a 1-quart double-boiler top. Beat slightly with wire whisk until frothy. Place over warm, not boiling water, and stir-cook about 5 minutes, or until whites are warmed. Remove from heat; stir in 1 cup granulated sugar, ½ teaspoon salt and ½ teaspoon vanilla extract. Beat with electric mixer or in large blender until meringue forms stiff peaks. Use whenever a meringue is needed. This recipe makes enough for two 9-inch pies or three 8-inch pies; or to put together and cover an 8-inch layer cake. Any unused meringue may be covered and refrigerated up to 24 hours.

SCOTTISH APPLE PUDDING

3 cups coarse-chopped peeled
   cored cooking apples
½ cup sugar
¼ teaspoon ground cinnamon
1 egg, well beaten
2 tablespoons butter or
   margarine at room
   temperature

¼ cup sugar
¼ cup flour
¼ teaspoon salt

Butter moderately a low 1-quart baking dish that can go-to-table. Pack in half the apple. Cover with sugar and cinnamon, mixed; pack in remaining apple. Beat egg; stir until creamy with butter or margarine, additional sugar, flour and salt. Spoon over apple. Bake 45 minutes in a moderate (350°) oven, or until apple is soft and top an appetizing golden brown. Serve warm.

BAKED BANANA PUDDING

2 tablespoons butter or margarine at room temperature	1 cup rather dry cake crumbs
	1 cup mashed banana pulp
¼ cup cornstarch	2 tablespoons lemon juice
1¼ cups boiling water	¼ cup canned crushed pineapple
2 eggs, separated	2 tablespoons sifted powdered sugar
⅛ teaspoon salt	
¾ cup sugar	Cream (optional)

Mix together butter and cornstarch. Stir into boiling water; boil up once. Cook 5 minutes over boiling water. Beat egg yolks with salt; mix in sugar and add. Butter a 1-quart baking dish. Line with cake crumbs. Combine egg mixture, banana pulp and lemon juice; transfer to baking dish. Spread with pineapple, then with meringue made from egg whites beaten stiff with powdered sugar. Brown in a slow (325°) oven about 12 minutes. Serve warm or cold as is or with cream.

CLARICE'S PARADISE PUDDING

This delightfully different dessert comes from Portugal. Although basically easy to prepare, it's wise to summon help beforehand if you don't have an electric beater, for much of the success of the recipe depends upon the beating of the whole eggs until they hold their shape—and that takes a lot of beating!

2 cups almonds, fine-ground	10 egg yolks
1 tablespoon flour	4 egg whites
¼ teaspoon salt	3 cups sugar
2 tablespoons cinnamon	1 quart water
1 tablespoon soft butter	

Combine and mix thoroughly first five ingredients. Beat eggs and whites together till stiff enough to hold their shape—do not underbeat! Meanwhile, boil sugar and water till mixture, when poured from a spoon, spins a thread. Combine almond mixture and eggs; slowly fold syrup into this. Pour into well-buttered cake tin and bake in a preheated 350° oven 35 to 40 minutes, or until toothpick inserted comes out dry.

BAKED INDIAN PUDDING

The traditional New England dessert—a time-saving version.

1 quart whole milk
½ teaspoon salt
⅓ cup molasses
1 teaspoon ground ginger
⅓ cup sugar
½ cup enriched or whole corn meal

2 tablespoons butter or margarine
1 cup cold milk
Half and half or whipped cream or chopped preserved ginger

Heat 1 quart of milk in double boiler until bubbles form around edge. Stir in salt, molasses, ginger and sugar; gradually stir in corn meal. Stir-cook until thickened. Add butter. Transfer to a buttered 2-quart baking dish. Set it in pan. Pour around boiling water to two thirds the depth of dish. Bake 45 minutes in a hot (400°) oven; then stir in additional milk. Continue to bake uncovered 45 minutes more. Serve warm or cold with half and half or whipped cream. Or try garnishing with chopped preserved ginger—delicious.

BAKED LEMON RICE PUDDING

1½ cups cooked flaky rice
1 large egg, beaten
½ cup sugar
¼ teaspoon salt

3 cups milk
Fine-grated rind and juice of ½ medium-sized lemon

Mix ingredients in order given. Pour into a buttered 3-pint baking dish that can go-to-table.

Set dish in baking pan. Pour in water to half the depth of the dish. Slow-bake about 1¼ hours at 325 to 350°, or until firm in center and pale brown. Serve warm or cold. Pass cream.

MOLASSES RAISIN PUDDING

½ cup orange juice
2 cups seedless raisins
1 apple, peeled, cored and
  chopped
1 tablespoon grated orange
  rind
2 eggs, slightly beaten
½ cup unsulphured molasses
1 cup chopped nuts (any kind)
½ cup ground suet
  (beef fat) (2 ounces)

¾ cup fine bread crumbs
½ cup presifted flour
1 teaspoon baking powder
½ teaspoon baking soda
¼ cup sugar
½ teaspoon each salt and
  cinnamon
¼ teaspoon each allspice and
  ground cloves

Pour orange juice over raisins, apple and orange rind; let stand 1 hour. Combine eggs and unsulphured molasses; stir in nuts, suet and bread crumbs. Sift in remaining ingredients; mix well. Spoon into two well-oiled 1-pound cans (✳303). Cover with aluminum foil; tie securely. Or divide the mixture between two 1-pound coffee cans. Cover securely with lid or aluminum foil. Place on rack in deep kettle; pour in boiling water to half the depth of cans. Cover; steam 2 hours, adding more boiling water if necessary. Serve warm and accompany with softened ice cream or Hard Sauce (see Index). Serves 12. Will keep refrigerated for a week. Re-steaming time is 30 minutes.

NESSELRODE PUDDING

A festive freezer dessert.

3 egg yolks
¼ teaspoon salt
⅔ cup sugar
2 cups light cream or half and
  half
⅓ cup almond paste
  (purchased)

⅔ cup chopped preserved
  marrons (purchased)
2 tablespoons marron syrup
1 cup heavy cream
1 teaspoon vanilla
⅓ cup mixed candied fruits

In top of double boiler, beat egg yolks with salt and sugar until foamy. Scald light cream and gradually pour into egg yolks, beating constantly. Stir-cook over simmering water until mixture coats spoon—about 5 minutes. Remove from heat and blend in almond paste and the marrons and syrup, forced through a sieve. Cool, then chill. Whip cream with vanilla, fold into custard mixture and pour into a freezer tray. Freeze till frozen around edges but still mushy in center. Transfer to a bowl and thoroughly mix in candied fruits. Return to freezer tray or, if preferred, 1-quart mold, and freeze till firm.

BAKED PERSIMMON PUDDING

Ripe persimmons are generally eaten raw, but they are also delicious in puddings, cakes, sherbet, custard, preserves, fruit cups and salads. This is nice as a finale to a poultry or game dinner.

1 cup all-purpose flour	2 large eggs, beaten
½ teaspoon salt	1 cup milk
½ teaspoon baking soda	½ teaspoon grated lemon peel
¾ cup sugar	2 tablespoon butter or
1 cup persimmon purée (2 or	margarine, melted
3 persimmons)	Whipped cream

Sift together flour, salt, soda and sugar. Peel persimmons, mash and put through sieve. Measure 1 cup persimmon purée and add with remaining ingredients except whipped cream to sifted flour mixture. Mix well. Turn batter into a well-oiled, lightly floured, 8×8×2-inch pan. Bake 50 minutes in a moderate (350°) oven. Cool 5 minutes. Cut into squares. Serve warm, topped with whipped cream, or Hard Sauce (see Index).
Note: If persimmons are unavailable, you can substitute apricot-apple purée (junior food) with a happy result.

ENGLISH PLUM PUDDING

3 cups flour
1 teaspoon salt
½ teaspoon allspice
½ teaspoon grated nutmeg
½ teaspoon ground cinnamon
2 cups stale bread crumbs
2 cups seeded raisins
1 cup currants

2 cups brown sugar
2 cups chopped beef suet
1 cup shredded candied citron,
    orange and lemon mixed
½ cup chopped figs
Grated rind of 1 lemon
6 eggs
1 cup grape juice or brandy

Sift together the flour, salt and spices, add the bread crumbs, the raisins cut into halves after seeding, the currants, sugar, suet very finely chopped, the shredded candied peel, the figs, and lemon rind. Mix thoroughly, then moisten with the well-beaten eggs and grape juice. Turn into well-oiled molds having tightly fitting covers, fill not more than two thirds. Steam or boil for 8 hours. This pudding may be made some time before it is needed and reheated by a further boiling of at least 1 hour. Serve with Hard Sauce (see Index) or any desired liquid dessert sauce.

COLONIAL PUMPKIN BREAD PUDDING

1 (1-pound) can puréed
    pumpkin
2 cups milk
2 tablespoons butter or
    margarine, melted
1 cup fine crumbs of rather
    dry enriched bread
    (no crusts)
1 teaspoon ground cinnamon
½ teaspoon ground cloves
2 eggs, separated

½ cup brown sugar or ¾ cup
    brownulated sugar
¼ teaspoon salt
½ cup coarse enriched bread
    crumbs
1 tablespoon butter or
    margarine, melted
1 tablespoon brown or
    brownulated sugar
Any whipped topping

Combine pumpkin, milk, butter, crumbs, cinnamon and cloves. Separate eggs; beat yolks together with ½ cup brown sugar and salt, and add to the pumpkin mixture. Beat egg whites stiff; fold in.

Transfer to buttered 3-pint baking dish. Mix coarse bread crumbs with additional butter and spread over top. Dust with additional brown sugar. Bake in a slow (325 to 350°) oven for 50 minutes, or until firm in center and golden brown on top. Serve warm with any whipped topping.

QUEEN OF PUDDINGS WITH MERINGUE

1½ cups rather dry enriched bread crumbs
3 cups milk
2 eggs, separated
⅔ cup sugar
¼ teaspoon salt
½ teaspoon any flavoring extract
¼ teaspoon baking soda
1 tablespoon warm water
½ cup soft red fruit jelly
⅛ teaspoon cream of tartar
1 tablespoon sugar
Whipped cream (optional)

Stir crumbs into milk and heat until almost boiling. Separate eggs; beat yolks creamy (set aside whites). To yolks, add sugar, salt, flavoring and baking soda dissolved in warm water. Stir into the crumb-milk mixture. Pour into a buttered 3-pint baking dish. Set in pan; surround baking dish with boiling water to depth of 2 inches. Bake 35 minutes in a moderate (350°) oven. Remove, and spread top surface of pudding lightly with jelly.

Beat reserved egg whites stiff with cream of tartar and additional sugar, making a meringue. Spread this over jelly on top of pudding. Return this to oven; bake 15 minutes more. Serve warm as is, or with whipped cream.

OLD-FASHIONED RICE PUDDING

½ cup rice
1 quart milk
½ cup sugar
¼ teaspoon each nutmeg and cinnamon
½ teaspoon salt
½ cup raisins (optional)

Put rice in a big buttered earthen baking dish, pour over milk, and stir in sugar, spices and salt. Bake in a slow (300°) oven 4 to 5 hours, stirring now and then. When done, it is thick, creamy and golden in color. If desired, ½ cup of raisins may be stirred in 1 hour after baking begins. Pass cream.

CHARLOTTE RUSSE

1 cup heavy cream
2 tablespoons sugar
¼ teaspoon vanilla extract
6 tablespoons applesauce or
   preserves

Macaroons or ladyfingers
6 candied cherries

Whip the cream until nearly stiff. Add the sugar and vanilla. Beat stiff. Arrange individually as follows: Put 1 tablespoon very thick applesauce or preserves into sherbet dishes; line with halves of macaroons or ladyfingers. Fill with the cream. Top with a candied cherry.

CHOCOLATE MOUSSE

1 (6-ounce) package (1 cup)
   semi-sweet chocolate morsels
2 teaspoons instant coffee
½ cup sugar

2 tablespoons water
½ teaspoon vanilla extract
3 eggs, separated
Whipped cream rosettes

Combine chocolate morsels, coffee, ¼ cup of the sugar and water in a 1-pint saucepan. Place over low heat, cook—stirring constantly until chocolate melts and sugar dissolves. Remove from heat. Beat until smooth. Add vanilla and egg yolks, one at a time, beating after each addition. Beat egg whites until peaks form. Gradually add remaining ¼ cup sugar, beating until very stiff. Fold in chocolate mixture. Refrigerate in small dessert dishes. Top each with whipped cream rosette. Keeps up to 12 hours!

MOCK CHOCOLATE BRANDY SOUFFLÉ

Quick and elegant!

1 cup heavy cream, whipped
2 tablespoons brandy or cognac
2 cans chocolate pudding
3 egg whites, whipped stiff
  with ½ cup sugar (added
  gradually)

Bittersweet chocolate shavings
  or slivered toasted almonds

Whip cream, add brandy. Fold into pudding. Fold egg whites into this mixture; pour into bowl; chill. Garnish with chocolate shavings or almonds. Serves 8.

Substitute 2 teaspoons instant coffee dissolved in 1 tablespoon water for brandy and this becomes Mock Mocha Soufflé!

STRAWBERRY FOOL

2 pints strawberries
½ cup sugar
½ cup water
1 cup heavy cream

½ cup heavy cream, whipped
  and sweetened
6 reserved strawberries

Wash, drain and hull strawberries. Reserve 6 for garnish. Place in a 1½-quart saucepan with sugar and water. Bring to boil; reduce heat, simmer 5 minutes. Remove from heat; strain. Set strawberries aside. Return strained liquid or syrup to saucepan; boil rapidly until reduced to ½ cup. Combine with cooled strawberries; chill.

When ready to serve, whip cream and fold in strawberry mixture. Spoon into parfait glasses. Top each serving with some additional whipped cream and 1 of reserved strawberries.

IRISH COFFEE PUDDING

A "cold soufflé" in gourmet cookery.

6 eggs, separated
¾ cup sugar
1½ teaspoons instant coffee dissolved in 1 cup water or 1 cup very strong black coffee
2½ tablespoons powdered gelatin

⅓ cup Irish whiskey or Irish Mist liqueur
1¼ cups heavy cream, whipped
2 tablespoons crushed walnuts
1 cup heavy cream, whipped

Separate yolks from whites of eggs. In a 2-quart bowl cream yolks with sugar. Blend instant coffee with water; or use strong black coffee. Heat it but do not boil. Completely dissolve gelatin in hot coffee and add all to yolks and sugar mixture. Beat well and put bowl over pan of boiling water. Continue beating until mixture begins to thicken. Add whiskey or liqueur and beat until mixture is thick and creamy. Remove from heat and when cooled a little, put over cracked ice and continue to stir. When mixture is very thick and on point of setting, whip 1¼ cups cream, add 2 tablespoons walnuts and fold it in. Lastly, fold in well-beaten egg whites.

Pour into 7-inch soufflé case or soufflé dish that has a collar of strong folded waxed paper tied around it. Paper should come up 3 inches above top of soufflé case. Lightly oil a jam jar or bottle, and press it down into center of pudding. Refrigerate 4 hours or more to set. Remove paper collar by easing around the circumference with a knife dipped in hot water. Remove jar (or bottle) and fill center with the additional whipped cream mixed with additional chopped walnuts. Decorate exposed sides of pudding with crushed walnuts that you press on with the palm of your hand. Serves 8 to 10.

Note: The alcohol from the whiskey used in Irish Coffee Pudding evaporates while cooking. If desired, use ⅓ cup melted chocolate bits instead. In this case, it becomes "Mocha Bavarian Cream."

RASPBERRY CHARLOTTE

1 (10½-ounce) package frozen raspberries, thawed, drained and slightly crushed
1½ teaspoons unflavored gelatin
2 tablespoons reserved raspberry juice

1 teaspoon lemon juice
¼ cup sugar
1½ cups heavy cream, whipped
18 ladyfingers, halved, or 18 strips of spongecake 1½ inches long

Drain frozen raspberries. Save juice. Crush raspberries. Combine gelatin and raspberry juice. Stir over hot water until gelatin dissolves. Add raspberries, lemon juice and sugar. Whip cream until stiff; stir in gelatin-raspberry mixture. Line sherbet glasses or small deep dessert dishes with halved ladyfingers or strips of spongecake. Pile in gelatin-raspberry mixture. Refrigerate 1 hour or more before serving.

ICE CREAM PECAN MERINGUE TORTE

What is the difference between a cake and a torte? Both belong to the general family of cakes; but instead of being made with flour, tortes are often made with fine-chopped nut meats and fine dry crumbs of some type folded into a meringue base, and baked in layers. These are put together with special fillings.

3 egg whites
⅛ teaspoon salt
1½ cups sifted confectioners' sugar
1½ cups fine-crushed shortbread cookie crumbs
1 cup fine-chopped pecans

2 squares semi-sweet chocolate, chopped
½ teaspoon vanilla extract
1 quart pistachio ice cream, softened
Chocolate Sauce

Beat egg whites and salt until foamy throughout. Gradually add sugar, beating about 10 minutes, or until stiff shiny peaks are formed. Stir in crumbs, pecans, chocolate and vanilla. Line large baking sheet with smooth brown paper. Draw 2 8-inch circles on this; rub lightly with oil. Divide meringue in 2 circles, spreading evenly so edges are same thickness as centers. Bake 18 to 20 minutes in a moderate (350°) oven. Partly cool on rack. While still slightly warm, carefully loosen edges of meringues with spatula. Leave on paper until thoroughly cooled.

To assemble torte, remove meringue layer from paper. Set on large serving plate. Spread over half of softened ice cream. Top with second meringue layer. Spoon remaining ice cream on top. Freeze 3 hours or until firm. Serve Chocolate Sauce over torte. Serves 10 to 12.

Chocolate Sauce: Combine 4 squares semi-sweet chocolate and 6 tablespoons water in saucepan. Place over low heat; stir until smooth. Add ¼ cup granulated sugar; stir until dissolved. Stir-boil gently 4 minutes. Remove from heat. Beat in 2 tablespoons butter. Serve hot. Makes about ¾ cup.

SACHER TORTE

One of the most elegant of nuts, filberts are highly prized in the European haute cuisine. Viennese, French and German tortes, pastry and cookie recipes are redolent with the fine flavor and texture of filberts. The most famous of the cakes, Sacher Torte, has become an American favorite.

¾ cup butter or margarine	⅓ cup ground toasted filberts
1 teaspoon vanilla extract	(see note)
¾ cup granulated sugar	½ cup apricot preserves,
6 eggs, separated	heated, sieved and cooled
6 (1-ounce) squares semi-sweet	Chocolate Glaze for Sacher
chocolate, melted and cooled	Torte
1 cup sifted cake flour	Topping

Cream butter, vanilla and ½ cup of the sugar until light and fluffy. Beat in egg yolks one at a time. Mix in cooled chocolate. Gently stir in cake flour, and ⅓ cup ground toasted filberts.

Beat egg whites until foamy. Gradually add remaining ¼ cup of the sugar to egg whites, beating until stiff but not dry. Into egg whites fold chocolate mixture. Pour this resulting batter into an oiled 8-inch spring-form pan. Bake in a slow (325°) oven 1 hour and 10 minutes, or until cake tests done. Cool 10 minutes. Then turn out of pan onto large serving plate. Spread cake with apricot preserves. Let stand 1 hour to allow preserves to set. Frost top and sides of cake with Chocolate Glaze. Serve each slice with Topping. Serves 8 to 10.

Note: To toast filberts, spread in shallow pan and bake in hot oven 10 to 15 minutes. Stir occasionally. Then grind or grate them.

Chocolate Glaze for Sacher Torte: In top of double boiler, melt 6 (1-ounce) squares semi-sweet chocolate over hot water. Remove from heat; add 2 tablespoons butter and stir until melted. Add 1 tablespoon each hot water and light corn syrup. Mix well. Use as directed.

Topping:

   1 cup heavy cream, whipped
   1 tablespoons confectioners' sugar
   ½ cup toasted filberts, chopped (about 2 ounces)

Into whipped cream, fold confectioners' sugar and additional chopped toasted filberts.

PEANUT BRITTLE

   2 cups sugar
   ⅔ cup water
   Pinch of cream of tartar
   2 tablespoons unsulphured
     molasses
   2 tablespoons cream or
     evaporated milk

   1¼ teaspoons baking soda
   Pinch of salt
   1 cup shelled, roasted peanuts

Cook sugar, water and cream of tartar, quickly to 280° by a candy thermometer; then add molasses and cream or evaporated milk. Boil up again quickly and cook to 295°, stir in soda, salt and peanuts. Turn onto an oiled platter, cool and spread 1/8 inch thick. Cut in squares. Makes about 1 1/2 pounds.

PRALINES FROM THE DEEP SOUTH

2 cups sugar
1/2 cup unsulphured molasses
1/4 cup water
2 tablespoons butter or
   margarine

1 cup roasted peanuts, pecan meats or coconut (shredded or flaked)

Combine first four ingredients in a 2-quart saucepan. Cook without stirring, to make syrup, over a medium heat until 1/2 teaspoon when dropped in cold water forms a soft ball (238° by a candy thermometer). Cool to 200° (about 5 minutes if placed in a pan of cold water). Stir in peanuts, pecans or coconut. Rub 1 tablespoon of syrup against side of pan until it is light in color and begins to grain. Quickly stir this throughout the mixture. Drop from a teaspoon onto a cookie sheet covered with heavy waxed paper or aluminum foil. Let stand 2 to 3 hours, or until firm. Makes 2 dozen 3-inch pralines.

CHOCOLATE FUDGE

1/4 cup butter or margarine
3 squares unsweetened
   chocolate
2 cups confectioners' sugar
1/3 cup instant nonfat dry milk

1/2 cup corn syrup
1 tablespoon water
1 teaspoon vanilla extract
1/2 cup chopped nuts
   (optional)

Melt butter and chocolate in top of double boiler or saucepan over boiling water. Meanwhile, sift confectioners' sugar and nonfat dry milk together; set aside. Stir corn syrup, water and vanilla into chocolate mixture over boiling water. Gradually blend in sifted dry ingredients, stirring until blended and smooth. Remove from heat, mix in nuts if desired. Turn into greased 8×8×2-inch pan. Cool. Cut into squares. Makes about 1 1/4 pounds.

BLACK WALNUT CHOCOLATE FUDGE

2¼ cups sugar
¼ cup butter
16 large marshmallows or
   2 cups midget marshmallows
½ teaspoon salt
1 cup undiluted evaporated
   milk

1 (6-ounce) package semi-
   sweet chocolate chips (1
   cup)
1 teaspoon vanilla extract
1 cup black walnut meats,
   broken or coarse-chopped

Mix sugar, butter, marshmallows, salt and evaporated milk in a 3-quart saucepan and stir over medium heat until bubbly. Boil and stir 7 minutes more. Remove from heat; add chocolate chips and vanilla; stir until chips melt. Stir in black walnut meats. When well blended, pour into buttered flat glass baking dish (approximately 7×12 inches). Let stand to cool thoroughly and "firm-up" before cutting into 1-inch squares. This fudge freezes well and retains its fresh consistency after thawing. Makes about 2 pounds.

DIVINITY FUDGE

2½ cups sugar
¼ teaspoon salt
⅓ cup light corn syrup

½ cup water
2 egg whites, beaten stiff
1 teaspoon vanilla

Combine sugar, salt, corn syrup and water in saucepan over low heat. Cook-stir till mixture comes to a boil, washing down any crystals that form on inside of pan. Continue to cook until ½ teaspoon, when dropped in cold water, forms a hard ball—254° on candy thermometer. Pour over stiffly beaten egg whites, beating constantly. When beginning to stiffen, quickly add vanilla and drop by teaspoons onto waxed paper. For variation, make with brown sugar, and/or fold in 1 cup broken nut meats, raisins, or chopped dried dates, apricots or prunes. Makes about 1 pound.

HAWAIIAN FUDGE

A notable contribution to American confectionery from our fif-
tieth state.

4 cups sugar
1 (14-ounce) can crushed
  pineapple, well drained
1 cup heavy cream
2 tablespoons butter

1 cup chopped macadamia
  nuts
1 tablespoon preserved ginger
  (optional)

In saucepan, mix sugar, pineapple and cream. Stir over low heat
to dissolve sugar. Bring to boil; cook, over medium heat, stirring
and washing down crystals from pan, till candy thermometer
registers 238°, or till mixture forms a soft ball in cold water. Remove from heat; cool to lukewarm. Add butter. Beat till mixture
loses its gloss. Quickly add nuts and stir in together with ginger if
desired. Spread into a buttered 8-inch square pan; cool and cut
into 1½-inch squares.

Cookies

The well-filled cookie jar has a place in history and perhaps in your own memory. (Did *your* granny have a cookie jar waiting for you?) Everybody likes cookies—and no commercial bakery has yet caught the specialness of the homemade variety. Here are cookies your family will love. You can bake three or four dozen for far less than the price you'd pay for bought cookies. All of them will keep fresh for days in a closed metal container.

ANISEED COOKIES

2 cups sifted flour	¾ cup chilled butter
1 cup sugar	1 egg
¾ teaspoon ground aniseed	1 tablespoon milk

Sift flour, sugar and aniseed into mixing bowl. Add butter; chop in with pastry blender until fine flakes form. Beat and add egg and milk. Stir into flour mixture to form a thick dough. Shape into small balls a scant ½ inch in diameter. Place 2 inches apart on unoiled cookie sheet. Flatten to $\frac{1}{16}$-inch thickness with bottom of small glass covered with aluminum foil, edges pressed up against the side. Bake 6 to 8 minutes in a hot (400°) oven, or until lightly browned at edges. Do not overbake. Cool. Store in a closed container. Makes 5 dozen.

BUTTERSCOTCH KRINKLE-TOP COOKIES

¾ cup shortening	1 teaspoon cinnamon
¾ cup sugar	½ teaspoon ginger
½ cup unsulphured molasses	½ teaspoon salt
1 egg, slightly beaten	1 (6-ounce) package
2¼ cups sifted all-purpose	butterscotch-flavored morsels
flour	Granulated sugar
1½ teaspoons baking soda	

Combine and mix shortening and sugar until light and fluffy. Mix in molasses and egg. Combine and sift in flour, baking soda, cinnamon, ginger, salt; mix thoroughly. Stir in butterscotch morsels. Refrigerate 2 hours. Form into small balls about 1 inch in diameter. Roll in granulated sugar. Transfer 1 inch apart to lightly oiled baking sheets; bake 10 to 12 minutes in a moderate (375°) oven. Makes approximately 5 dozen cookies.

CHOCOLATE CROQUANTS

1 cup brown sugar (no lumps)
½ cup sifted flour
¼ teaspoon salt
½ teaspoon vanilla extract
3 eggs

1 cup crushed blanched almond meats
3 (1-ounce) squares semi-sweet cooking chocolate

Combine all ingredients except chocolate and mix into a dough. Refrigerate 6 minutes. Roll into small balls and flatten them onto an oiled pan. Bake in a moderate (375°) oven; remove from pan immediately when baked. Let cookies cool, then pair them off. Melt chocolate; spread between each pair of cooled cookies; press together, and let stand until chocolate is firm. Makes about 5 dozen cookies.

GOLD COOKIES

¼ cup butter or margarine at room temperature
½ cup sugar
½ teaspoon vanilla extract
2 egg yolks, well beaten

¾ cup sifted flour
¾ teaspoon baking powder
Pinch of salt
24 whole nut meats

Stir together butter, sugar, extract and egg yolks; work in dry ingredients sifted together. Chill 30 minutes. Shape into marble-sized balls, using small teaspoonful for each. Top each with nut meat and put 1 inch apart on oiled cookie sheet. Bake about 12 minutes in a moderate (350 to 375°) oven. Makes 2 dozen.

PECAN WAFERS

1 cup butter at room
    temperature
1 cup sugar
1 teaspoon vanilla extract
2 eggs, well beaten
2 cups sifted flour

3 teaspoons baking powder
½ teaspoon salt
½ cup fine-chopped pecan
    meats
Halved pecan nuts

Mix butter and sugar; add vanilla and eggs. Sift dry ingredients together; add nut meats; add to first mixture. Chill 1 hour. Form into marble-sized balls by rolling between the hands; transfer to an oiled baking sheet; press half a pecan into the top of each. Bake in a hot (375°) oven for 10 minutes, or until golden brown. Makes about 5 dozen.

CHEWY DARK SWEET BROWNIES

½ cup sifted flour
½ teaspoon baking powder
¼ teaspoon salt
2 eggs
¼ cup sugar
⅓ cup butter or margarine,
    melted

2 (3-ounce) packages dark
    and sweet chocolate pudding
½ teaspoon vanilla extract
About 16 pecan halves

Sift together flour, baking powder and salt. Beat eggs until thick and frothy. Beat in sugar. Add butter or margarine. Add chocolate pudding and vanilla. Add sifted dry ingredients and mix. Spread evenly in a well-oiled baking pan, either a 12½×8¼-inch pan, which makes slim, chewy brownies, or a 10×6×1½-inch pan, which makes fatter, slightly softer brownies. Press pecan halves into batter so that when brownies are cut each piece will center a pecan. Bake 35 minutes in a slow (325°) oven. While still warm, cut into squares. These are moist, and will keep fresh days under refrigeration. Or cool, wrap-seal and freeze up to a month. Makes about 16.

SPICED GLACÉ FRUIT BARS

2½ cups sifted all-purpose
    flour
½ teaspoon baking soda
½ teaspoon salt
½ teaspoon ground cloves
½ teaspoon ground ginger
1 teaspoon ground cinnamon
¾ cup unsulphured molasses
⅓ cup shortening (any kind)

1 cup sugar
1 large egg, well beaten
½ cup nuts, chopped medium-
    fine
½ cup mixed glacé fruit
1 cup sifted confectioners'
    sugar
4 teaspoons water

Preheat oven to 350°. Sift together flour, soda, salt and spices. Combine molasses and shortening and heat in large saucepan. Stir in sugar; cool to room temperature. Mix in egg. Stir nuts and fruit into dry ingredients. Gradually stir into molasses mixture. Spread in two oiled, lightly floured 9×9×2-inch pans. Bake 30 minutes in the oven. Cool 10 minutes in pans. Turn onto wire rack. Mix confectioners' sugar with water; brush over tops while warm. Cool; cut each panful into 16 bars.

GOLDEN DATE BROWNIES

⅓ cup butter or margarine
1 cup brown sugar, packed
    down
2 large eggs
1 teaspoon vanilla extract
¾ cup sifted flour

¼ teaspoon baking soda
¾ teaspoon salt
1 cup pitted dates, sliced
½ cup walnut meats, chopped
Blanched almonds

Heat butter and brown sugar together slowly in pan until butter melts. Remove from heat; beat eggs and vanilla, stir into first mixture until well blended. Sift flour with baking soda and salt. Add to eggs; beat to smooth batter. Stir in dates and nuts. Turn into well-oiled 9-inch square pan. Bake 25 minutes in a moderate (350°) oven. When baked, remove from oven. Let stand in pan until lukewarm. Then turn onto wire cake rack to cool thoroughly. Cut into small squares with sharp knife.

To garnish, when lukewarm press blanched almond meat into center of each square. Finish as directed. Makes 2 dozen brownies.

CHOCOLATE BROWNIE MINIATURES

Three parts—crust, filling and glaze.

Nut Crust:

   3 tablespoons butter or margarine at room temperature
   3 tablespoons sugar
   ¾ cup fine-chopped walnut meats

Cream butter and sugar and add nut meats. Mix well. Line a 9-inch square baking pan with two strips of aluminum foil, 4 inches wide, and extending ½ inch above rim of pan. Press nut mixture evenly into lined pan.

Chocolate Brownie Filling:

   ½ cup butter or margarine at room temperature
   1 cup sugar
   3 eggs
   2 (2-ounce) squares unsweetened chocolate, melted and cooled

   1 teaspoon vanilla extract
   ⅓ cup sifted flour
   ½ teaspoon baking powder
   ⅛ teaspoon salt

Cream butter and sugar. By hand, beat in eggs, one at a time. Add melted chocolate and vanilla. Combine dry ingredients; stir into chocolate mixture. Turn and spread into nut-lined pan. Bake 35 to 40 minutes at 325°. (The filling should be slightly moist when done.) Cool in pan. Lift from pan by means of the ends of foil; trim brownie edges, if necessary, to make even.

Chocolate Glaze: In top of double boiler, combine ½ cup semi-sweet chocolate morsels, 2 teaspoons butter and 1 tablespoon corn syrup. Place over hot (not boiling) water until the chocolate melts; stir until mixture is smooth. Pour this over cool Chocolate Brownie Filling; spread glaze to cover top. Let stand until firm. Cut into 1 or 1½-inch squares. Top each with a small piece of nut meat. Makes 25 1½-inch squares.

DOUBLE RICH CHOCOLATE BROWNIES

2 (6-ounce) packages semi-sweet chocolate morsels (2 cups)
⅓ cup butter or margarine
½ cup sugar
2 eggs
1 teaspoon vanilla extract
½ cup sifted flour
½ teaspoon baking powder
¼ teaspoon salt
½ cup chopped nutmeats

Put 1 package semi-sweet chocolate morsels and shortening in a 1-quart saucepan. Place over low heat; stir until melted. Remove from heat. Add and mix in sugar. Add eggs, one at a time, beating well after each addition. Stir in vanilla. Sift together flour, baking powder and salt; add to chocolate mixture; mix until smooth. Stir in nut meats and remaining package of semi-sweet chocolate morsels. Spread in an oiled 8-inch square pan. Bake in a 375° oven 25 to 30 minutes. Cool. Cut into 2-inch squares. Makes 16.

CALIFORNIA FIG BARS

A typical autumn dessert.

1 cup light brown sugar
½ cup sifted flour
2 teaspoons baking powder
1 egg, beaten
2 tablespoons butter or margarine, melted
1 teaspoon vanilla extract
3 medium-sized tart apples, diced but not peeled
½ cup packaged flaked or fresh coconut
⅔ cup small-chopped dried figs
Whipped or ice cream

Combine the sugar, flour and baking powder; add the next six ingredients. Mix thoroughly; do not beat. Turn into an oiled

Bake 40 minutes in a moderate (375°) oven,
are fork-tender. Cut into 12 bars.
ld with whipped or ice cream.

OATMEAL BARS

⅓ cup butter or margarine,
  melted
2 cups uncooked oatmeal
½ cup firmly packed brown
  sugar
¼ cup dark brown syrup

½ teaspoon salt
1½ teaspoons vanilla extract
1 (6-ounce) package semi-
  sweet chocolate pieces
  (1 cup), melted
¼ cup chopped nut meats

Pour butter over oatmeal; mix thoroughly. Add sugar, syrup,
salt and vanilla; blend. Pack into greased 11×7-inch baking pan.
Bake in a preheated 450° oven about 12 minutes. (If glass baking
pan is used, preheat to 425°.) Mixture will be brown and
bubbly. Cool thoroughly.

Loosen edges; invert pan and tap firmly against bread or cutting board. Spread with melted chocolate. Sprinkle with nut
meats. Chill; cut in small bars. Store in refrigerator. Makes 3
dozen.

TOM GAD'S CONGO SQUARES

2¾ cups sifted flour
2½ teaspoons baking powder
½ teaspoon salt
⅔ cup shortening
2¼ cups brown sugar

3 eggs
1 cup nut meats
1 (12-ounce) package semi-
  sweet chocolate morsels

Mix and sift flour, baking powder and salt. Melt shortening and
add brown sugar. Stir until well mixed. Allow to cool slightly.
Add eggs, one at a time, beating well after adding each egg. Add
dry ingredients, then nut meats and chocolate. Pour into a
greased 10½×15½×¾-inch pan. Bake at 350° 25 to 30 minutes. Mixture should have a shiny look; do not overcook! Cut in
squares while warm. Makes 3 dozen.

MIKE'S BROWN SUGAR COOKIES (4-WAY COOKIES)

From home economist Eileen Wilson of Denton, Texas, comes this versatile recipe from the Gulf region.

1 cup butter	3 eggs, beaten
1 cup sugar	3 cups flour
1 cup brown sugar	1 teaspoon soda

Cream butter and sugars, and add eggs. Add sifted dry ingredients. Drop by teaspoonfuls on greased cookie sheet. Bake in a 350° oven 12 to 15 minutes. Makes about 4 dozen.

Fruit Cake Cookies: Add 2 cups of fruit mix and 1 cup chopped pecans.

Chocolate Chip Cookies: Add 1 (12-ounce) package of chocolate chips and 1 cup chopped pecans.

Pineapple-Orange Cookies: Add 1 cup drained crushed pineapple and grated rind of one orange. (This cookie is good frosted with a thin powdered sugar-orange juice mixture.)

Raisin-Spice Cookies: Add 1 cup raisins and 1 teaspoon cinnamon and ½ teaspoon allspice.

ENGLISH TEA CAKES

2¼ cups flour	1 egg and 1 egg yolk
1½ teaspoons baking powder	½ teaspoon vanilla extract
⅛ teaspoon salt	½ cup milk
½ teaspoon nutmeg	2 tablespoons powdered sugar
¾ cup sifted powdered sugar	½ cup whole nut meats or
½ cup shortening	raisins

Sift together flour, baking powder, salt, nutmeg and ¾ cup powdered sugar. Chop in shortening with pastry blender until mixture looks flaky. Beat egg and egg yolk. Add vanilla and milk.

Beat into first mixture until it is smooth and free from lumps.
Drop by heaping teaspoonfuls onto oiled cookie sheet. Keep
1 inch apart to allow spreading room. Dust with additional
powdered sugar; top each cake with a nut meat or raisin. Bake
12 minutes in a moderate (375°) oven, or until light brown.
These cakes will keep weeks in a close-covered canister. Makes
about 4 dozen.

COCONUT MACAROONS

Whites of 2 eggs	1 cup prepared coconut
⅔ cup powdered sugar	⅛ teaspoon salt

Beat the whites of the eggs until stiff, sift and add the sugar, beat
in the coconut and salt. Drop by teaspoonfuls onto waxed paper
laid on a baking sheet and bake 20 to 30 minutes at 325°. Makes
2 dozen.

Peanut Macaroons: Substitute fine-chopped shelled roasted peanuts for the coconut.

CHOCOLATE CHIP/OATMEAL COOKIES

½ cup shortening at room temperature	½ teaspoon baking soda
½ cup brown sugar	½ teaspoon salt
½ cup granulated sugar	1½ cups rolled oats
2 eggs	1 (6-ounce) package chocolate chips
1 tablespoon water	¼ cup chopped nut meats (any kind)
½ teaspoon vanilla extract	
1 cup sifted flour	

Stir shortening until creamy. Add sugars gradually; beat and
add eggs. Stir until fluffy. Stir in water and vanilla. Sift together
flour, soda and salt; add to mixture. Stir in rolled oats, chocolate
chips and nut meats. Drop from teaspoon onto oiled baking sheet
—keep cookies 2 inches apart. Bake in a moderate (375°) oven
about 12 minutes. Makes 3½ dozen.

CREOLE KISSES

Whites of 2 eggs
1 cup sugar
1 teaspoon baking powder
1 teaspoon vanilla extract

1 cup broken or chopped
pecans or 2½ cups
cornflakes

Beat whites of eggs until stiff enough to hold peaks, but not dry. Combine sugar and baking powder and add slowly to egg whites, folding in gently. Fold in vanilla, then nuts or cornflakes. Drop mixture from teaspoon on oiled cookie sheet. Bake in a slow (250°) oven until partly dry and firm enough to retain shape. Remove from cookie sheet while still hot. Makes about 3 dozen.

HERMITS

½ cup shortening
½ cup brown sugar, firmly
packed
¼ cup unsulphured molasses
1 egg
1¾ cups sifted all-purpose
flour

½ teaspoon baking soda
½ teaspoon salt
½ teaspoon cinnamon
½ teaspoon nutmeg
1 cup seedless raisins, chopped
¾ cup walnuts, chopped
¼ cup cold coffee or milk

Work shortening with back of spoon until fluffy and creamy. Add sugar and molasses gradually while continuing to work with spoon until light. Add egg. Sift dry ingredients and add raisins and walnuts; then add alternately with coffee to sugar mixture. Drop by rounded teaspoonfuls 1½ inches apart onto a greased or oiled cookie sheet and bake in a moderately hot (400°) oven for 10 to 12 minutes. Makes about 4 dozen cookies.

HONEY DROP COOKIES

1 cup butter or margarine at
room temperature
½ cup sugar
2 eggs, separated
½ tablespoon fine-grated
lemon rind
3 tablespoons lemon juice
3¼ cups sifted flour

¼ teaspoon salt
1 teaspoon baking soda
1 cup liquid honey
1 cup medium-chopped nut
meats (any kind)
60 half nut meats for topping
(optional)

Stir butter and sugar together until smooth and creamy. Beat egg yolks until light; add to butter and sugar with grated lemon rind and lemon juice. Sift together 3 cups of the flour, salt and baking soda. Add to first mixture, alternately with honey. Beat egg whites stiff and fold in. Mix remaining flour with the chopped nut meats and stir in. Drop 2 inches apart by teaspoonfuls onto slightly oiled cookie sheet. Top each cookie with a half nut meat if desired. Bake 15 minutes in a moderate (350 to 375°) oven, or until golden brown. Remove from oven and cool 1 minute. Remove from cookie sheet with spatula. Makes about 5 dozen cookies.

HONEY-SPONGE DROP COOKIES

2 eggs, separated
½ cup butter or margarine
at room temperature
½ cup sugar
Grated rind of ½ orange
½ cup milk
½ cup liquid honey
2 cups sifted flour

2 teaspoons double acting
baking powder
1 teaspoon ground cloves or
pastry spice
½ teaspoon salt
¾ cup whole nut meats or
raisins or halved pitted dates
or flaked coconut

Cream together egg yolks, butter and sugar until smooth and fluffy. Combine and mix grated orange rind, milk and honey. Sift together flour, baking powder, spice and salt. Add to first mixture alternately with orange rind, milk and honey combination. Beat egg whites until peaks form, and fold in. Drop by teaspoon onto oiled large cookie sheet, keeping the cookies 2 inches apart to allow for spreading. Top each cookie with a nut meat, raisin or date; or dust with flaked coconut. Bake 12 minutes in a moderate (375°) oven. Remove from pan while warm. Makes 4 dozen. These cookies will keep fresh in a tight-closed jar for 3 weeks.

LACE WAFERS

1 cup sifted flour
1 cup chopped flaked coconut or fine-chopped nuts
½ cup light or dark corn syrup
½ cup firm-packed brown sugar
½ cup butter or margarine
1 teaspoon vanilla extract

Mix together sifted flour and coconut or nuts. Combine corn syrup, brown sugar and butter in heavy saucepan. Bring to boil over medium heat, stirring constantly. Remove from heat. Gradually blend in flour-coconut mixture, then stir in vanilla. Drop batter onto a foil-covered cookie sheet by scant teaspoonfuls 3 inches apart. Bake in a moderate (350°) oven 8 to 10 minutes. Cool on wire rack until foil may easily be peeled off, 3 to 4 minutes. Remove foil, continue to cool cookies on wire rack covered with paper toweling. Makes 4½ dozen 3-inch cookies.

MIDWESTERN RAISIN-DROPPED COOKIES

1 cup sifted all-purpose flour
⅔ cup enriched corn meal
¼ teaspoon baking soda
1 teaspoon baking powder
¼ teaspoon salt
⅓ cup shortening at room temperature
⅓ cup sugar
⅓ cup brown sugar
1 egg
½ cup sour cream
½ teaspoon vanilla extract
⅔ cup raisins
2 tablespoons cinnamon-sugar

Sift together flour, corn meal, soda, baking powder and salt. Beat shortening with sugars and egg until light and fluffy. Add flour mixture alternately with sour cream, mixing thoroughly.

Stir in vanilla and raisins. Drop by half tablespoonfuls 2 inches apart on oiled cookie sheet. Dust with cinnamon-sugar. Bake in a moderate (375°) oven 10 to 12 minutes. Makes 3 dozen.

NEVADA HONEY COOKIES

½ cup shortening at room
  temperature
½ cup sugar
½ cup liquid honey
1 egg
1 cup sifted flour

½ teaspoon baking soda
½ teaspoon baking powder
¼ teaspoon salt
1 cup quick-cooking rolled oats
1 cup canned shredded coconut
½ cup chopped nut meats

Mix shortening, sugar and honey together until light. Add egg and beat well. Sift flour, soda, baking powder and salt together. Combine with creamed mixture. Stir in rolled oats, coconut and nut meats. Drop by tablespoonfuls 2 inches apart on oiled cookie sheet. Bake in a moderate (350°) oven 15 minutes, or until cookies are golden brown. Remove from cookie sheet while warm but not hot. Makes 30 cookies.

OLD-FASHIONED BROWNIE COOKIES

⅓ cup butter or shortening
¾ cup sugar
4 tablespoons milk
2 eggs, well beaten
2 (1-ounce) squares chocolate,
  melted

1 cup pastry flour
Pinch of salt
¾ cup chopped nut meats
1 teaspoon vanilla extract

Cream the shortening, add the sugar gradually, then the milk, the well-beaten eggs, melted chocolate and the flour and salt sifted together. Last add the nut meats and vanilla. Drop by teaspoonfuls onto shallow oiled pans and bake 12 to 15 minutes in a moderately hot (350 to 375°) oven. Or add 2 additional tablespoons of milk and spread the mixture in a shallow oiled baking pan, bake 15 minutes, and when cold cut into squares. Makes 16.

SOFT MOLASSES COOKIES

1 cup (2 sticks) butter or
    margarine at room
    temperature
½ teaspoon salt
3 teaspoons soda
2 teaspoons ground ginger
1 teaspoon powdered mustard
1 teaspoon instant coffee

½ teaspoon ground cloves
1 cup sugar
1 cup light molasses
1 egg, unbeaten
4¾ cups sifted flour
¾ cup water
Walnut halves or raisins

Mix first seven ingredients together until fluffy. Gradually blend in sugar and molasses. Beat in egg. Add flour alternately with water. Beat batter ½ minute. Drop onto oiled cookie sheets from a teaspoon, being careful to keep cookies round. Press a walnut half or a raisin in center of each. Bake 15 minutes, or until done in a moderate (350 to 375°) oven. Makes 5 dozen large cookies.

SPICED FRESH ORANGE COOKIES

¾ cup butter or margarine
    at room temperature
1 cup sugar
1 teaspoon grated orange rind
1 teaspoon grated lemon rind
½ teaspoon salt
½ teaspoon baking soda

1 teaspoon ground nutmeg
1 egg, beaten
¼ cup orange juice
½ cup sour cream
2 cups sifted flour
1 cup seedless raisins

Stir butter until fluffy. Gradually blend in sugar. Add next five ingredients. Mix well. Beat in egg. Combine orange juice and sour cream. Add alternately with flour, mixing well after each addition. Stir in raisins. Drop from teaspoon onto lightly oiled baking sheets. Bake 9 minutes in a moderate (375°) oven, or until brown around edges. Makes 3 dozen.

BUGIES (FRIED COOKIES)

3 egg yolks, beaten light
¼ teaspoon salt
½ teaspoon cinnamon
1 teaspoon water

About 1¼ cups flour
Vegetable oil for deep frying
Powdered sugar

Mix egg yolks, salt, cinnamon and water; stir in flour (enough
to make a thick paste). Turn onto slightly floured surface. Roll
very thin; cut in narrow strips—about 6 inches long. Fry in deep
oil, 390°, or hot enough to brown a cubelet of bread in 40 seconds. Drain on crumpled paper; dust with powdered sugar.
Makes about 3 dozen.

COLOMBIA ORANGE PUFFS

2 cups sifted enriched flour
2 tablespoons butter
½ teaspoon salt
2 tablespoons sugar

⅓ cup orange juice
Cold water, if needed
Sifted powdered sugar

Combine flour, butter, salt, sugar and orange juice and work
into smooth dough. If too stiff, add a few drops cold water.
Transfer to pastry board and roll out as thin as possible. Cut in
rounds, stars, squares or any desired shape. Fry in deep fat
heated to 360° for about 5 minutes. Drain on paper toweling;
then dust with sifted powdered sugar. Makes 4 dozen.

BROWN-EDGE COOKIES

1 cup butter or margarine at
    room temperature
1 teaspoon vanilla extract
1 cup brown sugar
2 eggs, beaten

3 cups sifted flour
¼ teaspoon baking soda
1 teaspoon baking powder
½ teaspoon salt

Stir butter with the vanilla, brown sugar and eggs until well
mixed. Sift together dry ingredients. Work into first mixture.

Form into roll 2 inches thick. Wrap in aluminum foil; refrigerate 2 hours, or until very firm. Slice very thin using sharp knife. Place cookies 2 inches apart on oiled baking sheet. Bake 7 minutes in a moderate (375°) oven, or until browned on edges but still light in center. Cool.

Kept in tightly closed tin canister, these cookies will stay fresh 2 weeks. Makes 5 dozen.

ICEBOX COOKIES

1 cup butter	1 teaspoon baking powder
1 cup light brown sugar	1/3 teaspoon salt
1 teaspoon vanilla extract	1/2 cup fine-chopped almonds
2 eggs, well beaten	or granulated sugar
3 cups all-purpose flour	(optional)
1/4 teaspoon baking soda	

Stir the butter until creamy; gradually work in the sugar and add the vanilla and the eggs, well beaten. Sift the dry ingredients together and combine with the first mixture. Form into a roll 2 inches in diameter; wrap in waxed paper and chill a few hours or until firm enough to slice. Then slice paper thin. Transfer to an oiled pan or cookie sheet and sprinkle with the almonds, or dust with granulated sugar. Bake in a hot (375°) oven for 10 minutes, or until a delicate brown. Makes 4 dozen.

PENUCHE NUT ICEBOX COOKIES

1 cup shortening	3 cups all-purpose flour
1 cup light brown sugar	1/4 teaspoon baking soda
(packed)	1 teaspoon baking powder
1 large egg, beaten	1/3 teaspoon salt
1/2 teaspoon vanilla extract	1/2 cup chopped nut meats

Stir shortening until smooth and creamy. Add brown sugar, which should be sifted. Beat egg, and add to mixture. Add vanilla. Then sift together dry ingredients except nut meats, and stir in. Shape this dough into a roll about 2 inches in diameter, wrap in aluminum foil and chill in refrigerator a few hours. When dough is firm, slice thin with a very sharp knife. Place on a large oiled pan and sprinkle with the chopped nuts. Bake 10 minutes in a hot (375°) oven. Makes 2½ to 3 dozen.

GINGERBREAD MEN

With a little ingenuity, a little time and some cookie cutters, you can make gingerbread men, bells, stars and Christmas trees—all by following this recipe.

1 cup mild, light molasses	2½ teaspoons ground
1 cup butter or margarine	cinnamon
4¾ cups sifted flour	2½ teaspoons ground ginger
1 teaspoon double acting	2 teaspoons ground nutmeg
baking powder	1 cup dark brown sugar, firmly
1½ teaspoons salt	packed
¾ teaspoon baking soda	1 large egg, beaten slightly

Heat molasses slowly in saucepan large enough for mixing cookies. Remove from heat. Add butter or margarine and stir until melted. Cool. Sift together next seven ingredients. Mix with brown sugar and stir into molasses mixture. Add egg. Chill 2 hours, or until stiff enough to handle. Roll ¼ to ⅛ inch thick on lightly floured smooth surface. Shape with gingerbread man cookie cutter. Place on lightly oiled cookie sheets and bake 12 to 15 minutes in a preheated moderate (350°) oven. Decorate as desired with raisins, currants or frosting. Makes 48 gingerbread men 6 inches tall—plus a few bells, Christmas trees and stars from the leftover scraps of dough.

OLD-FASHIONED GINGERSNAPS

½ cup butter or shortening	½ teaspoon salt
⅔ cup brown sugar	½ teaspoon baking soda
⅓ cup molasses	1½ teaspoons ground ginger
2½ cups pastry flour	About ⅓ cup milk

Beat the shortening and sugar together until creamy, add the molasses, and the dry ingredients sifted together, alternately with the milk. Chill for 1 hour, then roll out thin and cut into squares or rounds. Bake in an oiled pan in a moderate (350°) oven 8 to 10 minutes, and remove from the pan while the snaps are still warm. Makes 2½ dozen.

LITTLE SCOTCH SHORTBREADS

1½ cups sifted cake flour
½ cup cornstarch
½ teaspoon salt
1 cup unsalted butter

½ cup sugar
Tiny candies or chopped nut
  meats (optional)

Sift together the already sifted cake flour, cornstarch and salt. Add unsalted butter and chop in with pastry blender. Then work in sugar continually, working dough with a wooden spoon until it is fine and smooth. On board, flatten dough ½ inch thick. Cut into cakes with a 2½-inch cookie cutter. Crimp edges with fingers and lift each cake carefully to baking pan. If desired decorate with tiny candies or chopped nut meats. Bake 40 to 45 minutes in a slow (325 to 350°) oven, or until very lightly browned. Makes 2 dozen shortbreads.

SOUR CREAM COOKIES

1 large egg
1 teaspoon baking soda
½ tablespoon hot water
1 cup dairy sour cream
1¾ cups granulated or light
  brown sugar

½ teaspoon salt
1 teaspoon ground nutmeg
4 cups sifted flour

Beat egg lightly. Dissolve baking soda in hot water. Add to sour cream. Add egg, sugar and salt. Stir-beat in nutmeg and flour. Cover; chill 1 hour or more. Then transfer to floured surface. (If necessary work in a little extra flour if dough is too soft to roll.)

Roll ⅓ inch thick. Shape into rounds with a 2-inch cutter.

Place on oiled baking sheet. Bake 8 to 10 minutes in a moderate (375°) oven, or until lightly browned. Makes about 4 dozen. These cookies may be stored indefinitely in close-covered canister.

SUGAR COOKIES

3⅔ cups sifted cake flour
2½ teaspoons double acting
  baking powder
½ teaspoon salt
⅔ cup butter or margarine at
  room temperature

1½ cups sugar
2 eggs, unbeaten
1 teaspoon vanilla extract
4 teaspoons milk
½ cup granulated sugar

Sift together flour, baking powder and salt. Cream butter, add sugar gradually, beating well. Add eggs, one at a time, beating thoroughly after each. Add vanilla. Add flour mixture alternately with milk, mixing well after each addition to make a dough. Chill 3 to 4 hours, or overnight. Roll dough wafer-thin on lightly floured surface, cut with a floured 3-inch scalloped cutter and dust with white granulated sugar. Bake 5 to 8 minutes on ungreased cookie sheets at 400°. Makes 6 dozen cookies.

BUTTERSCOTCH SAND COOKIES

4 cups sifted flour
1½ cups granulated sugar
1⅓ cups butter or margarine
1 whole egg plus 1 egg yolk
¾ cup unsulphured molasses

1½ teaspoons vanilla extract
¼ cup sugar
1 teaspoon vinegar
½ cup confectioners' sugar

Sift together flour and sugar. Chop butter or margarine into flour and sugar with pastry blender until mixture resembles coarse meal. Beat egg and yolk. Combine with molasses, vanilla, additional sugar, and vinegar. Stir into flour mixture to make a dough. Refrigerate overnight or until stiff enough to handle. Roll ¹⁄₁₆ inch thick on smooth surface dusted lightly with some confectioners' sugar. Roll only a small piece of dough at a time and shape with cookie cutter. (Keep remaining dough refrigerated.) Bake 6 to 7 minutes on lightly oiled cookie sheets in moderate

(375°) oven, or until edges are browned lightly. Cool. Store in tightly closed tin box to keep crisp. Makes about 60 cookies.

Note: Lift cookies while hot from the cookie sheet, using broad spatula. If cooled before lifting, the cookies will crumble.

IRISH OAT COOKIES

½ cup shortening, soft
⅔ cup sugar
2 eggs, unbeaten
1 teaspoon vanilla extract
2 cups sifted enriched flour

½ teaspoon salt
½ teaspoon baking soda
1 cup uncooked quick or old-fashioned rolled oats
Sugar (optional)

Preheat oven to moderate (375°). Mix shortening and sugar together until creamy. Mix in eggs and vanilla. Sift together flour, salt and baking soda. Mix into creamed mixture thoroughly. Stir-mix in oats. Roll out on lightly floured smooth surface to ⅛ inch thickness. Cut with a 2-inch round cutter first dipped in flour. Place cookies 1 inch apart on oiled cookie sheets. Dust with granulated sugar if desired. Bake 12 to 15 minutes. Makes 4 dozen.

CHINESE ALMOND CAKES

1 teaspoon almond extract
2 cups butter or 1 cup each
    butter and margarine
4 cups flour

1½ cups sugar
½ teaspoon salt
Blanched almonds, halved

Work the flavoring into the shortening, then rub this very thoroughly into the flour. Add the sugar and salt and knead and work to a paste. No moisture will be required. Form into a thick roll, cut into slices ½ inch thick, lay the slices 1 inch apart on a greased cookie sheet. Press half a blanched almond into each cake, and bake 30 minutes in a moderate (350°) oven. Makes about 4 dozen.

Cakes and Frostings

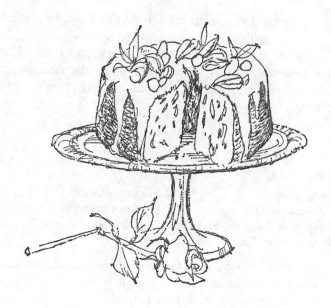

Cakes

Over the years I've earmarked some special recipes for cakes that I know you'll enjoy making and eating. A word of advice: follow the recipes exactly. All measurements are level, sift all flour *before* measuring. Don't experiment—do as the directions tell you, in the order given, and you'll have a successful mouth-watering cake.

ANGEL CAKE

8 egg whites
½ teaspoon flavoring
1 cup granulated sugar
¾ cup pastry flour

⅛ teaspoon salt
⅔ teaspoon cream of tartar
1 tablespoon cornstarch

Beat the whites of eggs until so stiff that they remain stationary even when the bowl containing them is inverted. Add the flavoring, then the sugar, a little at a time, beating it well into the egg whites. Sift the flour, salt, cream of tartar and cornstarch three times, fold very gently into the first mixture, turn carefully into a large unoiled angel cake pan and bake about 45 minutes in a slow (325°) oven, covering the cake with foil during the first 15 minutes of baking. When done leave the cake in the pan and invert it, resting the edges on two cups during the cooling, should it not be the kind of pan with raised removable slides. Makes a 9-inch ring.

STRAWBERRY TALLCAKE

1 (10-ounce) package angel food cake mix prepared according to package directions

⅓ cup port or Madeira or orange juice

1½ cups heavy cream

¼ cup sugar

2 pints fresh strawberries, hulled

2 tablespoons toasted slivered blanched almonds

Slice cake in 2 equal layers; sprinkle each layer with 2 tablespoons of the wine or orange juice. Whip cream with sugar and remaining wine or orange juice until stiff. Crush 1 cup of strawberries and fold in, making strawberried whipped cream. Spread this on top of each of the 2 cake layers. Slice 1 cup of strawberries onto 1 layer; top this with second layer. Arrange remaining strawberries atop cake. Strew with almonds. Serves 12 to 15.

TIPSY PARSON

2 8-inch round spongecake layers

½ cup beach plum jelly (if available. If not, any tart jelly such as currant or grape)

½ cup toasted shredded almonds

1 package vanilla pudding mix

1 cup half and half or evaporated milk

1¼ cups milk

¼ cup Marsala or sherry

Spread one layer of cake with half the jelly, sprinkle with half the almonds. Cover with remaining layer, spread with rest of jelly and sprinkle with remaining almonds. Prepare pudding according to directions but use 2½ cups of liquid in all, including milk and Marsala or sherry in above quantities. Cool, covered with a round of waxed paper, to prevent top from hardening. Before serving, pour sauce over cake. Serves 8.

OLD VIRGINIA TIPSY CAKE

5 eggs, separated
¼ teaspoon salt
2 cups sugar
2 cups sifted flour
3 teaspoons baking powder

½ cup cold water
1 teaspoon vanilla extract
1 pint sherry wine
Whipped cream with brandy
  or brandy extract

Beat egg yolks, salt and sugar together until very light. Sift flour and baking powder together; add alternately with water and vanilla, adding a little water first. Fold in stiffly beaten egg whites. Pour into unoiled angel food pan; bake in moderate (350°) oven for 50 to 60 minutes. Invert pan on rack until cool. Remove from pan. A few hours before serving, pour sherry wine over cake and let it stand. Serve with whipped cream laced with brandy.

Note: You can take the "tipsy" out of the cake by using equal parts of strained orange juice and apple juice with a whiff of grated nutmeg instead of the sherry. Serves 8.

SPONGECAKE

6 eggs, separated
1 cup sugar
1 teaspoon vanilla extract or
  other desired flavoring

1 cup bread flour
½ teaspoon salt

Separate the whites from the yolks of the eggs, beat the whites until stiff and dry, the yolks until thick. Add the sugar gradually to the yolks of eggs, beating until the mixture is very light and fluffy. Add the flavoring, then blend in the whites of eggs carefully. Sift the flour and salt 3 times and fold in gently. Turn at once into a good-sized loaf cake pan that has been well oiled, dusted with powdered sugar, and the loose sugar thoroughly shaken out. Bake about 1 hour, having the oven moderately hot (350°) to begin with, then increasing the heat to 375° when the cake is about half done; lower it toward the end of the baking so that it does not become too dark a color. Makes 1 spongecake.

ZUPPA INGLESE

First cousin to the traditional English trifle. Elegant for display service at table. Or to make an entrance with a hostess wagon when guests arrive after dinner for dessert and coffee.

1 spongecake, 10 × 10 inches square	1 cup heavy cream
½ cup sweet vermouth	1 tablespoon sugar
½ cup dark rum	½ tablespoon rum
1 cup jam or preserves of desired choice	Candied violets
	Angelica
Cream Custard (see Index)	Cherries glacé

Split the spongecake into 3 layers. Place 1 on a handsome deep plate. Pour over ⅓ cup each vermouth and rum. Spread with jam or preserves; cover with half the custard. Repeat with the second layer and remaining custard. Then put the top layer in place; pour over the remaining vermouth and rum. Chill at least 2 hours. Whip the cream stiff with sugar and additional rum. Spread over the cake. Decorate with alternating clusters of candied violets, the leaves and stems cut from the angelica or citron, and clusters of red cherry "berries" embellished with the same. Better scald the angelica with hot water and dry it before using, for pliability. Serves 8.

ALMOND APPLE CAKE

½ cup butter	2 egg yolks
½ cup sugar	3 egg whites
½ cup blanched, ground almonds	2½ cups stewed hot apples
	½ cup soft fine bread crumbs
½ teaspoon grated lemon peel	2 tablespoons butter
2 tablespoons lemon juice	

Blend butter and sugar. When smooth, add almonds, lemon peel, and juice. Beat until light and fluffy, adding egg yolks, one at a time. Whip egg whites stiff and fold in, making an egg batter.

Slightly sweeten hot stewed apples to taste; spoon into a buttered 2-quart baking dish. Lightly brown bread crumbs in additional butter and stir in. Top with egg batter. Bake 25 minutes in moderate (350 to 375°) oven, or until puffed and golden. Serves 8 to 10.

APPLE CRUMB COFFEE CAKE

The Cake:

½ cup sugar	1 cup flour
3 tablespoons shortening at room temperature	1½ teaspoons baking powder
	¼ teaspoon salt
1 egg, beaten	¼ cup milk

Mix together sugar and shortening; add egg. Beat well. Sift together flour, baking powder and salt; add alternately with milk to first mixture. Pour into an oiled 8×8×2-inch pan.

The Filling:

2 cups canned applesauce	½ teaspoon ground cinnamon
½ cup brownulated sugar	⅛ teaspoon ground cloves
1 teaspoon lemon juice	

Combine all above ingredients; mix well. Spoon over cake batter.

Crumb Topping:

½ cup sifted flour	½ cup chopped pecan meats
⅓ cup brownulated sugar	
3 tablespoons butter or margarine	

Mix all ingredients together until crumbly. Spread evenly over applesauce layer. Bake 50 minutes in moderate (375°) oven. Enjoy it warm on the day it is made. Serves 6 to 10.

BRITISH APPLE CAKE

½ cup shortening or margarine at room temperature
1 cup sugar
2 eggs
2½ cups sifted flour
1 teaspoon baking soda
1 teaspoon double acting baking powder
½ teaspoon salt

½ teaspoon ground ginger or ground cinnamon or ground cloves
½ cup milk
1¼ cups coarse-grated peeled raw tart apple
1 teaspoon grated lemon rind
2 tablespoons granulated sugar

Stir the shortening and sugar until creamy and light. Separate the eggs. Beat the whites stiff and the yolks lemon-colored. Add the yolks to the shortening mixture. Beat thoroughly. Combine and sift together the dry ingredients. Add gradually to the first mixture, alternately with the milk. Beat 5 strokes after each addition. Last, fold in the grated apple, lemon rind and the beaten egg whites. Transfer to an oiled 7×11-inch shallow pan. Dust with 2 tablespoons granulated sugar. Bake 50 to 60 minutes in a moderate (350°) oven, or until a pick inserted near the center comes out clean. Serve hot or cold. Serves 8.

APPLESAUCE CAKE

1 cup sugar
½ cup butter or margarine
1 cup applesauce
1 teaspoon baking soda
1 cup seeded raisins
½ cup currants

2 cups pastry flour
1 teaspoon salt
¼ teaspoon ground cloves
¼ teaspoon ground nutmeg
1 teaspoon ground cinnamon
1 teaspoon ground ginger

Cream the sugar and butter until light, add the applesauce with which the soda has been mixed, then the raisins and currants mixed with the flour, salt and spices sifted together. Beat hard— the batter will become thinner as the process continues. Bake in a large oiled cake pan in a moderate (350°) oven about 1 hour. This cake will keep for several weeks and slices of it may be steamed, if desired, and served as a pudding with a hot fruit sauce. Serves 8.

DANISH APPLE CAKE

2 cups fine day-old bread
  crumbs (not dry)
1 teaspoon ground cinnamon
½ cup sugar
1 pint cinnamon-flavored
  applesauce

2 tablespoons butter or
  margarine, melted
1 cup strawberry or any jam
Whipped cream

Rub a quart baking dish with butter or margarine. Combine crumbs, cinnamon and sugar. Pat a ¼-inch layer in baking dish. Over this spoon a layer of applesauce; continue until all crumb mixture and applesauce are used. Make the top layer crumbs. Press together with spoon. Pour over melted butter or margarine. Bake 30 minutes in a moderate (375°) oven. Half cool, and unmold. Spread with the jam; finish with whipped cream. Serves 8.

DUTCH APPLE CAKE IN FOUR STEPS

Step 1:

Prepare ½ recipe Rich American Pie Pastry (see Index), or use 1 package pie pastry mix. Roll a scant ¼ inch thick and line a low round 10-inch cake pan with pastry. Bake in moderate (350°) oven about 30 minutes. Cake shell should be only slightly browned.

Step 2:

4 tablespoons butter
1 pound 2 ounces peeled,
  cored and quartered apples
  (about 5 small)
1 tablespoon raisins

½ teaspoon cinnamon
½ tablespoon sugar
¼ teaspoon nutmeg
Juice of 1 lemon

Melt butter in a 2-quart saucepan. Add quartered cored apples, raisins, cinnamon, sugar and nutmeg. Sprinkle with lemon juice. Cover; slow-simmer until apples are barely tender. Cool to room temperature.

Step 3:

1½ pints milk	¼ teaspoon vanilla extract
5 eggs	¼ teaspoon salt
½ cup granulated sugar	

In electric blender, mix all the ingredients of the third step and then put through fine strainer, making uncooked custard mixture.

Step 4:

Spread apple mixture evenly in cake shell. Cover with custard mixture. Bake in moderate (350°) oven from 45 minutes to 1 hour. Serve at room temperature.

Note: If you do not have blender, beat eggs with rotary beater until frothy with sugar, vanilla and salt; then beat in milk. Serves 8 to 10.

HUDSON VALLEY APPLE CAKE

1 cup sifted flour	½ cup raisins
2 tablespoons sugar	¾ cup sugar
¼ teaspoon baking powder	1 teaspoon cinnamon
½ teaspoon salt	1 lemon, juice and grated rind
¼ teaspoon vanilla	¼ cup white wine (or apple
½ cup butter or margarine	juice)
4 cups thin-sliced peeled	2 egg yolks
cooking apples	1 tablespoon sugar
¾ cup chopped almonds	1 cup heavy sweet cream or
(optional)	sour cream

In a quart bowl, mix flour, sugar, baking powder, salt and vanilla. Add butter or margarine; chop in with pastry blender until fairly fine consistency. Spread over bottom of a buttered

9-inch round pan, about 2 inches deep. Mix together apples, almonds, raisins, additional sugar, cinnamon, lemon juice and rind, and wine or apple juice. Spread into pastry-lined pan. Bake 10 minutes in a hot (425°) oven. Meantime, mix egg yolks, 1 tablespoon sugar and cream. Spoon over apple topping. Continue baking 35 minutes at 350°. Cool and cut in wedge-shaped pieces. Serves 8.

BLUEBERRY CRUMB CAKE

2½ cups sifted all-purpose
    flour
1 cup sugar
2 teaspoons baking powder
1 teaspoon salt
1 teaspoon ground nutmeg
⅔ cup vegetable shortening
⅓ cup molasses

⅔ cup milk
4 eggs
1 teaspoon vanilla extract
2 cups fresh cultivated
    blueberries or dry-pack
    frozen blueberries
Topping

Mix flour, sugar, baking powder, salt and nutmeg. Add shortening, molasses and milk. Beat 2 minutes with electric mixer. Add eggs and vanilla and beat again for 2 minutes, making a batter. Pour half the batter into well-oiled 13×9×2-inch pan. Sprinkle blueberries over batter. Spoon remaining batter over blueberries. Spread batter evenly in pan. Combine Topping ingredients and sprinkle over batter. Bake 45 to 50 minutes in preheated moderate (350°) oven, or until edges of cake shrink slightly from pan. Serve warm. Serves 8 to 10.

Topping:

¾ cup firm-packed brown
    sugar
½ cup quick-cooking oatmeal

½ cup chopped pecan meats
¼ cup melted butter

ORANGE-GRAPE CAKE FIESTA

2 cups sifted flour	⅔ cup shortening
½ teaspoon salt	1⅓ cups sugar
2 teaspoons double acting baking powder	3 eggs
	⅔ cup milk
1 tablespoon grated orange rind	Creamy Frosting
	Toasted blanched almonds
1 teaspoon grated lemon rind	Fresh grapes in season

Sift together the first three ingredients. Next, stir together the orange and lemon rind, shortening and sugar until fluffy. Beat the eggs, one at a time, into the shortening mixture. Alternately add the milk with the flour mixture, beginning and ending with the flour mixture. Beat 20 strokes after all are added. Pour the batter into a well-oiled, lightly floured 9×3-inch tube pan. Bake 45 to 50 minutes in a moderate (350°) oven, or until done. Cool 10 minutes. Turn onto a wire rack to finish cooling. When cold, cover with Creamy Frosting. Decorate with toasted blanched almonds and clusters of fresh grapes. Serves 12.

Creamy Frosting:

¼ cup butter or margarine	¼ cup milk or half and half
3½ cups sifted confectioners' sugar	Pinch of salt
	1 teaspoon vanilla extract

Mix the butter until fluffy. Add the confectioners' sugar alternately with the milk until the mixture is of spreading consistency. Blend in the salt and the vanilla extract. Spread over top and sides of the Orange-Grape Cake Fiesta.

ORANGE MARMALADE SUNSHINE CAKE

¾ cup butter or margarine
1 cup sugar
1 tablespoon grated orange
 rind
1 teaspoon vanilla
3 eggs, unbeaten
1 cup orange marmalade
½ cup raisins (optional)
3 cups sifted flour

1½ teaspoons baking soda
1 teaspoon salt
1 cup buttermilk
1 recipe Ambrosia Frosting
 (see Index)
¼ cup shredded or packaged
 coconut
12 peeled orange sections

Combine butter, sugar, orange rind and vanilla; mix-stir until very fluffy. Add eggs, one at a time, beating in thoroughly after each addition. Stir in marmalade, and raisins if desired. Sift together flour, baking soda and salt. Add alternately to first mixture with buttermilk. Oil a 9-inch tube pan; line bottom with waxed paper cut to fit. Turn in the batter. Bake 1 hour in moderate 350° oven. Let cake cool 10 minutes in pan; then loosen top edges and turn out on rack. Spread with Ambrosia Frosting. Dust with coconut, and just before serving, ring the top with orange sections. Serves 12.

MELLOW YELLOW PUMPKIN CAKE

A delightful, spicy cake to welcome in the fall.

1¾ cups sifted enriched flour
2 teaspoons baking powder
1 teaspoon baking soda
½ teaspoon salt
2 teaspoons ground cinnamon
½ teaspoon ground nutmeg
¼ teaspoon ground allspice
¼ teaspoon ground ginger

½ cup shortening at room
 temperature
1⅓ cups sugar
2 eggs, unbeaten
1 cup sieved cooked or canned
 pumpkin
⅔ cup buttermilk

Sift together flour, baking powder, baking soda, salt and spices. Mix together shortening and sugar until light and fluffy. Add unbeaten eggs, one at a time, beating well after each addition. Combine pumpkin and buttermilk. Add alternately with flour mixture to shortening and sugar. Transfer to well-oiled, paper-lined 9-inch square pan, and bake 45 minutes in a moderate (350°) oven. Cool. Serve as is, or with a lemon sauce. Serves 8 to 10.

RAISIN TUDOR FRUIT CAKE

A long recipe—but not too much work and really outstanding.

2 (15-ounce) packages dark seedless raisins
1 (15-ounce) package golden seedless raisins
2⅔ cups dried figs
2 cups pitted dates
3 cups candied cherries
3 cups mixed candied fruits and peels
4 cups broken walnuts or pecans
4 cups sifted flour
1 teaspoon salt
2 teaspoons cinnamon
2 teaspoons ground cloves
1 teaspoon nutmeg
1 teaspoon allspice
1 pound soft butter or margarine
1 pound sifted brown sugar
2 tablespoons grated orange peel
1 tablespoon grated lemon peel
12 eggs, separated
1 cup thick strawberry jam
1 cup canned pineapple juice
¾ cup orange juice
2 tablespoons lemon juice

Chop all raisins coarse or leave whole, as desired. Clip stems from figs; cut figs in strips. Cut dates in strips; cherries in half, and mixed fruits and peels in medium-sized dice. Combine fruits and nuts. Sift flour with salt and spices. Add 1 cup of the flour mixture to fruit and nut mixture stirring until they are coated. To make batter, beat butter, sugar, grated orange and lemon peel until light and fluffy. Beat in well-beaten egg yolks. Add coated fruit-nut mixture, jam and fruit juices to batter. Using hands, mix thoroughly until well combined. Add remaining 3 cups flour mixture, mixing in well. Fold in stiffly beaten egg whites until completely blended. Makes 4½ quarts batter.

Spoon batter into 1 (13-cup) ring mold and 1 8½×4½×

2½-inch loaf pan, which have been oiled, lined with smooth brown paper and oiled again. Bake in slow (250°) oven with shallow pan of water put in a corner of the bottom of the oven (see note) for about 3½ to 4 hours, or until cakes are done when tested with a pick which comes out clean after it is inserted. Let cakes stand ½ hour before turning out on wire racks to cool. When completely cold, wrap in waxed paper for storing. Serves 16.

Note: When placing fruit cake in oven to bake, be sure you do not put it directly over the pan of water on the bottom of oven. The water is there to create a little steam so cake will not be dry. By the way, the cake is raised by using beaten egg whites in the manner of the olden days.

STRAWBERRY SHORTCAKE

What collection of recipes best loved by Americans would be complete without this all-time favorite? Easier than ever to make today, Strawberry Shortcake is a hearty and nutritious dessert that can originate, with a minimum of effort, in every American kitchen.

1 quart strawberries, rinsed, drained, hulled and slightly crushed, or 2 (10-ounce) packages frozen strawberries, thawed
1 cup sugar (omit sugar if frozen strawberries are used)
2⅓ cups biscuit mix

3 tablespoons sugar
3 tablespoons butter, melted
½ cup milk
1 cup whipping cream
3 tablespoons confectioners' sugar, sifted
1 teaspoon vanilla extract
Butter at room temperature

An hour or so before serving, mix crushed berries with sugar and set in refrigerator to chill. Mix from time to time.

Combine biscuit mix, sugar, butter and milk to form a dough. Knead on floured board about 10 times. Roll out to ½ inch thickness. Cut into 6 rounds with a 3-inch floured cutter. Bake 10 minutes on ungreased baking sheet at 450°. Meanwhile, whip cream, adding confectioners' sugar gradually, till stiff. Add vanilla.

To assemble, split and lightly butter biscuits while warm. Spoon half the crushed berries over bottom halves. Cover with top halves and spoon remaining berries over tops. Cover with the whipped cream. Serve immediately. Serves 6.

LEMON ICEBOX CAKE

A long recipe, but easy to do. It consists of a crumb lining, custard and cottage cheese filling.

1 cup graham cracker crumbs	2 tablespoons milk
3 tablespoons confectioners' sugar	⅛ teaspoon salt
2 tablespoons melted butter or margarine	1½ cups cottage cheese
	½ cup sweetened condensed milk
1 envelope unflavored gelatin	2½ tablespoons lemon juice
1½ tablespoons cold water	½ teaspoon grated lemon rind
1 egg, beaten	½ teaspoon vanilla
1 egg yolk	1 large egg white
1½ tablespoons sugar	

Blend crumbs, confectioners' sugar and butter or margarine. Reserve 3 tablespoons of this mixture. Press remainder into 9-inch square pan to make thin lining. Combine gelatin and cold water. Mix together egg, egg yolk, sugar, milk and salt. Stir-cook in double boiler until thickened. Add gelatin, stirring until dissolved. Cool. Beat cottage cheese, condensed milk, lemon juice, lemon rind and vanilla until well mixed. Add custard. Beat egg white stiff and fold into cheese mixture. Pour into crumb-lined pan. Dust reserved crumbs on top. Chill until set. Serves 8 to 10.

CHOCOLATE ICEBOX CAKE

2 (6-ounce) packages semi-sweet chocolate bits	18 ladyfingers or spongecake strips
4½ tablespoons hot water	1 cup heavy cream, whipped stiff
7 eggs, separated	½ cup chocolate shavings
1 teaspoon vanilla extract	

Melt chocolate with hot water in double boiler. Beat egg yolks and stir in; cook-stir 7 minutes or until thickened. Remove from heat; add vanilla; cool. Line a 1½- or 2-quart loaf pan with waxed paper. Use 2 wide strips of paper, laying one lengthwise, the other crosswise, leaving enough paper to cover top from both ends and sides. Beat egg whites until soft peaks form; fold carefully into chocolate mixture. Pour into paper-lined pan. On top put ladyfingers or spongecake strips cut to fit. Fold paper over. Refrigerate at least 4 hours. When ready to serve, cut away top paper and turn out mold onto chilled platter. Remove remaining paper; frost with whipped cream. Garnish with chocolate shavings. Serves 8.

CHOCOLATE CREAM ROLL PARISIENNE

7 ounces sweet chocolate	Powdered sugar or dry cocoa
1 tablespoon water	1 cup heavy cream, whipped
7 eggs, separated	and sweetened
¾ cup sugar	

Combine chocolate and water; melt in double boiler. Separate eggs; add sugar to yolks; beat together until very light. Beat into chocolate. Whip egg whites stiff in good-sized bowl. Fold in chocolate mixture. Mix gently but thoroughly, making a batter. Lightly oil a 12×15-inch cookie sheet. Cover with waxed paper and lightly oil again. Spread batter evenly on cookie sheet, leaving an inch margin all around. Bake 15 minutes in a moderate (350°) oven.

When done, cover with a slightly dampened cloth until cool. Remove cloth. Dust cake with powdered sugar or a little dry cocoa. Turn out; spread with whipped cream. Roll up. Place fold side down on serving dish. Dust with powdered sugar; chill; serve within 2 hours. Serves 10 to 12.

JELLY ROLL

1 teaspoon baking powder
¼ teaspoon salt
3 eggs
½ cup sugar
½ cup light corn syrup

1 teaspoon vanilla
1 cup sifted cake flour
Sifted confectioners' sugar
1½ cups tart jelly

Grease 1 15½×10½×1-inch baking pan; line bottom with waxed paper and grease again. Mix baking powder, salt and eggs together with an electric mixer or rotary beater. Beating constantly, add sugar gradually, then add light corn syrup, 1 tablespoon at a time, beating until mixture is thick and light in color. Beat in vanilla. Fold in cake flour.

Pour batter into prepared pan. Bake in a moderate (375°) oven about 15 minutes, or until cake springs back when touched lightly with a finger. Immediately turn upside down onto a cloth generously sprinkled with sifted confectioners' sugar. Remove waxed paper. Roll up cake in a clean towel, starting at one narrow end; cool 15 minutes. Unroll and spread with jelly, covering cake almost to the edges. Roll up cake again; wrap cloth around roll. Cool completely on wire rack. Makes 10 to 12 servings.

CHERRY VALENTINE CAKE

2 cups sifted enriched flour
1 tablespoon baking powder
1 teaspoon salt
½ cup shortening
1 cup sugar

½ teaspoon almond extract
2 eggs
¾ cup milk
Butter Frosting (see Index)
Cherry Filling

Sift together flour, baking powder and salt. Mix shortening, sugar and extract until light and fluffy. Beat in eggs thoroughly one at a time. Add flour mixture to creamed mixture alternately with milk. Beat well after each addition. Pour into two oiled and floured 8-inch heart-shaped (or round) pans. Bake 30 to 35 minutes in moderate (350°) oven, or until pick inserted in center comes out clean. Cool, slice layers horizontally in half. Spread Cherry Filling between layers, reserving about ¼ cup filling to decorate top of cake. Spread top and sides of cake with Butter Frosting. When almost set, use reserved Cherry Filling to edge top of cake with heart design.

Cherry Filling:

⅓ cup sugar
¼ corn cornstarch
⅛ teaspoon salt
1 (1-pound) can pitted sour
 red cherries

Few drops red food coloring
⅓ cup flaked coconut

Mix sugar, cornstarch and salt. Drain cherries; mash slightly. Measure syrup and add enough water to make 1½ cups liquid; blend into sugar mixture. Stir-cook 5 minutes, or until thick and smooth. Add few drops food coloring to give desired color. Stir in drained cherries and coconut. Cool. Serves 12.

COUNTY FAIR SURPRISE CAKE

½ cup butter at room
 temperature
1½ cups very fine granulated
 sugar
3 eggs, separated
¾ cup buttermilk
1¾ cups sifted all-purpose
 flour
¾ teaspoon baking soda

¾ teaspoon baking powder
¾ teaspoon ground nutmeg
1 teaspoon ground cinnamon
2 tablespoons cocoa powder
1 teaspoon vanilla extract
1 teaspoon lemon extract
1 cup medium-chopped walnut
 meats
County Fair Chocolate Icing

Stir butter until smooth. Add sugar. Beat egg yolks until light and stir into buttermilk. Sift flour with baking soda, baking powder, nutmeg, cinnamon and cocoa; resift twice. Stir about ¼ cup of dry ingredients at a time, alternately with ¼ cup combined buttermilk and yolks, into butter mixture. Stir resulting batter just until smooth. Do not overbeat. Stir in vanilla extract, lemon extract and chopped nut meats. Carefully, but thoroughly, fold in egg whites beaten stiff but not dry.

Turn batter into three buttered and floured 8-inch cake pans. Bake 20 to 25 minutes at 375°, or until pick inserted near center comes out clean. Turn out on cake rack; cool completely before putting together and frosting with County Fair Chocolate Icing. Serves 10.

County Fair Chocolate Icing: Melt 12 ounces semi-sweet chocolate pieces in top of double boiler over simmering water. Remove pan from water. Blend 1 pint cold dairy sour cream into chocolate. Cool completely before using on cake. Spread thick layer of icing between each layer, reserving balance to frost top and sides of cake.

COFFEE-NUT GINGERBREAD

1 package gingerbread mix	1 cup medium-chopped nuts
1 cup strong coffee	(any kind)
1 egg, beaten	Applesauce

Make up gingerbread mix following package directions, with following exceptions: use strong coffee instead of water, and stir egg into batter. Then fold in ¾ cup of nut meats. Transfer to a 7×11-inch shallow pan that has been oiled and floured. Strew remaining nut meats over top. Bake 30 to 35 minutes in moderate (350°) oven. Cool slightly. Serve warm as is cut in squares along with saucedishes of very cold applesauce. Or serve cold and accompany with whipped topping or lemon sauce. Serves 8 to 10.

MARY BALL WASHINGTON'S GINGERBREAD, 1784

My colleague, food editor Frances M. Crawford, has been responsible for some delightful articles in *American Home* magazine, among them a story on the American Museum at Claverton Manor in Bath, England. Here is a recipe for one of the many sweets, taken from early American cookbooks, that are served in the museum's tea rooms. And what could be more typically American?

½ cup butter or margarine
½ cup dark brown sugar, firmly packed
½ cup light molasses
½ cup honey
¼ cup sherry
½ cup warm milk
3 cups sifted all-purpose flour
2 tablespoons ground ginger
1½ teaspoons ground cinnamon

1½ teaspoons ground mace
1½ teaspoons ground nutmeg
1 teaspoon cream of tartar
3 eggs, well beaten
2 tablespoons grated orange rind
¼ cup orange juice
1 cup sultanas or raisins (optional)
1 teaspoon baking soda
2 tablespoons warm water

Preheat oven to 350°. Grease a 13×9×2-inch pan; line with waxed paper; grease paper. Cream butter or margarine until light. Add brown sugar; beat well. Add molasses, honey, sherry and milk. Beat very well. Sift flour, ginger, cinnamon, mace, nutmeg and cream of tartar together. Add alternately with beaten eggs to sugar mixture. Add orange rind and juice, raisins if desired and baking soda dissolved in warm water. Pour into prepared pan. Bake 45 to 50 minutes, or until cake is firm in center. Cut into squares. Serves 12.

DROPPED ENGLISH POUND CAKES

4½ cups flour
3 teaspoon baking powder
⅓ teaspoon salt
½ teaspoon ground nutmeg
1½ cups sifted powdered sugar
1 cup shortening

3 eggs
1 teaspoon vanilla extract
1 cup milk
½ cup sifted powdered sugar
About 60 whole nut meats or raisins

Sift together flour, baking powder, salt, nutmeg and powdered sugar. Chop in shortening with pastry blender until mixture looks flaky. Beat eggs until creamy; add vanilla and milk. Beat this into first mixture, stirring until smooth and free from lumps.

Drop by heaping teaspoonfuls onto large, low baking pan or cookie sheet. Keep 1 inch apart to allow room for spreading. Dust with additional powdered sugar and top each one with a nut meat or raisin. Bake in moderate (375°) oven for 12 minutes, or until a light golden brown. Remove at once from pan with spatula.

This makes about 5 dozen cakes, which will keep fresh for weeks if stored in a closed metal container.

HALF POUND CAKE

2 cups sifted cake flour	1 cup granulated sugar
¼ teaspoon salt	1 teaspoon pure vanilla extract
1 cup butter at room	¼ teaspoon ground nutmeg
temperature	5 eggs, well beaten

Sift together the flour and salt. Stir the butter and sugar and flavorings together until very light and fluffy. Beat in ¼ the flour-salt blend with the eggs. Add the remaining flour-salt. Beat at least 50 strokes to insure a fine grain. Line the sides and bottom of a 7×11-inch loaf pan with waxed paper. Spoon in the cake batter, making it higher at the sides than in the middle. Bake 1¾ to 2 hours in a slow (325°) oven, or until a pick inserted in the center comes out clean. Cool 5 minutes. Remove from the pan. Peel off waxed paper at once. Serves 8 to 10.

FIVE-MINUTE DEVIL'S FOOD CAKE

2 cups sugar	1 teaspoon baking soda
½ cup butter or margarine	½ cup buttermilk
2 eggs	1 teaspoon vanilla extract
3 tablespoons cocoa	1 cup boiling water
2 cups sifted flour	

Cream sugar and butter or margarine; add eggs. Mix cocoa with flour and soda. Then alternately add buttermilk and cocoa mixture. Stir in vanilla. Quickly stir in boiling water; beat rapidly ½ minute. Pour into two oiled 8-inch square pans. Bake in a moderate (350°) oven for 25 minutes. Cool; frost as desired. Serves 8 to 10.

FRY PAN CAKE

Many folks—bachelor girls, young marrieds or senior citizens—living in a one-room apartment with no oven, occasionally long for a home-baked cake. Just get out the electric fry pan and try this recipe! It keeps moist for several days.

2½ cups sifted cake flour	1½ cups granulated sugar
2½ teaspoons double acting baking powder	2 eggs, unbeaten
1 teaspoon salt	1 cup milk
½ cup butter or margarine at room temperature	1 teaspoon vanilla extract
	Confectioners' sugar

Sift flour once, measure, add baking powder and salt, and sift again. Stir butter until very soft, gradually mixing in sugar. Add eggs, one at a time, beating thoroughly after each. Add flour mixture, alternately with milk, small amount at a time, beating after each addition until smooth. Stir in vanilla.

Oil an 11-inch electric fry pan with vegetable oil; dust with flour. Cover pan and preheat to 280°. Pour in batter. Cover; bake 35 to 40 minutes, or until crust is dry and springs back when touched lightly with finger. Loosen cake around edges with spatula; invert fry pan on cake rack. Let stand 10 minutes, then lift off fry pan. To finish, sift over confectioners' sugar. Serves 9 to 12.

GRAHAM CRACKER LAYER CAKE

A favorite since the gay twenties when homemakers rolled their own crackers.

⅓ cup shortening
1 cup sugar
2 eggs, separated
1½ cups graham cracker
  crumbs (you can roll your
  own, or buy packaged
  crumbs)
1½ teaspoons double acting
  baking powder

⅓ teaspoon salt
½ cup milk
1 teaspoon vanilla extract
½ cup raspberry or strawberry
  jam
1 cup heavy cream, whipped

Cream shortening; gradually work in sugar. Separate eggs. Add yolks, slightly beaten, to sugar mixture. Combine graham cracker crumbs, baking powder and salt. Add alternately with milk and vanilla to first mixture. Fold in egg whites, whipped stiff; transfer to two oiled and floured layer cake pans. Bake 25 minutes in moderate (375°) oven, or until firm in center and brown on top. Remove from pans. Cool; put together with jam. Top with whipped cream. Serves 8.

LADY BALTIMORE CAKE

1 cup butter or margarine
2 cups sugar
1 cup milk
1 teaspoon rose water or
  vanilla extract
3 cups pastry flour

3 teaspoons baking powder
¼ teaspoon salt
5 egg whites
Lady Baltimore Filling and
  Frosting

Cream the butter and sugar together until very light; add the milk and flavoring, then the flour, baking powder and salt sifted together, and last fold in the whites of the eggs beaten until stiff. Bake in three oiled layer cake pans in a moderate (350°) oven about 25 minutes. Remove. Put together and cover with Lady Baltimore Filling and Frosting. Serves 12 to 16.

Lady Baltimore Filling and Frosting:

3 cups sugar	½ cup tenderized figs
1 cup boiling water	½ cup chopped nut meats
3 egg whites	(any kind)
1½ cups quartered raisins	

Boil sugar and water together until they thread (if using a candy thermometer, cook to 230°). Pour over the whites of eggs, which have been beaten until stiff; then beat until the combination is cool. Add raisins, figs and nut meats, and use both filling and frosting as directed.

MARBLE SPICE CAKE NEW ENGLAND

6 tablespoons butter or margarine at room temperature	¼ teaspoon salt
	2½ teaspoons baking powder
½ teaspoon pure vanilla extract	½ cup milk
	¾ teaspoon ground cloves
1 cup sugar	½ teaspoon ground cinnamon
3 eggs, beaten	⅓ teaspoon ground nutmeg
1¾ cups sifted flour	1 tablespoon granulated sugar

Stir together first four ingredients until well mixed. Sift together flour, salt and baking powder. Add alternately with milk to first mixture; beat 40 strokes. Remove half the batter to a second bowl; mix in spices. Lightly oil a 7×11-inch baking pan. Spread in a layer of plain batter, then swirl on spiced mixture. Dust with additional granulated sugar. Bake 35 to 40 minutes in moderate (375°) oven, or until golden brown and pick inserted near center comes out clean. Cool. Serve as is, sliced; or cut in squares and accompany with butter pecan ice cream or with butterscotch sauce, chopped nuts and a swirl of whipped cream! Serves 10 to 12.

MOCHA CREAM CAKE

1 package sweet cooking
  chocolate
½ cup boiling water
1 cup butter or margarine
2 cups sugar
4 egg yolks, unbeaten
1 teaspoon vanilla extract

2½ cups sifted cake flour
1 teaspoon baking soda
½ teaspoon salt
1 cup buttermilk
4 egg whites, beaten stiff
Coffee Whipped Cream

Melt chocolate in boiling water. Cool. Mix butter and sugar until light and fluffy. Add egg yolks, one at a time, beating after each. Add vanilla and melted chocolate, and mix until smooth. Sift flour and soda with salt. Add alternately with buttermilk, beating after each until batter is smooth. Fold in egg whites. Spoon into two 8×8×2-inch square pans, bottoms lined with paper. Bake 45 to 50 minutes in a moderate (350°) oven. Cool. Split each layer horizontally, making 4 layers. Spread Coffee Whipped Cream between layers and over top of cake. Refrigerate 30 minutes or more before serving. Serves 12 to 16.

Coffee Whipped Cream:

3 teaspoons instant coffee
2 cups heavy cream

4 tablespoons sugar
½ teaspoon vanilla extract

Place coffee, cream, sugar and vanilla in a chilled deep bowl. Beat until the cream holds its shape. Makes 4 cups.

THREE-LAYER SPICE CAKE

3 cups sifted all-purpose flour
2½ teaspoons baking powder
1 teaspoon salt
½ teaspoon ground cumin seed
½ teaspoon ground ginger
½ teaspoon ground mace
½ teaspoon ground cinnamon
2 teaspoons vanilla extract

¾ cup butter or margarine
1¾ cups sugar
3 eggs
1¼ cups milk
Never-Fail Frosting (see Index)

Sift together flour, baking powder and salt. Mix together spices and vanilla with butter. Gradually mix in sugar. Beat in eggs one at a time. Add flour mixture alternately with milk. Beat this batter 30 seconds. Turn into three well-oiled, lightly floured, round 9-inch layer cake pans. Bake 25 minutes in preheated moderate (375°) oven, or until a cake tester inserted in the center comes out clean. Cool in pans 10 minutes. Turn out onto a wire rack to finish cooling. Then spread Never-Fail Frosting between the layers and over tops and sides. Let stand 4 hours to firm the frosting. Serves 12 to 16.

ELECTION DAY CAKE

Before the women won the right to vote, it was customary in New England for the ladies to bake special Election Day cakes to serve when the men returned from the polls. This yeast-raised fruit cake was served only on Election Day. This recipe makes 1 10-inch tube cake.

1½ cups warm water (105 to 115°)

2 packages or cakes active dry or compressed yeast

2¼ cups unsifted flour

1 cup sugar

¾ cup (1½ sticks) margarine at room temperature

2 eggs

1½ teaspoons ground cinnamon

1 teaspoon salt

½ teaspoon ground nutmeg

¼ teaspoon ground cloves

¼ teaspoon ground mace

1½ cups raisins

¾ cup medium-chopped pecan meats

¼ cup chopped candied citron

Confectioners' sugar

Measure warm water into warmed large mixing bowl. Sprinkle or crumble in yeast; stir until dissolved. Stir in 1½ cups of the flour; beat until smooth. Cover; let rise in warm place, free from draft, about 30 minutes, or until light and spongy. Gradually work sugar into margarine. Add eggs and beat until frothy. Mix margarine mixture into yeast sponge. Beat in remaining flour, cinnamon, salt, nutmeg, cloves and mace; continue to beat until smooth. Stir in raisins, pecans and citron.

Turn into an oiled 10-inch pan. Cover; let rise in warm place, free from draft, until doubled in size, about 1½ hours. Bake about 50 minutes in moderate (375°) oven, or until medium browned and loaf does not stick to sides of pan. Cool 5 minutes. Then turn onto cake rack to cool. Turn right side up and sift over confectioners' sugar as a finish. Serves 12 to 16.

ANGEL BITES

½ cup sifted all-purpose flour
¼ cup sugar
¼ teaspoon ground cardamom
⅛ teaspoon ground cloves
⅔ cup egg whites at room
temperature (about 5)

⅛ teaspoon salt
½ teaspoon cream of tartar
½ cup sugar

Preheat oven to 375°. Sift flour; ¼ cup sugar, cardamom and cloves together 3 times for thorough mixing. Set aside. In a 2-quart bowl, combine egg whites, salt and cream of tartar; beat until soft peaks form. Add additional ½ cup sugar gradually, beating constantly until sugar is blended into egg whites and mixture holds *firm* peaks. Gently fold in flour mixture; mix well. Spoon batter into 24 1¾×⅞-inch small muffin or gem pans. Bake 15 minutes, or until tops are golden and spring back when gently touched with fingertips. Turn pans over and rest each end on cups, letting cakes cool upside down. When cool, cut around gently with a small, sharp knife and remove. Store in a covered container. Makes 24 angel bites.

Note: Make with angel food mix if desired, stirring in ¼ teaspoon ground cardamom and ⅛ teaspoon ground cloves.

DATE CUPCAKES

One-bowl method.

¼ cup butter or margarine at
room temperature
1½ cups brownulated sugar or
1¼ cups soft brown sugar
2 medium-sized eggs
½ cup milk or water
1 cup shredded pitted dates
(pasteurized)

1¾ cups sifted flour
3 teaspoons baking powder
⅛ teaspoon salt
½ teaspoon ground cinnamon
¼ teaspoon each ground
nutmeg and cloves

Combine all ingredients in a 2-quart bowl and beat thoroughly by hand (about 150 strokes). Transfer to an oiled cupcake pan (2½-inch cups); dust each with ¼ teaspoon granulated sugar. Bake 25 minutes in a moderate (375°) oven, or until a pick when inserted comes out clean. Makes about 1 dozen.

GLAZED PECAN-ORANGE CUPCAKES

¼ cup butter, margarine or shortening
½ cup sugar
1 egg
1 tablespoon grated orange rind
1½ cups sifted flour
¼ teaspoon salt
1 teaspoon baking powder
¼ teaspoon baking soda
½ cup chopped pecan nut meats (optional)
½ cup orange juice or diluted orange concentrate
Orange Syrup Glaze

Measure butter into a 2-quart mixing bowl. Gradually work in sugar with spoon. Beat and add egg and orange rind. Sift together flour, salt, baking powder and baking soda, and stir in pecans if desired. Add alternately with orange juice to first mixture. Mix thoroughly, making a batter.

Oil 2 sets of 12 2-inch muffin pans and fill ⅔ with batter. Bake 20 to 25 minutes in a moderate (325°) oven. Cool 2 minutes in pans. Then remove cupcakes and cool thoroughly. They are then ready to dip into the Orange Syrup Glaze.

To do this, insert a two-tined fork in each cupcake and dip it quickly in and out of the Orange Syrup Glaze striking fork against edge of pan to shake off any excess syrup. Place on cake rack to cool. Makes 24 cupcakes. They keep moist for a week when covered and refrigerated.

Orange Syrup Glaze: In a pint-sized saucepan, combine ½ cup orange juice, 1 cup sugar and 1 tablespoon grated orange rind. Stir over low heat until the sugar dissolves. Increase heat and boil rapidly 5 minutes. Use as directed above.

AMBROSIA FROSTING

1½ cups sugar	⅛ teaspoon salt
2 egg whites	2 teaspoons crushed grated
5 tablespoons orange juice	orange rind

Mix sugar, egg whites, orange juice and salt in top of a 1-quart double boiler. Beat with rotary beater until sugar dissolves. Place over boiling water and cook 7 minutes, beating constantly until frosting stands in peaks. Remove from hot water. Add grated orange rind and beat until thick enough to spread. Makes enough frosting to cover top and sides of a 9-inch tube cake, or to fill and frost two 8- or 9-inch layer cakes.

BUTTER CREAM

This is a type of ornamental icing used in decorating French pastry made of squares of sponge- or plain cake covered with plain or fondant icing.

¼ pound unsalted butter	¾ pound sifted confectioners'
¾ ounce cornstarch	sugar
White of 1 large egg	

Beat together the ingredients until the right consistency to put through the pastry bag and tube. Tint with any vegetable coloring. Flavor as desired. Makes 1½ cups.

Chocolate Butter Cream: Add a little melted chocolate.

Mocha Butter Cream: Flavor with coffee extract and add a little caramel to color.

BUTTER FROSTING

½ cup butter at room
  temperature
4 cups sifted confectioners'
  sugar

1 egg, unbeaten
2 teaspoons vanilla
4 tablespoons whipping cream

Thoroughly mix butter and sugar together. Stir in egg and vanilla. Add cream as frosting becomes thick. Sufficient to fill and frost a 9-inch layer cake generously.

CHOCOLATE FROSTING

1½ cups sugar
2 tablespoons cocoa
¼ teaspoon salt

1 teaspoon vanilla
2½ tablespoons boiling water
  (about)

Sift the sugar, cocoa and salt together; add the vanilla, and moisten with the boiling water. If desired, use part evaporated milk or cream and part water in making this frosting. Sufficient to frost an 8-inch layer cake.

SPICED CHOCOLATE ICING

½ cup butter
2 (1-ounce) squares or 2
  plastic packages no-melt
  unsweetened chocolate
1 tablespoon honey
½ teaspoon vanilla extract

⅛ teaspoon each ground cloves
  and instant coffee
3½ cups sifted confectioners'
  sugar
7 tablespoons cream or half
  and half

Heat butter in saucepan until pale brown. Add chocolate and cook-stir until melted. Stir in honey, vanilla, cloves and instant coffee. Beat in confectioners' sugar alternately with cream or half and half. Sufficient to fill and frost a 9-inch layer cake.

GLOSSY CONFECTIONERS' SUGAR GLAZE

Place 2 cups sifted confectioners' sugar in small bowl. Add 2½ tablespoons heated milk gradually, mixing well, or until the glaze is thin enough to spread over the cake. If too thick to spread, add a few more drops milk.

MAPLE FROSTING

1 egg white
Few grains salt
½ cup maple-blended syrup

Beat egg white with salt until stiff enough to hold up in peaks. Pour syrup in a fine stream over egg white and beat about 2½ minutes at high speed in an electric mixer. Makes about 2 cups frosting or enough to cover the top and sides of an 8×8×2-inch cake. Use at once; do not store longer than 3 to 4 hours.

NEVER-FAIL FROSTING

1 egg white
1 cup sugar
⅛ teaspoon salt
½ teaspoon cream of tartar
1 teaspoon pure vanilla extract
½ teaspoon grated lemon peel
½ cup boiling water

Place all ingredients in small bowl of electric mixer. Beat at high speed until frosting stands in very stiff peaks. Use as directed. Makes enough for a 9-inch 3-layer cake.

Pies

What would America be like without pie—especially apple pie? It's hard to imagine. But don't limit yourself—pumpkin pie, cream pies, fruit pies are part of the panoply of pie recipes offered in this chapter.

All recipes in this chapter are for eight servings unless otherwise stated.

RICH AMERICAN PIE PASTRY

Easy to make, suitable for all kinds of pies—½ recipe equals 1 pastry shell!

2 cups all-purpose flour
¼ teaspoon salt
¾ cup shortening (lard preferred)

5 tablespoons cold water, or as needed

Sift together flour and salt into a 2-quart bowl. Add lard or other shortening and chop it in with pastry blender or 2 knives until mixture looks mealy. Add 2 tablespoons of the cold water; mix in lightly with fork; then add 1 more tablespoon of water. More water may be needed to make dough stick together, but use as little as possible.

Put pastry on sheet of waxed paper. Fold up once, pat together and chill 30 minutes or more. Then remove from waxed paper and roll out a scant ¼ inch thick on lightly floured surface and use as desired. Makes enough pastry for a 2-crust, 9-inch pie.

PASTRY SHELL

1⅓ cups sifted flour
½ teaspoon salt

⅓ cup corn oil
2 tablespoons cold water

Combine flour and salt in mixing bowl. Blend in corn oil, mixing thoroughly with fork. Sprinkle all the water on top; mix well. Press firmly into a ball with the hands. If pastry is slightly dry, mix in 1 to 2 tablespoons additional corn oil.

Flatten dough slightly, and immediately roll out to a 12-inch circle between 2 pieces of waxed paper. Wipe the table with a damp cloth to keep the paper from slipping. Peel off the top paper; place the circle of pastry in a 9-inch pie pan, paper side up. Peel off the paper; fit the pastry loosely into the pan. Trim the pastry ½ inch beyond the rim of the pan, if necessary. Flute the edge. Makes enough for a 1-crust, 9-inch open pie.

GRAHAM CRACKER PIECRUST

Roll 16 graham crackers very fine. Combine and mix ¼ cup sugar and ½ cup room-soft butter or margarine (do not melt it). Lightly butter a 9-inch pie plate; line with the crumbs. Press them against the sides and bottom with a spoon to make an even layer. Chill and use as is for a cream pie. For other pies bake 8 minutes in a moderate (375°) oven.

ZWIEBACK PIECRUST

1½ cups rolled zwieback crumbs	¼ teaspoon salt
½ cup sugar	2 tablespoons butter or margarine at room
1 teaspoon ground cinnamon	temperature
¼ teaspoon nutmeg	1 egg white, slightly beaten

Blend ingredients in order given. The finished mixture should resemble fine sand. Proceed as above.

BAR HARBOR AMBROSIA PIE

½ recipe Rich American Pie
   Pastry (see Index) or a mix
1 teaspoon fine dry bread
   crumbs
1 tablespoon unflavored gelatin
¼ cup cold water
2 cups milk
1 teaspoon fine-grated orange
   rind

2 eggs, separated
⅛ teaspoon salt
1 cup sugar
¾ cup heavy cream, whipped
   and sweetened
½ cup packaged flaked
   coconut
1 large orange, peeled and
   sectioned

Make a 9-inch piecrust shell crimping the edges. Pat bread crumbs on the bottom of it. Bake 18 to 20 minutes in a 375° oven. Cool. While it is baking, make the filling.

Stir the gelatin into cold water. Scald milk and orange rind in a double boiler. Separate eggs; beat yolks until creamy. Stir in ¼ cup of hot milk and add salt and sugar. Return mixture to double boiler; cook-stir until it slightly coats a metal spoon. Stir in softened gelatin. Refrigerate until as thick as an unbeaten egg white. Spoon the ambrosia filling into baked pie shell. Spread with whipped cream, dust with coconut and decorate with orange sections. Refrigerate 4 hours, or until stiff enough to cut.

TEN-MINUTE APPLE PIE

1 8-inch graham cracker crumb
   shell, ready-made or make
   from packaged crumbs
   according to directions
⅛ teaspoon nutmeg

2 cups sweetened applesauce,
   boiling hot
1 egg, separated

Add nutmeg to applesauce. Separate egg. Beat white stiff, yolk until lemon-colored. Fold yolk into beaten egg white. Stir-pour applesauce in egg. Transfer to graham cracker shell. Cool. Decorate with whipped topping or thin layer of sweetened whipped cream.

APPLE PIE WITH STREUSEL TOPPING

½ recipe Rich American Pie   ¾ cup brown sugar
    Pastry (see Index) or a mix   ¼ teaspoon ground cinnamon
3 cups sliced peeled tart apples   Streusel Topping

Roll pastry a scant ¼ inch thick and line an 8-inch pie plate with
it. Flute pastry at edges; puncture in 6 places on bottom.

Combine apples, sugar, cinnamon and arrange in pastry-lined
plate. Make Streusel Topping and spread over apples. Bake 15
minutes in hot (425°) oven; reduce heat to 350°. Bake 25 to
30 minutes until lightly browned and apples are tender when
pierced with fork. Serve warm or cold.

Streusel Topping: Combine ¼ cup uncooked quick oatmeal,
⅓ cup flour, 3 tablespoons brown sugar, ¼ teaspoon ground
cinnamon and ¼ cup margarine or butter. Chop together with a
pastry blender to make crumbs. (Mix the Streusel Topping in
the not-washed bowl used when mixing pie pastry, scraping in
any dough left on the sides. The topping will be easier to mix,
the crumbs larger and more moist.) Use Streusel Topping as
directed above.

BANANA CREAM PIE

¼ cup sugar   ¼ teaspoon vanilla extract
¼ teaspoon salt   4 ripe bananas
3 tablespoons flour   1 9-inch baked pie shell
1½ cups milk   2 tablespoons lemon juice
1 egg yolk   Whipped cream, sweetened and
1 tablespoon butter   flavored (optional)

Mix sugar, salt and flour. Add the milk slowly. Cook until
thickened, stirring constantly. Cook for about 3 minutes, then
add some of the hot mixture to the lightly beaten egg yolk, while
stirring. Add to hot mixture and cook for another minute. Add
butter and vanilla. Cool. Slice bananas into the pie shell, sprinkle

with the lemon juice. Pour mixture over bananas. Chill before serving. If desired garnish with sweetened, flavored whipped cream.

BUTTERSCOTCH MERINGUE PIE

1 9-inch baked pie shell
1 cup undiluted evaporated milk
1 cup cold water
7 tablespoons flour
¼ teaspoon salt
2 large eggs, separated
1 tablespoon cold water

1½ cups brownulated or 1 cup packed brown sugar
1 tablespoon butter or margarine
½ teaspoon vanilla extract
¼ teaspoon cider vinegar
2 tablespoons sifted confectioners' sugar

Bake a 9-inch pie shell using a standard recipe or mix. While baking, prepare the following:

Combine evaporated milk and water; scald 1½ cups. Mix remaining ½ cup with flour and salt to make smooth paste. Then stir into scalded milk. Cook-stir until mixture thickens. Beat egg yolks light with cold water, add sugar and stir in. Cook-stir 2 minutes. Then add butter, vanilla and vinegar. Half cool, stirring twice. Pour this filling into baked pastry shell. Top with plain meringue made by beating 2 remaining egg whites stiff together with confectioners' sugar. Dot pie with meringue making small puffs; then lightly brown 10 to 12 minutes in slow (325°) oven; cool. Serve it the day it is made.

CHOCOLATE CHARLOTTE PIE

1 envelope unflavored gelatin
½ cup sugar
¼ teaspoon salt
⅔ cup undiluted evaporated milk
⅓ cup water
2 eggs, separated
1 6-ounce package semi-sweet chocolate morsels (1 cup)

1 teaspoon vanilla extract
⅔ cup icy cold evaporated milk, whipped
1 9-inch baked pie shell
Whipped cream, chocolate curls, chopped nuts (optional)

Mix together gelatin, ¼ cup of sugar, and salt in top of double boiler. Stir in ⅔ cup evaporated milk, water and egg yolks; mix well. Add semi-sweet chocolate morsels. Place over boiling water and cook, stirring occasionally, until chocolate melts; add vanilla. Remove from heat; beat with rotary beater until chocolate is blended in. Cool until mixture is chilled and mounds slightly when dropped from a spoon. Beat egg whites until stiff but not dry. Gradually add remaining sugar; beat until very stiff. Fold into chocolate mixture; fold in ⅔ cup whipped evaporated milk. Turn into baked pie shell. Refrigerate 4 to 6 hours or until firm. If desired garnish with whipped cream, chocolate curls and chopped nuts.

CHOCOLATE SILK PIE

¼ pound butter (no substitute)	1 teaspoon vanilla extract
¾ cup sifted powdered sugar	2 eggs
2 (1-ounce) squares cooking chocolate, melted	1 9-inch baked pastry shell
	1 cup heavy cream, whipped

Cream butter; add sugar; beat until light and smooth. Add melted chocolate and vanilla. Beat until smooth. Add eggs, one at a time; beat 5 minutes after each. Pour into baked pastry shell. Chill in refrigerator. Coat with whipped cream.

COCONUT CUSTARD PIE

½ cup grated coconut	1 cup sugar
1 pint milk	¼ teaspoon vanilla extract
1½ tablespoons cornstarch	½ recipe Rich American Pie
3 eggs	Pastry (see Index) or a mix
¼ teaspoon salt	

Scald the grated coconut and milk and thicken with the cornstarch blended with 1 tablespoon of the milk. Pour this into the eggs, salt, and sugar beaten together, and when cold, add the vanilla. Pour into a crust-lined plate and bake from 40 to 45 minutes in an oven heated to 375° for the first 15 minutes, then moderated to 350° for the remaining time. When done, the lower crust should be brown and firm and the pie filling solidified so that a knife when inserted comes out clean. The pie should not be allowed to boil during the baking process or it will curdle.

ICE CREAM PIE

1 (6-ounce) package semi-
  sweet chocolate morsels
  (1 cup)
2 tablespoons shortening

2 cups crisp rice cereal
½ cup chopped walnuts
1 quart ice cream (any kind)

Fit piece of aluminum foil inside and over rim of a 9-inch pie plate, smoothing with fingers to make a lining. Trim off excess corners with scissors. Turn semi-sweet chocolate morsels into pie plate and spread. Dot with shortening. Heat in 350° oven 3 minutes, or until melted. Remove from oven; blend chocolate morsels and shortening with back of teaspoon. Gently stir in crisp rice cereal and walnuts. Spread mixture over bottom, up sides, and just over rim of pie plate to form a shell. Refrigerate until set. Invert pie plate and carefully peel foil from shell. Discard foil. Slip shell back into pie plate. Fill with scoops of ice cream. Serve at once.

LEMON MERINGUE PIE

5 tablespoons cornstarch
¼ cup cold water
¼ teaspoon salt
1½ cups boiling water
1¼ cups sugar
1 tablespoon butter
Juice of 2½ lemons
Grated rind of ½ lemon

3 eggs, separated
3 tablespoons sugar or 4
  tablespoons powdered sugar
½ teaspoon vanilla
½ recipe Rich American Pie
  Pastry (see Index) or a mix,
  baked

Blend the cornstarch with cold water and stir into the boiling water with salt; cook rapidly, stirring constantly until it thickens. Then add the sugar, butter, lemon juice and rind and pour into the beaten egg yolks. Cool, and pour into baked crust. Heap on the meringue, made by using 2 of the egg whites whipped stiff but not dry, then gradually adding the 3 tablespoons sugar or 4 tablespoons powdered sugar and vanilla. Bake 10 to 15 minutes in a 350° oven.

MARLBORO PIE

1 cup sugar
1 tablespoon flour
Juice and grated rind of
  1 lemon
2 cups tart applesauce

3 eggs, separated
½ recipe Rich American Pie
  Pastry (see Index) or a mix
3 tablespoons powdered sugar
¼ teaspoon lemon juice

Add sugar, flour, lemon juice and rind to applesauce. Beat egg yolks slightly; add to mixture; pour into a 9-inch pie plate lined with pastry. Bake at 425° for 10 minutes, then at 350° until firm in center, about 25 minutes. Cover with meringue made of egg whites, beaten stiff with powdered sugar and additional lemon juice. Brown in slow (325°) oven. Serve cold.

FLORIDA LIME PIE

3 eggs, separated
1 (15-ounce) can condensed
  milk
¾ cup fresh lime juice

Grated rind of 1 lime
1 9-inch baked pastry shell or
  graham cracker shell
Meringue

Beat egg yolks until frothy. Add condensed milk and beat again. Add lime juice and rind, beat until smooth. Pour mixture into baked 9-inch pastry shell or graham cracker shell. Top with Meringue; bake about 12 minutes in slow (325°) oven, or until Meringue is golden brown.

Meringue: Beat reserved egg whites until stiff but not dry. Add ⅓ cup sugar, beating constantly. Spread over top of the lime pie. Bake as directed above. Cool.

SOUTHERN PECAN PIE

½ recipe Rich American Pie
  Pastry (see Index) or a mix
4 eggs
1 cup unsulphured molasses
1 cup white corn syrup
¼ teaspoon salt

1 teaspoon vanilla
2 tablespoons melted butter or
  margarine
1 cup halved pecan nut meats
12 pecan nut meats

Make pie pastry as usual; roll it a scant ¼ inch thick, then line an 8-inch pie plate. Prepare filling as follows: beat eggs until frothy; stir in molasses and white corn syrup, salt, vanilla and melted butter. Mix in cup of halved pecan nut meats. Pour into prepared pie plate. Bake 45 minutes in a moderate (375°) oven, or until firm in center when tested with toothpick. Decorate with additional nut meats. Cool thoroughly.

PUMPKIN PIE

¾ cup sugar
1 tablespoon cornstarch
½ teaspoon salt
½ teaspoon ground cinnamon
¼ teaspoon ground ginger

3 eggs, slightly beaten
1½ cups canned pumpkin
1½ cups milk
1 unbaked 9-inch pastry shell

Mix sugar, cornstarch, salt, cinnamon, ginger and eggs in a mixing bowl. Add pumpkin and milk. Mix well and rub through a sieve. Pour into pastry shell. Bake 15 minutes in a hot (400°) oven; set oven temperature control at moderate (350°). Bake about 40 minutes, or until knife inserted into filling 2 inches from edge comes out clean. Center of pie will be soft, but will be firm when pie cools.

PUMPKIN PIE DE LUXE

½ recipe Rich American Pie
Pastry (see Index) or a mix
1½ teaspoons unseasoned dry
bread crumbs
2 cups cooked fresh sieved or
canned pumpkin
1 cup light brown sugar

5 eggs, separated
½ teaspoon salt
1 teaspoon ground cinnamon
¼ teaspoon ground cloves
⅓ teaspoon ground ginger
1 cup heavy cream, whipped

Line a 10-inch deep pie plate with pastry; build up (flute) edge.
Dust bottom with unseasoned dry bread crumbs, and press in
lightly. Combine pumpkin, sugar, egg yolks (well beaten), salt,
cinnamon, cloves and ginger. Fold in egg whites, whipped stiff;
add cream; transfer to pie plate. Bake 15 minutes in hot (400°)
oven, then reduce heat and bake 35 minutes longer, or until light
brown on top and firm in center when tested with a pick. Serve
warm or cold. If made the day before, reheat in a slow oven.

SHOOFLY PIE

1¼ cups sifted enriched flour
⅔ cup sugar
¼ teaspoon nutmeg
⅛ teaspoon ground cloves
1 teaspoon cinnamon
⅓ cup butter or margarine

⅔ cup unsulphured molasses
¾ cup cold water
½ teaspoon baking soda
½ recipe Rich American Pie
Pastry (see Index) or a mix

Heat oven to very hot (450°). Mix first five ingredients. Cut
butter into the dry mixture to make crumb consistency. Combine
molasses, water and soda; pour into a 9-inch pie plate lined with
unbaked pastry. Lower heat to 425°, bake for 15 minutes. Reduce to 350° and bake 20 minutes, or until done.

STRAWBERRY CREAM PIE

1 9-inch baked piecrust
2 tablespoons granulated sugar
2 tablespoons fine bread
  crumbs
½ recipe Cream Custard (see
  Index)

3 cups strawberries, washed
  and hulled
1 cup red currant jelly
1 tablespoon kirsch
Confectioners' sugar

Sprinkle the bottom of the pie shell with granulated sugar and bread crumbs. Pour Cream Custard into the shell. Arrange strawberries so that they completely cover cream. Heat currant jelly slowly until it is melted. Strain it and add the kirsch. Coat the strawberries with jelly, using a large basting brush. Put some confectioners' sugar into a small wire sieve and sprinkle around edge of pie. Chill.

SWEET POTATO PIE

½ recipe Rich American Pie
  Pastry (see Index) or a mix
2 cups milk
1 cup mashed sweet potato
½ cup sugar
1 tablespoon cornstarch

1 teaspoon butter
⅓ teaspoon powdered
  cinnamon
½ teaspoon powdered nutmeg
½ teaspoon salt
Grated lemon rind

Line a pie plate with the crust. Add the milk to the sweet potato, together with the remaining ingredients, and pour into the pie plate.

Bake from 40 to 50 minutes in an oven heated to 375° for the first 15 minutes and moderated to 350° for the remaining time. When done, the lower crust should be brown and firm and the pie filling solidified so that a knife when inserted comes out clean.

BLUEBERRY PIE

3 cups blueberries
1 cup sugar
2 tablespoons cornstarch
Pastry for 2-crust, 9-inch pie
1 tablespoon lemon juice or
  ¼ teaspoon grated lemon
  rind

Pinch salt
1 tablespoon butter

Wash, pick over and drain blueberries. Mix with sugar and cornstarch. Line a pie plate with crust and heap the berries high into it. Sprinkle with lemon juice or grated rind, then salt, and dot with butter. Fit over the upper crust, wet edges with cold water and press together. Carefully make slashes to let steam out. Bake in 450° oven for 10 minutes, then reduce to 350° to finish baking for 20 to 30 minutes.

BLUEBERRY PIE ST. MORITZ

1 package pie pastry mix
1 teaspoon fine-grated orange
  rind
⅓ cup fine-chopped nut meats
  (any kind)
4 cups fresh cultivated
  blueberries, rinsed and
  drained

1 cup sugar
¼ cup cornstarch
½ teaspoon ground nutmeg
2 tablespoons butter
3 tablespoons confectioners'
  sugar

Prepare the pastry following package directions; add orange rind and nuts before adding liquid called for in directions. Roll out half the pastry and with it line a 9-inch pie plate. Moisten edge of pastry with a little cold water.

To prepare the filling, mix blueberries with sugar, cornstarch and nutmeg. Turn into pastry-lined pan. Dot top with butter. Roll out remaining pastry and cover top of pie; crimp edges together. Cut 3 slits in top of pie pastry for steam escape. Bake 1 hour in a moderate (375°) oven. Remove from oven; cool. Then sift over the confectioners' sugar.

CHERRY-RHUBARB PIE

½ recipe Rich American Pie Pastry (see Index) or a mix
1 (1-pound) can pitted tart red cherries, sweetened
3½ cups chopped tender young rhubarb, skin left on
1 cup granulated sugar
Grated rind of ¼ lemon
4 tablespoons quick-cooking tapioca
Pinch of salt
2 tablespoons butter (optional)

Roll pie pastry to ¼ inch thickness. With two thirds of this, line a 9-inch pie plate. Reserve remainder for lattice topping. Drain cherries (save liquid to add to a fruit cup). Combine cherries, rhubarb, sugar, lemon rind, tapioca and salt, and spread into pastry-lined plate. Dot, if desired, with butter. Top with lattice-work crust made of strips of remaining pastry. Bake 10 minutes in hot (400°) oven. Then reduce heat to 375° and bake 30 minutes more. Serve at room temperature.

FRESH APPLE PIE

1 pint peeled, cored and sliced apples
¾ cup granulated sugar
⅓ teaspoon nutmeg or cinnamon
Juice and rind of ½ lemon
1 recipe Rich American Pie Pastry (see Index) or a mix
2 tablespoons flour
3 tablespoons cold water

Slice the apples thinly. Mix with the sugar and spice and lemon. Prepare the crust. Strew 2 tablespoons of flour over the lower crust (a dusting). Put in the fruit mixture, add cold water, put on the top crust, dust with sugar and bake for 35 to 40 minutes in a hot (375°) oven.

FRESH CHERRY PIE

1 pint pitted cherries	2 tablespoons flour
1⅓ cups sugar	3 tablespoons cold water
1 recipe Rich American Pie	
Pastry (see Index) or a mix	

Mix the cherries and sugar. Prepare the crust. Dust the lower crust with flour. Put in the cherry mixture, add cold water, unless the fruit is very juicy. Place the top crust on, dust with sugar and bake for 35 to 40 minutes in a hot (375°) oven.

PARTY PEAR PIE

4 fresh Anjou pears	½ teaspoon rum flavoring
Pastry for 2-crust, 9-inch pie	⅓ cup cream
¾ cup brown sugar	2 tablespoons butter
3 tablespoons flour	Cheddar cheese slices or ice
¼ teaspoon nutmeg	cream

Peel, core and slice pears. Arrange in pastry-lined pie pan. Combine and mix brown sugar, flour and nutmeg. Stir in flavoring and cream. Spoon sugar mixture over pears. Dot with butter. Cover with top crust; seal. Cut out 6 pear-shaped pieces for steam escape. Bake 10 minutes at 450°; 40 minutes longer at 350°. Serve warm or cold with a slice of Cheddar cheese or a scoop of ice cream.

PINEAPPLE PIE

1 recipe Rich American Pie	¾ cup sugar
Pastry (see Index) or a mix	¼ cup pineapple juice
2 tablespoons fine dry bread	2 soda crackers, rolled fine
crumbs	1 egg, beaten
2½ cups small-diced or	1 tablespoon milk
crushed canned pineapple	1 teaspoon sugar

Line a 9-inch pie plate with pastry. Strew with crumbs and press them in; this helps to keep crust crisp. To pineapple add sugar, pineapple juice and soda crackers; beat egg and add it. Transfer mixture to crust-lined pie plate. Cover with top crust. Press the edges together with a fork. Slash the center. Brush with milk. Dust with additional sugar. Bake 10 minutes in a hot (425°) oven. Then reduce heat and bake 25 minutes at 375°. Cool before serving.

FRESH PLUM PIE

2 pounds pitted plums, halved
1 cup sugar
⅛ teaspoon salt
1 tablespoon quick-cooking tapioca
1 teaspoon melted butter or margarine
1 teaspoon grated lemon rind

1 recipe Rich American Pie Pastry (see Index) or a mix
1 teaspoon fine dry bread crumbs
2 tablespoons cold water or any fruit juice
1 tablespoon milk
Granulated sugar

If the plum skins are tough, remove them. Combine the plums with all the remaining ingredients except the pastry, crumbs, water, milk and additional sugar. Line a deep 9-inch pie plate with the pastry. Dust with the bread crumbs; press in lightly. Spoon in the prepared fruit. Add the 2 tablespoons cold water or fruit juice. Fit on the pastry top or make a lattice crust. Brush with the milk and dust with the additional granulated sugar. Bake 10 minutes in a hot (425°) oven. Then reduce the heat and bake 30 to 35 minutes at 375°.

LATTICE-CRUST FRESH RHUBARB PIE

Pastry for 2-crust, 9-inch pie
5 cups diced fresh rhubarb, leaves discarded (1½ pounds)
1¼ cups sugar
¼ teaspoon salt

3 tablespoons quick-cooking tapioca
2 tablespoons butter or margarine
1 teaspoon crushed grated lemon peel

Line a 9-inch pie plate with pastry rolled scant ¼ inch thick. Combine remaining ingredients. Turn into pastry-lined pie plate.

Roll remaining pastry ⅛ inch thick. Cut into strips ½ inch wide and arrange over top of pie in lattice fashion. Trim pastry, turn under and flute edge. Bake 15 minutes in preheated very hot (450°) oven. Reduce heat to moderate (350°) and bake 30 minutes, or until rhubarb is tender and crust is brown. Serve cooled to room temperature.

RHUBARB AND STRAWBERRY PIE

Pastry for 2-crust, 9-inch pie	1½ cups fresh strawberries
1 teaspoon fine dry unseasoned bread crumbs	2¼ cups (1-inch) unpeeled pieces fresh rhubarb
1½ cups sugar	Butter
Pinch of salt	1 teaspoon milk
⅓ cup flour	1 tablespoon sugar

Roll out pie pastry and line a 9-inch pie plate. Enough pastry remains to make a top crust. Dust bottom with fine dry crumbs and lightly press them in to absorb excess moisture from pie filling and so prevent sogginess. Stir together sugar, salt and flour. Spoon half of the strawberries and rhubarb into pie plate. Dust over half the sugar mixture. Spoon on remaining strawberries and rhubarb; dust over remaining sugar mixture. Dot with butter. Roll out remaining pastry and fit it loosely over pie. Slash in 6 places for steam escape. Flute edges. Brush over with milk. Dust over additional sugar. Bake 50 minutes in a hot (425°) oven. Serve cold (not chilled) the day it is made.

SPRING APPLE-STRAWBERRY PIE

2½ cups or 1 (No. 2) can thin-sliced peeled, cored tart cooking apples	⅛ teaspoon salt
	½ teaspoon cinnamon
1 cup sliced fresh strawberries or drained halved frozen strawberries	2 tablespoons water or fruit juice
	½ recipe Rich American Pie Pastry (see Index) or a mix
1 cup sugar	1 egg yolk
1 tablespoon flour	1 tablespoon milk

Combine fruits, sugar, flour, salt, cinnamon and water or juice. Transfer to well-buttered deep 9-inch pie plate or baking dish, preferably square. Cover with pastry rolled scant ¼ inch thick. Press down over edge of dish to seal in juices. Slash 3 times for steam escape. Brush lightly with egg yolk slightly beaten with milk. Bake 10 minutes in hot (450°) oven. Reduce heat to 375° and bake 35 minutes more. Serve warm.

Note: The pie pastry for this deep-dish pie is usually slightly sweetened; so, if desired, add ½ tablespoon sugar to dry ingredients of pastry or to the mix when preparing.

DEEP DISH APPLE-RAISIN PIE

3 cups peeled, cored and thin-sliced tart cooking apples	½ teaspoon ground nutmeg
½ cup dark raisins	2 tablespoons any fruit juice
½ cup brown sugar	½ recipe Rich American Pie Pastry (see Index) or a mix
1 tablespoon flour	Milk
⅛ teaspoon salt	

Combine apples, raisins, sugar, flour, salt, nutmeg and fruit juice. Transfer to a buttered 3-pint baking dish, preferably square. Cover with pastry, rolled a scant ¼ inch thick. Press it over edge of baking dish to keep in juice. Make 3 slashes in center to allow for steam escape. Brush lightly with milk for even browning.

Bake 10 minutes in preheated hot (450°) oven. Then reduce heat to 350° and bake 35 minutes more. Serve warm as is, or accompany with half scoops of vanilla or butter-pecan ice cream.

DEEP DISH BLUEBERRY PIE

Fill a baking dish or shallow casserole with blueberries that have been washed and picked over. When the dish is half filled with fruit, add sugar to taste, cover with more fruit, then pour ½ cup water into the dish for each quart of fruit used. Cover with a plain piecrust, wetting the edges of the dish so that the crust will

stick to it. Make 3 slashes in center to allow for steam escape.
Bake in a moderate (350 to 375°) oven for about ½ hour.

CHESS TARTS

½ recipe Rich American Pie
   Pastry (see Index) or a mix
1½ cups light brown sugar
½ teaspoon ground nutmeg
⅓ cup melted butter

4 eggs, beaten
2 tablespoons lemon juice
Crushed, grated rind of 1
   lemon

Line 1 dozen very small individual tart pans with pastry, rolled
thin. Combine and mix remaining ingredients. Ladle into pastry-
lined tart pans. Bake in slow (325 to 350°) oven, or until crust
is lightly browned and tarts are firm in center when tested with
toothpick. Cool and serve. Makes 12.

ORANGE ICE CREAM TARTS

1⅔ cups sifted flour
½ teaspoon salt
1 (3-ounce) package cream
   cheese at room temperature
⅔ cup butter at room
   temperature

1 tablespoon crushed, fine-
   grated orange rind
1 tablespoon orange juice
1 quart vanilla ice cream
1 cup orange marmalade,
   melted

Sift flour and salt into mixing bowl. Mix cream cheese and butter
until smooth; stir in orange rind. Chill. Chop cream-cheese-
butter mixture into dry ingredients. Add orange juice, ½ teaspoon
at a time; mix gently with fork. Shape dough into ball. Wrap in
foil; chill 1 hour or more or until firm. Divide into 8 equal
portions. Roll each on lightly floured board into a round piece,
5½ inches in diameter and ⅛ inch thick. Fit over outside of tart
shell pans, 4 inches in diameter and 1½ inches deep. Trim off
edge of pastry; puncture pastry with fork in 6 places. Put upside
down on baking sheet. Bake in hot (425°) oven, until lightly
browned, about 10 minutes. Cool. Fill with vanilla ice cream.
Top with melted orange marmalade. Serves 8.

RASPBERRY COCONUT TURNOVERS

1 cup enriched flour
½ teaspoon salt
½ cup shortening
1 cup uncooked rolled oats
½ cup shredded coconut
½ cup sugar

3 tablespoons water
¼ teaspoon almond extract
(optional)
12 tablespoons firm raspberry
jam

Sift together flour and salt. Add shortening and chop in with a pastry blender until the mixture resembles corn meal. Mix in rolled oats, the coconut and sugar. Add the water, and almond extract if desired. Knead the dough slightly until it barely holds together.

Divide the dough into 12 parts. Roll each out to form a circle about 5 inches across. Place 1 tablespoon firm raspberry jam on each circle. Fold over and seal the edges together by pressing with the tines of a fork. Prick with fork to allow the steam to escape. Place on a cookie sheet or baking pan. Bake in a hot (400°) oven for 12 to 15 minutes, or until the edges are delicately browned. Makes 12.

RHUBARB-MINCE TARTS

1 recipe Rich American Pie Pastry (see Index) or a mix
1 teaspoon fine dry plain bread crumbs
3 cups Rhubarb-Mince Filling

Line 8 2½-inch tart pans with pie pastry, rolled ¼ inch thick on floured surface. Dust pastry with bread crumbs; press them in. Spoon in Rhubarb-Mince Filling. Cover with a crisscross pastry topping made by rolling out remaining pastry dough and cutting it into long narrow strips. Press onto edges of pastry-lined pans. Bake 10 minutes in hot (400°) oven. When crust begins to brown, reduce the heat to 350° and bake 15 minutes more. Serve cold, but not refrigerated. Makes 8 tart shells.

Rhubarb-Mince Filling:

1 pound apples, peeled, cored, and fine-chopped

1 pound tender rhubarb, leaves and skin removed and small-diced

Grated rind and pulp of 1 orange

Juice of 1 lemon, strained

1 cup dark raisins

½ cup dried currants

¼ cup small-cubed citron

2½ cups brown or 2¾ cups brownulated sugar

½ cup water

1 teaspoon ground cinnamon

½ teaspoon each ground cloves and allspice

¼ teaspoon ground nutmeg

In a 3-quart saucepan, combine all ingredients; simmer uncovered 30 minutes. Cool before using. Enough for two 9-inch or three 8-inch pies according to size. Will keep covered up to 1 month when refrigerated.

APPLE TURNOVERS

2 cups all-purpose flour

½ teaspoon salt

2 teaspoons double action baking powder

¾ cup shortening (any kind)

5 tablespoons milk

6 medium-sized baking apples, peeled, cored and sliced

6 tablespoons brown sugar

1 teaspoon ground cinnamon

¼ teaspoon ground nutmeg

2 tablespoons butter

Sift together flour, salt and baking powder. Cut in shortening. Stir in milk to moisten dough. Roll ¼ inch thick on lightly floured surface. Cut into 6 5-inch squares. Place 1 peeled, cored, sliced apple in center of each square. Mix together brown sugar, cinnamon and nutmeg, and dust over apple. Dot with butter. Fold pastry corners over to make a triangle; press edges together with fork. Place ½ inch apart on cookie sheet. Slide into 450° oven. Immediately reduce heat to 375°; bake 35 minutes. Serves 6.

Fruits

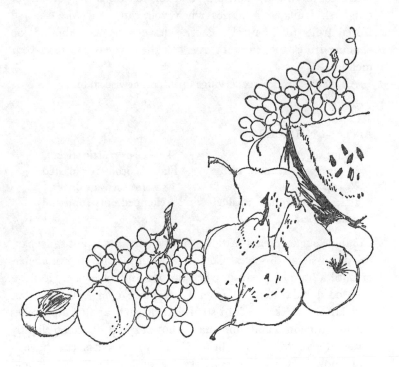

From our national fruit bowl comes a constant year-round succession of fruits. Fruits, whether fresh or cooked, are good as part of almost any meal—and are good for you! Use the garden- or tree-fresh fruits and berries when you can, otherwise thawed frozen fruits fill in nicely. Packers have done a creditable job canning fruits, too, so don't overlook them when you plan your menus.

All recipes are for six servings unless otherwise stated.

APPLES-ON-STICKS

2 cups sugar
⅛ teaspoon cream of tartar
¾ cup water
12 small red apples, washed
    and dried

Skewers or plastic sticks
Flaked coconut or toasted
    sesame seeds or fine-
    chopped nuts (optional)

Combine sugar, cream of tartar and water in a 1-pint saucepan. Stir until sugar dissolves. Cook to 320° by candy thermometer, or until a little of mixture, when dropped in cold water, forms a very hard ball. Remove from heat; place over boiling water. Quickly thrust skewer into stem end of each apple; dip apples one at a time into and immediately out of syrup. Place on slightly buttered pan to become firm. (Very young chefs can have a hand now: after apples-on-sticks are dipped in the syrup and almost dry, but still a bit sticky, they may be dusted with flaked coconut or toasted sesame seeds or fine-chopped nuts.) Makes 12.

BAKED APPLES

For baking, apples should be washed and cored. However, they may have the entire skin left on; or the upper third of the skin may be pared off, and the remainder left on, to help the apples keep their shape. If not pared at all, puncture each apple in 4 places with kitchen fork before baking, to allow steam escape and so prevent "bursting." Do not cover apples while baking. Apples become glazed when the surrounding sugar, or syrup, or honey and water is spooned over the apples 4 times when baking.

To bake apples: Place apples in a baking dish. Into center of each apple, spoon 1 tablespoon white or 1½ tablespoons brownulated sugar, or honey, or 1 tablespoon any fruit-flavored jelly, or jam or marmalade.

For 6 apples, pour around ¾ cup sugar dissolved in 1 cup water or in any unsweetened fruit juice mixed with ¼ teaspoon ground cinnamon or cloves. Bake in slow (325 to 350°) oven about 1 hour, or until tender, and a pick can be easily inserted in center. Baste 4 different times with syrup from baking dish.

CODDLED APPLES

6 medium-sized rosy apples	Few peelings orange rind
2 cups boiling water	Plain or whipped cream or
½ cup sugar	custard

Wash and core apples and simmer slowly until tender, about 30 minutes, in syrup made of next three ingredients, turning apples often so that they will cook evenly. When done, transfer apples to a platter, and boil down syrup until it is thick and dark. Pour over apples. Serve very cold with plain or whipped cream or boiled custard.

POACHED WHOLE APPLES

1 cup sugar	1 tablespoon fresh lemon juice
2 cups boiling water	6 medium-sized baking apples
1 (2-inch-long) stick	(Rome Beauty, McIntosh or
cinnamon	York Imperial)
3 tablespoons red currant jelly	

Measure sugar, water, cinnamon, currant jelly and lemon juice in a 2½-quart saucepan. Stir to dissolve sugar. Cover, bring to boiling point and boil 1 to 2 minutes. Wash, peel and core apples. Add 3 to syrup. Cover and cook 8 to 12 minutes or until apples are tender, turning to cook uniformly. (Cooking time depends on type of apple.) Remove to serving dishes with a slotted spoon. Repeat, using remaining apples. Spoon syrup over each. Crisp ginger cookies are a perfect accompaniment.

BAKED BANANAS

3 large ripe bananas
Juice of 1 fresh lime
½ cup light brown sugar
⅓ cup dry sherry or white grape juice
¼ teaspoon ground cinnamon
¼ teaspoon ground nutmeg
¼ teaspoon ground cloves
¾ teaspoon grated orange rind
1 tablespoon butter or margarine
1 cup heavy cream, whipped
⅓ cup grated fresh or flaked packaged coconut

Peel the bananas; cut in halves, lengthwise, then cut crosswise, making 4 pieces. Dip in the lime juice.

Place in a 10×6×2-inch baking dish that can go-to-table. Pour the remaining lime juice over the bananas. Combine the sugar, sherry or grape juice, spices and orange rind and pour over the bananas. Dot with the butter. Bake 15 to 20 minutes in a moderate (350°) oven. Top each portion with sweetened whipped cream dusted with the grated fresh or flaked packaged coconut.

CHERRIES JUBILEE

1 (1-pound) can pitted dark sweet cherries
¼ cup sugar
2 tablespoons cornstarch
¼ cup brandy, kirsch or cherry brandy
Vanilla ice cream

Drain cherries, reserving syrup. Blend sugar and cornstarch in saucepan; gradually stir in reserved cherry syrup, mixing well.

Cook and stir over medium heat till mixture thickens and bubbles. Remove from heat and stir in cherries. Turn into heatproof bowl or top pan of chafing dish. Make sure bottom pan of chafing dish is filled with hot water; keep hot over flame. Heat brandy or kirsch in small metal pan with a long handle, or pour heated brandy into a large ladle. Carefully ignite heated brandy and pour over cherry mixture. Stir brandy into sauce and serve immediately over ice cream. This recipe makes 2 cups of sauce.

FALL FRUITS GRILL

2 large cooking apples	2 bananas
3 tablespoons butter or	4 halves canned peaches
margarine, melted	⅛ teaspoon salt
2 tablespoons fine cookie	1 tablespoon lemon juice
crumbs	6 tablespoons powdered sugar

Core but do not peel apples. Slice crosswise in ⅓-inch pieces. Dip in melted butter, then crumbs. Peel bananas. Cut in halves lengthwise; brush with butter. Drain peaches; brush with butter. Place all on buttered broiler pan, dust with salt. Broil 6 inches from source of heat about 12 minutes, or until apple is tender. Serve hot, sprinkled with lemon juice and powdered sugar. Serves 4.

SPICED GRAPES

2 cups Ribier grapes	1 stick cinnamon
1 cup sugar	¼ teaspoon each whole cloves
1 cup water	and allspice
½ cup cider vinegar	

Wash the grapes, drain, prick each once with the point of a knife and place in a 1-quart jar or bowl. Combine the sugar, water, vinegar and spices. Bring to boiling point; boil 2 minutes; pour over the grapes. Cool, cover and refrigerate at least 48 hours before using. Serve with meats or poultry. Makes 2 cups.

MARINATED ORANGE SLICES

Prepare a day in advance.

Peel 6 firm navel oranges; slice thin. With scissors snip membranes from centers. Chill and arrange slices in a circle on deep, round dessert plate. Pour over all the juice of 2 oranges and ½ tablespoon lemon juice. Cover each slice with orange marmalade. Marinate and refrigerate overnight.

Serve in glass dishes, with a garnish of coconut or shredded almonds. Or, if you like, sprinkle the orange slices with 3 tablespoons Grand Marnier.

BAKED VALENCIA ORANGES

This entree accompaniment can become a dessert.

6 Florida Valencia oranges	6 tablespoons light brown
6 tablespoons chopped dates	sugar
or nuts	¾ cup Florida orange juice
2 tablespoons butter or	
margarine	

Make 8 vertical cuts through orange skin from blossom end to about 1 inch from bottom; pull peel down; remove white membrane from orange and turn pointed orange skin ends in. Loosen orange sections at top center and pull apart slightly. Place in shallow baking dish. Fill each center with 1 tablespoon of chopped dates or nuts. Dot top of each orange with 1 teaspoon butter; dust with 1 tablespoon brown sugar. Pour orange juice over all. Bake in slow (325°) oven 30 to 35 minutes, basting 3 times during baking. Serve with roast veal, ham or broiled chicken. The entire orange is eaten, including the skin.

Baked Valencia Orange Coconut Dessert: Follow the preceding recipe with these exceptions: Instead of dates or nuts, use package flaked coconut and add 3 extra tablespoons brown sugar.

ICE-CREAMED PEARS

6 halves large peeled fresh or
canned pears
1 pint fruit-flavored ice cream
or sherbet
½ cup orange marmalade

¼ cup frozen orange juice
concentrate
1 tablespoon Cointreau
(optional)

Chill the pear halves. Arrange in serving dishes hollow side up. Fill with the ice cream or sherbet. Stir together the marmalade, orange juice concentrate and the Cointreau and spoon over.

HALF-FROZEN PINEAPPLE AND WATERMELON

4 cups bite-sized cubes seeded
watermelon
1½ cups chunks fresh
pineapple, sweetened, or
halved chunks of canned
pineapple

1 (6-ounce) can thawed
frozen orange or tangerine
juice
⅓ cup kirsch or white grape
juice

Combine all the ingredients in a large freezer tray. Freeze 30 minutes or until crystals form on the edge; stir lightly with a fork. Continue to freeze 30 minutes more, or until very cold and slightly crystalline throughout. Serve at the table from the freezer tray.

PRUNE WHIP

1 cup pitted cooked sweet
prunes
2 tablespoons sugar
1 teaspoon lemon juice

2 egg whites
Sweetened whipped cream
(optional)

Drain prunes; chop fine. Add sugar and lemon juice. Beat egg whites until stiff and dry. Fold in prunes. Turn into lightly buttered 1-quart baking dish or 6 (6-ounce) ramekins (individual casseroles). Bake in moderate (350°) oven 35 minutes for baking dish; 18 to 20 minutes for ramekins. Serve at once as is or garnished with sweetened whipped cream. Serves 4.

BAKED PEARS OREGON

3 large winter pears
¼ cup brown or brownulated
  sugar
1 teaspoon grated lemon rind
¼ teaspoon ground ginger
3 tablespoons coarse-chopped
  filberts

2 tablespoons butter
½ cup orange juice
Whipped sweet or sour cream
  (optional)

Wash, halve and core pears. Peel 3 halves. Arrange alternately with unpeeled halves in shallow baking dish that can go-to-table. Mix sugar, lemon rind, ginger and filberts. Spoon into hollows of pears. Top each with ½ teaspoon butter. Pour in orange juice. Cover. Bake 1¼ hours, or until tender, in moderate (375°) oven. Serve warm as is or with whipped sweet or sour cream.

HOT FRUIT COMPOTE

1 (8-ounce) can apricots
1 (8-ounce) can pitted black
  cherries
3 cups peeled sliced tart apples

Juice and grated rind of 1
  lemon
¾ cup brown sugar
¾ cup sour cream (optional)

Combine fruits, juice, grated rind and sugar in a 1½-quart casserole; cover. Bake 1 hour in moderate (350°) oven, or until mixture is the consistency of a thick and rich dessert. Serve warm with or without sour cream.

STRAWBERRIES ROMANOFF

2 pints fresh strawberries
1 cup confectioners' sugar
1 cup heavy cream

1 teaspoon almond extract
2 tablespoons Cointreau or
  orange juice

Gently wash strawberries in cold water; drain, hull. Place berries in medium bowl, sprinkle sugar over and toss gently. Refrigerate 1 hour, stirring occasionally. In chilled bowl, whip cream until stiff with rotary beater. Add almond extract and Cointreau or orange juice. Fold whipped cream mixture into strawberries. Serve at once. Makes 8 servings.

MARINATED STRAWBERRIES WITH CUSTARD CREAM

2 pints fresh strawberries (hulls and stems on)
1/3 cup sweet red wine or a fruit nectar
Custard Cream

Combine strawberries and wine in shallow dessert dish; chill. Serve with Custard Cream for dipping.

Custard Cream:

3 eggs
1/4 cup sugar
1/4 teaspoon salt
2 cups milk

1 tablespoon butter, cut in bits
1/2 teaspoon fine-grated lemon peel

In a saucepan, beat together eggs, sugar and salt. Gradually stir in milk; cook-stir over medium heat until custard coats a metal spoon. Add butter and grated lemon peel; stir until butter melts; chill. Use as directed.

Beverages

Beverages are very much a matter of individual taste but some are just right as accompaniment for a special dish or occasion. Try serving them in a variety of ways—as punch, in mugs, in frosted glasses—to add fun and color to the table.

Perhaps a good cup of coffee is the most universally appreciated and often the hardest to find. Here is a sure-fire recipe for the elusive good cup of coffee, and a few variations on this popular beverage theme.

COFFEE

Good coffee is fresh, sparkling, full of life and mellow, the aroma enticing, the color dark golden brown and clear as crystal. The essentials for preparing perfect coffee are: A good grade of coffee of the grind suited to the kind of pot to be used. The right pot, spotlessly clean. Freshly drawn water brought to a galloping boil.

The brand of coffee depends upon your own taste. Only experience will prove which you like best. However, it must be fresh, and either packed in vacuum cans or otherwise protected, or freshly roasted and ground, in the appropriate coarseness to suit the type of coffee maker. Keep it in a tightly closed can or canister away from heat and sun.

As to the coffee maker, choose one that contains approximately the amount of coffee beverage usually served, for best results are obtained when used to capacity.

Making Coffee: Allow 2 level tablespoons of ground coffee per ¾ to 1 cup of boiling water (depending upon how strong you like it), no matter what method is used.

Vacuum Method: Start with fresh measured cold water in the lower bowl. When water boils, insert top bowl with measured coffee. Lower heat. When water rises into the top, stir well. Turn off heat in 3 minutes.

Percolator Method: Measure water. Boil. Add basket with measured coffee. Cover. "Perk" 6 to 8 minutes. Remove coffee basket from percolator. Cover and serve.

Drip Method: Set the pot in a pan of boiling water where it will keep hot. Measure into the drip part of the pot the proper amount of coffee. Pour in required amount of rapidly boiling freshly drawn water. Cover and let the water drip through.

Iced Coffee: Prepare strong coffee, using ⅓ more ground coffee than when making it for breakfast. Half fill tall glasses with ice cubes or cracked ice; pour the boiling coffee over; then add cream and sugar to taste.

Or make coffee regular strength. Cool in a nonmetallic container for not more than 3 hours; or if the container is tightly covered, chill in refrigerator. Serve in tall glasses with ice cubes, adding sugar and cream to taste.

CAFÉ BRÛLÉ

> After-dinner coffee
> Sugar tablets
> Brandy

Serve the coffee very hot. Each guest places a sugar tablet in a spoon and then pours over enough brandy to fill the spoon. This is ignited. When the flame subsides and the sugar melts, the contents are stirred into the coffee. Remember that the spoon is hot!

CAFÉ DIABLE

6 sugar tablets
Grated rind of 1 orange
⅓ teaspoon ground cloves
⅓ teaspoon ground cinnamon

1 tablespoon Curaçao
3 tablespoons brandy
3 cups strong after-dinner
coffee

In a small double boiler or in the top of a chafing dish combine the sugar, orange rind, spices, Curaçao and brandy. Cook together until the sugar has melted. Pour into the coffee and serve. This is enough for 6 demitasse services.

CAFÉ ROYALE

After-dinner coffee
Cognac or other brandy

Into each demitasse pour cognac to taste. A half tablespoon per serving is ample.

COFFEE COLOMBIANO

Coffee Ice Cubes
1½ cups strong cool Colombian coffee
1 tablespoon sugar or an approximate amount of non-caloric sweetener

Fill an electric blender with the cracked Coffee Ice Cubes; add the cooled strong coffee and sweetener. Blend until thick and foamy. Pour into chilled slim glasses. Serves 2 to 4, depending on size of glasses.

Coffee Ice Cubes: Prepare coffee as usual. Pour into ice cube trays, cool and freeze 4 hours, or until firm. Then use instead of plain ice cubes to avoid diluting the fine flavor of Coffee Colombiano.

IRISH COFFEE

Heat a stemmed (6-ounce) heat-resistant glass goblet with hot water. Pour in 1 jigger (2 tablespoons) Irish whiskey. Add 2 teaspoons sugar. Pour in strong coffee to 1 inch of brim. Stir. Top to the brim with whipped cream beaten until not quite stiff, letting it blanket the top. (Do not stir after adding the cream as the true flavor of Irish Coffee is obtained by drinking the coffee and whiskey through the suave coolness of the cream.)

FROSTED COFFEE LATIN AMERICA

Prepare 1 quart strong coffee and well-sweeten to taste with honey. In a 2-quart bowl beat 2 egg whites until soft peaks form. Beat in the boiling hot coffee and serve at once. There will be an enticing froth on top.

TURKISH COFFEE

This method of making coffee is attractive when conducted at the table on a small electric table stove.

Turkish Coffee is made with very finely pulverized coffee of mild flavor and excellent quality. The usual utensil is a *jezve*—a tall, decorative open pot of metal with a handle to permit easy pouring, wider at the base than at the top, which causes the steam from the boiling liquid to rise and make a foam.

As the pulverized coffee is served in the beverage, this helps to keep it in suspension. Any tall, narrow utensil may be used instead of a *jezve*.

Put 1 teaspoon pulverized coffee into the pot with a heaping teaspoon of granulated sugar for each person. Add a 2-ounce demitasse of cold water for each person; bring rapidly to boiling point, the more foam the better. Pour a little of it into each demitasse and boil up again. Do this 3 times. Serve at once.

The sediment remaining in the cups is not used.

CIDER FRUIT PUNCH

½ cup sugar
½ cup boiling water
1 cup orange juice
1 pint canned pineapple juice

⅓ cup lemon juice
2 quarts sweet cider
1 quart bottle sparkling water,
    chilled

Melt the sugar in the boiling water. Combine the fruit juices and stir. Refrigerate. Just before serving, add the sparkling water. Fills about 30 punch glasses.

SPICED CIDER PUNCH

¼ teaspoon nutmeg
½ teaspoon cinnamon
6 cloves
¾ cup sugar
2 cups warm water
1½ cups fresh orange juice

¾ cup fresh lemon juice
1½ cups cider or apple juice
3½ cups cold water
1½ teaspoons Angostura
    bitters
Lemon peels

In a saucepan combine nutmeg, cinnamon, cloves, sugar and warm water. Boil 5 minutes. Strain; chill. Add orange juice, lemon juice, cider or apple juice, cold water and bitters. Pour into glasses two thirds filled with ice cubes. Garnish with a twist of lemon peel. Makes 12 (6-ounce) servings.

EGG CHOCOLATE

3 (1-ounce) squares
    unsweetened chocolate
3 cups whole milk
Pinch of salt

½ cup granulated sugar
½ teaspoon cinnamon
1 teaspoon vanilla extract
3 eggs

Cut chocolate into bits. Place in double-boiler top; add milk. Cook over hot water until chocolate melts; stir often. Add salt, sugar, cinnamon and vanilla. Beat eggs in a 1½-quart pitcher. Stir in hot chocolate. With rotary beater beat until frothy; serve at once in small cups. Serves 6.

EGGNOG

10 egg yolks	1 quart heavy cream
Few grains salt	½ cup rum or cognac
¾ cup sugar	(optional)
1 quart or ⅘ quart California	Grated nutmeg to taste
sherry	

Beat thick the yolks and salt; then beat in sugar a little at a time. Beat in the sherry. Chill 3 hours or longer; stir occasionally. To serve, fold in the heavy cream, whipped stiff. Add the rum or cognac if desired. Serve at once. Sprinkle with grated nutmeg. Serves 10 to 16.

Sherry Eggnog: For each person allow 1 well-beaten egg, ½ tablespoon sugar, 2 tablespoons sherry, a few grains each of salt and nutmeg; beat all together. Add ⅔ cup chilled milk. Shake or put in mixer. Serve with a dusting of nutmeg.

CHERRY VANILLA NOG

8 eggs	⅓ cup maraschino cherry
⅔ cup sugar	syrup
¼ teaspoon each ground	1 quart milk
cardamom, cloves and	1 cup heavy cream
cinnamon	3 tablespoons sugar
3 teaspoons vanilla	Nutmeg

Beat eggs with sugar, spices and 2 teaspoons of the vanilla; stir in cherry syrup and milk. Refrigerate. Combine cream, additional sugar and remaining vanilla in deep quart bowl. Refrigerate 30 minutes; then whip. Stir into egg mixture with ice; ladle into glasses. Dust with nutmeg. Serves 10 to 16.

FRUITY BARLEY WATER

In older days, regular barley was boiled in water until soft; the liquid was then drained off, flavored to taste with lemon juice and sugar, and sipped as a refreshing cold beverage throughout the day. Many a Scottish lass credited her fine complexion to this sensible and simple beverage. Not only in Scotland, but in England as well, ladies still enjoy the benefits of this simple beverage—it is even used by royalty.

1½ teaspoons salt	4 oranges
6 cups boiling water	½ cup sugar
½ cup regular barley	2 grapefruits
2 lemons	

Add salt to boiling water; stir in barley; cover; cook over low heat about 1 hour, or until barley is soft. Drain, reserving liquid. Use barley for soup or stew. Grate rinds of 1 of the lemons and 2 of the oranges into barley liquid. Stir in sugar. Cool thoroughly. Strain barley liquid to remove rinds. Squeeze juice from lemons, oranges and grapefruits. Combine with barley liquid. Makes 1¾ quarts. Cover; store in a jar in refrigerator up to 1 week.

GINGER-ALE FLOAT

⅔ cup strained lemon juice	1 cup heavy cream
2 ripe bananas, peeled and mashed	1 pint orange ice or sherbet
1 cup powdered sugar	1 cup chilled ginger ale
	12 orange segments

Blend, then refrigerate for 1 hour, lemon juice, bananas and powdered sugar. Stir in cream, orange ice and ginger ale. Pour into tall glasses. Garnish with orange segments. Serves 6.

LEMONADE

Allow the juice of 1 lemon and 1 tablespoon of sugar to each person. Pour enough boiling water on the sugar to melt it, combine with the lemon juice and a half glassful of crushed ice, fill with plain or charged water, shake in a cocktail shaker if possible and serve.

Cherry Lemonade: To each serving add 2 to 4 tablespoons of chopped sweet ripe cherries.

Raspberry Lemonade: To each serving add 2 to 4 tablespoons of slightly crushed red raspberries.

Pineapple Lemonade: To each serving add 2 to 4 tablespoons of shredded canned or fresh pineapple.

Strawberry Lemonade: To each serving add from 2 to 4 tablespoons of crushed strawberries.

Peach Lemonade: To each serving add 2 to 4 tablespoons of chopped and crushed ripe peaches.

CHILLED FRESH LEMON FROSTED

¾ cup sugar	6 scoops lemon sherbet
¾ cup fresh lemon juice	12 fresh or cystallized mint
3 cups water	leaves
Lemon rinds (from the squeezed lemons)	

Combine sugar, lemon juice and ¾ cup of the water. Mix, and bring to boiling point. Boil 2 minutes. Remove from heat and add lemon rinds. Let stand 5 minutes. Discard lemon rinds. Add remaining water, making lemonade. Chill. Put 1 scoop lemon sherbet in each of 6 5- to 6-ounce glasses. Fill with chilled lemonade. Garnish with fresh or crystallized mint leaves.

LEMON SHAKE

This frosty cooler only rates about eighty calories per portion.

2 eggs	½ cup sugar
½ cup ice water	3 cups milk
⅓ cup lemon juice	

Beat eggs until frothy. Add water, lemon juice and sugar, mixing thoroughly. Beat slowly into milk. Serves 5.

SPICED MOLASSES APPLE JUICE

¼ cup molasses	Pinch of ground cloves
¼ cup water	4 cups chilled apple juice
1 teaspoon ground ginger	10 lemon slices
¼ teaspoon ground cinnamon	10 cinnamon sticks

In saucepan, combine and heat molasses, water and spices. Bring to boil and simmer 4 minutes. Cool. Meantime, turn apple juice into ice cube tray and freeze until ice crystals form. Fill 8-ounce glasses with the apple juice and stir in the spice flavoring. Garnish the glasses with lemon slices and cinnamon sticks. Serves 8 to 10.

ORANGEADE

6 tablespoons sugar	Juice of ½ lemon
Boiling water	1½ cups crushed ice
Juice of 4 oranges	3½ cups cold water

Dissolve the sugar in enough boiling water to cover it, add the fruit juices and the crushed ice with the cold water; shake until thoroughly cold and serve. Serves 6.

PINEAPPLE BUTTERMILK

Thin peeled rind of ½ lemon
4 tablespoons lemon juice
¾ can light corn syrup

1 cup canned crushed
  pineapple
2½ cups buttermilk

Chill all ingredients. Combine in electric blender; buzz 15 seconds or until smooth. Serves 4.

TEA

It's easy to brew a perfect cup of tea if you follow a few basic rules. For each cup of tea, use 1 tea bag or 1 full teaspoon of tea (the best you can buy—even the most expensive teas are economical). Use an extra tea bag or teaspoon of tea for the pot too.

1. A good brew never comes from just hot water. The water must be boiling merrily.

2. Pour the boiling water over the tea.

3. Steeping tea is important. Cover the teapot and steep at least 3 minutes. Remove the tea bags, or pour the tea into another pot, and serve with milk or lemon wedges and sugar.

Iced Tea: Iced tea is its best if you use 3 teaspoons of tea or 3 tea bags for every 2 cups of tea you want to make. The water must be boiling merrily. Pour the boiling water over the tea, just as you do in making hot tea. Steep 3 minutes or more. Keep the pot covered and, while the tea is steeping, put ice cubes into iced-tea glasses or a big pitcher. Steeped and brewed to perfection, the tea is now ready to pour over the ice. Serve iced tea with wedges of lemon and sprigs of mint.

HOT OR CHILLED TOMATO JUICE PIQUANT

1 (46-ounce) can tomato juice

1 medium-sized green pepper (not seeded), chopped fine

1 onion, peeled and medium-chopped

6 outer stalks celery, chopped fine, or 1 cup celery leaves, packed down

½ tablespoon cider vinegar

2 tablespoons sugar

2 teaspoons salt

¼ teaspoon pepper

2 bay leaves

6 whole cloves

4 peppercorns

Combine ingredients in order given in 3-quart kettle. Bring to slow boil; simmer 10 minutes. Strain through fine sieve. Serve hot or chilled. Keeps refrigerated 2 weeks. Makes about 1½ quarts.

SPICED TOMATO JUICE

To 1 (46-ounce) can tomato juice, stir in 2 tablespoons prepared horseradish, ½ teaspoon freeze-dried chopped shallots and 3 drops Tabasco. Cover and refrigerate 24 hours. Stir well before serving. Makes about 1½ quarts.

HOT BUTTERED RUM

For each serving, heat a whiskey glass, put a lump of sugar into it and fill two thirds with boiling water. Add thin pat of butter and 2 ounces rum. Stir and sprinkle with nutmeg.

LEMON SYLLABUBS

1 cup sugar

½ pint light cream

3½ lemons, squeezed

1 cup sweet white wine, as Malaga

½ cup sherry

Combine the sugar and cream. Grate rinds of 2 lemons and combine with the lemon juice, the wine and the sherry. Add to the cream and beat slowly and steadily until very frothy. Chill and serve in punch cups. Makes about 3 cups.

WHIP SYLLABUBS

1 pint heavy cream, whipped
½ cup powdered sugar
Juice and rind of 1 lemon

½ cup Madeira, cognac or any red wine, such as Port

Beat the cream stiff; add the sugar and lemon juice and grated rind and gradually the wine. Fill "posset" glasses a little more than half full. Heap with the whipped cream froth and serve at once. This is a famous New Year's drink of the seventeenth century. Makes about 1 quart.

MULLED WINE

1 quart Madeira, sherry or
  Tokay
¼ teaspoon nutmeg

4 eggs
¼ cup brandy
Sugar to taste

Bring the wine and nutmeg together almost to boiling point. Beat the eggs light and mix with the brandy. Pour the heated wine into them. Return to a double boiler and cook over hot water for 2 minutes, beating constantly with a rotary egg beater. Add sugar to taste. Serve hot in small cups. Pass lightly buttered toast or unsweetened wafers. Serves 10.

YULETIDE WASSAIL

6 apples, pared and soft-baked
¼ teaspoon nutmeg
½ teaspoon ginger
½ teaspoon cinnamon
¾ cup granulated sugar

1 pint ale or beer
Grated rind of 1 lemon
1 quart ale
¾ cup sherry or any sweet red or white wine

Prepare the apples as usual for baking, filling the centers with sugar; and bake in a moderate (350 to 375°) oven until tender. Allow them to cool. Add the nutmeg, ginger, cinnamon and sugar to the pint of ale or beer and let it stand where it will get hot; but not boil. Stir occasionally. When hot, add the lemon rind, remaining ale and the sherry. Stir occasionally again till very hot; then add the apples and serve from a big bowl. Serves 8.

Conserves, Pickles
and Relishes

Conserves, pickles and relishes are part of a well-established tradition of home cooking. Their preparation is neither complicated nor costly, and storage is rarely a problem. These homemade condiments add color and variety to meals that can't be matched by commercially prepared items. Use them immediately or keep them on the shelf for those future country-style meals.

CRANBERRY CHUTNEY

2 cups fresh cranberries, halved
3 slices canned pineapple, small-diced
6 dried peaches, snipped small
½ cup coarse-chopped crystallized ginger
½ cup dark raisins
½ cup sliced blanched almonds
½ cup molasses
1 cup wine vinegar
1 teaspoon curry powder
1 teaspoon dry mustard
1 teaspoon ground cloves
1 teaspoon ground cinnamon
1 teaspoon salt

In a bowl, combine cranberries, pineapple, peaches, ginger, raisins and almonds. In a 2-quart saucepan, stir together remaining ingredients and bring to boil. Simmer-boil 10 minutes; remove from heat and stir in cranberry mixture. Bring to rapid boil; boil 10 minutes. Remove from heat. Cover; let stand several hours to merge the flavors. Refrigerated, this keeps indefinitely. Makes 1 quart.

RAISIN CHUTNEY

4 quarts sour apples, pared,
cored and chopped
4 sweet green peppers, seeded
and minced
⅔ cup minced onion
1½ pounds raisins, chopped
1 tablespoon salt
1½ cups brown sugar

Juice of 4 lemons
3 cups cider vinegar
1½ cups fruit juice or tart
jelly
Grated rind of half orange
1½ tablespoons green ginger
⅓ teaspoon cayenne

Combine all the ingredients. Simmer until thick like chili sauce, and seal in sterilized jars.

Tomato Chutney: Use ¼ the apples in the preceding recipe and substitute 3 quarts of tomatoes. Makes about 10 pints.

MARINATED MUSHROOM CAPS

These gain even finer flavor if prepared well in advance and refrigerated 24 hours before serving.

1¼ cups salad oil
1 pound medium-sized
mushroom caps (save the
stems for other uses)
Juice of 1 large lemon

1 bay leaf
½ teaspoon crushed thyme
leaves
2 tablespoons vinegar

Heat the salad oil until hot enough to brown a ½-inch cube of bread in 1 minute, 350°. Add the mushroom caps. Strain in the juice of the lemon; fry 1 minute. Remove from the heat; stir in remaining ingredients. Cover and cool. Transfer to a glass jar. Refrigerate 24 hours. Serve on a relish tray or as a garnish to a tossed salad or cold platter. Makes 1 pint.

PICKLED CHERRIES COLONIAL

2 pounds large sweet cherries
2 cups mild cider vinegar
2 cups water

2 cups granulated sugar
Cherry extract
Almond extract

Wash cherries; stem and remove pits. Place cherries in bowl or large glass jar. Add vinegar and water. Refrigerate at least 24 hours. Drain, but reserve vinegar. Arrange cherries in pint jars in layers with sugar. Cover with vinegar. Put on lids. Stir every day for a week (don't refrigerate). Let stand 4 weeks. Then to each jar add 2 drops cherry extract and 1 drop almond extract. Use to garnish meats and salads. These cherries keep indefinitely. Makes about 4 pint jars.

MUSTARD PICKLE

2 pints sliced cucumbers
2 pints sliced medium-sized
    green tomatoes
2 pints sliced peeled onions
2 pints medium-chopped
    cabbage

⅓ cup salt
1 cup powdered mustard
1½ cups brown sugar
3 tablespoons ground turmeric
1 quart cider vinegar

In a 6-quart kettle, layer vegetables and salt. Cover; let stand 12 hours; then drain. In 2-quart bowl, mix together mustard, brown sugar and turmeric. Gradually stir in vinegar. Pour over the vegetables. Simmer 2 hours, or until thoroughly cooked and mixture is quite thick. Pour at once into sterilized jars and seal. Makes 1½ quarts.

SPICED ORANGE WEDGES

Place 4 unpeeled Florida oranges in a 2-quart saucepan. Pour in water to cover. Bring to rapid boil. Boil gently 20 minutes, or until oranges can be easily pierced with fork; drain and cool. Cut oranges in eights.

Combine 2 cups sugar, 1¼ cups water, ½ cup vinegar, 1

teaspoon whole cloves and 3 (3-inch) pieces stick cinnamon. Stir over low heat until the sugar dissolves. Bring to a boil. Add the pieces of orange; simmer 20 minutes more; remove cinnamon. Transfer to a jar; cover. Keeps refrigerated indefinitely. Makes 5 to 6 cups of relish.

PICKLED PEACH PRESERVE

2 tablespoons cider vinegar
6 cloves
½ bay leaf

1 (2-inch) stick cinnamon
1 (No. 2½) can cling peach halves

In a 1-quart saucepan combine the vinegar and spices. Drain in the syrup from the peaches. Simmer 5 minutes; remove the spices.

Meantime, cut the peaches in bite-sized pieces. Add the peaches to the syrup; boil 1 minute. Cover; cool. Refrigerate in a jar for 24 hours. Keeps up to 2 weeks. Makes 1 quart.

WATERMELON SWEET PICKLE

Rind of a large watermelon
Cold water
Sweet Pickle Syrup

Use rind left after serving, removing outer green, and pink portions. Cut into 1-inch pieces, cover with water, ½ cup of salt to the quart, and soak overnight. Drain, add fresh water, and cook until barely tender. Drain again, cook until clear in Sweet Pickle Syrup and seal in sterilized jars.

Sweet Pickle Syrup: Bring to a boil 7 cups sugar, 2 cups cider vinegar, ¼ teaspoon oil of cloves, ½ teaspoon oil of cinnamon. Stir till sugar is dissolved. Makes 5 quarts.

FRESH-PACK DILL PICKLES

17 pounds (3- to 5-inch-long) small green cucumbers

2 gallons 5 per cent brine (¾ cup pure granulated salt per gallon water)

6 cups vinegar

¾ cup pure granulated salt

¼ cup sugar

9 cups water

2 tablespoons whole mixed pickling spice

2 teaspoons whole mustard seed per quart jar; or

2 peeled sections garlic per quart jar if desired; or

3 heads dill plant (fresh or dried) per quart jar; or

1 tablespoon dill seed per quart jar

Wash cucumbers thoroughly with vegetable brush. Drain. Cover with brine. Let stand overnight. Combine vinegar, salt, sugar, water and mixed pickling spice tied into clean, thin, white cloth; heat to boiling. Pack cucumbers into hot clean quart jars. Add mustard seed, dill heads or seed or garlic to each jar. Cover with boiling brine to within ½ inch of the top of the jar. Adjust jar lids. Process in boiling water 20 minutes. (This is for altitudes less than 1,000 feet above sea level. To adjust, add 1 minute per 1,000 feet above this altitude.) Count processing time as soon as hot jars are placed in the actively boiling water. Remove jars and complete seals if necessary. Set jars upright, several inches apart, on a wire rack to cool. Makes about 16 quarts.

FRESH APPLE RELISH FOR MEATS

4 Washington Delicious apples

1 medium-sized onion, peeled

1 green pepper, seeded

2 stalks tender celery

¼ cup sweet pickle relish

½ cup sugar

½ cup cider vinegar

Wash, halve and core but do not peel apples. Put with onion, pepper and celery through food chopper (medium blade). Combine and mix with sweet pickle relish, sugar and vinegar. Cover.

Refrigerate overnight to blend flavors. Serve with meats. Makes 5 cups.

MAY BEET RELISH

2 quarts peeled chopped
  cooked beets
1 quart chopped raw cabbage
1 green pepper, cored and
  chopped
1 cup prepared grated
  horseradish
1 cup fine-minced onion
  (optional)

½ teaspoon black pepper
¼ teaspoon cayenne pepper
3 teaspoons salt
1 cup sugar
Cold mild cider vinegar to
  cover

Combine and stir together ingredients, except vinegar, in order given. Transfer to glass jars. Add vinegar, barely covering. Close-cover and keep in cold place. Makes about 3½ to 4 quarts.

CORN RELISH

8 cups fresh corn cut off cob
  (12 ears)
2 cups chopped cabbage
  (½ small head)
1½ cups diced celery
1½ cups chopped seeded green
  pepper
1¾ cups peeled diced onion
2 cups cider vinegar
½ cup water

⅓ cup fresh lemon juice
1 cup sugar
2 tablespoons salt
2½ teaspoons whole celery
  seeds
5 teaspoons powdered
  mustard
⅛ teaspoon ground cayenne
  pepper
1 teaspoon ground turmeric

In large deep kettle, combine and mix first ten ingredients. Boil slowly 25 minutes, stirring often. Add spices; continue cooking 15 minutes, or until mixture thickens. Transfer to hot sterilized jars. Seal at once. Store at least 6 weeks before using. Makes 7 (½-pint) jars.

RAW CRANBERRY RELISH

2 cups fresh cranberries
½ unpeeled orange
1 cup sugar

Grind cranberries and orange with medium blade of food chopper. Add sugar. Mix well. Let stand 4 hours or overnight for flavors to blend. Keep jarful in refrigerator to use as needed. Makes 1½ cups.

BARBECUE CUCUMBER RELISH

3 good-sized cucumbers
¼ cup peeled grated onion
¼ cup cider vinegar
1 teaspoon dill seed
1½ teaspoons salt
½ teaspoon pepper

Chop cucumbers fine. Let stand 1 to 2 minutes and drain. Add the other ingredients and mix well. Put this in the refrigerator at least 4 hours before serving so that the flavors have a chance to blend. It will get better if it stands a couple of days. Makes about 2 cups.

SHARP PEPPER RELISH

12 red sweet peppers
12 green sweet peppers
1 pod hot pepper
6 medium-sized onions
1 cup sugar
3 teaspoons salt
1 tablespoon pickling spice
2 cups sharp vinegar

Wash and drain vegetables. Remove seeds from peppers; peel onions; chop all vegetables fine. Cover with boiling water. Let stand 5 minutes. Drain. Cover again with boiling water. Let stand 10 minutes. Drain again. Add sugar, salt and spice (tied in a bag) to vinegar. Simmer 15 minutes. Add vegetables. Simmer 10 minutes. Bring to boil. Pour, boiling hot, into scalded pint glass jars; seal at once. Makes about 3 pints.

PICCALILLI

8 quarts green tomatoes
1½ quarts sweet green peppers
3 onions, peeled and sliced
3 cups chopped cabbage
3 cups chopped celery
¾ cup salt
1 cup brown sugar

2 cups granulated sugar
1 ounce each white mustard
  seed and allspice
1½ ounces each broken stick
  cinnamon and whole cloves
Cider vinegar to cover

Remove the bloom ends from the tomatoes and the seeds and pith from the peppers; wash and fine-chop. Add the onions, cabbage, and celery, mix with the salt and stand overnight; drain, add the sugars, and the spices tied in a bit of cheesecloth, cover with the vinegar and simmer until the vegetables are tender. Remove the spices and seal in sterilized jars. Makes about 6 quarts.

ELIZABETH LANSING'S PICCALILLI

8 pounds small green
  tomatoes, sliced
4 onions, peeled and sliced
1 cup salt
4 green peppers, fine-chopped
1 cup mustard seed

3 teaspoons black pepper
2 teaspoons whole cloves
2 teaspoons cinnamon
1½ pints cider vinegar
1 cup sugar

Place tomatoes and onions in layers in sieve or colander and sprinkle salt between each layer (1 cup in all). Drain 24 hours. Add remaining ingredients except sugar, mix thoroughly but gently, and simmer in heavy pot ½ hour. Add sugar, stir to dissolve completely, pour into sterilized jars. Makes 8 pints.

APPLE BUTTER

8 pounds apples
4 quarts sweet cider
3½ pounds sugar

1 teaspoon ground cloves
1 teaspoon ground allspice
1½ teaspoons cinnamon

Weigh, wash, and slice the apples. Combine with cider or water, and cook rapidly until mushy. Rub through a sieve, then add the sugar and spices, cook until thick, stirring often. Transfer to sterilized jars and seal with sterilized rubbers and tops; if it is to be used soon, pour into sterilized jars; when cool, wipe the tops with vinegar and cover with paraffin. Makes about 10 pints.

NO-COOK GRAPE OR BOYSENBERRY JELLY

1 package powdered pectin
2 cups water
1 (6-ounce) can frozen grape
  or boysenberry fruit juice
  concentrate

3¼ cups sugar

Dissolve pectin in lukewarm water in a 2-quart bowl this way: add pectin to water slowly, stirring constantly until pectin is completely dissolved. Allow to stand 45 minutes, stirring occasionally. Stir, do not beat. Thaw fruit juice concentrate by placing can in cold water. Pour juice into a 1-quart bowl. Add 1½ cups sugar to thawed juice. Add remaining 1¾ cups sugar to dissolved pectin. Stir until dissolved. Add juice-sugar mixture to pectin-sugar mixture. Pour into jelly glasses; or 4- to 8-ounce plastic containers; or use waxed paper cups with set-in lids. It is not necessary to cover the jelly with paraffin. The glasses can be merely covered with aluminum foil. Allow jelly to stand at room temperature until it has properly set. The time required is at least 6 hours. If jelly is prepared in afternoon, it is best to allow it to stand overnight to set. Makes about 5½ cups.

PEACH/ORANGE/GINGER JAM

1 large seedless tart orange
1 cup water
8 cups peeled pitted chopped
  peaches
7 cups sugar

4 tablespoons chopped
  crystallized ginger
¼ teaspoon ground ginger
½ teaspoon salt

With razor-sharp knife, remove thin yellow rind of half the orange. Peel rest of orange. Chop peel fine and combine with thin rind. Add water; cook over low heat until peel is mushy-soft. Add more water if needed. Turn all ingredients except orange into a 4-quart kettle. Pour orange into strainer; hold over kettle, and press out as much pulp and juice as possible. Slow-boil almost to "jelly stage," when a few drops, on chilled plate, form jelly. Stir to prevent sticking. Do not overcook; jam thickens more after cooling. Skim off foam; pour hot jam to within ⅛ inch of top of pint or ½-pint fruit jars. At once, put dome lids on jars; screw bands tight. Invert jars a few minutes to test for leakage; then stand upright to cool. Makes 3 to 3½ pints jam.

TANGERINE JAM

    8 to 10 Florida tangerines
    4 cups sugar
    1 (2½-ounce) package powdered pectin

Remove peel from tangerines; discard white fibers. Cut sections in 3 pieces; remove seeds. There should be 3½ cups (1¾ pounds) prepared fruit. Measure sugar and set aside. Place fruit in large saucepan over high heat. Add powdered pectin and stir until mixture comes to a hard boil. At once, stir in sugar. Bring to a full rolling boil and boil hard 1 minute, stirring constantly. Remove from heat; skim, ladle quickly into heated sterilized glasses. Cover with melted paraffin at once. Cool. Store in a cool place. Makes about 5 8-ounce glasses.

PLUM JELLY

Traditional method.

    4 cups plum juice
    1½ cups water
    3 cups sugar

Use any variety of tart plums, about 3¾ pounds for each batch of jelly. About ¼ should be under-ripe to supply pectin, the "jellying" factor in fruits, the rest of the plums fully ripe for flavor. Wash, drain and mash plums; combine in a 4-quart kettle with water. Cook over low heat 20 to 30 minutes until plums are mushy. Scald regular jelly bag and wring out as dry as possible; pour in hot plums; let juice drip through without pressing bag. This takes several hours. To save time, twist and squeeze bag to extract juice; however, jelly will be less clear. To turn juice into jelly, measure juice and sugar into kettle. Place over high heat and stir until sugar dissolves. Boil rapidly until syrup "sheets" when dropped from side of the spoon.

Remove from heat; quickly skim off foam; pour boiling hot jelly to within ⅛ inch of top of ½-pint scalded tapered fruit jars; put dome lids on jars; screw bands tight. Invert jars for a few minutes to test for leakage; set upright to cool. Makes about 2 pints, or enough to fill 4 or 5 ½-pint jars.

CANTALOUPE/PLUM JAM

2 medium cantaloupes (2 cups purée)	4 cups sugar
	1 tablespoon lemon juice
2 pounds red plums (2 cups purée)	

Remove rind from melons, halve melons, remove seeds, and cut flesh into chunks. Purée in a blender or food mill. Remove pits from plums and purée the flesh. Put both fruits in a 4- to 6-quart kettle and bring to a boil. Add sugar and lemon juice. Gently boil the mixture until the desired consistency, from 30 to 45 minutes. Skim off any froth from the top. Pour into sterilized pint jars and seal. Makes 2 pints.

GRAPE CONSERVE

3 quarts firm wild grapes	Grated rind and juice of
1 cup water	2 oranges and 1 lemon
1 pound seeded raisins	1½ cups chopped nut meats
5 pounds sugar	

Remove seeds from the grapes and simmer for ½ hour with the water. Add the raisins and sugar, cook until thick—about 45 minutes. Put in the orange and lemon rind and juice, simmer 5 minutes, stir in the nut meats at the last moment. Turn into small glasses and seal. Makes about 3 pints.

CHERRYVIN JAM

2 pounds fresh sweet cherries	¼ teaspoon allspice
¼ cup lemon juice	5 cups sugar
1 (1¾-ounce) box powdered fruit pectin	1 cup burgundy or chianti wine

Wash, stem, pit and put cherries through food chopper. (There should be 3 cups.) Combine with lemon juice, pectin and allspice. Bring to rolling boil. Stir in sugar and wine; bring to rolling boil again; boil rapidly 1 minute. Remove from heat; skim off foam. Ladle into hot sterilized ½-pint (8-ounce) jars. Seal at once. Let stand 25 minutes, then shake gently to distribute fruit evenly.

Index